Irrigation Tanks in Semi-Arid Ecosystems

Irrigation Tanks in Semi-Arid Ecosystems

A Pioneering Study Of Six representative Water bodies in Tamil Country, For Basic Data, Inferences and Management

C. B. S. R. Sharma [Retd]
Department of Ecology and Environment,
Pondicherry University

T. R. K. Yoganand,
World Wide Fund for Nature, South East Asia,
Yangon, Myanmar

M. Amruth
Forest Research Institute, Peechi, Trissur, Kerala

KALPAZ

ISBN: 978-93-5324-246-6

First Published, 2020

Published by

Kalpaz Publications
C-30, Satyawati Nagar,
Delhi – 110052
Ph.: 011-47034999, 9811692060
www.kalpazpublications.com
E-mail: kalpaz@hotmail.com

Printed at: G. Print Process, Delhi

DEDICATION

Dr. Neelakantan

Director, Madras Insitute of Developmental Studies
Professor Bharatidasan University

Dr. Paul Appasamy

Director, Madras Insitute of Developmental Studies
Director, Madras School of Economics
Vice Chancellor, Karunya University

Mr. Cyril Antony

Chairman, INTACH, Pondicherry
Social Activist, Journalist and Editor

Contents

पांडिच्चेरी विश्वविद्यालय
PONDICHERRY UNIVERSITY
(केंद्रीय विश्वविद्यालय) (A Central University)

பேராசிரியர் குர்மீத் சிங்
துணைவேந்தர்
आचार्य गुरमीत सिंह
कुलपति
Prof. GURMEET SINGH
Vice-Chancellor

आर.वेंकटरामन नगर,
R. Venkataraman Nagar,
कालापेट / Kalapet,
पुदुच्चेरी -६०५ ०१४.
Puducherry - 605 014.
भारत. India.

Foreword

Indeed I am very happy to put a few introductory words for a book "Irrigation Tanks in Semi-Arid Regions" by one of our most senior Professors, for he, is still active in academics, a rarity anywhere in the world. The work embodied here was done about 25 years ago, resulting in a project report considered as one of the best from our University and a most relevant one to our times.

I was told that he was chosen to do this work not due to his expertise, but to his reputation for honesty and integrity and values following the dictum that anyone good in one subject can equally be good in another, if one strives. He is a man of Genetic Toxicology confined to laboratory, but executed a field work in Wetland Ecology, exceptionally.

I am surprised that this locally relevant work was pioneered by a man not conversant with region and society, surprising the local talents. Because of the many virtues in this project report, the earlier Avatar of this book has been a source for piracies, plagiarism of many sorts, I was given to understand.

The other workers of this field work, now become co-authors. I find they are already distinguished with many years of fruitful service awaiting. I am sure that the academia and society will greatly benefit from their efforts.

Despite being a layman I realize that data on soil, water and biodiversity, Illustrations and bibliographies are very elaborate and impressive. Therefore this work can be used by others to initiate their works. This book provides many lines of investigation, a kind of guide book for the uninitiated and pioneers.

11 March, 2020

Gurmeet Singh

Acknowledgments

Basic knowledge on tanks was gained by us from Prof. Sivasubramaniam, Madras Institute of Development Studies, Chennai, TN. Mr. Cyril Antony, the former President of INTACH, Pondicherry contributed greatly in the organization of this work, both during documenting as well as in formatting.

Drs. Manimekalan and Jayaprakash Rajan collected soil and water samples from field for analysis in the laboratories of the government. I owe a debt of gratitude to them.

Mr. Murugaian, a computer expert has done me the greatest service in converting a double-column project report into the present book form.

Preface to the Current Edition

Why this book ? When this work incorporated in this publication, was done 25 years ago, why to re-report? Yes. This work is still relevant and it will continue to be relevant. But the single prime reason is the immoralities and crimes going on most of which unknown to me. The few known to me were reported but Vice- Chancellors are unwilling to take any preventive or corrective action. Friends advised me to obtain a copy right first. So is this book.

The present work though done during mid-Nineties did not inspire people to improve upon and apply to other tanks which would have helped to classify waterbodies and standardize the system as a whole. On the other hand

> Some chapters were copied into their books; Tables on plants were converted into descriptive form; Illustration and other methods pioneered here were copied claiming to be their own; Some tank data were simply attributed to some other un-worked tanks to obtain degrees. Just change the name of the tank – copy the data - one gets a new dissertation. Atleast one doctoral degree was obtained using our report under the combined guidance of a colleague and a Scientist in the French Institute. This Arabindo Ashram student, has even impersonated another to obtain a copy of this report ! I informed this to his teacher in the Ashram. If I have done the same in the French Institute, he would have lost his job!

Most of the people indulged in these crimes are known to me because they were all my junior and sub-junior colleagues from the erstwhile Salim Ali School of Ecology of late 1980s.. Some of them give lectures on tanks as if they are authorities on these ecosystems. But I am helpless because I am treated as an alien and my co-workers do not wish to cross with their country-cousins.

For many years the local Government ran a Tank Rehabilitation Program with the aid of Dutch Government. Pondicherry is a small territory and tanks, about 80, are also small. Yet the program endlessly continued that the foreign aid ceased. There was an adviser by name Dr. Peter. I met him to give copies of my Project Report – one for him and another to the library. He was displeased and annoyed with me when I asked a few questions on their work. How do you rehabilitate without first gathering baseline data and restore them without judging their status? I suspect a racket here.

Further, this comes under the Department of Science and Environment of Pondicherry Government. Here too I have been told of several scandalous happenings. A nexus between these two cannot be ruled out.

In both these, people from Ecology Department of the University have considerable roles. My suspicions of some frauds are likely to be real. But neither the University nor the Government will investigate! All that I can do is publish the project report as a Book to obtain Copy Right.

> Tanks in India were about 200,000 and in Tamil Country [Tamil Nadu & Pondicherry], about 40000, now dwindled to less than half due to encroachments under political patronage.
>
> Another "***Tragedy of Commons***"

No where in India are governments serious about restoring them to normalcy for local peoples' benefit, except Telangana and to a lesser extent Tamilnadu. The value of tanks is perennial. An ecosystem can develop around the tank, as a nucleus. Therefore this work should be regarded as a modest attempt to revive interest in the nature around the people and develop an ecosystem mind-set.

Professor C. B. S. R. Sharma [Retd]

07-03-2020

Department of Ecology and Environmental Sciences
Pondicherry University 605 014
Cbsrsharma42@gmail.com

Preface to the Project Report

Water that comes to us through rainfall, melting snows, flowing rivers, lakes, engineered reservoirs, channels and groundwater is garnered in wetlands and tanks. Tanks combine some of the above characteristics rainfall, channeled water and reservoir systems -thereby influencing human settlements in the semi arid tropics since times immemorial. The Tamil Nadu region in India is known to have over 35,000 tanks around which the local destinies often revolve, Therefore a knowledge of the static and the dynamic aspects of these tank systems in time and space is expected to improve the tank systems. Hence the present effort, although limited to only six water bodies could serve as a model for extending the scope to all the other important water bodies, considering the climatic and geopolitical factors influencing the agro-economy of Tamil Nadu.

Six water bodies, usually referred to as wetlands or tanks, were taken up from July 1993 for the present representative study of the vast diversity of tanks. These are Kaveripakkam, Pillaipakkam, Kaliveli, Ousteri, Mirattunilai and Kambikudi. The surveys and analyses cover soil, water, plants, animals, agriculture, aquaculture, social forestry and perceptions of local people on all these and the reservoirs as a whole. To the best of our knowledge there are no previous records of any work of this sort to serve as model or guide. Our pioneering studies yielded baseline data on the characteristics of and activities around each water body. These are likely to motivate and influence scientific and policy inputs and field practices warranted in each tank. A general discussion on the ground facts, possible imperatives and perspectives relevant to all wetland irrigation systems has been attempted.

The present report is organized into eight chapters starting with (A) Introduction, (B) Methodology, followed by (C) Observations on six water bodies, (D) Discussion, (E) Perspectives, (F) Summary (G) References and winding up with (H) Appendices. In the chapter on Observations, baseline data on soil, water, plants, animals (butterflies; fishes, amphibians, reptiles, birds and mammals), cultural aspects (agriculture, aquaculture, social forestry, human settlements and pollution) and Perceptions of local people pertaining to the water bodies are presented. All these are followed by a Discussion of the data and their implications. Supporting Tables, Figures and Photographs are incorporated at appropriate places. The fifth chapter on Perspectives is an evaluation of the likely inputs that the water bodies need in times to come. The chapter on References includes only the literature relevant to one or other aspect in the text, We have not included in this report (a) data on Bahour, Kirurnambakkam and Sriperumbudhur tanks because they are not comparable to those on other water bodies, (b) information on bore wells, water markets, land grabbing, encroachments and aquaculture as they are limited to only Ousteri and Kaliveli.

To understand any tank, the local people should be contacted for eliciting their experiences. This is done with the aid of a questionnaire prepared specially for the purpose. The ecological dynamics of the wetland ecosystems as a whole are to be identified next. Any reclaiming efforts of tanks will depend on its self-regenerating capacity through the hibernating stocks in the soil, therefore a select bibliography on wetlands, tanks and seed banks is provided. Notes on plants and animals are written based on field observations and standard texts.

Illustrations of biodiversity are made from plant herbarium, Field photos and a few published sources, as photography of all animals is difficult and arduous. All these constitute the chapter under Appendices. The entire biodiversity has been classified taxonomically.

Some planned works could not be executed because the Research Assistants did not stick . to their assignments continuously due to factors beyond control. A few items could not be executed for paucity of funds and constraints on time while certain achievements became possible though not planned. I believe that the present report has the basic information and data to provide insights into a very large number of aspects of wetland life required for policy inputs.

I would like to acknowledge the assistance extended to me in this project by Messers Yoganand, Manimekhalan, Rajan and Amruth. All animal data were collected by Yoganand who also took most of the photographs. Amruth had to put in enormous hard work in compiling the data collected by others, prepare the notes, classify biodiversity and collect references. Some ideas like Expert System and Rapid Evaluation belong to him. He carried out the works even after he joined for full-time research at Kerala Forest Research Institute. Ms. Vidya Sridhar, a student of our school provided me ungrudging and efficient assistance. Last but not the least, my wife, Ramadevi gave unstinted support to all of us whenever needed.

This project is funded by the Madras Institute of Development Studies, Adayar, Madras on behalf of the Ministry of Environment and Forests, Government of India, New Delhi. I would like to place on record my gratitude to Professors Vaidyanathan, Neelakantan and Paul Appasamy, all of MIDS, for their understanding support and assistance extended to me for accomplishing this assignment. I am also indebted to the Tamil Nadu Agricultural University's Regional Soil Testing Laboratory, Cuddalore, Government of Tamil Nadu's Laboratory at Kancheepuram and the Krishi Vigyan Kendra of Pondicherry for analysing the soil and water samples. Mr.Cyrii Antony, local convenor of INTACH has helped me in many ways towards the preparation of this report. He and Dr.Sivasubramaniam of MIDS, Madras have gone through this report and brought to my notice several errors. Mr.Edwin and Mr.Shanmugam of Arun Typographies, have done all the typesetting and pagemaking work with great competence.

The people in the villages nearby the tanks and most of the officials whom we contacted were very cooperative. For all the merits of this report credit should go to the team of Research Assistants led by Yogan and while I am responsible for shortcomings, if any.

I had to face problems, both predictable as well as unforeseen almost at every stage of this assignment. Although I do not wish to apportion blame. on anyone, my experiences underscore the inability of academicians adhering to old values to deal with the market forces entrenched in the Universities in India.

Professor C. B. S. R. Sharma
Salim Ali School of Ecology
and Environmental Sciences
Pondicherry University

Date: O4-04-1997
Pondicherry – 605014

Chapter - I

Introduction

The Second Citizens Report on the state of India's Environment gives us a glimpse of the status of water in India. It appears that only about 10% of the annual precipitation is utilised for want of proper storage systems. Therefore wells, ponds and tanks - the age old storage systems - constitute important components in water management. However managing them is usually difficult due to the vagaries of rainfall. To mitigate these problems, conservation of storage capabilities may have to be accompanied by several ecological inputs in a holistic manner. Consequently obtaining knowledge on all aspects of small water bodies natural and man-made becomes a basic imperative. Ecologically considered as kidneys of nature and estimated to be over 200,000 (Zamindari, Village and Public Works) they mostly occur in Peninsular India.

A. The Indian Situation

1. *Water bodies of India*

The oldest man-made tank in India is supposed to be twenty centuries old, found near Allahabad. In Bellary and Telengana some ltanks date back to 12th and 13th centuries. Most tanks occur in the Coastal districts of Tamil Nadu and Andhra Pradesh, South Central Karnataka, Telengana, Eastern Vidarbha, North-eastem Uttar Pradesh and Eastern Rajasthan. The erstwhile Madras Presidency had about 53,000 tanks accounting for 50% of irrigation source which however dwindled to a mere 10% even while the cropped area increased eight fold. In Telenqana the acreage under tanks increased from 4,000 ha in 1895 to 3,64,000 ha in 1940s. The national coverage however decreased from 4.8 million hectares (mha) in 1958-59 to 3.9 mha in 1978-79.

There are about 1.7 mha of cultivable areas, including 0.5 mha of swamps and wetlands in India. In all about 400 species of fish alone, flourish here. Further, they are winter resorts for birds; they harbour reptiles, mammals and other fauna; provide food and fodder; help in flood control and production of organic material. They are natural filters and regulate water regime. These are supposed to be the most productive systems. The underground productivity is 3-5 times greater; unfortunately they are neither nutritious nor easily degradable!

Gradually the water bodies have been filled up and built upon. Foreshores have been encroached. Tubewells have increased multifold. The common property of tanks became systematically difficult to maintain. Droughts, siltation, abolition of zamindari system and non-functional Panchayats have added to the disuse of tanks even though they are economically profitable and ecologically resourceful for storage and charging wells.

2. *Periodical Concerns*

The 1944 Famine Enquiry Commission recommended construction of tanks and their proper maintenance through appropriate legal inputs. The Grow More Food Campaign initiated in 1943 and subsequently integrated into the First Five Year Plan recommended greater attention to minor irrigation works and their maintenance. The Second Irrigation Commission also surveyed the status of tanks in India. In some districts of Andhra Pradesh tanks disappeared along with Zamindaris. In Gujarat only 20% of a total of 1142 tanks were in good shape in 1964-65. In Madhya Pradesh 26.4% of irrigated area was accounted for by tanks in 1952 dwindling to a half by 1968-69. In Vidarbha the acreage under tank irrigation has fallen from 1, 57,000 ha in 1954 to 97,000 in 1960. In Karnataka the irrigable area increased from 5, 05,000 ha in 1905 to 12, 34,000 ha in 1968-69. But the share of tanks increased only by 91,000 hectares from 2, 60,000. Where there is concentration of habitations, the land value of the tank is greater than its water and is irrevocably encroached upon.

3. *State of knowledge*

There is no comprehensive and reliable data collected on an annual basis on the tanks/wetlands in India for making appropriate technological and developmental inputs. In fact there is no study available on the State of Tanks in India. On the contrary destruction of wetlands is fastest in India. Bhumbla and Pisharody recommended specific practices of management of these resources in about 300 districts in India for augmenting groundwater and helping subsistence farmers. But these envisage comprehensive water collection and distribution. Soil conservation and habitat vegetating. Yet planners and policy makers seem to be unconcerned about tanks in spite of telling figures on regional shortages, periodical droughts and ominous portents.

B. Tamil Nadu Scenario

1. *Background*

Taml Nadu has a geographic area of 13 million hectares and a population of over 60 million. In all, 35% of the state's income and 60% of the working population come from the rural sector. The population growth rate (1.75%) is lower than the national average and the population density (372/sq.km) higher. The net area sown constitute 44% of the geographical area i.e., 5.7 mha with an intensity of 121%. The average land holding is 1.08 ha per family and the per capita income is just about Rs. 15,00.

(a) **Climate:** Maximum temperature vary around 44.Q.Cexcept in hill stations and the average rainfall, 950 mm. Evaporation increases from coastal to inland zones. Based upon these and the sources of rainfall, Tamil Nadu can be divided into three zones: (1) the western part, which lies east of western Ghats, benefited by the south-west monsoon (2) the eastern coastal belt receiving the North-East monsoon and (3) the intermediate drought prone plateau with poor rainfall. The latter zones are often visited by cyclonic rainfalls and have a great concentration of tanks.

(b) **Soil:** The main soil types fall broadly into four major groups: red, alluvial, lateritic and black cotton soils. Tanks are more common in red soils where the need is greater 3rising from their low moisture retention capacity.

(c) **Crops:** Paddy is the most common crop occupying about 40% of the agricultural area with an average yield far lower than in many other parts of India. Due to lower fields and greater demand, rice growing is spread over more land consuming more water than usually necessary. Groundnuts, millets, pulses, cotton and sugarcane are the other important crops. The marketing of yields is done either through the governmental agencies and/or regulated market and/or local traders and/or sold to rice mills.

(d) **Green Revolution:** There is a general belief that most crops underwent a stable increase of yields due to the intensification of inputs, such as fertilizers, pesticides, better seeds, mechanisation of agriculture, etc. Consequently the gap among landowners, small farmers, marginal farmers, tenants and laboures gradually increased. Due to such increases of inequities in the rural work force the socioeconomic setting of villages has been growing worse.

The practices of interdependence observed in villages for local self sufficiency, cooperation between irrigators on a watercourse, traditional land-owning pattern, etc., have been replaced by subservience of local Panchayats to the emergent class of affluent farmers and the increasing transfer of local responsibility to district administration. The social-political network has fractured, leaving its members in many ways irresponsible, disunited and disgruntled.

(e) **Governmental Policies:** Credit facilities and technical assistance for agricultural development are made available through banking and extension services so as to develop local resources, increase employment, accumulate assets and stimulate non-agricultural enterprises in villages and small towns. From these the following are expected :(1) wider spread of benefits of enterprise among small farmers and owners, (2) more equitable distribution of land, water and biomass resources, (3) overall growth in the villages and (4) wider availability of water for domestic and irrigation purposes. The priorities are to retain the population in the rural areas and diversify rice producing areas. Water thus became a highly political commodity in the rural ecosystems. Therefore it is given cheap, the land tax is not re-evaluated and electricity is subsidised in the agro-ecosystems.

2. *Irrigation*

The state is served by 33 river systems but only six are significant: Kaveri, Ponnayar, Vellar, Vaigai, Tamraparani and Kodayar. Most of the potential south west monsoon is missed due to the Ghats. Out of the 20,000 million cubic meters (Mcum) of surface water available, 19,000 Mcum (95%) is harvested. Many canal systems connected to reservoirs have been successfully developed and all the good sites have been utilised. Therefore, farming operations have shifted to other systems such as underground water. But the haphazard way of drilling and over- tapping of the aquifers has led to the fall of water table. Consequently costs of well deepening and water lifting have increased.

3. *Tanks*

Tanks are structures that collect and store runoff water and bound by earthen embankments. There may be additional engineering works. This water is either used for paddy cultivation or for supplementary irrigation of dry crops. Since the income from irrigated crops is higher than from rain-fed crops, surface reservoirs have an impact upon productivity, employment and income in the rural sector.

There are about 40,000 tanks scattered throughout the State, of which only 7,400 have an ayacut of more than 40ha. The ratio between ayacut and water spread areas ranges between S and 1 for bigger tanks. Though the total potential under minor irrigation is one mha, the productivity is only one third of its potential because of improper management. Further, increased density of population deters tank construction because land becomes more difficult to acquire; in fact tank land is encroached! Moreover tank irrigation requires a strong local authority to generate collective action for tank building, to efficiently distribute the water by optimally allocating it among beneficiaries and over seasons, and to properly maintain the irrigation system. Princely states in pre-independence days enjoyed a stronger local authority than the British Indian provinces which favoured large scale irrigation schemes and export crops more than food production.

The mode of water regulation continues to be under the control of the local community itself, though the practices differ from place to place depending on the local situation. Individual beneficiaries sometimes form themselves into ad hoc committees or empower the headman of the village. Clashes do exist within and between villages when they share a tank facility. These self managing societies are, in general, decaying. The larger land owners have naturally found it convenient to acquire control 01 more land by encroachments and more water by sinking wells in the command areas at the expense of others.

Tamil Nadu's 40,000 tanks, accounting for one third of the irrigated area have been moulding the rural societies. The socio-political, technological and economic backgrounds have recently undergone a major change during the green revolution that has led to the breaking up of the traditional balances. This may further be aggravated under the impact of the new economic policies now pursued by the rulers. As 95% of the surface water in Tamil Nadu is already being harvested, the need to improve the management and the efficiency of these systems is plainly urgent.

Most tanks are small fanner managed systems. The area, the associated people and the agro-economic conditions around the tanks are variable only slightly. Hindrances from administrative agencies are also limited. Therefore reviving these centuries-old systems will not be difficult. But these systems are spread all over Tamilnadu and most of !hem are in a state of disrepair. Appraising each of these forty thousand tanks is impossible.

Though 60% of Tamil Nadu is drought prone, only a third of the annual precipitation is utilised. It is therefore imperative to lay stress on storage of rainfall. That is why the state became a land of ponds and tanks. Unfortunately, however many of these are being filled up and built upon. Thus Tamil Nadu has been suffering more than its share of water shortage. Therefore the dynamic aspects of these systems in time and space have become very relevant so as to enhance their utility to local people. The tanks should therefore become subjects of inputs. The question that arises now is whether the tank systems a part of human settlements or the latter revolve around the former. Answers to this and other questions raised before, can render the efforts to improve the tank system more fruitful. Hence the present effort premising that villages are parts of the irrigating wetland systems.

C. *Perspectives*

The International Union for Conservation of Nature(IUCN), World Wide Fund for Nature (WWF) and Ramsar Convention (1971-89) recognised the importance of wetlands - reclamation and management of water bodies. Therefore the Government of India formed a National Commission on Wetlands in 1989 to be aided by State level Steering Committees based on the feedings from the Area Development Authorities. The various management aspects were to be implemented and managed through four Acts of parliament - The Environment Protection Act (1986), The Forest Conservation Act (1980), The Wetland Conservation Act (1972) and The Water Act (1974). While IUCN has detailed criteria for wetland identification and management, the Indian Government detailed the needs of research on a score of issues and has even settled for a management plan. This helped raise data on some important wetlands, but none on the vast mass of small water bodies.

The WWF had listed and classified about 100 wetlands in 1989, which included a few irrigation tanks and estimated the wetland area to be about 3.0 mha. which is nearly 100% more than the previous estimations. The first among the nine types of wetlands in India, interestingly, happens to be tanks, reservoirs and other similar water bodies. These differed in size and shape depending upon the topography and are mostly under local organisations and powers. Tanks in India currently account for 11.7% of irrigated area i.e. 3.3 mha.

Thus it is obvious that there is a need for first extending scientific inputs to the smaller water bodies in all their aspects. In other words an ecological approach has to be followed to study them followed by complementary engineering inputs, if the tanks are to be revitalised in full and used in a sustainable manner.

D. Objectives

The following aspects of six water bodies in the Tamil Nadu - Pondicherry region are attempted here so as to obtain an ecological perspective on their revivability:

1. Obtaining the baseline data on water, soil, plants, animals, agriculture, aquaculture and social forestry;
2. Eliciting the perceptions of local people on all the above aspects of the tanks;
3. Documenting the diversity within and among the tanks;
4. Developing a perspective necessary for the revitalisation of the water bodies on a long-term, sustainable and holistic basis.

Chapter - II

Methodology

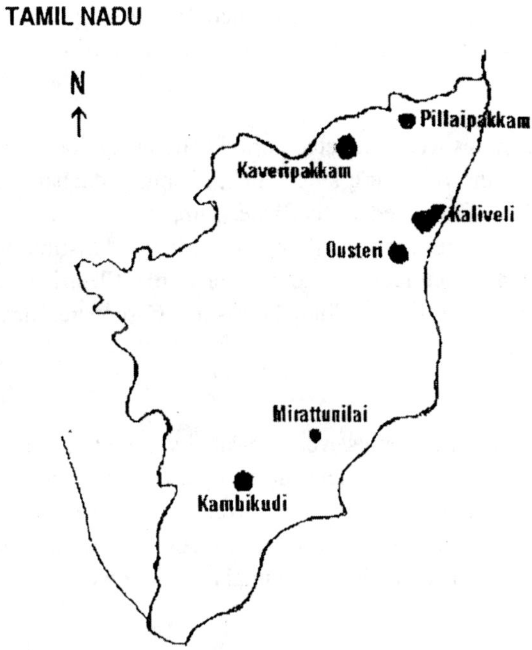

Fig. II.1: Water Bodies Under Study.

A combination of different methods was adopted in the collection, analysis, interpretation and presentation of data. These include field survey of the tank environment for collecting soil and water samples, plant specimens, animal observations and elicit anecdotal information's, analysis of Soil and water samples, identification of biota and interviewing the people and officials concerned with the tanks.

A. Field Survey

Reconnaissance of the tank was carried out during the first few field visits. Rough sketches of the tanks were drawn indicating various habitats and engineering features of tanks. Background information on the history, engineering, hydrological and climatic details of the tank were collected from local administration and public work departments.

B. Soil

Soil samples were collected and tested for variations in important physical and chemical parameters. Soil was collected from four regions foreshore, bed, ayacut and wastelands. Samples were collected from 30 cu.cm pits and analyzed for the following parameters: texture, pH, Electrical conductivity, Nitrogen, Phosphorus and Potassium. Samples from each of the above mentioned four regions were collected periodically using methods of the Indian Standards Institution (1966).

C. Water

Water samples were collected periodically using 500 ml cans from at least 3 of the following sites - inlet channel, stagnant water, outlet channel, dug or bored wells. Water samples are analyzed as per the standard methods prescribed by Indian Standard Institution (1966) for physical and chemical parameters such as pH, Electrical conductivity, Calcium, Magnesium, Sodium, Potassium, Carbonate, Bicarbonate and Chloride.

D. Flora

All habitats of all tanks were repeatedly surveyed for enumerating flowering plant species. The survey involved collection, preservation and identification of specimens. A recent work on the regional flora (Matthew 1992) was used for identification. Habit and habitat of the species was noted along with animal associations.

E. Soil Seed Banks

A preliminary study to enumerate species richness of seeds in the soil of two tanks-Kaliveli and Ousteri was made. Soil samples were collected from 25X25 cm quadrats up to a 5 cm depth and the samples were moistened to satisfy germination needs. Seedlings were identified with the help of Matthew (1992). 4 samples each were made from Kaliveli and Ousteri. Three sites were monitored in Kaliveli for natural germination and 2 sites in Ousteri. The results were used to calculate Shannon-Weiner index for biodiversity.

F. Fauna

Six animal classes were selected for studying species richness by checklisting species during field surveys. These are Butterflies, Fishes, Amphibians, Reptiles, Birds and Mammals.

1. Butterflies

Butterflies were looked for and net-trapped in and around the tanks. Their developmental stage, interactions with plants and other animals were also recorded. Specimens were identified with the help of a standard work (Sathyamoorthy, 1966).

2. Fishes

The fish catch of local fishermen were screened for various species. Also, local people were enquired and employed to bring any species which they claimed to be present in the tank. Specimens are identified with the help of Chandy's work (1970).

3. Amphibians and Reptiles

Various habitats like agriculture fields, afforested lands and other areas were randomly surveyed for these. These were also recorded during other field surveys. Identifications were made with the help of Daniel's work (1983).

4. Birds

Birds were sampled randomly in various habitats in the mornings and evenings and identified using the treatise of Ali and Repley (1987). Observations were made on their food habits and migratory status.

5. Mammals

Various habitats in and around the tanks were surveyed for mammals. Also observations of local people were noted and cross that of ours. Mammals were identified with the help of Prater's work (1980).

G. Human Ecology

1. Culture Systems

Agriculture, Aquaculture and social forestry of each tank was surveyed on the field and enquired from the local people and government officials.

2. Perceptions

Perceptions of local people on their tank ecosystem were obtained by using a monitoring schedule. Background information provided in the official statistics were checked with the village headman or old and knowledgeable people. The respondents were predetermined according to their socio-political status. Two or three people from each category were interviewed. Their perceptions on plants, animals, soil, water, cultured systems, animal husbandry, social forestry, pollution & health and other aspects of tank management were obtained. The respondents are: 1. ex-Kamam, 2. ex-Maniakarar, 3. Sarpanch, 4. Panchayat Board President/Member, 5. Delegate of Farmers' Association, 6. Cooperative Society President, 7. Political Functionary 8. MLA / ex-MLA / MP / ex-MP, 9. Landlord / Small Farmer / Labourer, 10. Irrigation owner / irrigation labourer, 11. Educated Men / Women / Employed / Unemployed, 12. Oldest Citizenry: Women / Men, 13. Government officer Irrigation / Agriculture / Health / Public works / Revenue / Education / Others.

H. Data Processing

Soil and water data were statistically analyzed by calculating the mean and standard deviation of each parameter. To avoid error due to extremities the data falling outside the range of first mean (+ standard deviation) were ignored and another mean was calculated. Such data of each parameter were qualitatively analyzed by comparing with the standards for agricultural purposes; given in this chapter elsewhere. The animal and plant observations were tabulated and taxonomically categorized. A summary of such analysis is given in the case of each tank. All these data were compared.

I. Documentation

1. Sketching

The physical and geographical features of the tanks and its immediate surroundings, the microhabitats identified in each tank, soil and water sampling sites, locations of specimen collection, sampling locations of seed banks were mapped. The sketches are not made according to any scale.

2. Photography

Photographs of the important tank features including bunds, vegetation and few animals were taken. These are presented along with descriptive legends. Photography was done using - Nikon Zoom Camera.

J. Standards

Table II.1: Soil Nutrients.

Fertility status	*Nitrogen*	*Phosphorus*	*Potassium*
Very low	12.50 - 80.00	0.16 - 2.24	0.9 - 29.7
Low	81.25 - 125.0	2.40 - 4.48	30.6 - 48.6
Medium	126.25 - 188.5	4.64 - 8.96	49.5 - 116.1
High	>188 - 9.12	0.00 - 13.44	117 - 144.9
Very high	-	>13.6	>145

All values in Kg/ac

Table II.2: pH Value.

Quality	*Range*
Extremely acidic	below 4.5
Very strongly acidic	4.5 - 5.0
Strongly acidic	5.1 - 5.5
Moderately acidic	5.6 – 6.0
Slightly acidic	6.1 - 6.5
Neutral	6.6 – 7.3
Slightly Alkaline	7.4 – 7.8
Moderately Alkaline	7.9 – 8.4
Strongly alkaline	8.5 – 9.0
Very strongly alkaline	9.1 and above

Table II.3: pH tolerance limit of some crops.

Crops	*Range*
Paddy	6.5 - 8.2
Coconut	6.0 - 7.5
Groundnut	5.3 - 7.0
Cotton	5.0 - 6.5
Sugarcane	6.0 - 8.0
Banana	6.0 - 7.5

Table II.4: E. C. Tolerance limits of crops*.

All crops grow well	<02
Sensitive crops affected	0.2 – 0.4
Many crops affected	04 – 0.8
Only salt tolerant crops – unaffected	0.6 – 1.6
All crops – affected	>1.0

* mmh/cm at 25°C

K. Others

1. **Conversion Tables:** Metric to Imperial

Length			
1 Meter	=	3.28 ft.	
1 Foot	=	30.48	centimeters
1 Mile	=	1.609	kilometers
Area			
1 Acre	=	0.405	ha
1 Hectare	=	2.47	Acre
1 Sq. Km	=	100 ha	
1 Sq. Mile	=	259 ha = 640 acres	
1 Sq. Foot	=	0.093	Sq. meters
Volume			
1 Million Acre ft.	=	1233.48	Million cubic metres
1 Cubic foot	=	28.32	litres
1 Cubic Metre	=	219.97	Gallons
		35.32	cubic ft.
1 Million cubic meters	=	810.71	Acre ft.
1 Gallon	=	4.55	liters
1 Liter	=	0.22	Gallons
1 Million Gallons	=	160514	Cu. ft
		4546.09	Cubic meters

2. Valuing Resources

An attempt is made to give value ratings to each component of the tanks as they exist now. Summing up a composite value emerges for each water body. This is purely subjective at the movement.

3. Rapid Evaluation System

A rapid evaluation system was attempted and applied for the 6 water bodies under the study. As a pioneering attempt evaluation system restricts itself to three major aspects pertaining to the tank. They are (1) the system, (2) the user value, and (3) attitude of the people.

All three aspects are identified as the functions of a number of factors. They are qualitatively categorized into three groups and each group is given a scoring ranging from 0 to 2 or 0 to 4. The total scoring obtained in each category will help to determine the status of the tank. This scoring is ultimately expressed as the percentage of maximum obtainable scoring. A key is provided to assess the status of the tank and its components.

Chapter - III

Water Bodies

1. KAVERIPAKKAM
2. PILLAIPAKKAM
3. KALIVELI
4. OUSTERI
5. MIRATTUNILAI
6. KAMBIKUDI

1. KAVERIPAKKAM

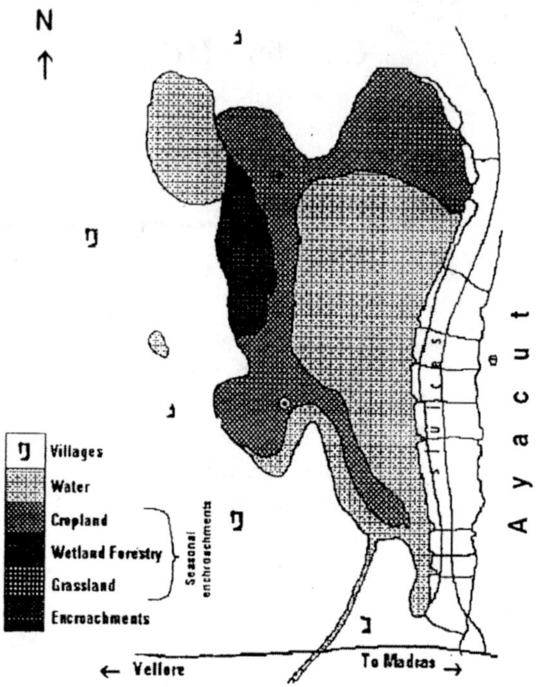

Fig. 1.1: Ecography of Kaveripakkam Tank

A. Introduction

Kaveripakkam tank is located at Kaveripakkam village, in the North Arcot District about 100 km. south-west of Madras on the Madras - Bangalore highway. This tank, connected with the Palar Anicut system, has been known to exist for nearly 600 years. With total water spread area of 16.05 sq. km. the tank is capable of storing 32.9 M.Cu.M. of water. It receives supply from its own catchment's of 31.80 sq. km. and from Palar Anicut situated 9 km. away through the Kaveripakkam supply channel. Average depth of the tank is 9.3 m., when the tank is full. 14 villages are associated with this tank mainly for agriculture. Water is supplied to the nearby agricultural fields through 10 sluices constructed along the 8.35 km. long bund. Total water yield from the combined catchments is 214 M. cu. m. But the original storage capacity of the tank has decreased considerably due to siltation and encroachments. Tank water is available for agriculture for 6-8 months after the rainy season. The climatic factors of the area are typical of the semi-arid tropics with a seasonal rainfall of 53-55 days/year totaling to an annual rainfall of 107.8 cm. Mean temperature of the area is 32°C. Major crops of the ayacut are Sugarcane and Paddy. Of the 42.31 sq. km. of arable land a second crop is raised in 25.42 sq. km. (Table 1.7 Fig 1.1).

B. Characteristics

1. Soil (Table 1.1 and 1.8a, Fig 1.2a)

Soil from all the habitats - foreshore, bed and ayacut-is sandy clayey and loamy in texture. pH ranged between 5.9 and 8.8, Electrical conductivity between 0.1 and 0.6. Among the nutrients, Nitrogen varied between 11.0 and 142.0 Kg/Ac, Phosphorus between 1.0 and 55.0 Kg/Ac and Potassium between 17.0 and 480.0 Kg/Ac.

Table 1.1: Characteristics of Kaveripakkam – Soil@

	Parameter	*Foreshore*	*Bed*	*Ayacut*	*Mean (SD)*
1.	Texture	SCL	SL	SCL	
2.	pH	6.4 - 8.8	5.9 - 8.8	6.4 - 8.5	7.5 (0.88)
3.	E.C.*	0.1 - 0.3	0.10 - 0.6	0.2 - 0.5	0.23 (0.07)
4.	Nutrients#				
	N	20.0 -137.5	11.0 -142.0	14.0 -122.5	77.65 (17.7)
	P	1.3 -17.0	1.0 - 55.0	1.0 - 47.0	6.56 (4.62)
	K	60.0 -327.0	17.0-367.0	29.0 - 480.0	109.05 (38)

@ For more details refer Table 1.8a and Fig.1.2a *mm/cm # Kg/Acre

2. Water (Table 1.2 and 1.8 b, Fig 1.2 b)

Water inflow is from October to January, i.e., during the North-East monsoon. pH of water varies between 7.9 and 9.4, concentration of Calcium, Magnesium, Sodium and Potassium vary between 0.4 and 3.5, 0.5 and 7.5,2.0 and 8.5 and 0.03 and 0.1 Me/I respectively. Concentrations of Carbonate, Bicarbonate and Chloride vary between 0.04 and 1.6, 0.6 and 7.2 and 0.2 and 9.0 Me/l respectively.

3. Flora (Table 1.3 and 1.8c, Fig 1.2c)

There are a total of 95 species of plants belonging to 81 genera and 44 families. They are distributed in four habitats. Maximum occur in the foreshore (71) and minimum in the tank bed (21). There are six categories of plants including two hydrophytes. Twenty four of these appear to be comparatively of greater importance ecologically and / or economically.

Table 1.2: Characteristics of Kaveripakkam – Water[@]

Parameter	*Stagnant*	*Inlet*	*Outlet*	*Well*	*Mean(SD)*
pH	7.5 – 9.4	7.9 – 8.0	7.6 – 9.4	7.7 – 8.4	8.23 (0.53)
E.C.	0.2 – 0.5	1.3 – 1.4	0.6 – 1.1	0.2 – 1.5	0.78 (0.31)
S.A.R.	0.6 – 4.0	2.4 – 3.7	3.0 – 5.6	1.6 – 5.2	4.03 (1.25)
Cations (me/l)					
Ca	0.5 – 2.3	4.0 – 4.1	0.4 – 1.7	0.5 – 3.5	2.82 (1.69)
Mg	0.7 – 2.1	1.9 – 4.0	0.5 – 4.7	1.0 – 7.5	1.86 (1.12)
Na	4.8 – 5.5	4.9 – 6.2	3.8 – 5.5	2.0 – 8.5	4.72 (1.10)
K	–	0.03 – 0.1	0.1 – 0.1	–	0.07 (0.03)
Anions (me/l)					
CO_3	1.6	–	0.04 – 1.6	0.3 – –	0.98 (0.56)
HCO_3	0.8 – 2.9	6.8 – 7.2	0.7 – 6.9	0.6 – 5.8	3.26 (2.25)
Cl	0.2 – 5.5	5.7 – 7.0	3.0 – 4.8	0.2 – 9.0	3.81 (1.99)

@ For more details refer Table I.8c and Fig. 1.2c.

Table 1.3: Characteristics of Kaveripakkam – Flora[@]

Habit	*Taxonomy*				*Habitat*			
	Spp	Gen	Fam	Fs	Bl	Cl	Wl	Importan t
Grasses or Sedges	13	12	2	4	10	6	2	4
Herbs	41	34	20	31	7	20	12	6
Shrubs	23	17	10	19	2	12	9	20
Climbers	6	6	6	6	-	3	2	2
Trees	12	12	7	11	2	4	3	6
Total	95	81	44	71	21	47	28	24

@ For more details refer Table 1.8b and Fig. 1.2c

Spp: species **Gen:** genera **Fam:** families **Fs:** foreshore **BI:** bed lands **CI:** croplands **WI:** wastelands

4. **Fauna (Tables 1.4a, 1.4b and 1.8d-i)**

There are a total of 110 species belonging to 92 genera and 55 families. They are found in four habitats guilds. Of these 110, 15 are butterflies, 6 fishes, 5 amphibians, 8 reptiles, 70 birds and 6 mammals. Fishes and amphibians are present in water and croplands. The immediate surroundings pf the tank bund harbour largest number of animal species'(79} followed by agricultural fields (56). Most of the birds are resident (55) and insectivorous in food habit (35).Others feed on fruits, nectar, aquatic and terrestrial organisms etc.

Table 1.4a: Characteristics of Kaveripakkam – Fauna@

Animals	*Taxonomy*			*Habitat*			
	Spp	Gen	Fam	TW	HS	AF	TB
Butterflies	15	13	6	2	7	6	12
Fishes	6	5	3	6	-	2	-
Amphibians	5	3	1	4	-	3	-
Reptiles	8	8	5	2	3	5	6
Birds	70	59	35	23	16	36	57
Mammals	6	6	5	-	4	4	4
Total	110	92	55	37	30	56	79

@ For more details refer Tables 1.8d – i

TW: tank water **HS:** human settlements
AF: agricultural fields **TB:** thickets and bushes

Table 1.4b: Characteristics of KAVERIPAKKAM – BIRDS@

Migratory Status	*Taxonomy*			*Food Habit*					
	Spp	Gen	Fam	F	N	I	A	T	
Resident	55	46	24			9	28	17	14
Local Migratory	5	5	6			1	4	1	-
Migratory	10	6	5		-	-	1	6	-
Total	70	59	35		17	10	35	24	-

@ For more details refer Tables 1.8h

F: Frugivores N: Nectarivores I: Insectivores A: Aquatic feeders T: Terrestrial feeders

5. Culture Systems (Table1.5 and Fig.1.1)

(a) Agriculture: Agriculture is the major occupation of villagers. The crop variety and cropping patterns change according to the water availability. Paddy and sugarcane are the major crops and the minor crops are mulberry, coconut, groundnut, ragi and castor Most of these crops depend solely on the tank water for irrigation Tail-end farmers depend on well water from pre-summer months In such areas less water requiring crops like groundnut are cultivated. A total area of 49.31 sq. km. is under single crop and another 25.42 sq. km land is under double crop. Nowadays the cropping pattern is changing in favour of plantain.

Table 1.5: Characteristics of Kaveripakkam - Culture Systems

Agriculture	*Aquaculture*	*Wetland Forestry*		*Human Settlements*	
	Natural	*Location*	*Plant*		
Plantain	Catfish	Bank, Bed	Acacia	1. Kaveripakkam	8. Alapakkam
Paddy	Mullet	Bund, Cuter	Prosopis	2. Kattalai	9. Athipattu
Sugarcane	Tilapia	Slope		3. Kondapuram	10. Panniyur
Mulberry	Carps			4. Cheri	11. Kilveeranam
Brinjal				5. Iralacheri	12. Kadaperi
Groundnut				6. Maganipattu	13. Sirukarumbur
Ragi				7. Duraiperumpakam	14. Pudupattu

(b) **Aquaculture:** Aquaculture is practiced by the State Fisheries Department. The cultured species are Cirrihina mirigal, Catla catla and Tilapia mossambica. Prawns, carps and catfishes are also available from tanks. Villagers harvest the tank fauna for food.

(c) **Wetland Forestry:** Acacia nilotica and Prosopis juliflora are the major fast growing trees cultivated in the foreshore, outer slope of the bunds and bed of the tank. Villagers depend on these for firewood.

(d) **Settlements:** There are 250 major and 600 minor land holdings in the ayacut belonging to people in the 14 villages.

6. Pollution

People suspect that the tanneries in the nearby villages are polluting by releasing their effluents in the tank vicinity. The water in some regions was reported to be warmer. Dead fishes were sighted in such places.

C. Perceptions

Table 1.6: People's perceptions on KAVERIPAKKAM

Soil: All locals have similar perceptions on soil fertility but have no knowledge of bio-fertilizers and modern organic farming. Some of them feel that the ash from sugar factory is a potential fertilizer for the fields. They use soil for construction purposes and as a fertilizer.

Water: Farmers are satisfied with the duration of water availability and its distribution. For drinking purposes people depend on Panchayat Water Supply and well water. There are more than 300 privately owned wells around Kaveripakkam village alone. The average depth of groundwater is 15-20 meters. Disputes regarding water distribution are resolved by Nattanmaikaran.

Plants: People are not satisfied with the plant cover around the tank. They prefer to have more trees for shade as weft as fuel wood. They use Prosopis as a fuel wood and help in its spread. Croton and Parthenium are the feared weeds.

Animals: Peoples awareness about animals and their seasonality is poor but they are aware of the wintering water fowls.

Agriculture: Most farmers depend on the tank and supplement their needs through wells. Most of them grow sugarcane, plantain and paddy. Pesticides are used by the farmers for controlling pests in fields and granaries. They feel these are ineffective. Cattle dung, foliage, and compost are used as manure traditionally. Sunflower, mulberry and soyabean have been introduced on an experimental basis. In water scarce months the tank bed is used for vegetable cultivation.

Aquaculture: Though naturally occurring fishery is exploited for almost 3-6 months in a year, people are unaware of the aquaculture potential of the tank.

Wetland forestry: The annual yield of Eucalyptus which is approximately 30 MT/Acre is used as firewood by locals.

Livestock: Cattle, buffaloes, sheep and poultry providing milk, meat, hide and eggs need more grazing lands.

Pollution: People are concerned about water pollution from the tanning units in Ranipet and neighbouring villages. Since these leather units provide employment for many villagers, protest remains muted.

Perspectives: 35-40% of the villagers are literate. Majority of the youth are unemployed and most of them work in brick kilns. Child labourers are common. Traditional water management systems like Kudimaramathu, Neerkatti, Natanmaikarar and Thotti are present. People feel that the channels should be cemented to reduce seepage. They prefer a centralised supply system to the present one. They also look forward to governmental inputs for raising fodder crops.

D. Inferences

A study of the characteristics leads to tentative inferences broadly falling under three categories-Ecology, Conservation and Development. In other words, the characteristics, resources, diversity and ecology have implications for conservation as well as development.

1. Ecology

Kaveripakkam is different from other tanks in having water for a greater part of the year because of a supply channel and greater rainfall. The larger size of the water body (16.05 sq. km), its antiquity and the intensive agriculture has bestowed on Kaveripakkam, considerable resources and diversity. These can be understood from the three subsystems of the tank.

(a) Subsystems

(i) **Water body:** The Kaveripakkam tank had an original water spread area of 16.05 sq. km. and an average depth of 9.3 meters at the maximum water level. This level greatly recedes in summer still leaving some amount of water. This perennial habitat supports hydrophytes like Marselia and Vallisneria and many mesophytes apart from phytoplankton. These account for the productivity of the ecosystem. A number of aquatic insects, amphibians and fishes are found in this habitat. Among the eight species of reptiles reported, two are water dwelling. 23 species of birds depend on these aquatic organisms for nourishment. Guano droppings from the birds are highly nutritious and these enhance productivity of the system. A total of 37 animal species are found dependent on this aquatic habitat.

(ii) **Agro-ecosystems:** More than 60 sq. km of land is cultivated with a variety of major and minor crops. Though frequently sprayed with various pesticides a rich diversity of animals and plants is maintained. 47 plants, mostly herbs and grasses, 5 reptiles, 4 mammals and 36 bird species, mostly insectivorous, occur here. Crop fields provide enough hideouts for these animals. Diversity in agricultural habitat is because of the high productivity and subsequent high population of insects and other animals. & these fuel a number of food chains leading to diverse interrelationships.

(iii) **Wetland forestry:** Social forestry plantations of Acacia arabica and Prosopis juliflora in the northern fringes of the tank are partially submerged during monsoon. Acacia arabica plantations are owned by the Government and harvested by the locals. Naturally occurring Prosopis is seen on the bunds and nearby wastelands. Despite low rewards from monoculture, plantations support high diversity. A few butterflies are closely associated with Prosopis. There are 71 plant species found here. A number of birds are found either roosting or nesting in these plantations contributing guano to the habitat. A number of reptiles and mammals too occur here. Considerable insect-plant associations are seen which form the basis of other ecological ramifications.

These three subsystems interact through ecological links. By and large these function as a single ecological unit; the tank ecosystem.

(b) Habitat Qualities

(i) Soil: Analysis of soil for six major parameters of quality - pH, EC Nitrogen, Phosphorus, Potassium and texture suggest that the soil is of medium quality. Although these parameters varied slightly between different subsystems, the mean values reveal the general nature. Thus the pH was 7.5 and EC, 0.23 indicating very slight alkalinity tolerated by all crops. However Nitrogen varied from very low to medium levels but the mean value is very low (77.65). Though Phosphorus and Potassium varied from very low to very high concentrations, their mean values were medium (Table 1.1 and Fig. 1.1a).

(ii) Water: The mean pH (8.25) and E.C (0.78 units) indicate that the tank water is moderately alkaline. However this is very much within the tolerance limits for crops like Paddy and Sugarcane. Ca, Mg, Na, CI and $HC0_3$ distributions are very erratic in different sites. In some places K and $HC0_3$ are totally absent. The wells have more of Na and Mg. High concentration of cations is attributed to the possible lime saturation from land drain. The low soil Nitrogen could be due to the slight salinity of water. However these findings need more intensive field observations and hydro-geological studies for confirmation. Generally it can be stated that the tank water is suitable for direct irrigation of Paddy and Sugarcane, and probably for potable purposes (Table 1.2 and Fig.1.1b).

2. Conservation

If the tanks are to continue to be useful to rural society, their subsystems and resources need to be conserved, maintained, restored and improved. Resources such as soil, water, flora and fauna constitute the resource base, on which all else develops. Since the tank is a cornerstone of the village ecosystem in many respects, tank related resource development calls for more attention. Besides supplying water, tanks also function as a base for firewood, fodder, organic manure and other plant resources.

(a) Habitats

(i) Water body: The water body is a long-standing one with considerable biological richness and moderate in quality. These are to be conserved. This is possible only by limiting the wetland forestry and seasonal agriculture to the foreshore regions using only leguminous plants, deepening the bed and strengthening the embankments with engineering inputs and botanical methods. Phytoplanktonic and hydrophytic inputs will gradually increase amphibian, Piscean fauna attracting avian visitors. The implications of all these to the tank health and local economy need not be over emphasised.

(ii) Land: Governmental operations around the tanks often do not bring in the desired results for want of local cooperation. To obtain this vital input it is better to strengthen the tank banks with a variety of soil binding, humus forming and economically useful plants so that this will be nurtured as a common property. Since these serve to strengthen the bank, both the ecology and the economy are taken care of. Motivating the local farmers towards larger objectives will be easy. Conserving the integrity of tank by caring for its banks and water holding capacity, works as an incentive for other such ecologically sound measures. A farmers cooperative in this water-wise area can build a model for other tanks and their users. Doing all these will be easier around this tank because it is in comparatively good condition.

(b) Resources

(i) Soil: Soil varies from black clayey to sandy in various localities and is generally moderate in nutrients. A wide varlet of food and cash crops are therefore cultivated. Soil erosion is not noticed in the tank vicinity. But in recent years a new threat has emerged. An increasing application of pesticides and fertilisers can seriously damage soil by reducing its biological activity. The soil is used for construction purposes to an extent that it provides considerable employment to local people.

(ii) Water: Tank water lasts for 6-8 months after the monsoon. The water storage capacity of the tank is said to have declined by nearly 9 M.c.m. since its construction. The water quality depends on a number of factors such as dissolved salts, sediments, evapo-transpiration rate, soil quality etc. In general the water is suitable for irrigating all crops. The potability is not tested, but appears promising. But wells appear to be a negative influence on the tanks as systems.

(iii) **Plants:** While all the 95 plant species can be considered ecologically and/or economically important, about 15 of them are of obvious utility. Some are directly used by villagers in large amounts and others are extracted only in small amounts (e.g. medicinal plants). Some exploit-able ones are not known to the locals. Fodder plants are very less. A description of plant utilities are given in the appendices. Local people have faith in folk medicine and traditional systems of health management both of which are based on plants. Unfortunately there is a dearth of these and they are further dwindling. There- fore it would be useful to restore all the species of medicinal plants which existed once. This involves establishment of a medicinal plant garden.

(iv) **Animals:** With its 110 animal species from six classes, Kaveripakkam can be considered rich in animal diversity. Avifauna contribute 63% of the total fauna. These are only a part of the vast spectrum of fauna flourishing here. The species richness of the system can be gauged from this fact. All animal species have their etched roles in the local ecology. Some animals are directly helpful and others indirectly to human interests. Insectivorous birds help in the control of insect pests of crops. Nitrogen rich guano deposited by the roosting water fowls helps in enriching soil. Yet Nitrogen levels in the soil are comparatively lower as mentioned earlier. Nectarivorous insects like butterflies help in cross pollination of plants. Also seed dispersal is facilitated by the fruigivorous birds.

Conservation of the present diversity appears urgent. Some selected species shall be protected from poaching especially the Pin tailed duck, Garganey teal, Common poachard, Whiskered tem and Red crested poachard. These wintering birds not only enrich the fertility of the tank surroundings with their droppings but also help in controlling many noxious insects of Paddy and Sugarcane. Thus the winter congregation of the birds plays an important role in the local economy. This seasonal bird population needs protection. A two pronged strategy should be adopted by declaring the tank as a protected area in the winter months and also by making locals aware of the importance of the birds in their own interests.

Programmes for monitoring the bird populations, ringing studies for assessing the migratory patterns, assessment of habitat health and productivity to support the animals for food and nesting place are warranted. Planting more trees, restoring the natural vegetation etc. may improve the situation. Thus Kaveripakkam Bird Sanctuary is a feasible development project enabling the conservation of not only local, but global resources.

3. Development

We have maintained that villages are part of the tank system and that this wetland should be conserved and regenerated holistically, i.e., according to ecological principles. As a corollary any rural development programme should be tank oriented so that people will not overlook its importance.

(a) **Agriculture:** The agro-ecosystem is rich in water and yet maintains double cropping only in part due to agricultural practices. It is also intensive using pesticides and fertilisers. However, double cropping can be achieved in the entire ayacut through water economy and cultivating less water-needing crops. Since chemicals pollute water body unleashing chain reactions, these need substitution by botanical pesticides, bio-fertilizers, vermiculture and composting. The tank has a few sugar mills in its vicinity. The ash and other solid wastes from them composted with green manure and animal wastes can be used in the agricultural fields. Vermiculture is a natural additive in this exercise of reducing polluting chemicals and increasing fertility and plant protection.

(b) **Aquaculture:** Water is available for a long time in Kaveripakkam. Six fish species, some of them introduced, and amphibians live here. Therefore the locals should be impressed upon that they should multiply the native species and enrich the productivity so that they may enjoy continuous access to them as a commons.

(c) **Sericulture:** Mulberry cultivation was introduced a few years ago along with soyabean and sunflower. It should be encouraged as it can provide a source of income to small farmers.

(d) **Apiculture:** Apiculture has received a setback in the humid areas but its potential in the semi-arid regions was not well studied. As plant diversity is high and water is available, bee keeping should be successful here. This practice can constitute another source of income even to the marginal people.

(e) **Ecotourism:** Kaveripakkam with its well engineered bunds and longer water availability can become a good recreation spot with some investments towards establishing minimal recreational facilities by planting shade trees and construction of benches for sitting, the tank premises can be converted into a picnic spot. The present guest house situated on the southern bunds can be renovated. For nature lovers and bird watchers it can be an excellent winter recreation station. But care should be taken to protect the tank from getting polluted and dumped with waste by visitors. Such programmes make local people aware of the importance of tanks for improving their local economy through ecological wisdom.

E. Summary

Table 1.7: Summary of Characteristics: Kaveripakkam

1. Location	:	Kaveripakkam village, NAA Dist., TN. 13'50' N X 79°22' E, Palar river basin					
2. History	:	600 years old (taken from an inscription on an ancient masonry sluice)					
3. Rainfall	:	107.8 cm/year (1981 - 1990 mean)					
4. Temperature	:	Yearly mean 320 C					
5. Ayacut	:	67.72 Sq. Km.					
6. Catchment	:	Free = 31.08 Sq. Km. Combined = 126.91 Sq. Km.					
7. Yield	:	214 M. Cum / Sq. Km.					
8. Tank	:	Depth = 9.3 m (Deepest level) Area = 16.05 Sq. Km.					
9. Tank bund	:	Length = 8.35 Km Width = 3.6 m.					
10. Supply channel	:	Kaveripakkam supply channel from Palar Anicut-4.83Km. away					
11. Storage capacity	:	Original -41.73 M. Cu as per Memories Recent – 32.9 M. Cu M in 1981 Present – Not known					
12. Duration of water	:	6 – 8 Months after monsoon					
13. Sluices	:	10, Channel length = 20 to 7200 meters					
14. Cultivated area	:	25.42 Sq. Km. 42.31 Sq. Km.					
15. Villages	:	14					
16. Soil	pH :	5.9 – 8.8	N :	11.0 – 142.0 Kg/Ac			
	E. C :	0.1 – 0.6	P :	0.96 – 55.0 Kg/Ac			
	Texture :	SCL	K :	17.0 – 480.0 Kg/Ac			
17. Water	pH :	7.9 – 9.4	Na+ :	2.0 – 8.5 Me/I			
	Ec :	0.2 – 1.5	K+ :	0.03 – 0.1 Me/I			
	S.A.R :	0.6 – 5.6	CO_3 :	0.04 – 1.6 Me/I			
	Ca :	0.4 – 3.5 Me/I	HCO3- :	0.6 – 7.2 Me/I			
	Mg :	0.5 – 7.5 Me/I	Cl- :	0.2 – 9.0 Me/I			
18. Flora	Grasses :	13	Climbers :	6	Hydrophytes :	2	
	Herbs :	42	Trees :	12	Shrubs :	23	
19. Fauna	Butterflies :	15	Fishes :	6	Birds :	70	
	Amphibians:	5	Reptiles :	8	Mammals :	6	

20. Culture systems

(a) Agriculture

1. Major Crops – Plantain, Paddy and Sugarcane
2. Minor Crops – Mulberry, Groundnut, Ragi and Castor and Vegetables like Brinjal

(b) Aquaculture

1. Natural : Catfishes, Mullets, Tilapia and Carps.
2. Cultured : Nil

(c) Wetland Forestry

Location : Tank bank and Bed

Species : Acacia Arabica and Prosopis Juliflora

F. Addenda

1. Tables : 1.8 a - i

Table 1.8: a Characteristics of KAVERIPAKKAM - SOIL

				Nutrients (kg/acre)			
Sam	***Tex***	***pH***	***E.C mmh/cm***	***N***	***P K***		
1	S	CL	7.1	0.30	20.0	5.0	73.0
2	O	CL	8.4	0.20	137.5	1.3	67.5
3	N	SCL	6.6	0.12	72.0	17.0	87.0
4	M	SL	6.4	0.18	85.0	11.0	310.0
5	M	SL	8.1	0.20	57.0	14.0	96.0
6	JL	SCL	8.7	0.19	104.0	6.0	96.0
7	JL	SCL	8.3	0.25	105.0	6.0	210.0
8	JL	SCL	8.5	0.21	109.0	6.0	327.0
9	JL	SCL	7.5	0.16	53.0	6.0	66.0
10	JL	SCL	8.5	0.16	74.0	6.0	105.0
11	JL	SCL	8.8	0.17	52.0	9.0	60.0
12	S	CL	6.6	0.10	11.0	2.0	17.0
13	O	CL	8.5	0.20	148.5	1.0	90.0
14	N	SL	6.3	0.62	67.0	6.0	150.0
15	M	SL	6.7	0.25	84.0	55.0	157.0
16	J	SCL	5.9	0.46	86.0	33.0	369.0
17	JL	SCL	8.3	0.28	85.0	8.0	126.0
18	JL	SCL	8.8	0.22	62.0	6.0	102.0
19	JL	SCL	8.2	0.30	56.0	6.0	174.0
20	JL	SCL	7.1	0.50	100.0	6.0	111.0
21	N	CL	7.6	0.20	14.0	1.0	29.0
22	O	CL	7.0	0.20	122.5	1.1	105.3
23	N	SCL	6.4	0.34	56.0	9.0	96.0
24	M	SL	6.4	0.26	77.0	11.0	109.0
25	J	SCL	8.1	0.26	114.0	47.0	279.0
26		SCL	8.2	0.46	85.0	32.0	360.0
27		SCL	8.5	0.24	84.0	32.0	480.0
		E.X	205.5	7.03	21.19	343.4	3771.5
		X	7.61	026	78.48	12.78	145.05
		SO	0.92	0.12	3324	14.03	99.21

1-11	: Foreshore	12-20	: Bed	21-27	: Ayacut
S	: September	O	: October	N	: November
M	: May	J	: June	JL	: July
Sam	: sample	E.C	: electrical conductivity	S	: sandy
CI	: clayey	L	: loamy	Tex	: texture

Table 1.8b: Characteristics of KAVERIPAKKAM - WATER

Sam		pH	E.C.	S.A.R.	Cations (me/l)				Anions (me/l)		
					Ca	Mg	Na	K	Co_3-	Hco_3 -	Cl
1.	S	8.0	0.2	-	1.2	2.1	-	-	-	0.8	0.2
2.	S	7.9	0.2	-	2.3	1.9	-	-	-	1.6	0.2
3.	M	9.4	0.8	0.6	1.1	0.7	5.5	-	-	0.9	4.8
4.	J	8.1	0.8	4.3	0.5	1.9	4.8	-	-	2.9	4.5
5.	JL	7.5	0.9	4.5	1.3	1.7	5.5	-	-	2.6	5.5
6.	S	8.0	1.4	2.4	4.1	4.3	4.9	0.05	-	6.8	7.0
7.	S	7.9	1.3	3.7	4.3	1.9	6.5	0.03	-	7.2	5.7
8.	O	8.2	0.7	3.6	1.7	0.6	3.8	0.12	-	3.7	3.0
9.	O	8.0	0.6	3.1	1.5	1.5	3.8	0.09	-	2.8	3.0
10.	J	9.4	0.8	5.6	1.1	0.8	5.5	-	1.6	0.9	4.8
11.	J	9.0	0.8	5.5	0.9	1.1	5.5	-	1.0	0.8	4.5
12.	J	8.6	0.7	5.0	0.4	1.6	5.0	-	0.4	2.0	4.6
13.	J	7.6	1.1	2.9	0.9	4.7	5.0	-	-	6.9	4.1
14.	O	7.9	0.8	-	1.5	1.4	-	-	-	0.6	0.2
15.	M	8.0	0.8	5.1	1.1	1.0	2.0	-	-	5.0	2.5
16.	M	8.4	1.5	4.7	3.5	3.0	8.5	-	-	5.4	9.0
17.	J	8.4	0.7	5.2	0.5	1.4	5.1	-	0.3	2.2	4.2
18.	JL	7.7	1.2	1.6	1.3	7.5	3.3	-	-	5.8	6.0
	E.X	156.4	22.5	56.45	90.15	31.6	66.2	0.29	4.9	58.7	64.8
	X	8.23	0.78	4.03	2.82	1.86	4.72	0.07	0.98	3.26	3.81
	SD	0.53	0.31	1.25	1.69	1.12	1.10	0.03	0.56	2.25	1.97

1-5: Stagnant **6-7:** Inlet **8-13:** Outlet **14-18:** Well

Table 1.8c: Characteristics of KAVERIPAKKAM-PLANTS

No	*Species*	*Habit*	*No*	*Species*	*Habit*
1.	Abutilon indicum	H	47.	Ischaemum angustifolium	G
2.	Acacia arabica	T	48.	Jasminum angustifolium	C
3.	Acalypha indica	S	49.	Jatropha glandulifera	S
4.	Achyranthes aspera	S	50.	Jatropha heterophylla	S
5.	Aerva lanata	H	51.	Justicia glabra	H
6.	Alangium salvifolium	T	52.	Justicia glauca	H
7.	Albizia amara	T	53.	Leucas aspera	H
8.	Alysicarpus vaginalis	H	54.	Lycopersicum esculentum	H
9.	Ammania baccifera	H	55.	Melothria madraspatana	C
10.	Andrographis paniculata	S	56.	Mimosa pudica	H
11.	Anisomeles indica	S	57.	Mollugo pentaphylla	H
12.	Apluda mutica	G	58.	Morinda coreia	T
13.	Arundo donax	G	59.	Nerium odorum	S
14.	Azadirachta indica	T	60.	Ocimum basilicum	H
15.	Blastania garcini	C	61.	Ocimum canum	H
16.	Boerhavia diffusa	H	62.	Ocimum sanctum	H
17.	Bombax ceiba	T	63.	Oldenlandia alata	H
18.	Borassus flabellifer	T	64.	Oldenlandia umbellata	H
19.	Cadaba fruticosa	S	65.	Opuntia coccinellifera	S
20.	Canthium coromandelium	S	66.	Pavonia zeylanica	S
21.	Carissa spinarum	S	67.	Parthenium hysterophorus	H
22.	Celosia argentea	H	68.	Parthenocissus sp.	C
23.	Chloris inflata	G	69.	Passiflora edulis	C
24.	Chloris virgata	G	70.	Perotis indica	G
25.	Citrulus lanatus	C	71.	Phoenix loureirii	S
26.	Coldenia procumbens	H	72.	Phoenix sylvestris	T
27.	Coleus barbatus	H	73.	Physalis minima	H
28.	Commelina persicariaefolia	H	74.	Pongamia pinnata	T
29.	Croton bonplandianus	H	75.	Prosopis juliflora	T
30.	Cyanodon dactylon	G	76.	Psilotrichum nudum	H
31.	Cyperus articulatus	G	77.	Randia malabarica	S
32.	Cyperus arenarius	G	78.	Saccharum officinarum	G
33.	Digitaria chinensis	G	79.	Sida acuta	H
34.	Echinops echinatus	H	80.	Sida cordifolia	H
35.	Eclipta prostrata	H	81.	Sida rhombifolia	H
36.	Elephantopus scaber	H	82.	Solanum nigrum	S
37.	Eleusine indica	G	83.	Solanum torvum	H
38.	Euphorbia hirta	H	84.	Syzygium cumini	T
39.	Evolvulus alsinoides	H	85.	Tacca pinnatida	H
40.	Fimbristylis aggregata	G	86.	Tamarindus indica	T
41.	Flueggea leucopyrus	S	87.	Tephrosia purpurea	H
42.	Gomphrena celosioides	H	88.	Thevetia neriifolia	S
43.	Heliotropium scabrum	H	89.	Tragia involucrata	H
44.	Hibiscus esculentus	S	90.	Tribulus terrestris	H
45.	Hibiscus hirtus	H	91.	Tridax procumbens	H
46.	Indigofera cordifolia	H	92.	Vrtex negundo	S

G (Grass) : 16 T (Trees) : 12

H (Herbs) : 42 Hy (Hydrophytes) : 2

S(Shrubs) : 19 C (Climbers) : 6

Table 1.8d: Characteristics of KAVERIPAKKAM - BUTTERFLIES

No.	Species	Common Name
1.	Byblia ilithyia	Common Castor
2.	Catopsilia crocale	Common Emigrant
3.	Danais chrysippus	Plain Tiger
4.	Delias eucharis	Common Jezebel
5.	Ergolis merione	Common Castor
6.	Euploea core	Common Indian Crow
7.	Hypolimnas misippus	Danaid Egg fly
8.	Mycalesis perseus	Common Bush Brown
9.	Papilio polytes	Common Mormon
10.	Polydorous aristolochiae	Common Rose
11.	Polydorous hector	Crimson Rose
12.	Precis lemonias	lemon Pansy
13.	Precis nierta	Yellow Pansy
14.	Talchinia violae	Tawny Castor

Table 1.8e: Characteristics of KAVERIPAKKAM - FISHES

No.	Species	Common Name
1.	Cattle catla	Catla Carp
2.	Cirrhina mrigal	Mrigal Carp
3.	Labeo rohita	Rohu Carp (Kendai)
4.	Ophiocephalus marulius	Avuri Viral
5.	Ophiocephalus punctatus	Koravai
6.	Tilapia mossambica	Tilapi Kandai

Table 1.8f: Characteristics of KAVERIPAKKAM - AMPHIBIANS

No.	Species	Common Name
1.	Bufo melanostictus	Common Indian Toad
2.	Rana hexadactyla	South Indian Frog
3.	Rana limnocharis	Paddy field Frog
4.	Rhacophorus sp.	Tree Frog

Table 1.8g: Characteristics of KAVERIPAKKAM - REPTILES

No.	Species	Common Name
1.	Ahaetulla nasutus	Common Green Whip Snake
2.	Amphiesma stolata	Buff striped Keel back
3.	Calotes versicolor	Garden lizard
4.	Hemidactylus frenatus	Southern House Gecko
5.	Mabuya carinata	Common Skink
6.	Melanochelys trijuga	Indian Pond Terrapin
7.	Ptyas mucosus	Common Rat Snake
8.	Xenochrophis piscatos	Checkered Keel back

Table 1.8h: Characteristics of KAVERIPAKKAM - BIRDS

No.	*Species*	*Common Name*	*Migration*	*Nutrition*
1.	Accipiter badius	Shikra	R	T
2.	Acridotheres tristis	Common Myna	R	FI
3.	Alauda gulgula	Eastern Skylark	LM	IAF
4.	Alcedo atthis	Small Blue Kingfisher	R	A
5.	Amaurornis phoenicurus	White Breasted Waterhen	R	A
6.	Anans acuta	Pin-tailed Duck	M	A
7.	Anas clypeata	Shoveler	R	A
8.	Anas penelope	Wigeon	R	A
9.	Anas querquedula	Garganey Teal	M	A
10.	Ardea cinerea	Grey Heron	R	A
11.	Ardeda grayii	Pond Heron	R	A
12.	Artamus fuscus	Ashy Swallow-Shrike	R	I
13.	Athene brama	Spotted Owlet	R	T
14.	Aythya ferina	Common Pochard	M	A
15.	Bubulcus ibis	Cattle egret	R	T
16.	Centropus sinensis	Crow Pheasant	R	T
17.	Ceryle rudis	Lesser Pied Kingfisher	R	A
18.	Chlidonias hybridus	Whiskered Tern	M	A
19.	Cisticola juncidis	Streaked Fantail Warbler	R	I
20.	Clamator jacobinus	Pied Crested Cuckoo	LM	FI
21.	Columba livia	Blue Rock Pigeon	R	TG
22.	Coracias benghalensis	Indian Roller	R	TI
23.	Coracina novaehollandiae	Large Cuckoo-Shrike	R	I
24.	Corvus macrorhynchos	Jungle Crow	R	AFI
25.	Corvus splendens	House Crow	R	AFI
26.	Copsychus saularis	Magpie Robin	R	I
27.	Cuculus varius	Common Hawk Cuckoo	R	FI
28.	Cypsiurus parvus	Palm Swift	R	I
29.	Dendrocitta vagabunda	Indian Tree pie	R	AF
30.	Dicrurus adsimilis	Black Drongo	R	NI
31,	Dicrurus leucophaeus	Grey Drongo	R	NI
32.	Dinopium benghalense	L.Golden-backed Woodpecker	LM	NI
33.	Egretta garzetta	Little Egret	R	T
34.	Egretta intermedia	Small Egret	R	T
35.	Eudynamis scolopacea	Keel	R	FI
36.	Francolinus pondicerianus	Grey Partridge	R	T
37.	Fulica atra	Coot	R	A
38.	Halcyon smyrnensis	White Breasted Kingfisher	R	A
39.	Haliastur indus	Brahminy Kite	R	A
40.	Himantopus himantopus	Black winged Stilt	R	A
41.	Hirundo rustica	Swallow	M	I
42.	Megalaima haemacephala	Crimson Breasted barbet	R	F
43.	Merops Orientalis	Green Bee-eater	R	I
44.	Milvus rnigrans	Pariah Kite	R	T
45.	Motacilla madraspatensis	Large Pied Wagtail	R	IA
46.	Nectarinia Iotenia	Loten's Sunbird	R	N

(Contd...)

47.	Nectarinia zeylonica	Purpleumped Sunbird	R	IN
48.	Netta rufina	Red creasted Pochard	M	A
49.	Oriolus oriolus	Golden Oriole	R	FI
50.	Orthotorhus sutorius	Tailor Bird	R	NI
51.	Phalacrocorax niger	Little Cormorant	R	A
52.	Phylloscopus trochiloides	Dull Green Leaf Warbler	R	I
53.	Ploceus philippinus	Baya Weaverbird	LM	IF
54.	Podiceps rulicotlis	Lillie Grebe	R	A
55.	Prinia socialis	Ashy Wren-Warbler	R	I
56.	Psittacula krameri	Rose-ringed Parakeet	LM	FG
57.	Pycnonotus caler	Redvented Bulbul	R	FIN
58.	Pycnonotus luteolus	White browed Bulbul	R	FIN
59.	Saxicola caprata	Pied Bush Chat	R	I
60.	Saxicolaides fulicata	Indian Robin	R	I
61.	Streptopilia chinensis	Spotted Dove	R	TG
62.	Streptopilia senegalensis	Little Brown Dove	R	T
63.	Sturnus pagodarum	Black headed Myna	R	FI
64.	Tephrodornis pondicerianus	Common Wood Shrike	R	I
65.	Tringa hypoleucos	Common Sandpiper	M	A
66.	Tringa stagnatilis	Marsh Sandpiper	M	A
67.	Turdoides affinis	White-headed Barbier	R	FIN
68.	Turdoides malcolmi	Large Grey Barbier	R	FIN
69.	Upupaepops	Hoopoe	R	TI
70.	Vanellus indicus	Redwattled Lapwing	R	T

R: 55 LM: 5 M: 10 F = 17 N = 10 I = 35 A = 24 T = 14

Table 1.8i: Characteristics of KAVERIPAKKAM - MAMMALS

No.	*Species*	*Common Name*
1.	Bandicoota indica	Bandicoot Rat
2.	Funambulus palmarum	Three-stripped Plam Squirrel
3.	Herpestes edwardsi	Mongoose
4.	Lepus nigricollis	Indian Hare
5.	Macaca radiala	Bonnet Macaque
6.	Rattus raltus	Common Rat

2. Figures: 1.2a-d

Collection locations of soil, water and plant samples and sites of photography

3. Photographs: 1.1-8

1 **& 2 Kaveripakkam:** A panoramic view, from the southern banks of Kaveripakkam after the onset of monsoon. Tank receives its water from the catchments and the Kaveripakkam supply channel from Palar anicut system. When the water level rises it inundates most of the agricultural fields & agro-forestry on fringe-lands.

3. **Inundated plantain cultivation in the tank:** since ground water level is high and the soil is humid even in summer, crops like sugarcane and plantain are grown. The embankment is visible on the right.
4. **The Kaveripakkam supply channel:** Major source of water of the tank is the Palar anicut system. Kaveripakkam tank systems include about 161 used and unused system and non-system tanks supplying water for approximately. 94 villages. The banks of supply channel are thickly vegetated with Prosopis. Bunds of the supply channel are well engineered.
5. **Agriculture fields:** Irrigated by Kaveripakkam tank. The tank is seen in the background. Foreground is 1tie agricultural area. Major crops are rice and sugar cane. Coconut is also grown on a large scale in many places. The tank bed is the major grazing ground !of village livestock.

6 & 7. The Lush green agricultural fields in the ayacut: from plantain to mulberry, a variety of crops are cultivated in these fields.

8. **Paddy fields:** In the ayacut of Kaveripakkam the lands are irrigated directly by tank water through sluices or indirectly through ayacut wells.
9. A google map of Kaveripakkam

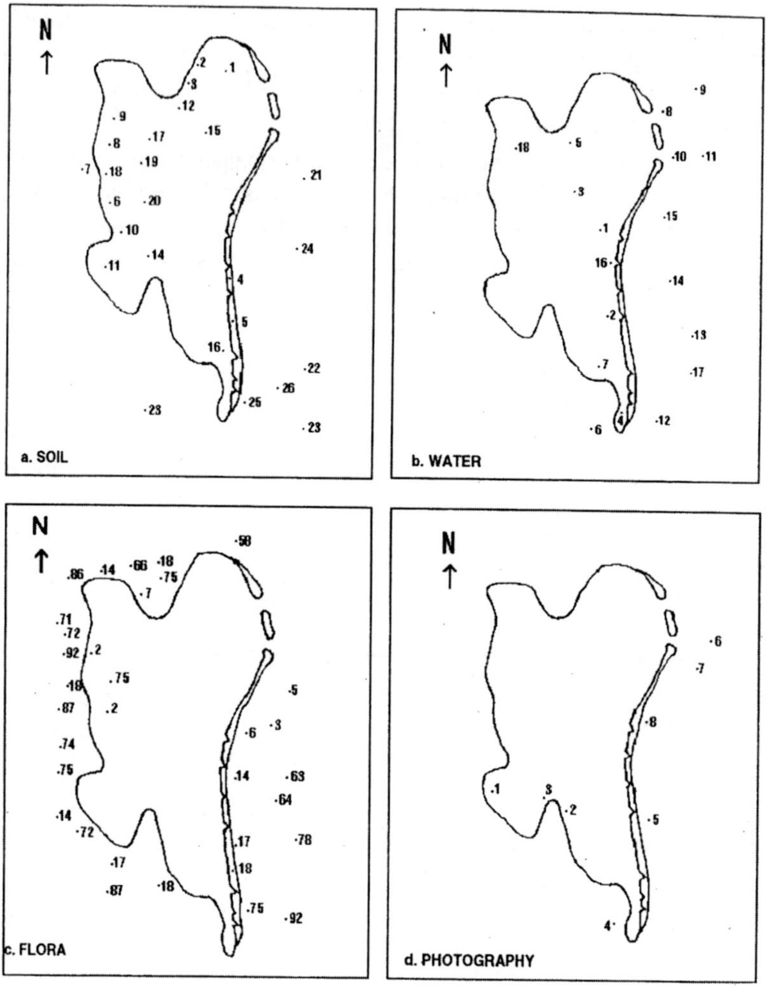

Fig. 1.2: Sampling sites at KAVERIPAKKAM

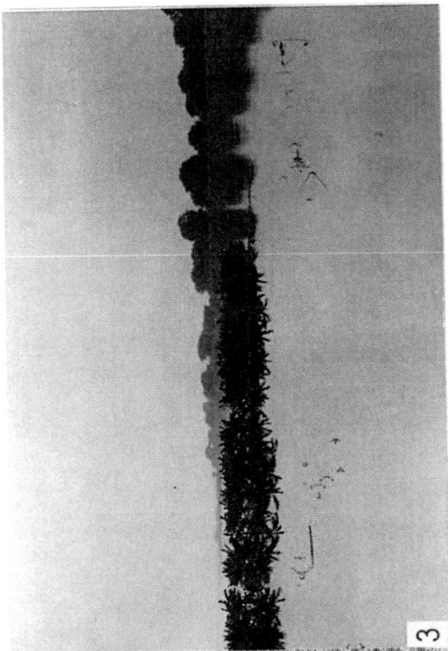

5

6

7

8

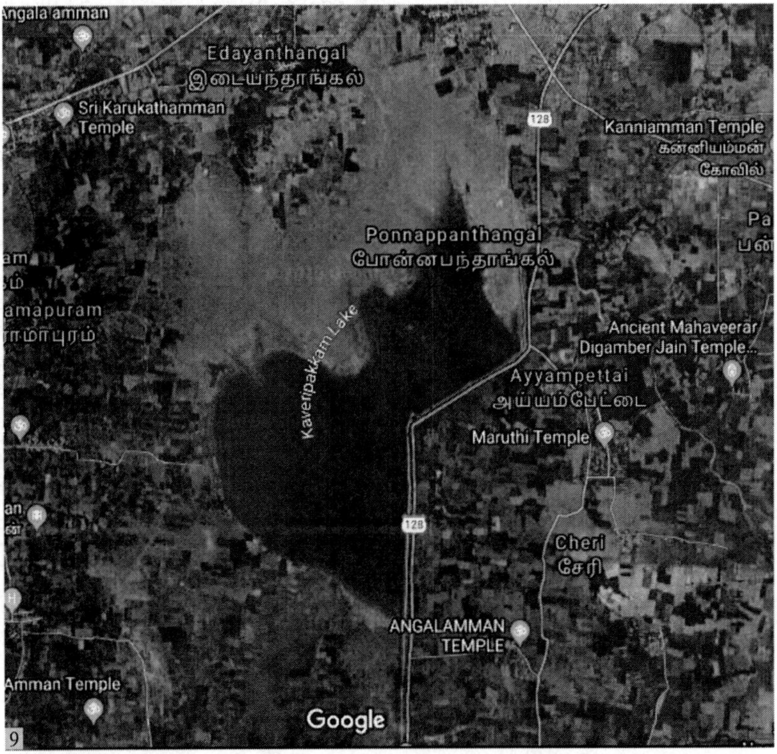
Edayanthangal
இடையந்தாங்கல்
Sri Karukathamman Temple
128
Kanniamman Temple
கன்னியம்மன் கோவில்
Ponnappanthangal
பொன்னபந்தாங்கல்
Kaveripakkam Lake
Ancient Mahaveerar Digamber Jain Temple...
Ayyampettai
அய்யம்பேட்டை
Maruthi Temple
Cheri
சேரி
ANGALAMMAN TEMPLE
Amman Temple
Google

2. PILLAIPAKKAM

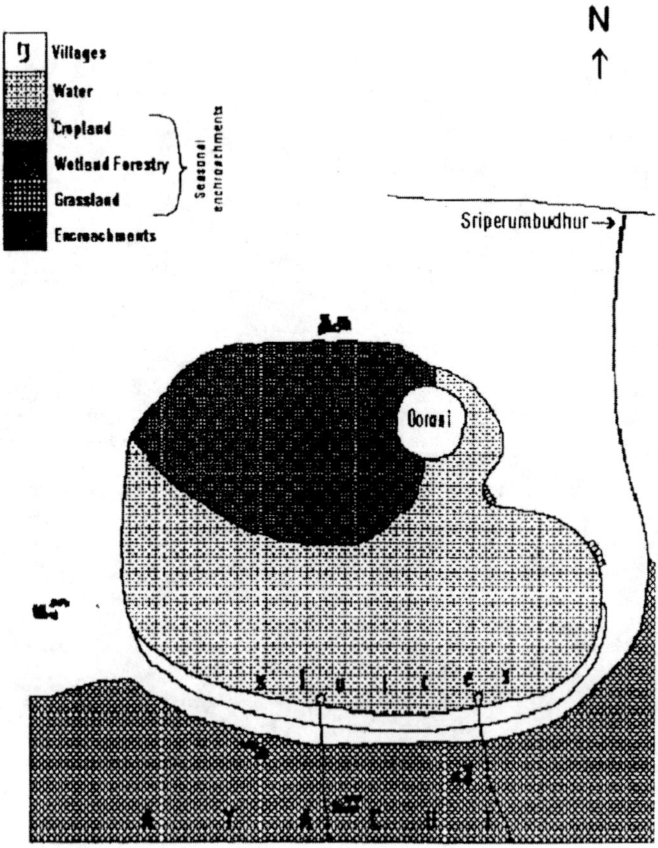

Fig 2.1: Ecography of Pillaipakkam.

A. Introduction

Pillaipakkam tank is located at Pillaipakkam village in the North Arcot district 3 Km south of Sriperumbudur on the Madras-Bangalore highway. The tank has been known to exist for about six hundred years. This tank is at the tail-end of Kambakkal channel of the Palar Anicut System. Total water spread of the tank is 9.79 sq. km. and the average depth of the tank is

4 meters when the tank is full. The tank has a man-made embankment of 3.66 Km length and an average width of 2.5 m. The storage capacity of the tank is nearly 3.77 M.Cu.M. Water is supplied through Kambakkal supply channel and also from its own catchment of 9.98 sq. km. Water is available in the tank for 3-4 months after the rainy season. The total ayacut of the tank is 4.45 sq. km. of which 1.77 sq. km of area harvests only a single crop. Only four villages depend on this tank for irrigation. The agro climatology of this area is similar to that of Kaveripakkam. Major crop in the tank vicinity is Paddy. Ragi, Cotton and Millets are the minor crops (Table 2.7, Fig. 2.1).

B. Characteristics

1. **Soil** (Tables 2.1, 2.8a and Fig. 2.2a).

   Soils of the foreshore, bed and wasteland are of sandy clay and loamy texture. All these except that of wastelands have a widely varying pH. Electrical conductivity varied between 0.1 and 1.5 (mm/cm). Nitrogen content varied between 14.0 and 126.0 Kg/Ac, Phosphorus between 1.4 and 56 and Potassium between 11 and 633.

Table 2.1: Characteristics of Pillaipakkam – Soil[@]

	Parameter	*FS*	*B*	*Ayacut (WL)*	*Mean (SO)*	
1.	Texture	SCL	SL	SL - CL	SCL	-
2.	pH	5.8 – 8.1	2.5 – 8.4	6.9 – 8.0	7.2 – 7.7	7.04 (0.8)
3.	E.C*	0.1 – 0.6	0.1 – 53.0	0.2 – 1.5	0.1 – 0.4	0.24 (0.1)
4.	Nutrients #					
	N	45.0 – 126	14 – 119	20 – 95	22 – 78	74.06 (17.8)
	P	3.4 – 43	1.4 – 16	2.8 – 56	3.1 – 9.0)	9.79 (4.91)
	K	33.0 – 594	88 – 162	53 – 633	11.0 – 143	131.06 (45.8)

@ For more details refer Table 2.8a and Fig.2.2a

**mm/cm* # Kg/Acre

2. **Water** (Tables 2.2, 2.8b and Fig. 2.2b)

   In the water samples from the inlet and outlet channels, stagnant water and the wells in the ayacut, pH varied between 6.7 and 9.0, electrical conductivity between 0.2 and 0.9, Calcium concentration between 0.3 and 2.3 Magnesium between 0.5 and 2.5, Sodium between 0.3 and 6.5 and Potassium between 0.3 and 0.9 Me/l, Bicarbonate between 1.0 and 9.8 Me/l and Chloride between 0.3 and 8.7 Me/l.

Table 2.2: Characteristics of PILLAIPAKKAM – Water@

Parameters	*Stagnant*	*Inlet*	*Outlet*	*Well*	*Mean(sd)*
pH	7.8 – 9.0	6.7 – 7.5	8.1	6.8 – 8.0	7.74 (0.82)
E.C.	0.3 – 1.1	0.2 – 1.9	0.2 – 0.2	0.2 – 1.1	0.40 (0.34)
S.A.R.	2.8 - –	2.8 - –	0.3 – 0.7	4.7 - –	1.63 (2.39)
Cations (me/l)					
Ca	0.3 – 0.9	0.6 – 2.3	0.5 – 0.8	1.0 – 1.5	1.77 (2.39)
Mg	0.5 – 2.5	0.4 – 1.7	0.8 – 1.2	1.5 – 2.3	1.41 (0.70)
Na	1.8 - –	0.7 – 0.8	0.3 – 0.5	6.5 - –	0.82 (0.49)
K	–	0.3 – 0.9	0.3 – 0.4	0.3 - –	0.49 (0.49)
Ations (me/l)					
CO_3	0.5 - –	–	0.48 (0)		
HCO_3	1.3 – 3.0	5.0 – 9.8	1.0 – 1.4	1.0 – 1.3	1.69 (0.99)
Cl	0.8 – 4.5	1.0 – 3.3	0.6 - –	0.3 – 8.7	1.41 (1.37)

@ For more details refer Table 2.8b, Fig.2.2b

3. **Flora** (Tables 2.3, 2.8c and Fig 2.3c)

A total of 67 flowering plant species belonging to 59 genera and 37 families are found in the vicinity of Pillaipakkam tank of which 6 are grasses, 35 herbs. 12 shrubs, 5 climbers, 8 trees and 1 hydrophyte. Of these, 19 plants are of considerable economic and ecological importance. Foreshore (52) and ayacut (49) have greater diversity than bed (15) and wastelands (16). The barren wastelands are dominated by Prosopis or Croton (Table 2.3).

Table 2.3: Characteristics of PILLAIPAKKAM – FLORA *

Important Habit	*Taxonomy*				*Habitat*			
	Spp	*Gen*	*Fam*	*FS*	*Bed*	*Ayacut*		*WL*
Grasses & Sedges	6	6	2	3	5	3	1	2
Herbs	35	29	15	26	5	31	7	6
Shrubs	12	11	11	12	2	8	3	5
Climbers	5	5	4	5	–	3 – 4	1 – 2	–
Trees	8	7	4	6	2	3	3	5
Hydrophytes	1	1	1	–	1	–	–	1
Total	67	59	37	52	15	49	16	19

@ For more details refer Table 2.8c. Fig 2.2c.

4. **Fauna** (Tables 2.4a, 2.4b, 2.8d-i).

There are 86 species belonging to 77 genera and 48 families. Of these, 54 are birds, 10 butterflies, 6 fishes, 4 amphibians, 7 reptiles and 5 mammals, inhabiting the four parts of the tank region. Broadly speaking, thickets (53) on the banks and the agricultural fields (52) harbour more species. The 54 bird species possess 5 types of feeding habits, most being insectivorous.

Table 2.4a: Characteristics of PILLAIPAKKAM - FAUNA@

Animals	*Taxonomy*				*Habitat*		
	Spp	*Gen*	*Fam*	*TW*	*Hs*	*AF*	*TB*
Butterflies	10	9	5	2	6	7	9
Fishes	6	5	5	6	-	2	-
Amphibians	4	2	2	3	2	4	-
Reptiles	7	7	5	1	4	5	6
Birds	54	46	27	16	14	31	33
Mammals	5	5	4	-	4	3	5
Total	86	77	48	28	30	52	53

@ For more details refer Tables 2.8d-i

Table 2.4b: Characteristics of PILLAIPAKKAM - BIRDS@

Migratory Status	*Taxonomy*				*Habitat*			
	Spp	*Gen*	*Fam*	*F*	*N*	*I*	*A*	*T*
Resident	40	39	20	9	6	21	11	17
Local Migratory	3	3	2	1	-	1	1	1
Migratory	11	7	5	-	-	3	9	-
Total	54	49	27	10	6	25	21	18

@ For more details refer Tables 2.Bh

5. **Culture systems** (Table 2.5, Fig 2.1).

   (a) **Agriculture**: Major crops are Paddy and Sugarcane. Two harvests are made in 2.67 sq. km. of the ayacut and one in the remaining 1.77 sq. km. Minor crops like Ragi, Cotton and other Millets are cultivated in marginal areas, sometimes as summer crops. Apart from the tank water, well water is also used for irrigating the tail-ends of channels.

   (b) **Aquaculture:** No systematic aquaculture is practiced in the tank though six species of fish occur here, among which Tilapia, catfishes and carps are edible.

Table 2.5: Characteristics of PILLAIPAKKAM - CULTURE SYSTEMS

Agriculture	*Aquaculture*	*Wetland Forestry*		*Human Settlements*
	Natural	*Location*	*Plant*	
Paddy	Catfish	Bank bed	Eucalyptus	Pillaipakkam
Plantain	Mullet		Acacia	Chinnapillaipakkam
Brinjal	Tilapia		Prosopis	Kaduvancherry
Groundnut	Carps			Odankaranani
Ragi				Navalur
Kambu				
Sugarcane				

(c) **Wetland forestry:** Social forestry plantations are raised by the government in the tank bed, especially on the western shallow regions with Acacia arabica and Eucalyptus. Villagers depend on these for firewood.

(d) **Settlements:** A total of five villages, viz. Pillaipakkam, Navalur, Chinnapillai pakkam, Kadangamcheny, and Odenkaranari depend on this tank for irrigation of their land holdings in the ayacut.

6. **Pollution:**

No account of pollution was reported from the tank vicinity. But an increasing use of pesticides and fertilisers was observed in the agricultural fields.

C. Perceptions

Table 2.6: People's perceptions on PILLAIPAKKAM

Soil: Soil is claimed to be fertile perhaps enriched by the animal wastes and tank bed sediments.

Water: Tank water is available for a maximum of 6 months .It is used for domestic purposes also. Water scarcity occurs only when monsoon fails. Disputes on distributing tank water are resolved by Nattanmaikkaran.

Plants: People are not aware of the ecological significance of plant cover. They wish to have more plants for their use but have not taken initiatives.

Animals: Except for birds and their winter migration, people are not aware of the seasonality of animals. Birds are poached upon by locals using nets and guns.

Agriculture: Agriculture is entirely dependent on tank water. Paddy, Sugarcane and Groundnut are the major crops. The crops are manured with synthetic fertilizers, animal wastes and tank bed sediments. The pest infestation has considerably increased over the last few years. People are unaware of biological control of pests and still depend on pesticides.

Aquaculture: People are not aware of the benefits of low input aquaculture.

Wetland Forestry: People depend on Prosopis, Acacia and Eucalyptus for firewood.

Animal husbandry: Villagers keep cows, buffaloes, sheep and poultry to get milk, meat, eggs and hide. Animal waste is utilised as manure.

D. Inferences

1. Ecology

(a) Subsystems

(i) **Water body:** When the tank is full, the water body occupies an area of nearly 9.89 sq. km. After the monsoon the water level recedes. The water body harbours fishes and amphibians. In winter many migratory birds use this habitat. Hydroloea zeylanica is a common hydrophyhte. Shrubs like Ipomoea grow in an aqua terrestrial habitat.

(ii) **Agro-ecosystem:** Agriculture is practiced in the ayacut and along the shorelines of the tank. A variety of crops like Plantain, Groundnut, Ragi, Kambu and Sugarcane contribute to the diversity of the agro-ecosystem. About 49 species of plants are found in the ayacut Some are weeds, while others like Jatropha and Vitex are used as live fencing. A number of animal species are also found, such as butterflies, amphibians, reptiles, birds and mammals. Some of these play a significant role as pests, their predators, dispersants of seeds and pollinators.

(iii) **Wetland forestry:** Three species of fast growing multipurpose trees- **Prosopis, Acacia and Eucalyptus** are cultivated on the tank embankments and shoreline. Of late a number of privately owned plantations have also cropped up. These systems are characterised by poor undergrowth and low faunal diversity comprising of a few small mammals and birds. Water birds depend on the trees for roosting and nesting.

(b) Habitat Qualities

(i) **Soil:** Soil is sandy loamy and clayey loamy with a neutral pH, which is suitable for all crops. Electrical conductivity has a mean value of 0.24 which is under tolerance limits. Soil is deficient in Nitrogen but rich in Phosphorus and Potassium whose concentrations vary from very low to very high in different locations.

(ii) **Water:** The mean values of pH (7.74) and E.C. (0.40) suggests that the tank water is mildly alkaline and suitable for irrigating all crops. There is no lime saturation in water. It is interesting to note that the water of Pillaipakkam appears better than that of Kaveripakkam, though both the tanks receive water from the same supply channel.

2. Conservation

(a) Habitats

(i) **Water body:** Water remains for a short time. This duration could be increased by maneuvering all the rainfall to drain into the tank. This could then serve as a habitat for fishes and amphibians for longer periods possibly becoming a natural source of food for the local people. More avifauna will naturally be attracted.

(ii) **Land:** The barren banks, susceptible to erosion, need to be vegetated by ground cover, shrubs and trees. In fact, the thickets present in some places could be replicated. The preferences should be for plants useful as soil binders, humus builders and fodder yielders. The habitat support to plants, butterflies, reptiles, mammals and birds may gradually increase the biodiversity and their productivity, that development inputs may be possible, in due course.

(b) Resources

(i) **Soil:** The soil is used for plastering houses, brick making, pottery, etc. Being deficient only in Nitrogen, it will need replenishments of nitrogenous fertilisers, directly or indirectly, on a long-term basis.

(ii) **Water:** It is found good for agricultural purposes as well as for human consumption both directly and indirectly.

(iii) **Plants:** Of the 67 plant species recorded, two grass species growing in wastelands and tank embankments are used for making broomsticks and a few others are used as fodder. Herbs are used as leaf vegetables, medicines, etc. Shrubs like Jatropha, Vitex and Opuntia are used for live fencing.(Prosopis is the major source of firewood for villagers). Local people have faith in medicinal plants. Unfortunately these are dwindling gradually. Therefore it is urgent to protect the medicinal plants and reintroduce the lost ones.

(iv) **Animals:** Besides restoring the depleted resources conservation of the present diversity is essential. Different animals are ecologically and economically important. A refugium for local animals will be apt. As far as birds are concerned, steps against poaching are necessary especially during the migratory season. Planting more trees, turfing the banks and regenerating the lost vegetation will improve the habitat for animal species. Thus Pillaipakkam Animal Refugium is a feasible development project enabling the conservation of resources. That the tank is near Sriperumbudur town may provoke better ideas of ecotourism.

3. Development

(a) Agriculture: People should be encouraged to cultivate less water-consuming crops, so that water can be conserved in the wells and underground for longer durations and for potable purposes. and raising a second crop in the entire ayacut. Misuse of chemical fertilizers and subsequent degradation in soil quality. In such instances it is necessary to popularise the alternative methods of fertilizing the soil. Compost made out of green manure and animal waste can be used. This can be clubbed with vermi-composting using earthworms. However these efforts need careful preparation, continuous interest and cooperative effort on the part of the local farming community of all the surrounding villages.

(b) Aquaculture: The tank retains water for less than six months. Six species of fishes constitute a naturally occurring fishery for the villagers. Aqua-cultural development, therefore, seems feasible.

(c) Sericulture: It should be possible to raise mulberry plantations atleast for a few months as in case of Kaveripakkam as a new source of income to local people without affecting the local ecology

(d) Apiculture: Availability of water, well vegetated banks and semi-arid climate suits Apiculture. Suitable species for the semi arid zone can be introduced with governmental inputs. Since the success of beekeeping is connected with flowering plant diversity and water availability, these ought to be ensured first.

(e) Ecotourism: Pillaipakkam with its well engineered bunds and sea-sonal availability of water can develop into a good picnic spot with a few inputs. This involves (a) planting of shade trees (b) Construction of sitting benches (c) Turfing of banks, and (d) Improvement of the road from Sriperumbudur. For nature lovers and bird watchers it can bean excellent winter recreation station. Such programmes make people aware of the importance of tanks.

E. Summary

Table 2.7: Summary of Characteristics: PILLAIPAKKAM

1. Location	: 3 Km south of Sriperumbudur on the Madras-Bangalore Highway. Tail end of Kambakkal supply channel of Palar River Basin. Coordinates: 12’57' N X 79’57' E				
2. History	: Palar River Basin, 600 Years old				
3. Rainfall	: 106 cm/year, 52.8 days/year (average of 50 years)				
4. Temperature	: Yearly mean 32 C				
5. Ayacut	: 4.45 Sq. Km.				
6. Catchment	: Free = 9.69 Sq. Km. Combined = 28.98 Sq. Km.				
7. Yield	: 7.12 M Cu. M.				
8. Tank	: Area = 9.89 Sq. Km.				
9. Tank bund	: 3660 meters				
10. Supply channel	: Kambakkal channel				
11. Storage capacity	: 3.77 M. Cu. M.				
12. Duration of water	: 6-8 months				
13. Sluices	: 6, 0.5 - 1 Sq. Km/Sluice				
14. Cultivated area	: 10.4 Sq. Km.				
15. Villages associated	: 4				
16. Soil	pH :	5.8 - 8.1	N	:	14.0 -126.0 Kg/Ac
	E.C :	0.1 - 1.5	P	:	1.4 - 56.0 Kg/Ac
	Texture:	SCL - CL	K	:	11.0 - 633.0 Kg/Ac
17. Water	pH :	6.8 – 9.0	Na	:	0.3 – 6.5 Me/I
	E.C. :	0.2 – 1.1	K	:	0.03 – 0.4 Me/I
	S.A.R :	0.3 – 4.7	CO_3	:	0.5 – - Me/I
	Ca :	0.3 – 2.3 Me/I	HCO3-	:	0.8 – 1.3 Me/I
	Mg :	0.5 – 2.5 Me/I	Cl-	:	0.3 – 8.7 Me/I
18. Flora	Grasses :	6	Climbers	:	5
	Herbs :	35	Trees	:	8
	Shrubs :	12	Hygrophyte	:	1
19. Fauna	Butterflies :	10	Fishes	:	6
	Amphibians:	4	Reptiles	:	7
	Birds :	54	Mammals	:	5

20. Culture systems

(a) Agriculture

1. Major Crops – Paddy and Sugarcane
2. Minor Crops –Ragi and Castor and millet

(b) Aquaculture

1. Natural : Tilapia sp., Catfish and Carps
2. Cultured : Nil

(c) Wetland Forestry

Location : Tank Bed

Species : Eucalyptus and Acacia arabica

F. Addenda

1. Tables: 2.8a – i

Table 2.8a: Characteristics of PILLAIPAKKAM – SOIL

Sam	*Texture*		*pH*	*E.C mmh/cm*	*Nutrients (kg/acre)*		
					N	*P*	*K*
1	S	CL	6.8	0.50	70.0	3.4	220.0
2	O	CL	6.3	0.50	45.0	3.8	83.0
3	N	SCL	7.7	0.21	64.0	7.0	594.0
4	M	SL	8.1	0.57	70.0	43.0	74.0
5	J	SCL	6.2	0.29	126.0	18.0	33.0
6	J	SCL	5.9	0.24	98.0	16.0	162.0
7	J	SCL	6.2	0.16	126.0	17.0	390.0
8	JL	SCL	5.8	0.08	84.0	7.0	36.0
9	JL	SCL	5.8	0.15	98.0	7.0	168.0
10	JL	SCL	6.0	0.08	74.0	6.0	33.0
11	N	CL	8.1	0.50	28.0	1.4	150.0
12	S	SL	8.0	0.50	14.0	16.0	88.0
13	O	SCL	7.6	0.12	72.0	8.0	96.0
14	M	SL	7.9	0.23	77.0	12.0	96.0
15	M	SL	7.9	0.23	70.0	11.0	138.0
16	J	SCL	6.7	0.19	89.0	10.0	141.0
17	J	SCL	6.2	0.29	119.0	11.0	162.0
18	N	SL	7.4	0.40	20.0	3.8	53.0
19	N	CL	7.7	0.70	95.0	2.9	360.0
20	S	SL	6.9	0.22	70.0	56.0	192.0
21	M	CL	8.0	1.50	77.0	15.0	633.0
22	O	SCL	7.2	0.40	22.0	3.1	143.0
23	N	SCL	7.7	0.11	78.0	9.0	11.0
		E.X	156.3	6.38	1540	243	2829
		X	7.10	0.30	70.0	12.5	134.71
		SO	0.79	0.16	28.69	10.28	95.96

Table 2.8b: Characteristics of PILLAIPAKKAM - WATER

Sam		*pH*	*E.C.*	*S.A.R.*	*Cations (me/l)*			*Anions (me/l)*			
					Ca	*Mg*	*Na*	*K*	*Co_3-*	*Hco_3-*	*Cl*
1.	O	7.8	0.40	-	0.9	1.8	-	-	3.00	0.8	-
2.	O	8.0	1.10	-	0.7	2.5	-	-	-	3.70	4.5
3.	M	9.0	0.25	2.76	0.3	0.5	1.75	-	0.48	1.28	0.8
4.	S	6.7	0.94	3.33	2.3	1.7	0.70	0.03	-	5.00	3.3
5.	S	7.5	0.20	1.10	0.6	0.4	0.78	0.09	-	0.80	1.0
6.	M	8.1	0.22	0.34	0.8	1.2	0.34	0.03	-	1.40	0.6
7.	S	8.1	0.17	0.72	0.5	0.8	0.53	0.39	-	1.04	0.6

(*Contd...*)

8.	M	8.0	0.23	-	1.0	1.5	-	-	-	1.0	0.3
9.	M	6.2	1.10	4.7	11.5	2.3	6.50	0.25	-	1.28	8.7
	E.X	61.9	3.61	6.53	20.93	12.7	4.1	4.89	0.48	13.5	12.7
	X	7.74	0.40	1.63	1.77	1.41	0.82	0.49	0.48	1.69	1.41
	SD	0.82	0.34	1.42	2.39	0.70	0.49	0.49	0	0.99	1.37

1-3 : Stagnant 4-5 : Inlet 6-7 : Outlet 8-9 : Well

Table 2.8c: Characteristics of PILLAIPAKKAM - PLANTS

No	*Species*	*Habit*	*No*	*Species*	*Habit*
1.	Abutilon indicum	H	35.	Ipomoea pres-capre	H
2.	Acacia arabica	T	36.	Ipomoea camea	S
3.	Achyranthes aspera	S	37.	Jatropha glandulifera	S
4.	Agave angustifolia	H	38.	Jatropha heterophylla	S
5.	Alangium salvifolium	T	39.	Justicia glauca	H
6.	Amaranthus spinosus	H	40.	Leucas aspera	H
7.	Anisomeles indica	S	41.	Lycopersicum esculentum	H
8.	Argemone mexicana	H	42.	Melothria madraspatana	C
9.	Arundo donax	G	43.	Merremia tridentata	H
10.	Azadirachta indica	T	44.	Mimosa pudica	H
11.	Blastania garcini	C	45.	Mollugo oppositifolia	H
12.	Blepharis molluginifolia	H	46.	Mollugo pentaphylla	H
13.	Calophyllum inophyllum	T	47.	Ocimum basilicum	H
14.	Canthium coromandelium	S	48.	Ocimum canum	H
15.	Carissa spinarum	S	49.	Ocimum sanctum	H
16.	Celosia polygonoides	H	50.	Oldenlandia umbellata	H
17.	Ceratophyllum demersum	H	51.	Opuntia coccinellifera	S
18.	Chloris inflata	G	52.	Parkinsonia aculiata	T
19.	Cissus quadrangularis	C	53.	Parthenium hysterophorus	H
20.	Coccinia grandis	C	54.	Pavonia odorata	S
21.	Cocculus sp	C	55.	Pavonia zeylanica	S
22.	Coldenia procumbens	H	56.	Perotis indica	G
23.	Commelina persicariaefolia	H	57.	Prosopis juliflora	T
24.	Corbichonia decumbens	H	58.	Phoenix sylvestris	T
25.	Croton bonplandianus	H	59.	Physalis minima	H
26.	Digitaria chinensis	G	60.	Sida acuta	H
27.	Evolvulus alsinoides	H	61.	Sida cordifolia	H
28.	Fimbristylis aggregata	G	62.	Solanum torvum	H
29.	Garcinia indica	T	63.	Tephrosia purpurea	H
30.	Gmelina asiatica	S	64.	Tragia involucrata	H
31.	Heliotropium scabrum	H	65.	Tridax procumbens	H
32.	Heteropogon contortus	G	66.	Vernonia cinerea	H
33.	Hydrolea zeylanica	Hy	67.	Vitex negundo	S
34.	Indigofera cordifolia	H			

G (Grass) : 7 T (Trees) : 7 H (Herbs) : 34 Hy (Hydrophytes) : 1
S(Shrubs) : 15 C (Climbers) : 5

Table 2.8d: Characteristics of PILLAIPAKKAM - BUTTERFLIES

No.	*Species*	*Common Name*
1.	Byblia ilithyia	Joker
2.	Catopsilia crocale	Common Emigrant
3.	Danais chrysippus	Plain Tiger
4.	Danais plexippus	Common Tiger
5.	Delias eucharis	Common Jazebel
6.	Ergolis mariona	Common Castor
7.	Euploea cora	Common Indian Crow
8.	Papilio polytes	Common Mormon
9.	Polydorous hector	Crimson Rose
10.	Precis niarta	Yellow Pansy

Table 2.8e: Characteristics of PILLAIPAKKAM - FISHES

No.	*Species*	*Common Name*
1.	Cattle catia	Catla Carp
2.	Cirrhina mrigal	Mrigal Carp
3.	Labeo rohita	Rohu Carp (Kendai)
4.	OphiocephaJus marulius	Avuri Viral
5.	Ophiocephalus punctatus	Koravai
6.	Tilapia mossambica	Tilapi Kandai

Table 2.8f: Characteristics of PILLAIPAKKAM - AMPHIBIANS

No.	*Species*	*Common Name*
1.	Bufo melanosticus	Common Indian Toad
2.	Rana hexadactyla	South Indian Frog
3.	Rana limnocharis	Paddy field Frog
4.	Rana tigrina	Bull Frog

Table 2.8g: Characteristics of PILLAIPAKKAM - REPTILES

No.	*Species*	*Common Name*
1.	Ahaetulla nasutus	Common Green Whip Snake
2.	Calotes versicolor	Garden lizard
3.	Hemidactylus frenatus	Southern House Gecko
4.	Mabuya carinata	Common Skink
5.	Melanochelys trijuga	Indian Pond Terrapin
6.	Ptyas mucosus	Common Rat Snake
7.	Xenochrophis piscatos	Checkered Keel back

Table 2.8h: Characteristic of PILLAIPAKKAM - BIRDS

No.	*Species*	*Common Name*	*Migration*	*Nutrition*
1.	Accipiter badius	Shikra	R	T
2.	Acridotheres tristis	Common Myna	R	FI
3.	Alauda gulgula	Eastern Skylark	LM	IAF
4.	Alcedo atthis	Small Blue Kingfisher	R	A
5.	Anans acuta	Pin-tailed Duck	M	A
6.	Anas querquedula	Garganey Teal	M	A
7.	Anthus novaeseelandiae	Paddy field Pipit	R	I
8.	Ardea alba	Large Egret	LM	A
9.	Ardea cinerea	Grey Heron	R	A
10.	Ardeola grayil	Pond Heron	R	A
11.	Artamus fuscus	Ashy Swallow-Shrike	R	I
12.	Athene brama	Spotted Owlet	R	T
13.	Aythya ferina	Common Poachard	M	A
14.	Aythya fuligula	Tufted Poachard	M	A
15.	Aythya nyroca	White Poachard	M	A
16.	Bubulcus ibis	Cattle Egret	R	T
17.	Centropus sinensis	Crow Pheasant	R	T
18.	Ceryte rudis	Lesser Pied Kingfisher	R	A
19.	Chlidonias hybridus	Whiskered Tern	M	A
20.	Circus aaruginosus	Marsh Harrier	M	A
21.	Columba livia	Blue Rock Pigeon	R	TG
22.	Coracias benghalensis	Indian Roller	R	TI
23.	Corvus splendens	House Crow	R	AFI
24.	Cuculus varius	Common Hawk Cuckoo	R	FI
25.	Cypsiurus parvus	Palm Swift	R	I
26.	Dicrurus adsimilis	Black Drongo	R	NI
27.	Dinopium benghalense	L. Golden-backed Woodpecker	R	NI
28.	Egretta garzetta	Little Egret	R	T
29.	Egretta intermedia	Small Egret	R	T
30.	Elanus caeruleus	Black winged Kite	R	T
31.	Eudynamis scolopacea	Koel	R	FI
32.	Halcyon smyrnensis	White Breasted Kingfisher	R	A
33.	Hirundo restica	Swallow	M	I
34.	Merops orientalis	Green Bee-eater	R	I
35.	Merops philippinus	Blue tailed Bee-eater	M	I
36.	Milvus migrans	Pariah Kite	R	T
37.	Nectarinia lotenia	Loten's Sunbird	R	N
38.	Nectarinia zeylonica	Purplerumped Sunbird	R	IN
39.	Orthotorhus sutorius	Tailor Bird	R	NI
40.	Passer domesticus	House Sparrow	R	ITF
41.	Phalacrocorax niger	Little Cormorant	R	A
42.	Ploceus philippinus	Baya Weaverbird	LM	IF
43.	Prinia socialis	Ashy Wren-Warbler	R	I
44.	Psittacula krameri	Rose-ringed Parakeet	R	FG
45.	Phylloscopus trochiloides	Dull Green Leaf Warbler	R	I
46.	Saxicoloides fulicata	Indian Robin	R	I

(*Contd...*)

47.	Sturnus pagoranum	Black headed Myna	R	FI
48.	Streptopillia senegalensis	Little Brown Dove	R	T
49.	Tringa glareola	Wood Sandpiper	M	A
50.	Tringa hypoleucos	Common Sandpiper	M	A
51.	Tringa totanus	Common Redshank	R	A
52.	Turdoides affinis	White-headed Babbler	R	FIN
53.	Upupa epops	Hoopoe	R	TI
54.	Vanellus indicus	Redwattled Lapwing	R	T

R: 40 LM: 3 M: 11 F = 10 N = 6 I = 25 A = 21 T = 18

Table 2.8i: Characteristics of PILLAIPAKKAM - MAMMALS

No.	*Species*	*Common Name*
1.	Bandicoota indica	Bandicoot Rat
2.	Funambulus palmarum	Three-stripped Plam Squirrel
3.	Herpestes edwardsi	Mongoose
4.	Lepus nigricollis	Indian Hare
5.	Macaca radiala	Bonnet Macaque
6.	Rattus raltus	Common Rat

2. **Figures: 2.2a - d**

   Collection locations of soil, water and plant samples and sites of photography

3. **Photographs: 2.1-8**

   1 **& 2. Panoramic view of Pillaipakkam tank**, taken soon after the out break of monsoon. Tank has a total water spread area of 9.89. Sq. km. and capable of storing 3.77 M. Cu. m water is available in the tank for 6 - 7 months.

   3. **The northern part of the tank**, soon after the rain. The area is slushy. Catchments of the tank are not vegetated properly. This causes siltation of the tank during the rain.

   4. **& 5. The embankments on southern side**: tank is well engineered. Embankment is about 3.5 km. long. A sluice is seen on the left side.

   6. **The ayacut region irrigated by the tank water**. Major crop is paddy, ragi, cotton. Finger millets are also cultivated.

   7. **& 8. Pintail Ducks:** Winter visitors to the tanks. In the background are eucalyptus plantations. Most of these plantations are in private lands.

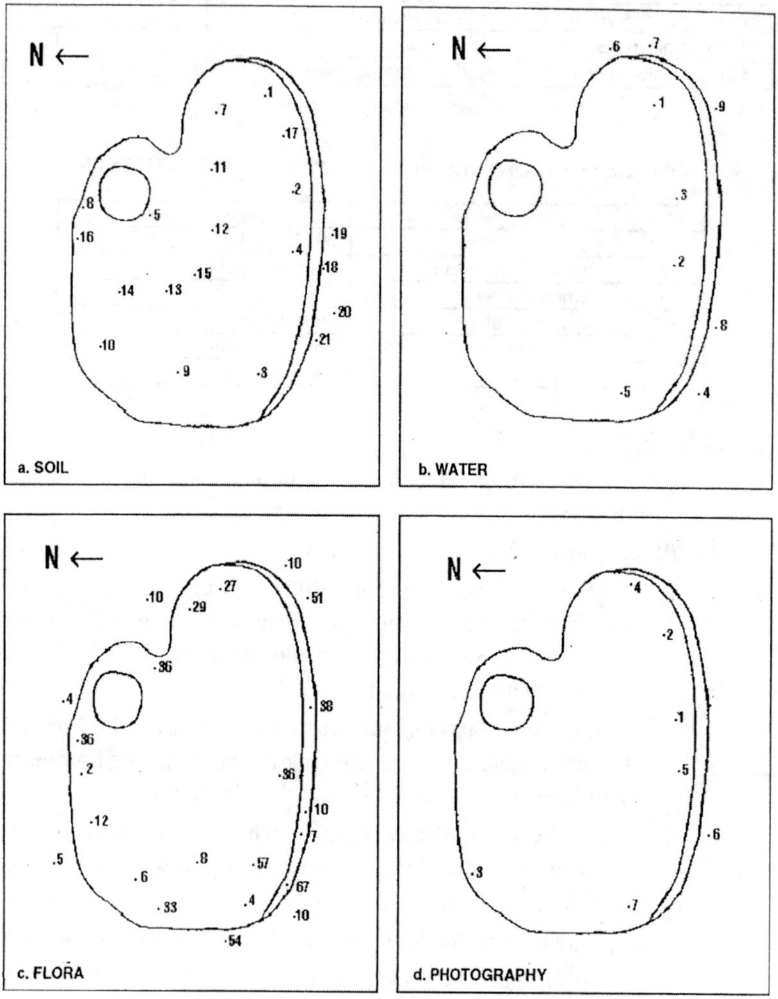

Fig. 2.2: Sampling sites at PILLAIPAKKAM

1
2
3
4

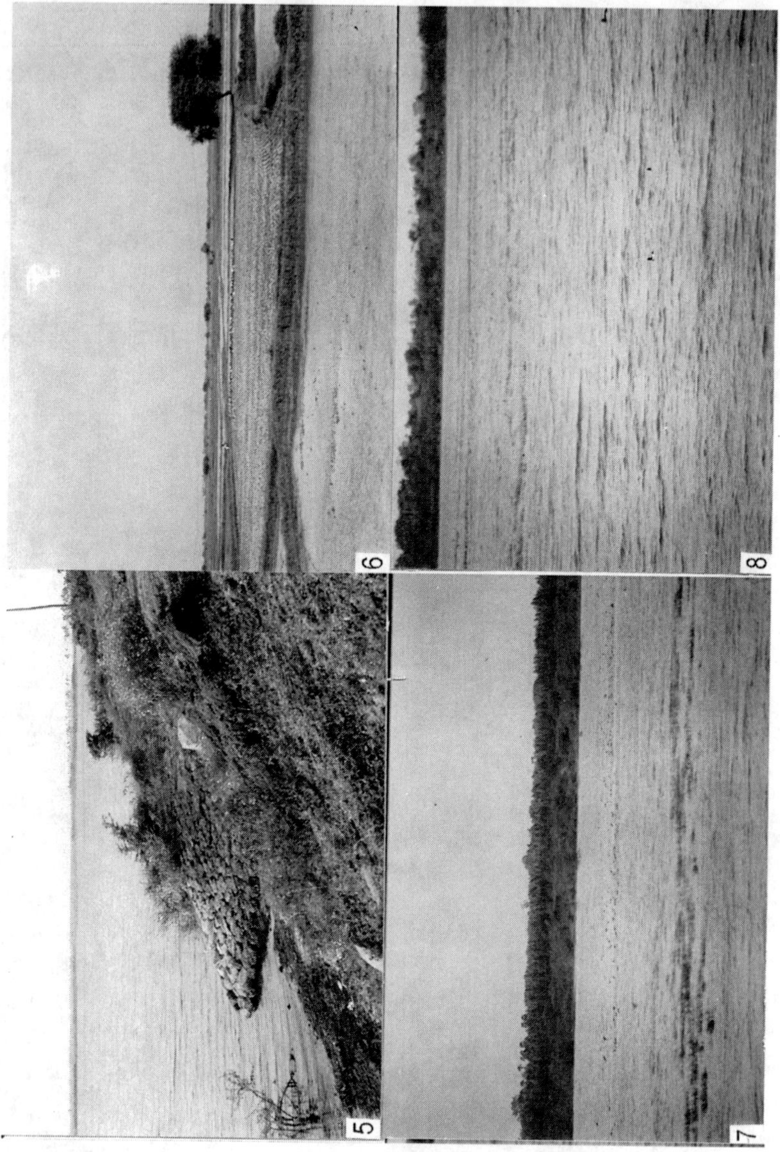
5
6
7
8

3. KALIVELI

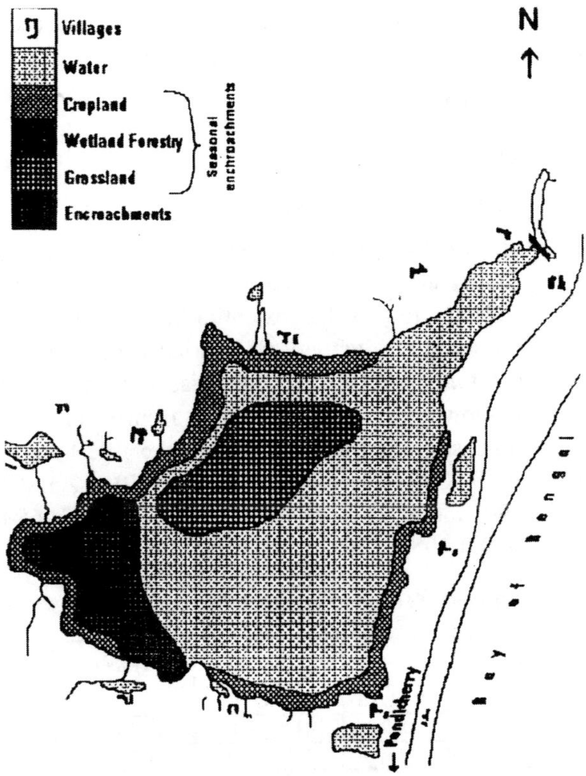

Fig. 3.1: Ecography of Kaliveli Tank.

A. Introduction

Kaliveli, a large fresh water swampy wetland (Kazhi = back waters, Vazhi = pathway) with an area of 7040 ha, is located in South Arcot District of Tamil Nadu about 20 km North of Pondicherry with a catchment of 75.7 Sq. Km. it can be likened to a non-system irrigation tank. However it has inter tidal mudflats, marshes and seasonally flooded reed beds. It is connected to Yedayanthittu estuary through a tidal creek Uppukali, 8 km further north. To prevent in flows from these in to the fresh water wetland a regulator was constructed at the creek mouth. Kaliveli is fed by precipitation of, North-east monsoons and cyclonic rains. Its catchment area includes Auroville plateau and the foreshore areas of the Bay of Bengal. The rainfall pattern is asymmetrical with an annual precipitation of around 130 cm, the major portion of which falls during October-November. As a result Kaliveli is wet upto a maximum of eight months supporting agriculture on the western shore-line, forestry in the south west, fishing activities in the north and grazing in some parts. Owing to estuarine links and good rainfall, the characteristics of this wetland are different from other water bodies.

(Fig 3.1 Fig 3.3 and Table 3.7).

B. Characteristics

1. **Soil** (Tables 3.1, 3.8a and Fig 3.2a)

The soil of the tank bed, foreshore and ayacuts on the west are sandy loamy and clayey in nature. pH has varied widely in the bed (4.5 - 8.4) and to a far less extent in the agricultural fields (5.9-7.4). Electrical conductivity also varied widely in the bed (0.1-5.3) and foreshore (0.1-3.2), but was consistently low in the ayacut, showing an increasing trend from south to north. The nutrients also varied more widely in the foreshore (N:30-135; P:1.2-62 & K:29-378) and in tank bed (N:50-162.5; P:1.9-129 & K:34-600) and to a far less extent in the ayacut (N:65-88; P:0.8-11; & K:9.0-105).

Table 3.1: Characteristics of Kaliveli – Soil@

	Parameter	*FS*	*B*	*Ayacut*	*Mean (SO)*
1.	Texture	SCL SL	SL	–	
2.	pH	5.0 – 8.0	2.5 – 8.4	5.9 – 7.4	7.16 (0.41)
3.	E.C	0.1 – 3.2	0.1 – 53.0	0.2 - –	0.83 (0.75)
4.	Nutrients #				
	N	30 – 135	50 – 162.5	65 – 88	76.68 (21.12)
	P	1.2 – 62	1.9 – 129	0.8 – 11	8.37 (6.81)
	K	29 – 378	34 – 600	9.0 – 105	108.7 (41.9)

@ For more details refer Table 3.8a and Fig.3.2a

**mm/cm* # Kg/Acre

2. **Water** (Table 3.2, 3.8b and Fig 3.2b)

The inflow into the lake depends mainly on the rainfall in the local catchment areas. During cyclones and when the fresh water inflow from catchment is less sea water from the estuary flows in through the Uppukali Creek on the North. The inflow season is from October to January during which period water quality shows spatio-temporal variations in all parameters studied. The pH of water has exhibited a narrow range both in the North (7.2 - 9.0) and South (6.9 - 8.7) Electrical conductivity, SAR, Ca, Mg, Na, K, CO_3, HCO_3, CI have demonstrated variations in the Northern and Southern regions, the ranges being wider in the former. However all values are not only very low but also of narrow range in the wells.

Table 3.2: Characteristics of KALIVELI – WATER[@]

Parameters	*North*	*South*	*Well*	*Mean(sd)*
pH	7.2 – 9.0	6.9 – 8.7	7.3	7.74 (0.82)
E.C.	1.3 – 15.4	1.9 – 5.3	0.5 – 0.6	0.40 (0.34)
S.A.R.	2.3 – 27.2	5.9 – 13.5	2.7 – 3.0	1.63 (2.39)
Cations (me/l)				
Ca	2.6 – 7.80	3.0 - –	0.7 – 1.3	2.48 (1.04)
Mg	2.0 – 29.0	4.0 – 12.2	1.3 – 1.6	3.78 (2.83)
Na	4.1 – 11.6	1.0 – 37.1	3.0 – 3.2	16.29 (15.3)
K	0.4 – 2.80	0.4 – 0.5	–	0.54 (0.19)
Ations (me/l)				
CO_3	0.4 – 1.20	1.2 –	–	2.2 (1.47)
HCO_3	0.3 – 6.20	1.2 – 4.00	1.5 – 4.1	2.2 (1.46)
Cl	6.7 – 122	3.5 – 37.9	2.1 – 3.5	17.24 (4.8)

@ For more details refer Tables 3.8b and Fig.3.2b

3. **Vegetation** (Table 3.3a, 3.8c and Fig 3.2c)

   (a) **Flora:** There are a total of 163 species belonging to 153 Genera and 79 families. These include hydrophytes (6) grasses and sedges (17) climbers (20) shrubs (34) trees (34) and herbs (52). Diversity exists not only in taxonomical level but also in habitat preferences. For example **Suaeda maritima** a halophyte occurs towards north near Kunimedu. Reeds are restricted to the middle part of the tank. Forest species like Racourtia indica, Memecylon umbellatum, Albezia amara etc. and some scrub jungle species are widely scattered in the thickets. The hydrophytes are two species of Nymphaea, Nelumbo, Vallisneria and a pteridophyte Marselia. The 6 habit types of the species are found in the four different habitat guilds. About 65 species are considered ecologically and economically important by the local people. The predominance of species typical to near North and West indicate another vegetation pattern.

(b) Soil Seed banks: Soil in the tank bed indicated the occurrence of seed banks of about 12 species in different frequencies. MolIugo, Tephrosia and Aristida are more frequent. Shannon Wiener index was found to be 1.943 (Table 3.3b).

Table 3.3a: Characteristics of KALIVELI - FLORA[@]

	Taxonomy				*Habitat*		*Important*	
Habit	***Spp***	***Gen***	***Fam***	***Fs***	***B***	***AF***	***Wl***	
Grasses or Sedges	17	14	2	13	8-10	5-8	7	5-7
Herbs	52	45	25	35-40	14-20	40+	15	17
Shrubs	34	32	18	28	5-8	29-32	12	8
Climbers	20	20	12	16	-	16	3-5	13
Trees	34	34	18	30-34	3-4	30-34	5-8	18
Hydrophytes	6	6	4	-	6	-	-	2
Total	163	153	79	131	48	130	47	65

@ For more details refer Table 3.8c and Fig. 3.2c.

Table 3.3b: Characteristics of KALIVELI - SEED BANKS

Species	*No. of Individuals*	*Relative Pi abundance*	*Pi In PI*
1. Aerva lanata	2	0.02	0.078
2. Aristida sp	19	0.15	0.285
3. Buibostylis barbata	5	0.04	0.129
4. Cleome viscosa	6	0.05	0.150
5. Euphorbia hirta	5	0.04	0.129
6. Eragrostis teneHa	7	0.06	0.169
7. Indigofera sp.	10	0.08	0.202
8. lsachne elelgans	18	0.15	0.285
9. MoHugo pentaphyHa	27	0.22	0.333
10. Perotis indica	3	0.02	0.078
11. Tephrosia purpurea	19	0.15	0.027
12. Unidentified Sp.	3	0.02	0.078
Total	124	E*Pi In Pi INDEX	1.943

4. **Fauna** (Tables 3.4a, 3.4b, 3.8d-i)

   There are 187 species distributed among 142 genera and 82 families. These include 19 Butterflies (from 6 families), 11 Fishes (from 8 families), 6 Amphibians (from 1 family), 16 Reptiles (from 9 families) and 15 Mammals (from 10 families). Many species are rare in distribution especially among mammals. For example, the bird Ruddy Shelduck and the mammal Small Indian civet cat are endangered species. There are totally 118 bird species belonging to 92 genera and 50 families. They have varied food habits but majority are feeders of aquatic organisms.

Table 3.4a: Characteristics of KALIVELI - FAUNA@

Animals	*Taxonomy*					*Habitat*		
		Spp	*Gen*	*Fam*	*TW*	*Hs*	*AF*	*TB*
Butterflies	(3)	19	13	6	4	12	13	16
Fishes	(1.5)	11	8	7	11	-	4	-
Amphibians	(6)	6	3	1	3	2	5	-
Reptiles	(1.7)	17	15	9	3	9	10	14
Birds	(2.4)	120	89	49	20	21	38	72
Mammals	(1.5)	15	14	10	1	8	11	15
Total		187	142	82	42	52	81	117

@ For more details refer Tables 3.8d-i

Table 3.4b: Characteristics of KALIVELI – BIRDS@

Migratory Status	*Taxonomy*				*Food Habit*			
	Spp	*Gen*	*Fam*	*F*	*N*	*I*	*A*	*T*
Resident	79	63	31	12	6	21	11	17
Local Migratory	11	11	10	-	-	2	6	4
Migratory	28	18	9	2	-	5	22	1
Total	118	92	50	14	6	28	39	22

@ For details refer Tables 3.8h

5. **Culture systems** (Table 3.5, Fig 3.1)

   (a) **Agriculture:** Millets, groundnut and cashew are the usual crops around the tank. Paddy is cultivated in south east and north east only during monsoons. The crops are affected by several diseases and pathogens. Fertilisers and pesticides are frequently used (Table 3.5).

   (b) **Aquaculture:** No aquaculture is practiced, but water body has many species of fishes like Tilapia, Anabas and Mullets and Crustaceans like crabs and prawns. These edible species are harvested by the locals (Table 3.5).

   (c) **Wetland forestry:** South - west part of the tank is full of Prosopis and Casuarina. In the foreshore Casuarina, Eucalyptus, Prosopis and Acacia plantations are maintained by Panchayats as well as private parties. Wastelands on the Auroville plateau have been completely revegetated with fast growing multipurpose tree species.

   (d) **Settlements:** There are about 14 villages around Kaliveli dependent on this tank for generations for agriculture. The tank is exploited for fisheries, guano-enriched silt, grazing

Table 3.5: Characteristics of KALIVELI - CULTURE SYSTEMS

Agriculture	*Aquaculture*	*Wetland Forestry*		*Human Settlements*
	Natural	*Location*	*Plant*	
Paddy	Prawn	Foreshore	Eucalyptus	1. Puttupattu
Millet	Mullet		Acacia	2. Chinna Kozhuveri
Groundnut	Tilapia		Casuarina	3. Periya Kozhuveri
Coconut	Carps		Prospis	4. Mattur
	Anabas	Bed	Prospis	5. Kazhupurampakkam
			Casuarina	6. Villavanam
				7. Ambakkam
				8. Esankadu
				9. Thilapakkam
				10. Konchumangalam
				11. Edacheri
				12. Puthukuppam
				13. Karatte
				14. Vandipakkam

and collection of resource reed and fire wood. Vast areas of tank have been reclaimed for agriculture by locals.

6. Pollution

There are no industries on the banks. But the run-offs from the surrounding agricultural fields may contain pesticides. Salinity due to the estuarine water intrusion is common.

C. Perceptions

Villages around the Kaliveli are inextricably associated with the wetland system. Drinking water supply and management of plantations by the Panchayats appear to be the two most popular desires.

Table 3.6 People's Perceptions and Practices at KALIVELI

Soil: 1.Salinityis increasing Guano reed bed. 2. Agricultural fields are fertile as rich silt from the lake and burned organic matter of the reed bed are added in summer.

Water: 1. Lake water is not directly utilised for agriculture. 2. Well water is the main source of irrigation. 3. Many villages on the southwest depend on centralized water supply for drinking water. 4. Motorised water pumping from the ground and selling is common.

Plants: 1. Plant cover is not satisfactory. 2. Fast growing trees to meet the growing demand for firewood are needed. 3. Traditional medicine and local knowledge systems are trusted. Gmelina, Justicia, Cissus, Gloriosa, Aerva, Asparagus, Tylophora etc. are used for curing various illnesses. 4. Reeds are collected for domestic use.

Animals: 1. Avifauna are seasonal. 2. Some aquatic organisms are edible. 3. Small Indian Civet Cat and the toddy cat are reducing in numbers. People from Pondicherry and other nearby towns come with guns for shooting birds.

Agriculture: 1. Coconut plantations are the current interest. Organic matter from the tank is used for enriching the fields. 2. Pesticides are also used in the fields.

Aquaculture: 1. There is no systematic aquaculture. 2. The naturally occurring fish are accessible to all.

Wetland Forestry: 1. More social forestry plantations are needed as a solution for firewood scarcity. 2. Fast growing fodder crops are needed as milk yield is less in summer due to fodder scarcity.

Others: 1. Repair of the regulator at the Agarum village in Uppukali creek. 2. Forestry plantations shall be managed by village Panchayats. 3. Drinking water supply is needed for salinity affected areas. 4. Grazing grounds are needed for cattle to yield more milk. 5. Drinking water supply is a great need. 6. Child labour is common. Literacy rate is 40 - 50%.

D. Inferences

By integrating the information on the various components of Kaliveli with the perceptions of local people, a clear picture of the system emerges. Such an understanding is necessary to build durable conceptual framework for interactions between people and nature on a sustainable basis and helps draw a package of imperatives.

1. Ecology

(a) Microhabitats: Microhabitats are the unique subsystems of this wetland. This is due to a combination of factors. This offshore depression is a geological phenomenon; rain water drains into this due to topography of the western & southern plateau, the salinity and cyclonic rainfall caused due to estuarine proximity and oceanographic reasons. Loamy soil and water naturally attracted human settlements which gradually depleted vegetation and fauna to different degrees. Yet it continues to be a stop over of migratory birds. It has rich flora and fauna - some common and others characteristic of each of microhabitats - tank-bed, reed bed, shorelines, inlets, satellite ponds and the cultured systems - Agriculture and wetland forestry. The soil is enriched due to Avian guano and leguminous plants. Area calculations of sub- systems, water-spread areas and depth variations have not been carried out so far. Yet Pattas are being issued to encroaching farmers!

(i) **Tank beds:** High evaporation due to exposure prevents growth of long-standing vegetation in the tank bed. Consequently only ground cover emerges during early summer and late monsoon which is grazed upon by the cattle. In Puttupattu and Koonimedu alone more than 200 heads of cattle are driven into the tank bed. The slushy substratum harbours many insects and amphibians attracting a number of birds, from the banks as well as winter visitors from different parts of the world.

(ii) **Reed beds:** Vast areas of the mid western lake bed are undergrowth. These grounds from another microhabitat within the lake. Some plants and animals are present exclusively in this habitat (See notes in the Appendix). The boundaries of reed bed indicate the limits of salt water intrusion as it is a typical glycophyte (Fresh water hydrophyte). This productive natural habitat is preferred by a number of water bird communities as breeding grounds because of availability of food and reduced disturbance.

(iii) **Satellite ponds:-** Another unique component of Kaliveli is presence of numerous perennial supply ponds on the banks mostly to the West and South. They teem with life in winter as well in summer and function as a refuge for many animal species. This is one of the features contributing to the faunal richness of Kaliveli.

(iv) **Wetland forestry:** Another microhabitat is the Prosopis juliflora growth on the south western side of Kaliveli. These are of limited growth due to seasonal inundation and cutting for fire wood. This habitat provides a safe nesting and roosting place for many water birds. In summer it becomes the breeding ground for small mammals. These plants coppice well, regenerate fast and contribute to the gradual increase of soil fertility. Growing leguminous plants ensure nitrogen fixation, fodder, fuel and habitats for animals. The cumulative effect is the gradual improvement of the soil physically, chemically and perhaps biologically.

(v) **Agricultural fields:** Agro-wetlands of Kaliveli form a very productive and unique habitat. The poromboke land fringes of Kaliveli owned by the Government are cultivated by villagers collectively. These function as a habitat for diverse weed flora and fauna including many birds and small mammals.

(vi) **Inlet Channels:** Kaliveli gets filled by water from far flung areas through natural channels. These inlet channels are highly vegetated on both sides and are dominated by Pandanus, Thespesia and Azadirachta which support a number of birds, reptiles and small mammals.

(vii) **Guano deposits:** Bird excreta (Guano) constitutes a major source of macro nutrients especially nitrogen. But the economic and ecological aspects of this natural bio-fertilizer have not yet been studied. Such a study may help in increasing the efficiency of guano collection and application.

(b) Habitat qualities

(i) **Soil:** The soil sandy loamy having a mean pH value of 7.16 indicating mild alkalinity, (though some sites have extreme values as 4.8 and 8:1) tolerated *by* many crops such as paddy, sugarcane, coconut, plantain, etc. Electrical Conductivity with a mean value of 0.83 is also under tolerance limits. Nitrogen content is low though varying widely from very low to medium level, at different locations. But phosphorus and potassium vary from very low to very high, the mean value suggesting adequacy. Thus the soil is agriculturally suitable though macronutrient richness is only moderate needing inputs.

(ii) **Water:** Relatively high values of pH (7.83) and EC·(2.45 units) indicate salinity thus substantiate the reported sea water intrusion to the lake. High concentrations of magnesium and calcium cations suggest sea water intrusion to the surface water. This is reported and verified in our field reports. The soil quality is reportedly good and thus it is suitable for agriculture, provided good-quality surface water is used for irrigating the fields.

2. Conservation

Due to anthropogenic pressures, this system is under stress as most other wetlands everywhere. But the resources also appear vulnerable from the data on soil, water and biota. Adding to all these is the ongoing construction of Coastal highway not far away from this wetland on the East. As this system has viable and vibrant subsystems the problem is more severe for two reasons. Firstly, they are interlinked and affect each other. Secondly none of them have been studied in detail so far. Conservation is naturally more urgent than realised.

(a) Habitats

(i) **Water body:** Although most of the rainwater shed in the wetland depression, is retained a part of it overflows into the estuary. Some rainfall from the surrounding areas is lost to the sea instead of draining into Kaliveli. Therefore the urgent need is to prevent both the losses: The salinity from the north can be easily prevented though engineering works. The habitat can thus be enriched.

(ii) **Land:** The soil is fertile on the foreshore areas Unfortunately this is being eroded into the lakebed which is being gradually salinised from north. Therefore physical prevention of soil excavation and/or movements, pollution by marine salts and preserving guano "opportunity value" are essential. The biological richness of Kaliveli is the consequence of several factors, such as its long historical existence and dynamics of nature which ultimately resulted in the formation of many habitat refuges within the system. These microhabitats have two levels of existence - spatial and temporal. The chemical parameters of water and soil show a clear variation through summer and monsoon and a spatial variation along a North to South gradient (Table 3.1). It appears that disturbance of any one of these triggers the degeneration. For example, if the bed continues to grow shallow due to siltation, the supply channels will start holding water and the tank's ability to hold rainfall will diminish. The possibility of the entire stretch of 7000 Ha. turning into an agricultural field first and barren land subsequently for want of water (where the tank no longer exists) cannot be ruled out in the coming decades. The only features which may remain will be the small satellite tanks on the south and west.

(b) Resources

(i) Soil: Soil in general is found suitable for agriculture except in the northern most portion where there is salt water intrusion. This soil in the tank bed is rich in phosphate due to the large amount of bird droppings. Villagers use this soil as a manure in their fields. Siltation from sloping banks and erosion from plateaus of catchment are the two factors which considerably alter the soil quality of this wetland.

(ii) Water: Unlike most other tanks under the present survey, water source of Kaliveli is through the drainage from numerous micro catchments. The water influx soon after the monsoon outbreak makes the wetland a fresh water lake temporarily. With the withdrawal of the monsoon, salt water from the Idayanthittu estuary enters the lake. During summer months agricultural fields on the fringes of Kaliveli are irrigated with water extracted from deep wells often dug in the tank bed itself. Ground water in some villages are found unfit for drinking due to the presence of dissolved solids. Thus the utility of water varies with its quality.

(iii) Plants: A large number of plants are used by local people and there are many others which have so far escaped local intelligence. They are of importance and constitute a great exploitation potential source for fuel, medicines, fodder etc. Reed beds are used as grazing grounds. Reeds are collected for thatching and the stumps are annually burnt for ash.

(iv) Animals: Many species of fishes, amphibians, reptiles and mammals are economically important. Many of these are not known to local people. Some of these may have potential for commercial exploitation through conservation. Guano from bird colonies is collected and used as manure in the fields.

Biotic diversity: Kaliveli holds a very diverse biota. Some of these are of economic importance to the local people. In some cases, locals do not know their value yet. This biodiversity can inspire several developmental inputs provided the resource capital is durable – Medicinal plants, reeds for thatching, fodder, fuel wood, fuel leaf and so on. The water body is also a natural breeding ground for many animal species. If the species richness is buttressed by richer population sizes, conservation could really be used for development. Preserving the habitats and their species becomes all the more urgent in the face of pressures from tourism and the East Coast Road.

The conservation efforts are hampered due to several factors. There are no measures pertaining to (a) encroachments, (b) microhabitats, (c) Current area of the tank and (d) its water holding capacity. Further, the sluice barrier preventing saline water intrusion from north is non-functional. In the coming decade the impacts of the East Coast Road are expected to be far reaching, threatening the very existence of this wetland.

3. Development

Rural development activities in the semi-arid South India should be based on conservation and development of micro watersheds. Some of these watersheds especially Kaliveli consist of the features around the water body beginning from the inlet channels, catchments, agriculture, aquaculture, animal husbandry, along with soil, water plants and animals. For managing such a complex system having some features of irrigation reservoirs, shallow wetlands, lakes and reservoir shore lines, realisation of the ecological linkages is essential. Strengthening the resource base therefore means conservation of habitat diversity and interlinks. Developmental alternatives and conservation measures should then be mutually contributing.

(a) Engineering Works to protect rainwater

(i) Checking the saline water intrusion from the Idayanthittu estuary into Kaliveli in early summer and during high tides is the first priority. For this purpose the regulator at Uppukali creek has to be immediately repaired. The regulator can also improve the water retention period of the lake which in turn will enrich aquatic fauna.

(ii) Digging more satellite tanks on the banks near inlet channels will help reduce the siltation in the tank bed. The rainfall draining into the sea instead of the tank can be diverted into these satellites. They can also serve as seed stocks of aquatic and amphibian fauna.

(iii) There is a need to keep water in the tank for longer durations. In other words there has to be systematic desilting/deepening. This is possible only by appropriate engineering inputs like a long horizontal well or a series of such structures with stone work.

(iv) Fresh water supply is an immediate necessity to the villages like Kozhuppurampakkam, Kozhuveri, Karattai etc. where ground water is not potable because of high level of dissolved salts.

Ecological studies on the wetlands can improve or alter the existing practices for the longevity of the system and welfare of the people. For example comparing the resources with habitat features and qualities highlight both problems and provides likely solutions. Most of these findings appear useful in the agricultural sector where a number of sustainable practices can be adopted. Some of these are given below.

(b) Agriculture

(i) Foreshore agriculture: As soon as water level recedes from the shorelines rice is planted. The field is irrigated subsequently by ground water through numerous mechanised wells. Continuation of this practice may gradually lead to saline water intrusion into a large tract which has already begun in the villages on the southern and western sides of Kaliveli. This is ecologically disastrous. Water should be conserved in the underground and wells for longer durations and for potable purposes. Therefore agriculture should shift to paddy varieties and other crops needing less water with help from the agricultural department. In that case two crops can be raised and both water and electricity can then be conserved. Due to their drainage characteristics in some cases only fodder species can be cultivated (e.g. Vetiveria, Cyanodon, etc.) forming vast grazing grounds.

With the availability of guano as a natural fertilizer, chemical fertilizers are not preferred by the local farmers. But the cropping pattern should also be ecologically suitable to this ecosystem - less water needing, short duration, soil conserving methods should be used. Thus ecological agriculture should avoid pesticides and use enriched tank bed as a fertilizer - gradually elevating the foreshore and contributing to the deepening of the tank bed.

(ii) Organic farming: Organic manuring is already practiced in a traditional way. Most of the farmers use tank sediment and burnt remains of the reed which are rich in Nitrogen and Potassium respectively. Besides cattle dung and poultry droppings are also used in fields, though the former is mostly used as substitute to firewood, a gross under utilisation of resource. In this scenario, the only input missing is vermiculture in order to totally eliminate chemicals, yet ensure long term productivity. Thus earthworm rearing is desirable and possible with some effort. Vermicompost is capable of assuring a better harvest as the nutrient content is more and it does not demand extra manpower. Several methods for vermicomposting of agricultural and other wastes are already available to choose from. With efficient guanal collections by creating small depressions and embankments to help concentration, a mass scale bird fertilizer unit can be developed with an everlasting potential. By increasing bio-control plant and animal populations, a lot can be achieved. For all this to happen an ecological ethos has to develop which only altruists can do. A prospect for developing a national model exists here.

(iii) Biological Control of Pest: In the present study neither the pesticide pollution of the water body nor the bio-control organisms have been investigated although pesticides are applied in the Paddy fields and many insectivorous animals and repellent plants are found in this wetland. Besides birds like, Dicrurus adsimilis, Cypsurus parvus, Coracius benghalensis, Athena brama reptiles like monitor lizards, and snakes rodents and Amphibians and plants such as Vitex are potential biocontrol agents. However a lot has to be understood on the entire issue of biological control of pests.

(c) Wetland Permaculture: The foreshore agriculture may not be sustainable because of changing land use patterns tending towards water intensive crops like coconut and sugarcane or casuarina and eucalyptus in the tank bed. Therefore strategies need to be altered. One such would be to cultivate an assortium of suitable tree crops along with leguminous fodder/fuel species since these are reasonably water-rich areas. A new system of wetland permaculture will then come into existence catering to the local needs and replacing the current imperfect and short-sighted practices.

(d) **Aquaculture:** There are many fishes, amphibians and molluscans naturally occurring here which are used locally. Since water remains for a few months and saline intrusion occurs only in north, horizontal wells can be dug at appropriate places to keep water for longer durations. These can be used for culturing molluscans fishes and frogs. In this process the tank gets deepened and delineated into a shoreline ayacut and tank proper. Such an input may have chain reactions for the system in the years to come.

(e) **Apiculture:** With a wide variety of flowering plants, there is a great potential for apiculture and income generation for villagers. The initial capital is meagre compared to other similar projects. As diversity of flowering plants is an important factor determining the success of apiculture, the satellite ponds are very suitable sites for the honey bee rearing.

(f) **Auroville and Puttupet:** In Puttupet, on the south eastern part of Kaliveli, a remnant patch of natural vegetation occurs. This is a typical dry evergreen forest formation dominated by Albizia amara community. This forest patch is protected because of the religious beliefs of the locals. This sacred grove of Puttupet suggests that this area might have been thickly forested a few decades ago. The vegetation change and siltation followed by that, can be fully assessed only by conducting a detailed palyno-logical survey of Kaliveli lake bed-sediments.

On the other hand, Wastelands on the Auroville plateau have been completely revegetated with last growing multipurpose tree species during their programme for water and soil conservation. This stands as a very good example for participatory management in fragile environments. It will be wise to replicate this experiment through Non Governmental Agencies and local panchayats on the barren lands around Kaliveli which are the major contributors of silt to the lake. This will be helpful not only in conserving water and soil but also in providing firewood to local women.

Sacred groves of Puttupet represent remnants of a forest vegetation preserved due to popular faiths, while Auroville represents revival of a lost habitat employing practical common sense and altruistic philosophy. The possibility of replicating these has to be explored wherever possible.

(g) **Coastal Highway and Tourism:** Kaliveli's shallow vastness attracts people from nearby places. Most of them are nature lovers and bird watchers. Varieties of migratory water fowls like spot billed pelican, painted storks, ducks, teals, flamingos and terns are the special attraction of this wetland. Therefore ecotourism can be developed in Kaliveli carefully avoiding any degradation to the ecosystem. Amateur bird watchers can be given facilities like peddler boats, make shift shelters and refreshments can be provided to tourists. A programme for wild life awareness development for tourists can be arranged using - demonstration of bird ringing and organizing slide shows. Otherwise East Coast Road currently under construction will gradually consume Kaliveli by encouraging un-ecological development detrimental to the eco-system.

E. Summary

Table 3.7 Summary of Characteristics: KALIVELI

1.	**Location**	: Tindivanam Taluk. Between Marakanam and Pultupet on the east coast, connected through a 8 km long tidal creek to Yedayanthittu estuary in the North 12'5' – 12'10' N X 79'47' E – 79'55'E
2.	**History**	: Natural Lake
3.	**Rainfall**	: 127 cm/year
4.	**Temperature**	: 35 C – 23 C
5.	**Area**	: 70.47 Sq. Km
6.	**Ayacut**	: Undetermined Foreshore
7.	**Catchment**	: Free = 116.40 Sq. Km. Intercepted = 636.28 Sq. Km. Combined = 754.69 Sq. Km. Equivalent = 244.0 Sq. Km.
8.	**Yield**	: 34.32 M Cu. M.
9.	**Lake**	: Width = 10.5 Km (Max) Length = 12.80 Km(Max) Area = 70.47 Sq. Km. (17,600 acres 7.050 ha) Depth = Avg. of One mt. No Bond, Sloping Banks
10.	**Storage capacity**	: 33.82 M. Cu. M.
11.	**Duration**	: 3/4 months
12.	**Command area**	: Uncertain foreshore area
13.	**Cultivated area**	: Not known, Mostly Shore-line agriculture. Changes with the water level.
14.	**Villages**	25+

15. **Soil**	pH	: 4.8 - 8.1	N	:	30 -162.0 Kg/Ac
	E.C	: 0.09 - 3.7	P	:	0.8 - 62.0 Kg/Ac
	Texture	: CL, L, SK	K	:	9.0 - 378.0 Kg/Ac
16. **Water**	pH	: 6.9 – 9.0	Na+	:	4.1 – 116.0 Me/I
	E.C.	: 1.3 – 15.4	K+	:	0.4 – 0.9 Me/I
	Hardness	: 610 – 760	CO_3-	:	0.0 – 1.2 Me/l
	S.A.R	: 2.3 – 27.0	HCO2-	:	0.3 – 6.2 Me/I
	Ca	: 2.6 – 7.8 Me/I	Cl-	:	6.7 – 122.0 Me/I
	Mg	: 2.0 – 29.0 Me/I	Na %	:	70.0 – 77.0
17. **Flora**	Grasses	: 17	Climbers	:	20
	Herbs	: 52	Trees	:	34
	Shrubs	: 34	Hygrophyte	:	6
18. **Fauna**	Butterflies	: 19	Fishes	:	11
	Amphibians	: 6	Reptiles	:	16
	Birds	: 120	Mammals	:	15

19. **Cultures**
   - (a) Agriculture
     1. Major Crops – Paddy and Ground Nut
     2. Minor Crops – Millets
   - (b) Aquaculture
     1. Natural : Anabas, Tilapia, Mugil and Prawns
     2. Cultured : Nil
   - (c) Wetland Forestry
     1. On the sloping banks and Private fields
     2. Acacia, Prosopis, Casuarina, Eucalyptus

20. **Others:** Regular near to the creek
   - (a) Prevention of entry of tidal waters (salinity)
   - (b) Prevention of crop field submersion (flood)
   - (c) Flood discharge: 1900 cusecs (Max)

   Poaching of birds and Monitor lizards, Shoreline agriculture

F. Addenda

1. Tables : 3.8a - i

Table 3.8a: Characteristics of KALIVELI - SOIL

					Nutrients (kg/acre)		
No.		*Texture*	*pH*	*E.C mmh/cm*	*N*	*P*	*K*
1	S	SCL	7.5	1.0	30.0	1.9	75.6
2	S	SL	7.3	1.0	35.0	2.4	86.4
3	S	S	7.3	1.5	30.0	1.4	112.5
4	O	SL	6.4	0.4	135.0	3.8	135.9
5	O	C	7.2	0.5	70.0	1.2	108.0
6	D	SL	5.7	0.6	109.0	16.0	222.0
7	M	S	6.8	0.7	59.0	5.0	29.0
8	M	F	5.7	0.1	61.0	6.0	64.0
9	M	SCL	6.0	0.5	56.0	23.0	268.0
10	M	SCL	7.6	0.4	56.0	21.0	228.0
11	M	SL	5.9	0.3	53.0	7.0	58.0
12	J	SCL	6.1	2.2	90.0	28.0	378.0
13	J	SL	5.0	2.3	98.0	28.0	150.0
14	J	S	6.0	0.3	46.0	62.0	57.0
15	JL	SL	6.9	3.2	133.0	10.0	321.0
16	JL	SL	7.6	1.0	104.0	17.0	33.0
17	S	C	7.6	2.0	152.0	2.7	108.0
18	S	S	8.4	0.3	52.5	1.9	161.8
19	O	SL	2.5	2.1	146.0	2.7	94.5
20	O	C	7.5	1.5	135.5	2.4	112.5
21	O	SL	6.5	2.0	104.0	11.0	378.0
22	O	SL	7.7	2.2	162.5	2.8	106.5
23	M	S	5.9	0.2	63.0	6.0	67.0
24	M	SL	4.8	0.1	50.0	3.0	34.0
25	M	SL	8.0	0.7	57.0	18.0	242.0
26	M	SCL	7.8	3.7	115.0	34.0	600.0
27	M	CL	7.2	3.6	76.0	28.0	600.0
28	J	CL	7.5	0.2	77.0	28.0	600.0
29	J	CL	7.2	23.0	128.0	28.0	600.0
30	J	CL	7.3	7.2	77.0	28.0	600.0
31	J	SL	7.6	53.0	87.0	129.0	579.0
32	J	S	8.1	1.6	32.0	28.0	600.0
33	J	SL	7.5	0.2	98.0	26.0	60.0
34	J	SCL	7.1	0.1	98.0	17.0	261.0
35	J	SL	5.9	0.2	88.0	19.0	168.0
36	JL	SL	6.6	0.4	95.0	18.0	172.0
37	JL	SCL	6.8	6.2	112.0	9.0	546.0
38	O	S	6.6	0.2	75.0	2.2	71.0
39	O	SL	5.9	0.2	85.0	8.0	9.0
40	D	SL	6.0	0.2	88.0	11.0	27.0
41	D	SL	7.3	0.2	65.0	0.8	108.0
42	D	SL	7.4	0.2	76.5	0.9	105.5
43	D	SCL	7.1	0.2	54.5	0.9	96.5
	E.X		400.74	52.76	3627.50	566.0	4793
	X		6.90	1.23	80.6	113.80	133.14
	SO		0.85	1.57	36.66	12.92	94.89

1-16: Fore Shore 17-37: Bed 38-43: Ayacut S: September O: October D: December M: May J: June JL: July

Table 2.8b: Characteristics of KALIVELI - WATER

Sam		*pH*	*E.C.*	*S.A.R.*	*Cations (me/l)*			*Anions (me/l)*			
					Ca	*Mg*	*Na*	*K*	*Co_3-*	*Hco_3-*	*Cl-*
1.	N	9.0	2.1	7.2	2.8	4.2	13.4	0.4	1.2	0.8	-
2.	D	8.9	5.5	17.1	2.6	9.6	42.2	0.5	0.4	3.70	4.5
3.	D	7.4	15.4	27.2	7.8	29.0	116.0	0.9	-	1.28	0.8
4.	D	7.2	1.3	2.3	4.0	2.0	4.1	2.8	-	5.00	3.3
5.	N	6.9	5.3	13.5	3.0	12.2	37.1	0.5	1.2	0.80	1.0
6.	N	8.7	1.9	5.9	3.0	4.0	11.0	0.4	1.2	4.0	13.5
7.	M	7.3	0.5	3.0	0.7	1.3	3.0	-	-	1.5	3.5
8.	J	7.3	0.6	2.7	1.3	1.6	3.2	-	-	4.1	2.1
	E.X	62.7	17.2	51.7	17.4	22.7	114	2.7	15.4	15.4	120.7
	X	7.83	2.45	7.39	2.48	3.78	16.29	0.54	2.2	2.2	17.24
	SD	0.81	1.34	5.36	1.04	2.83	15.29	0.19	1.47	1.46	14.81

1-6 : Stagnant 7-8 : Well 1-4 : Near North 5-6 : Near South N: November D: December M: May J: June

Table 3.8c: Characteristics of KALIVERI - PLANTS

No.	Name of the Species		No.	Name of the Species	
1.	Abrus precatorius	C	32.	Butea monosperma	T
2	Abutilon indicum	H	33.	Cadaba frusticosa	T
3.	Acacia nilotica	T	34.	Calophyllum inophyllum	T
4.	Acalypha indica	H	35.	Calotropis gigantia	S
5.	Achyranthus aspera	S	36.	Canthium coromandelicum	S
6.	Adhatoda zeylanica	S	37.	Capparis stylosa	S
7.	Aerva lanata	H	38.	Caralluma adscesionis	H
8.	Aeschynomene indica	S	39.	Cardiospermum halicacabum	C
9.	Ailanthus excelsa	T	40.	Carissa spinarum	S
10.	Alangium salvifolium	T	41.	Cassia auriculata	S
11.	Albizia amara	T	42.	Cassia fistula	T
12.	Aloe vera	H	43.	Cassytha filiformis	C
13.	Amaranthus spinosus	H	44.	Celosia polygonoides	H
14.	Amaranthus virdis	H	45.	Cephalandra indica	C
15.	Anacardium occidentale	T	46.	Ceropegia elegans	C
16.	Andrographis paniculata	S	47.	Chara sp.	Hy
17.	Anisomeles indica	S	48.	Chloris Inflata	G
18.	Aristida mutabilis	G	49.	Chloroxylon swettenia	T
19.	Aristolochia bracteolata	H	50.	Cissampelos Pareira	C
20.	Aristolochia indica	C	51.	Cissus quadrangularis	C
21.	Arundo donax	G	52.	Citrullus colocynthis	C
22.	Asparagus racemosus	C	53.	Cleome viscosa	H
23.	Asystasia gangetica	H	54.	Cocos nucifera	T
24.	Azadirachta indica	T	55.	Coldenia procumbens	H
25.	Boerhavia diffusa	H	56.	Combretum albidum	C
26.	Bombax ceiba	T	57.	Commelina clavata	H
27.	Borassus flabellifer	T	58.	Commelina ensifolia	H
28.	Borreria hispida	H	59.	Corbichonia decumbens	H
29.	Brachiaria ramosa	G	60.	Crotalaria pallida	S
30.	Breynea retusa	T	61.	Croton bonplandianus	H
31.	Bulbostylis barbata	G	62.	Cucumis sativus	C

(Contd...)

No.	Name of the Species	
63.	Cynodon dactylon	G
64.	Cyperus articulatus	G
65.	Dactyloctenium aegiptium	G
66.	Datura stramorium	S
67.	Dendrophthoe falcata	H
68.	Digera muricata	H
69.	Digitaria sp.	G
70.	Eclipta prostrate	H
7t.	Elephantopus scaber	H
72.	Eragrostis ciliaris	G
73.	Eragrostis riparia	G
74.	Eragrostis tenella	G
75.	Eucalyptus globules	T
76.	Eugenia bracteata	T
77.	Euphorbia antiquorum	T
78.	Euphorbia hirta	H
79.	Euphorbia thirukalli	S
80.	Evolvulus alsinoides	S
81.	Ficus benghalensis	T
82.	Ficus hispida	S
83.	Fimbristylis aggregata	G
84.	Flacourtia indica	T
85.	Flueggea leueopyrus	S
86.	Garcinia spicata	T
87.	Gloriosa superba	C
88.	Glycosmis pentaphylla	T
89.	Gmelina asiatica	S
90.	Gomphrena celosioides	H
91.	Heliotropium indieum	H
92.	Hemidesmus indieus	C
93.	Hydrilla verticillata	H
94.	Ichnocarpus fruteseens	S
95.	Indigofera tinctoria	H
96.	Ipomoea carnea	S
97.	Ipomoea pres-(ap~ae	H
98.	Jasminum angustifolium	C
99.	Jatropha curcus	S
100.	Jatropha gossypifolia	S
101.	Jatropha glandulifera	S
102.	Kyllinga nemoralis	G
103.	Kyllinga bulbosa	G
104.	Lantana camara	S
105.	Leonotis nepatifolia	H
106.	Lepidagathis Cristata	S
107.	Leucas aspera	H
108.	Luffa cylindrica	C
109.	Macaranga peltata	T
110.	Memycelon umbellatum	T
111.	Microcacca mercurialis	H
112.	Mimosa pudica	H
113.	Mollugo cerrina	H
114.	Mollugo distycha	H

No.	Name of the Species	
115.	Mollugo pentaphylla	H
116.	Morinda coreia	T
117.	Moringa oleifera	T
118.	Mukia maderaspatana	C
119.	Najas indica	Hy
120.	Nelumbo nucifera	Hy
121.	Nerium oleander	S
122.	Nymphaea pubescens	Hy
123.	Ocimum basilicum	H
124.	Ocimum tenuifolium	H
125.	Oldenlandia corymbosa	H
126.	Oldenlandia umbellata	H
127.	Olea,	T
128.	Opuntia monocantha	S
129.	Pandanas canarus	S
130.	Pavonia zeylanica	S
131.	Parthenium hysterophorus	H
132.	Pedalium murex	H
133.	Peristrophe paniculata	H
134.	Perotis indica	G
135.	Phoenix loureirii	S
136.	Phoenix sylvestris	T
137.	Phyllanthus Amarus	H
138.	Phyllanthus Pinnatus	S
139.	Phyasaits minima	H
140.	Pongamia Pinnata	T
141.	Porlulaca oleraceae	H
142.	Premna corymbosa	S
143.	Prospis juliflora	T
144.	Randia dumetorum	S
145.	Ricinus communis	S
146.	Sarcoslemma intermedium	C
147.	Sida acuta	H
148.	Sida cordifolia	H
149.	Sida rhombitolia	H
150.	Solanum surranttense	H
151.	Solanum amplexicaulis	H
152.	Stachtarpheta jamaicensis	H
153.	Suaedia maritime	H
154.	Syzygium cumini	T
155.	Tamarindus indica	T
156.	Thephrosia purpurea	H
157.	Thespesia populnea	T
158.	Tribulus terrestris	H
159.	Tridax procumbens	H
160.	Tylophora inidca	C
161.	Vallisneria natuns	Hy
162.	Vitiveria zizanoides	G
163.	Vernonia cinerea	H
164.	Vitex negundo	S
165.	Wattakaka volubilis	C
166.	Zizyphus Xylopyrus	S

G: 14 C: 1 H: 54 T: 34 S: 34 Hy: 6

Table 3.8d: Characteristics of KALIVELI - BUTTERFLIES

No.	*Species*	*Common Name*
1.	Catopsilia crocale	Common Emigrant
2.	Danais chrysippus	Plain Tiger
3.	Danais limniace	Blue Glassy Tiger
4.	Delias eucharis	Common Jezebel
5.	Ergolis merione	Common Caslot
6.	Euploea core	Common Indian Crow
7.	Eurema hecabe	Common Grass Yellow
8.	Hypolimnias misipus	Danaid Eggfly
9.	Hypolimnias bolina	Great Eggfly
10.	Mycalesis perseus	Common Bush Brown
11.	Papilio demoleus	Lime Butterfly
12.	Papilio polytes	Common Mormon
13.	Polydorous aristolochiae	Common Rose
14.	Polydorous hector	Crimson Hose
15.	Precis almana	Peacock Pansy
16.	Precis lemonias	Lemon Pansy
17.	Precis nierta	Yellow Pansy
18.	Precis orithya	Blue Pansy
19.	Telchinia violae	Tawny Castor

Table 3.8e: Characteristics of KALIVELI - FISHES

No.	*Species*	*Common Name(Tamil)*
1.	Anabas testudineus	Climbing Perch (panai eri Kendai)
2	Anguila sp.	Vilangu
3.	Clarias batachus	Masaarai Keluthy
4.	Macrones seenghala	Koombu Keluthy
5.	Mugil cephalus	Periya Madavai
6.	Mugil macrolepis	Madavai
7.	Mugil parsia	Pachai Madavai
8.	Ophiocephalus marulius	Avuri viral
9.	Ophiocephalus striatus	Viral
10.	Tilapia mossambica	Tilapi Kendai
11.	Wallago attu	Valai Keluthy

Table 3.8f: Characteristics of KALIVELI - AMPHIBIANS

No.	*Species*	*Common Name*
1.	Bufo melanosticus	Common Indian Toad
2.	Rana cyanophlyctis	Skipping Frog
3.	Rana hexadactyla	South Indian Frog
4.	Rana limnocharis	Paddy field Frog
5.	Rana tigrina	Bull Frog
6.	Rhacopharus sp.	Tree Frog

Table 3.8g: Characteristics of KALIVELI - REPTILES

No.	*Species*	*Common Name*
1.	Ahaetulla nasutus	Common Green Whip Snake
2.	Calotes versicolor	Garden Lizard
3.	Dendrelaphis lristis	Common Bronze back
4.	Echis carinatus	Saw-scaled Viper
5.	Eryx johni	John's Earth Boa
6.	Hemidactylus frenatus	Soulhern House Gecko
7.	Hemidactylus leschnaulti	Bark Gecko
8.	Lissemys punctata	Indian Mud Turtle
9.	Mabuya carinata	Common Skink
10.	Melanochelys trijuga	Indian Pond Terrapin
11.	Naja naja	Indian Cobra
12.	Ptyas mucosus	Common Rat Snake
13.	Sitana ponticeriana	Fan Throated Lizard
14.	Typhlina bramina	Common Worm Snake
15.	Vipera russelli	Russell's Viper
16.	Varanus benghalensis	Common Monitor Lizard
17.	Xenochrophis piscatos	Checkered Keel back

Table 3.8h: Characteristics of KALIVELI - BIRDS

No.	*Species*	*Common Name*	*Migration*	*Nutrition*
1.	Accipitet badius	Shika	R	T
2.	Acridotheres lristis	Common Myna	R	FI
3.	Acrocephalus dumetorum	Blyth's Reed Warbler	R	AI
4.	Aegithina tiphia	Common lora	R	I
5.	Alauda gulgula	Eastern Slylark	R	IAF
6.	Alcedo althis	Small blue Kingfisher	R	A
7.	Anas acuta	Pin-tailed Duck	M	A
8.	Anas clypeata	Shoveller	M	A
9.	Anas penelop€	Wigeon	R	A
10.	Anas poecilorhynca	Spot-billed Duck	LM	A
11.	Anas querquedula	Garganey Teal	M	A
12.	Anastomus oscii	Open billed Stork	LM	A
13.	Anlhus nwaeseelan	Paddy field Stork	R	I
14.	Ardea alba	Large Egret	LM	T
15.	Ardea cinerea	Grey Heron	R	A
16.	Ardeola grayii	Pond Heron	R	A
17.	Artamus fuscus	Ashy Swallow-Shrike	R	I
18.	Athene brama	Spotted Owlet	R	T
19.	Aythya nyroca	White pochard	M	A
20.	Bubulcus ibis	Cattle Egret	R	T
21.	Calidris minuta	Little Stint	R	A
22.	Caprimulgus asiaticus	.The common Night Jar	R	T
23.	Centropus sinensis	Crow Pheasant	R	T
24.	Ceryle rudis	Lesser Pied Kingfisher	R	A

(*Contd...*)

25.	Charadrius alexandrinus	Kentish Plover	M	T
26.	Charadrius dubius	Little Ringed Plover	LM	A
27.	Charadrius mongolus	Lesser Sand Plover	R	T
28.	Chlidonias hybridus	Whiskered Tern	M	A
29.	Ciconia ciconia	White Stork	M	A
30.	Circus aeruginosus	Marsh Harrier	M	A
31.	Circus macrourus	Pale Harrier	R	T
32.	Clamator jacobinus	Pied Crested Cuckoo	M	FI
33.	Columba livia	Blue Rock Pigeon	R	TG
34.	Copsychus saularis	Magpie Robin	R	I
35.	Coracias beghalensis	Indian Roller	R	TI
36.	Corvus macrorhynchos	Jungle Crow	R	AFI
37.	Corvus splendens	House Crow	R	AFI
38.	Cuculus varius	Common Hawk Cuckoo	R	FI
39.	Cursorius coromandalicus	Indian Curser	R	T
40.	Cypsiurus parvus	Palm Swift	R	I
41.	Dendrocitta vagabunda	Indian Tree pie	R	AF
42.	Dicaeum erythrorhynchos	Tickell's Flower pecker	R	NI
43.	Dicrurus adsimilis	Black Drongo	R	NI
44.	Dicrurus leucophaeus	Grey Drongo	R	NI
45.	Dinopium benghalense	L.Golden-backed Woodpecker	R	NI
46.	Egretta garzetta	Little Egret	R	T
47.	Egreta intermedia	Smaller Egret	R	T
48.	Eremopterix grisea	Ashycrowned Finch-Lark	R	IF
49.	Elanus caeruleus	Black winged kite	R	T
50.	Esacus magnirostris	Great Stone Plover	R	A
51.	Eudynamis scolopacea	Koel	R	FI
52.	Falco peregrinus	Peregrine Falcon	R	T
53.	Falco tinnunculus	Kestrel	LM	T
54.	Francolinus pondicerianus	Grey Patridge	R	T
55.	Gallinago gallinago	Fantail Snipe	M	A
56.	Gallinago sterrna	Pintail Snipe	M	A
57.	Gelochelidon nilotica	Gull billed Tern	M	A
58.	Halcyon smyrnensis	White Breasted Kingfisher	R	A
59.	Haliastur indus	Brahminy Kite	R	A
60.	Himantopus himantopus	Black winged Stilt	LM	A
61.	Hirundo daurica	Striated Swallow	LM	I
62.	Hirundo rustica	Swallow	M	I
63.	Lanius cristatus	Brown Shrike	R	TI
64.	Larus ichthyaetus	Great Black headed Gull	M	A
65.	Lonchura malabarica	White-throated Munia	R	IF
66.	Lonchura malacca	Black headed Munia	R	IF
67.	Megalaima haemocephala	Crimson Breasted Barbet	R	F
68.	Merops Orientalis	Green Bee-eater	R	I
69.	Merops Philippinus	Blue-tailed Bee-eater	M	I
70.	Milvus migrans	Pariah Kite	K	T
71.	Motacilla cinerea	Grey Wagtail	M	IA
72.	Motacilla citreola	Yellow headed Wagtail	M	I
73.	Motacilla flava	Yellow Wagtail	M	I

(*Contd...*)

74.	Motacilla madraspatensis	Large Pied Wagtail	M	IA
75.	Mycteria leucocephala	Painted Stork	R	A
76.	Nectarinia lotenia	Loten's Sunbird	R	N
77.	Nectarinia zeylonica	Purplerumped Sunbird	R	IN
78.	Nettapus coramandalinus	Cotton Teal	R	A
79.	Netla rufina	Red crested Pochard	M	A
80.	Numenius arquata	Curlew	M	FA
81.	Nycticorax nyclicorax	Night Heron	R	A
82.	Oriolus oriolus	Golden Oriole	R	FI
83.	Orthotomus sutorius	Tailor Bird	R	NI
84.	Pandion haliaetus	Osprey	R	A
85.	Passer domesticus	House Sparrow	R	ITF
86.	Pelicanus philipensis	Spot billed pelican	LM	A
87.	Phoenicopteres roseus	Greater Flamingo	LM	A
88.	Phylloscopus trochiloides	Dull Green leaf Warbler	R	I
89.	Pitta brachyara	Indian Pitta	R	I
90.	Ploceus philippinus	Baya Weaverbird	R	IF
91.	Podiceps ruficollis	Little Grebe	R	A
92.	Prinia socialis	Ashy Wren-Warbler	R	I
93.	Psittacula eupatria	L. Indian Parakeet	R	FG
94.	Psittacula krameri	Rose-ringed Parakeet	R	FG
95.	Pychnonotis cafer	Redvented Bulbul	R	FIN
96.	Pychnonotis Jocosus	Red wiskered bulbul	R	FIN
97.	Pychnonotis leuteolus	White browed Bulbul	R	FIN
98.	Saxicoloides fulicata	Indian Robin	R	I
99.	Sterna benghalensis	Indian lesser Crested Tern	M	A
100.	Sterna hirundo	Common Tern	M	A
101.	Streptopilia chinensis	Spotted Dove	R	T
102.	Streptopilia decaocta	Indian Ringdove	R	T
103.	Streptopilia senegalensis	Little Brown Dove	R	T
104.	Sturnus pagodarum	Black headed Myna	R	FI
105.	Tadorna ferruginea	Ruddy Shelduck	M	A
106.	Tephrodornis pondicerianus	Common Wood Shrike	R	I
107.	Terpsiphone paradisi	Paradise Flycatcher	R	I
108.	Threskiornis aethiopica	White Ibis	R	T
109.	Tringa glareola	Wood Sandpiper	M	A
110.	Tringa hypoleucos	Common Sandpiper	M	A
111.	Tringa ochropus	Green Sandpiper	M	A
112.	Tringa stagnatilis	Marsh Sandpiper	M	A
113.	Tringa tetanus	Common Redshank	M	A
114.	Turdoides affinis	White headed Babbler	R	FIN
115.	Turdoides caudatus	Common Babbler	R	FIN
116.	Turnix sylvatica	Little Bustard Quail	R	T
117.	Tyto alba	Barn Owl	R	T
118.	Upupa epops	Hoopoe	LM	TI
119.	Vanellus indicus	Red wattled lapwing	R	T
120.	Vanellus malabaricus	Yellow-wattled Lapwing	LM	T

R: 80 LM: 11 M: 29 F: 14 N: 6 I: 28 A: 3 T: 22

Table 3.8i: Characteristics of KALIVELI - MAMMALS

No.	*Species*	*Common Name*
1.	Bandicoota benghalensis	Indian Mole Rat
2.	Bandicoota indica	Bandicoot Rat
3.	Canis aureus	Jackal
4.	Felis chaus	Jungle Cal
5.	Funambulus palmarum	Three-stripped Palm Squirrel
6.	Herpestes edwardsi	Mongoose
7.	Lepus nigricollis	Indian Hare
8.	Mus booduga	Field Mouse
9.	Paradoxurus hermaphroditus	Palm Civet
10.	Pipistrellus coramandra	Indian Pipistrelle
11.	Rattus raltus	Common Rat
12.	Suncus murinus	Grey Musk Shrew
13.	Tatera indica	Indian Gerbille
14.	Viverricula indica	Small Indian Civet
15.	Vulpus benghalensis	Indian Fox

2. **Figures: 3.2a-d**

   Collection locations of soil, water, plants samples and sites of photography

3. **Photographs: 3.1-16**

   1. **A panoramic view of Kaliveli.** This snap was taken soon after the onset of monsoon.
   2. **Uppukali Creek - Soon After The Onset of Monsoon** Uppukali creek is a 50 - 100 meter wide channel in the north eastern side of Kaliveli, connecting this wetland to Yedayanthittu Estuary. During the high tide in summer, saline water reaches the northern part of Kaliveli through this creek. This salinity is a crucial factor deciding the biological composition of this wetland. The absence of reeds and presence of a typical Halophyte **Suaedia marina** is a good evidence for this. Fishes adapted to salinity have also been reported from Uppukali Creek.
   3. **Uppukali Regulator:** This regulator was constructed to serve two purposes (1) to check saltwater intrusion to Kaliveli during high tides. (2) To retain freshwater of the lake for more time by stopping the water flow to Yedayanthittu estuary. .But this regulator is not functional as shutters spoilt. Villagers use this as a pathway to cross the creek in monsoon. The impact of the Uppukali regulator on the hydrology of lake is not studied.

4. **A Supply Pond Near Thilapakkam:** drains to Kaliveli. In the background is Kaliveli.
5. **Kaliveli At Anumanthai:** flooding of tank bed soon after the onset of monsoon. Onset of the monsoon is immediately marked in Kaliveli by the flooding in paddy fields in the fringes. Level of groundwater table is also raised by the flooding. The plate shows a flooded well in the foreground.
6. **Inlet Channels Draining to Kalivei:** The channel is thickly vegetated with neem trees Randia, Canthium etc. in the lake bed this vegetation is replaced by Pandanus thickets. The sin deposition can be seen on the bed of Itleri. These inlet channels are used as cart ways when the tank bed is dried. Itleries provide good habitat refugia for many birds and small mammals.
7. **Kaliveli At Koonimedu:** Soon after the first rains of monsoon. Vast stretches of wet tank bed is shown in the background. In the foreground is the tank bed reclaimed for paddy cultivation the main weeds are Thespesia and Croton sps. Grazing grounds are seen in background. These grass beds form excellent grazing ground for cattle. More than two hundred heads of cattle are driven to the tank bed in Koonimedu and Puttupattu alone.
8. **Kazhuppuram Pakkam:** The southern banks of Kaliveli. In the foreground is the bed of an in let channel showing eroded banks and sitted bed. Main perennial vegetation is ipomoea. In the background is Kaliveli after the first showers.
9. **Paddy Culitivation in Foreshore:** Agricultural activities in Koonimedu. Major crop is paddy. The agricultural field shown in Photograph is reclaimed tank bed, but construction of small bunds and silt accumulation has made the fields out of reach from flood waters. The paddy fields are excellent breeding and foraging ground for many bids and small mammals. When not under cultivation the bed provides excellent grazing ground for the cattle.
10. **Siltation:** One of the most serious threats to this wetland. Due to siltation the water retention period reduces considerably. This can be detrimental to the water body. The plate shows breaching in the fore shore paddy fields.
11. **Poaching in Kaliveli:** Large scale poaching is reported from the tank during winter. Large birds like Egrets and Flamingos

are the targets. Poachers come not only from villages around the lake but also from nearby towns plate No.11 shows egrets shot dead plate. No.12 A median egret (Egretta intermedia) striped. Hundreds of such incidents goes unnoticed every year.

12. **Viverricula indica (E: Small Indian Civet):** Reported from Kaliveli. The scrub thickets and grasslands of Kaliveli provide ideal habitat. It shelters in holes or under rocks, lies up in grass or under bushes, many live near villages. Usually prey on mice, rats, squirrel, lizards, small birds and insects, fruits, roots and other vegetable matter. Civets are capable of controlling population of destructive rodents like rats and mice.
13. **Dicrurus adsimilis (Black Drongo):** Reported from all tanks. A very common bird near both of the water bodies seen flight foraging insects or attending grazing cattle. It is seen very commonly in the agricultural fields, feeding on insects.
14. **Clarius batrachus: (T: Masaarai keluthy):** Reported from Kaliveli, Ousteri and Mirattunilai. It is mostly a freshwater fish but tolerate salinity. Reported from both Kaliveli and Ousteri. This fish is capable of surviving with atmospheric oxygen for considerable time when removed from water. The fish is edible and believed to have medicinal properties.
15. **Macrones seenghala (T: Koombu kelldhy):** Reported from Kaliveli and Ousteri. A fish capable of tolerating saline/ brackish waters. Reported from both Kaliveli and Ousteri. This fish survives in Ooranles and satellite ponds in summer.
16. **A Fish catch from Ousteri tank (Tilapia mossambica - Tilapia Kendai):** This fish is reported from all tanks except Kambikudi. This is an African species introduced to the fresh water bodies for commercial fishery. Fish is capable of tolerating slight salinity. Now the fish is exploited for commercial aquaculture.
17. **Google Map of Kaliveli**

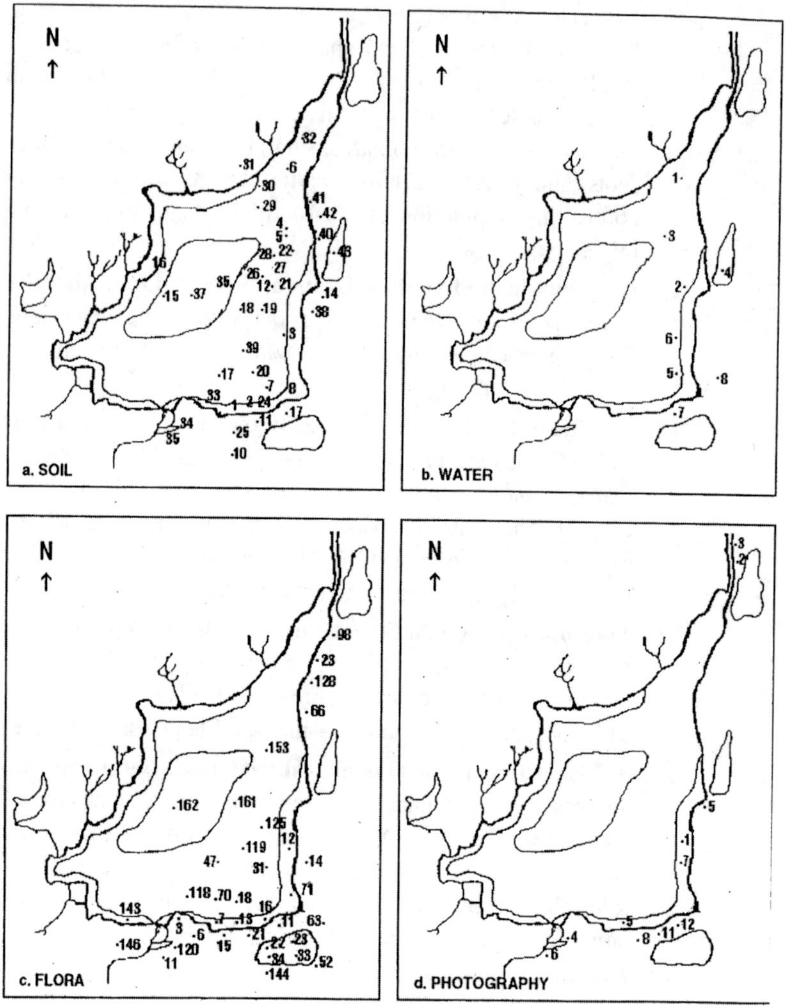

Fig. 3.2: Sampling sites at KALIVELI.

1
2
3
4

5

6

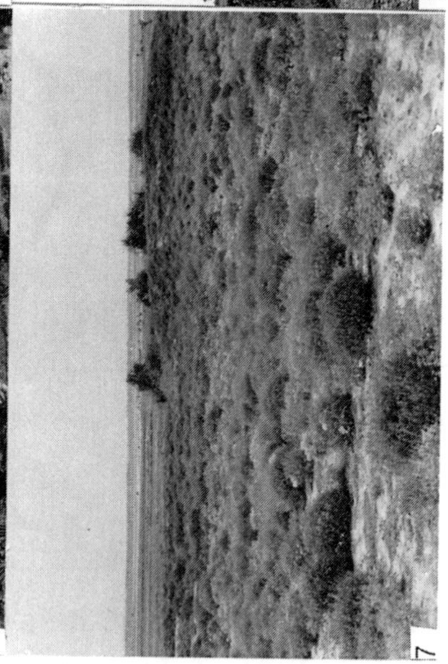

7

8

9
10
11
12

14
16
13
15

God's Church
Shri Mariyamman
Kovil Vandipalayam
Sri Throwpathiyamman
Kovil Kilappakkam
Bhagavan Parijatha
Kannan Temple
Sri Selliamman Temple
49
Atchikadu
Mandavi
Shri Kaseri Amman Kovil
Muthallamman kovil
Hidden Bay
Kaliveli Lake
கலிவேலி ஏரி
Chettikuppam
செட்டிக்குப்பம்
Shri Vellathan
Temple
Parijatha Kannan Temple
Koonimedu
K Resort
erumbakkam
Google
17

4. OUSTERI

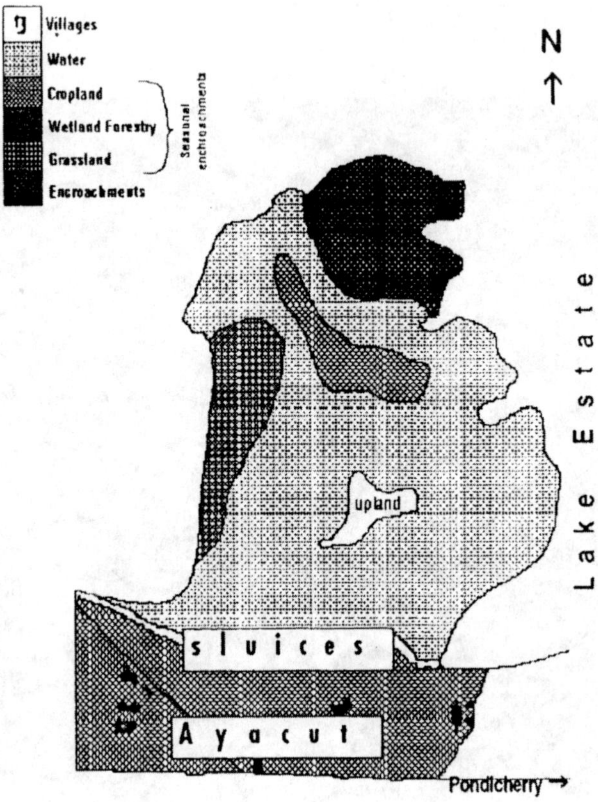

Fig 4.1: Ecography of Ousteri Tank.

A. Introduction

Ousteri tank is located 10 km west of Pondicherry in an area of 700ha, part of which is in Tamil Nadu State. The region has a tropical monsoon climate with an average rainfall of 125 cm/yr. The tank is characterized by the presence of input and output channels as well as seasonal rainfall. Water is generally available for 6-9 months per year and is used for agriculture and domestic purposes. The rain fall regime is dissymmetrical and the water level fluctuates with the rainfall. It is a major wintering spot for migratory birds and a rich source of inland fishes. It is also ringed with industrial units.

Ousteri dates back to the Chola period, developed by the Vijayanagar Empire, the Nayakas, as well as the French. Ananda Ranga Pillai seems to have improved it to facilitate irrigation of his lands nearby. It has thus been an important wetland for over 5 centuries enjoying official patronage. Unfortunately it is now facing problems in the catchment area and main water body (Fig. 4.1, Table 4.7).

B. Characteristics

1. Soil (Table 4.1, 4.8a and Fig 4.2a)

Soil is clayey. pH ranges from 5.6 to 804 and electrical conductivity from 0.2 to 5.20. The lime status was found to be Nil. Among the macronutrients, Nitrogen varies from 2.8 to 182 Kg/Ac, Phosphorus from 2.8 to 55 Kg/Ac and Potassium from 72 to 620. Table 4.1 and 4.8a show the characteristics of various regions of the tank. Sampling locations are shown in Fig A.2a.

Table 4.1 Characteristics of OUSTERI SOIL[@]

	Parameter	*FS*	*Bed*	*Ayacut*	*Mean (SD)*
1.	Texture	SCL	CSL	SCL	–
2.	pH	6.7 – 8.40	7.50 – 8.2	5.6 – 8.40	7.86 (0.77)
3.	E.C*	0.2 – 5.20	0.20 – 0.5	0.2 – 2.40	0.3 (0.09)
4.	Nutrients#				
	N	49 – 104.5	54.0 – 182	2.8 – 130.3	92.31 (23.1)
	P	3.0 – 17.0	2.80 – 6.0	3.5 – 55.0	4.97 (1.96)
	K	72 – 547	109.6 – 321	37 – 820	121.87 (46.1)

@ For more details refer Table 4.8a and Fig.4.2a *mm/cm # Kg/Acre

2. Water (Table 4.2, 4.8b and Fig 4.2b)

The water is slightly alkaline and saline with pH ranging between 7.3 and 8.7 and electrical conductivity between 0.3 and 3.5. The ranges of cations were found to be as follows - Calcium: 0.6 and 9 A Mel I, Magnesium: 004 - 6.2, Sodium: 0.1 - 1904 and Potassium: 0.02 - 0.11 Mel I. Anions like Carbonates ranged between 0.2 and 0.9 MelI, Bicarbonates between 1.7 and 9.20 and Chlorides between 0.8 and 2.2 Men.

Table 4.2: Characteristics of OUSTERI – WATER[@]

Parameters	*Stagnant*	*Well*	*Mean(sd)*
pH	7.3 – 8.7	7.4 – 7.50	8.2 (0.47)
E.C.	0.3 – 0.8	0.3 – 3.50	0.63 (0.65)
S.A.R.	0.1 – 4.7	0.9 – 6.90	1.98 (1.18)
Cations (me/l)			
Ca	0.6 – 1.9	2.0 – 9.40	1.14 (0.37)
Mg	0.4 – 2.1	0.6 – 6.20	0.45 (0.49)
Na	0.1 – 5.1	1.0 – 19.4	3.01 (4.44)
K	0.02 – 0.06	0.11 –	0.05 (0.03)
Ations (me/l)			
CO_3	0.2 – 0.8	0.9 –	0.48 (0.21)
HCO_3	1.7 – 4.8	2.8 – 9.20	2.24 (0.87)
Cl	0.8 – 2.3	1.0 – 25.7	1.39 (0.52)

@ For more details refer Tables 4.8b and Fig.4.2b

3. Vegetation (Table 4.3c and 4.8c)

(a) Flora: In total there are 101 species distributed in 95 genera and 55 families. These are terrestrial, semi-terrestrial and aquatic varieties colonizing the tank bed, margins and other areas i.e. there are 6 habit types distributed among 4 habitat guilds. Of these 52 are found to have considerable economic and/or ecological importance. Commonly found hydrophytes are Vetiveria zizanioides, Typha angustata, Marselia and two species of Nymphaea.

Table 4.3a: Characteristics of OUSTERI – FLORA.

	Taxonomy				*Habitat*		*Important*	
Habit	*Spp*	*Gen*	*Fam*	*Fs*	*B*	*Ayacut*	*Wl*	
Grasses or Sedges	11	9	2	5	8	5	3	3
Herbs	30	27	14	22	3	23	14	14
Shrubs	23	22	16	23	4 - 5	17	12	15
Climbers	13	13	10	10	-	10	4	6
Trees	20	20	9	16	-	15 - 20	12	12
Hydrophytes	4	4	4	-	4	-	-	2
Total	101	95	55	76	20	76	45	52

@ For more details refer Table 4.8c and Fig. 4.2c.

(b) Seed banks: Assaying barren soil in the tank bed for natural germination revealed the occurrence of seed-banks of 13 species in different frequencies. Many were weeds found in agricultural fields. Shannon Weiner index was calculated. (Table 4.3b).

Table 4.3b: Characteristics of OUSTERI: SOIL SEED BANKS.

Species	*No. of Individuals*	*Relative Pi abundance*	*Pi In PI*
1. Aristida sp	9	0.07	0.186
2. Buibostylis barbata	10	0.08	0.202
3. Cyperus sp.	8	0.06	0.169
4. Euphorbia hirta	13	0.10	0.230
5. Eragrostis teneHa	11	0.09	0.217
6. lndigofera sp.	4	0.03	0.105
7. lsachne elelgans	5	0.04	0.129
8. Leucas aspera	9	0.07	0.186
9. Perotis indica	18	0.14	0.275
10. Unidentified Species I	4	0.03	0.105
11. Unidentified Species II	9	0.07	0.186
12. Unidentified Species III	12	0.09	0.217
13. Tephrosia purpurea	18	0.14	0.275
Total	130	E*Pi In Pi INDEX	2.382

4. Fauna (Table 4.5a and 4.5b)

In total there are 153 species distributed among 123 genera and 78 families.

Though many species of grasshoppers, dragon flies, spiders, bugs and beetles were seen, only butterflies (18 species), fishes (10), amphibians (4), reptiles (20), birds (82) and mammals (11) were check listed. They were found in four habitat guilds. There are 90 species of birds belonging to 74 genera and 48 families. Their food habits range from Frugivory, nectarivory, insectivory (0 feeding on aquatic and terrestrial organisms. Many are aquatic feeders and insectivorous.

Table 4.4a: Characteristics of OUSTERI - FAUNA[@]

Animals Species	*Taxonomy*			*Habitat*			
	Gen	*Fam*	*TW*	*Hs*	*AF*	*TB*	
Butterflies	18	13	8	3	12	13	16
Fishes	10	8	7	10	-	3	-
Amphibians	4	1	1	3	2	3	-
Reptiles	20	17	8	3	8	12	16
Birds	90	74	47	19	18	26	38
Mammals	11	10	7	1	5	8	10
Total	153	123	78	39	45	65	80

@ For more details refer Tables 4.8d-i

Table 4.4b: Characteristics of OUSTERI - BIRDS@

Migratory Status	*Taxonomy*				*Food Habit*			
	Spp	*Gen*	*Fam*	*F*	*N*	*I*	*A*	*T*
Resident	53	50	31	16	10	29	13	14
Local Migratory	10	9	8	-	-	3	8	2
Migratory	19	15	9	1	-	4	16	1
Total	82	74	48	17	10	36	37	17

@ For details refer Tables 4.8h

5. Culture systems

Culture systems include artificial and semi-natural ecosystems like agriculture, aquaculture, social forestry and private plantations. These are inseparable part of the tank system both structurally and functionally (Tables 4.5, 4.6 & 4.7, Fig.4.1).

(a) **Agriculture**: Paddy, sugarcane, millet and groundnut are cultivated in an approximate area of 1550 ha. of registered ayacut. The villages - Gudappakam, Sendanattam, Villianur, Poraiyur, Oussudu, Odiyanpatlu and Ozhukarai in Pondicherry and Perumbaiin Tamil Nadu are benefited by this tank. A total of 1465 ha is approximately benefited and harvested twice a year. Water is supplied through seven sluices situated along the southern bunds of the tank. Crops are affected by pests and diseases. Fertilizers and pesticides are applied regularly. (Table 4.6).

Table 4.5: Characteristics of OUSTERI - CULTURE SYSTEMS.

Agriculture	*Aquaculture*		*Wetland Forestry*		*Human Settlements*	
	Natural	*Cultured*	*Location*	*Plant*		
Sugarcane	Catfish	-Nil-	Bank	Acacia	Oussudu	Ozhukarai
Paddy	Tilapia		[north]	Casuarina	Gundapakkam	Kadapperikuppam*
Millet	Carps			Eucalyptus	Sendanattam	Kondimedu*
Plantain					Villianur	Poothurai*
Maize					Poraiyur	Perambai*
					Odiyambattu	

* Villages belonging to South Arcot District of Tamil Nadu.

(b) **Aquaculture:** There is no managed aquaculture in Ousteri tank Tilapia mossambica a fish species introduced from Africa forms the main catch. The fish produce is leased out every year to private parties. (Table 4.5).

(c) **Social forestry:** Casuarina, Eucalyptus, Prosopis and Acacia plantations are maintained by Panchayats as well as by private parties. The North-Eastern banks are under Prosopis plantation while others are scattered (Table 4.5).

(d) **Settlements:** The eleven villages around the tank have depended on this tank for generations. The local people are benefited by the natural fisheries. The tank serves as the main source of recharging the groundwater from which they extract water through wells and bore wells. Lateral seepage is an important factor helping the surrounding agricultural fields.

6. Pollution

There was a hue and cry in the print media during mid-1993 that chemical wastes were being dumped near Ousteti tank and that they caused detrimental effects. Ultimately the episode ended with the ministerial clarification that pollution of the lake, if any, was under permissible levels. The details of the alleged episode are as follows:

(a) About 10 lorry loads of wastes, including yellowish white coloured polished stones have been seen for the last 6 months at Poonthurai road near the Aurobindo Ashram's estate.

(b) They were reported to have caused irritation to skin and throat of sometimes nausea.

(c) The implications are:

1. The dumping was done by the industries from the estates around-Mettupalayam, Thattanchavadi or Sedharapattu, Tondamanatham bottle factory, Hindustan lever and a dozen others situated around.
2. The lake is polluted when rainfall sweeps/washes them.
3. Vegetation, fisheries and agriculture are affected.

(d) This may have led to "reduced fish yields"

(e) Animals, especially birds are poached upon by foreigners.

(f) The wastes were supposed to have been dumped by an undisclosed unit of Tamil Nadu (from where?) Which is safely cleared by the PWD of Pondicherry (To where?) and the lake is within the limits of pollution standards' (7) A "Save Ossudu" campaign was also launched!

All of a sudden the clamour stopped. The only pollution observed was from domestic and animal sources and poaching is done by locals too and not by foreigners only. Analysis of water did not reveal any pollution. It is unfortunate that academicians and NGOs are involved in this three legged race for prominence and profits.

C. Perceptions

The local people are conscious of the utility of this water body as it has been an age old facility. Besides agriculture they wish to have greater utility of this wetland as a source of drinking water, fisheries etc. The locals feel that it is being degraded due to bore wells, which are owned by affluent people. The tank is perceived as a common property resource (Table 4.6).

Table 4.6: People's perceptions on OUSTERI

Soil: Soil is less fertile. Fertilizers and pesticides are applied. Organic farming by using compost as manure is the recent trend.

Water: Ground water irrigation is common. Desiltation of canal and channels is needed. Water from bore wells is hard. Many farmers buy water during summer. Urgent need for efficient distribution.

Plants: Plant cover is inadequate. More organized social forestry is required.

Animals: People are aware of noxious animals-Toddy cat, Jackals, Bandicoot rat, Mice and useful and edible ones like Fishes, Birds and Hare etc.

Agriculture: Mainly Paddy and Sugarcane. Crop rotation in Paddy fields with Groundnuts is practiced.

Wetland Forestry: Casuarina and Acacia are the main plantation trees. Private plantations also occur. Firewood is scarce. More area under plantations desired.

Livestock: Buffaloes, cattle and goats graze on tank bunds and beds. Ducks feed in water and on the tank bed.

Others: Lateral seepage of surface irrigation. Tail end farmers unsatisfied with surface irrigation canals and supplies which are irregular and unpredictable

D. Inferences

The Ousteri tank is an important determinant of the normal functioning of surrounding villages and agricultural fields. Though it is a man made wetland, during the long period of its existence it has developed characteristic flora and fauna, habitat systems and interactions. (Table4.1)

1. Ecology

(a) Subsystems

(i) **Agro-ecosystems:** A variety of crops are raised here dominated by paddy. Despite intense pesticide use a great number of plants and animals are found here. Crop fields serve as good hideouts for animals. Thus 76 plant species and 65 animal species of which 26 are birds favour agro-systems as regular habitats. Needless to emphasise that very diverse roots of interrelationships are sparked from here.

(ii) **Water body:** The tank receives water both from local catchment and also from the main feeder, the Suthukeny channel from the Veedur dam on the Sankaraparani river through a diversion at Suthukeny anicut. Water inflow is during the North-East monsoon from October to January. The ayacut area is about 15.68 sq.km. The capacity of the tank is 15.29 M.Cu.M. Plants such as Ipomea through ageing and decay may increase the BOD, COD, N, P etc. of water and cause pollution. Sunlight may gradually be prevented from penetrating into lower levels of water this reduces natural water currents and movement of fishes. These may usher in other ecological impacts with the passage of time.

(iii) **Sluice proximities:** Some of the sluices especially the first one, are comparatively deeper, holding more water and for longer durations attracting human activities such as washing clothes, kitchenware, etc. Water quality is different here. Other features must also be different as a consequence, though not investigated currently.

(iv) **Islands:** The water availability in the tank is more dependent on the supply from Veedur dam. When this supplies as well as local catchments are weak, patches of ground are exposed. They are mostly Ipomoea dominant islands giving refuge to many molluscs, insects, worms and water birds. The deeper parts of inlet channels nourish fishery and molluscs.

(b) Habitat Qualities

(i) **Soil:** Soil in general has a sandy loamy texture. pH of the soil varied from 5.60 to 8.40, the mean amounting to 7.86 indicating mild alkalinity, which is within the tolerance limits of paddy, sugarcane, coconut, plantain, etc. The mean Electrical Conductivity is 0.3. Nitrogen distribution varied widely from very low to medium level (2.8-182), Phosphorus (2.8-55) and Potassium (72-620) showed variations from very low to very high but their mean values indicate adequacy.

In general soil is Nitrogen deficient but adequate in Phosphorus and Potassium.

(ii) **Water:** High value of pH (8.2) is not substantiated by the E.C value (0.63 units) which is relatively low. Above readings indicate that water is slightly alkaline but not saline. High Carbonate and Bicarbonate values along with low cation concentration points towards the possibility of lime saturated water mixing with the tank water from adjacent areas. For better yield field should be pre treated with green manure or compost.

2. Conservation

(a) Habitats

(i) **Water body:** The tank receives water from two sources and continuity of both has to be ensured so as to maintain the aqua terrestrial life of nearly 40 species and adequate dilution of pesticide pollutants. This should not be normally difficult in the light of the ground realities. The most difficult task however will be to vacate the encroachments on the north which has reduced the water body by a third.

(ii) **Land:** The banks are barren and susceptible to erosion. Therefore the bank slopes and margins need to be vegetated by shrubs and trees preferably useful to the local people. The thickets existing in some places should be replicated. The preferences should be for utility as energy sources, soil binders, humus builders, fodder yielders etc. A checklist of ecologically and economically important plants, their importance and possibility of using them for vegetating the banks are given elsewhere (Appendix).

(b) Resources

(i) **Soil:** Soil texture is suitable for both agricultural and construction purposes. It is moderate in nutrient status. Nitrogen inputs are absolutely essential for agriculture. The tank soil is often used as an appendant to croplands.

(ii) **Water:** Feeder channels lack maintenance. Gingee river is silted along its entire length. A drastic reduction in the area under tank and canal irrigation and a phenomenal increase of tube wells has been noticed. Such an increase in the extraction of ground water leads to an intrusion of saline water and lowering of water table. Foreshore is illegally' occupied in the north. The physical structures - dam, embankments, sluices, inlet channels are intact. The area of the water body appears to have reduced due to encroachments during the last few decades. The volume of water held is further reduced by the shallowing of the bottom due to siltation from the shores, supply channels and human interferences. Water is clear when the tank is full and foulest when shallow. In between the aquatic weeds play an important role. When their growth reaches maximum level, nutrients like P deplete, checking their growth. If these nutrients are added due to domestic pollutants, limiting factors do not operate and weed pollution continues to plague the tank.

(iii) **Plants:** A large number of plants are found to be economically and ecologically important. The potential of some of these are not yet realised by the villagers. Ecologically important plants were identified by field survey and by cross checking with the locals. Local people have faith in folk medicine and traditional systems of health management both of which need plants. Unfortunately these plants are dwindling in number. Therefore it is necessary to restore all the species of medicinal plants that once existed, and propagate them with the current ones in a medicinal plant garden.

(iv) **Animals:** There are 153 species from the six classes currently surveyed. They all should be considered resources ecologically. From an economic point of view many may be useful in addition to those usually poached. The prospects of developing fish, amphibians and bird excreta as distinct resources are indeed great.

3. Development

(a) **Engineering Works:** Repairing the channel system and removing the islands are the two inputs required as the remainder are well maintained by the government. The local catchment needs to be intervened so as to channel all rainwater into Ousteri. To the credit of the PWD it should be acknowledged that their engineers have prepared a modernisation plan 5 years ago and yet nothing has been implemented for reasons not known.

(b) **Agriculture:** Once water is available, paddy is planted. Some times sugarcane also is cultivated using groundwater. These are unwise practices. Instead, people should be encouraged to cultivate less water-needing crops, so that water can be conserved in the wells and underground for longer durations and for potable purposes. Water should be priced to the farmers, so that they realise the value of the precious resource. The plant and animal associations seen in tank must have been greater when vegetation was denser. These associations form a basis for seed dispersal, pollination, food and habitat variations. They are relevant to agriculture both as pests as well as predators of pests. The potential bio-control agents are birds like (Dicrurus adsimilis, Cypsurus parvus, Coracias benghalensis, Athene bramar etc.) reptiles like (Monitor lizards, Rat Snake, etc.) and amphibians. Also insects capable of transforming into pests in due course need examination. As high input farming is loosing significance, vermicultural efforts over a length of time should be more productive. Other kinds of organic fertilizers, lime composts, etc. can substitute for chemical fertilizers.

(c) Aquaculture: The year round availability of water indicates very good aquaculture prospects in the tank. Thus a variety of fishes (Tilapia, Catfishes, Carps etc.) were introduced in the tank. An aquaculture farm was set up. But the project was abandoned for some unknown reasons. Naturally occurring fishery is exploited by villagers. Edible molluscans are also available from the tank.

(d) Apiculture: Availability of water, well vegetated banks and semi arid climate is suitable for apiculture. Suitable species for the semi-arid zone should be introduced. Governmental inputs are essential in initial stages. The Khadi and Village Industries Board can playa crucial role in this regard.

(e) Sericulture: Introducing mulberry cultivation of suitable varieties requiring less water inputs has to be explored. If this is possible even for a few months a new source of income generation will take roots. There is the Chinese experience in this regard using tank sediment and aqua cultural wastes. Recently, mulberry varieties suitable to semi-arid conditions have been developed.

(f) Tourism and recreation: Since Ousteri is surrounded by human settlements and has good communication system to Villupuram, Sedarapet and Pondicherry; prospects of developing it as a picnic spot are high. With some investments towards establishing minimal recreational facilities, Ousteri can be developed into an eco-tourist spot for both public and academic personnel. These can be centered on the southern embankment and it may boost local economy too.

E. Summary

Table 4.7: Summary of Characteristics: OUSTERI

1. Location : 12 Km West of Pondicherry, in Ousudu village 11° 57' N X 79° 45' E
2. History : About 500 years old. Vijayanagar King's reign
3. Rainfall : 125 cm/year (average of 20 years)
4. Temperature : 33°C – 23° C (average of 20 years)
5. Ayacut : 15.68 Sq. Km
6. Catchment : Free = 10.36 Sq. Km.
Intercepted = 5.18 Sq. Km.
Combined = 15.54 Sq. Km.
Equivalent = 11.4 Sq. Km.
7. Yield : 0.169 Mm/Sq.Km. (15.5 M clt/Sq.mile)
8. Tank : Area = 7 Sq. Km., depth upto 3 meters
9. Tank bund : length = 7023 Km., Width = 3 mt.
10. Supply channel : Suthukeny channel
11. Storage capacity : 15.29 M. Cu. M.
12. Duration of Water : 6 - 8 months
13. Sluices : 7
15. Cultivated area : as above and 25.30% of encroached North.
16. Villages associated : 7

17. Soil	pH	: 5.6 - 8.4	N	:	95 -166.0 Kg/Ac
	E.C	: 0.2 - 24.0	P	:	2.82 – 30 Kg/Ac
	Texture	: CL	K	:	72 - 321 Kg/Ac
18. Water	pH	: 7.3 – 9.1	Na+	:	0.1 – 5.10 Me/I
	E.C.	: 0.3 – 0.8	K+	:	0.02 – 0.11 Me/I
	Hardness	: 80 – 150	CO_3-	:	0.2 – 0.90 Me/l
	S.A.R	: 0.1 – 3.7	HCO_2-	:	1.5 – 4.80 Me/I
	Ca+	: 0.6 – 2.0	Cl-	:	0.8 – 2.70 Me/I
	Mg+	: 0.4 – 2.3	Na %	:	62.4 – - Me/l
	TDS	: 275 – 512			
19. Flora	Grasses	: 11	Climbers	:	13
	Herbs	: 30	Trees	:	20
	Shrubs	: 23	Hygrophyte	:	6
20. Fauna	Butterflies	: 18	Fishes	:	10
	Amphibians	: 4	Reptiles	:	20
	Birds	: 90	Mammals	:	11

21. Culture System

(a) Agriculture

1. Major Crops – Paddy and Sugarcane
2. Minor Crops – Pennisetum, Eleusine and Setaria

(b) Aquaculture

1. Natural : Tilapia mossambica, Catfish and Carps
2. Cultured : Nil

(c) Wetland Forestry

Location : Encroached tank area and private owned ayacut
Species : Acacia, Arabica and Casuarina

22. Current status

Good inflow, siltation, Ipomoea infestation, input channel silted, encroachments, pollution, poaching.

F. Addenda

1. Tables: 4.8a-i

Table 4.8a: Characteristics of OUSTERI-SOIL.

					Nutrients (kg/acre)		
No.		*Texture*	*pH*	*E.C mmh/cm*	*N*	*P*	*K*
1	S	C	8.0	0.2	101.3	3.0	118.8
2	S	SCL	6.7	5.2	49.0	6.0	547.0
3	S	SL	8.1	0.2	84.0	17.0	172.0
4	S	-	7.9	0.4	82.0	7.0	234.0
5	D	SL	8.4	0.2	95.0	9.0	72.0
6	D	SL	8.3	0.2	102.0	3.2	98.0
7	J	SL	8.3	0.2	104.5	3.4	94.0
8	S	C	8.0	0.4	166.3	2.9	115.2
9	S	-	7.5	0.4	79.0	6.0	321.0
10	D	-	7.8	0.2	54.0	6.0	294.0
11	D	-	7.8	0.3	60.0	6.0	294.0
12	JL	C	8.1	0.3	142.0	3.0	117.4
13	JL	SL	8.0	0.5	182.5	3.0	118.8
14	M	SL	8.2	0.3	128.3	2.8	109.8
15	S	C	8.0	0.3	126.3	3.5	108.9
16	S	SCL	5.6	2.4	53.0	6.0	620.0
17	J	S	5.9	0.5	56.0	5.0	37.0
18	J	SL	7.5	0.2	84.0	30.0	106.0
19	J	SL	7.6	0.6	91.0	55.0	532.0
20	JL	C	8.4	0.3	2.8	10.5	265.3
21	JL	SCL	8.4	0.3	100.0	11.0	304.0
22	J	SCL	8.3	0.3	130.3	8.5	177.5
		E.X	291.5	6.3	2075.4	123.1	3157.7
		X	10.05	0.32	94.34	6.16	166.19
		SD	0.35	0.12	40.50	3.54	87.42

1-7: Fore Shore 8-14: Bed 15-22: Ayacut.

Table 4.8b: Characteristics of OUSTERI - WATER.

Sam		*pH*	*E.C.*	*S.A.R.*	*Cations (me/l)*			*Anions (me/l)*			
					Ca	*Mg*	*Na*	*K*	*Co_3-*	*Hco_3-*	*Cl-*
1.	S	8.1	0.4	3.0	0.6	1.0	2.7	0.02	0.4	2.3	1.6
2.	S	8.0	0.3	0.1	1.9	0.4	0.1	0.04	0.8	1.5	0.8
3.	S	7.8	0.3	0.1	1.5	1.0	0.2	0.06	0.2	1.6	2.3
4.	N	8.4	0.8	4.7	1.0	2.0	5.1	0.05	0.5	2.6	2.3
5.	N	8.0	0.5	3.7	1.2	0.6	3.5	0.03	0.4	2.8	2.2
6.	N	7.8	0.3	1.2	1.7	0.9	0.2	0.06	-	1.6	1.0
7.	Ap	8.7	0.8	3.0	1.2	2.1	4.0	-	0.4	4.8	2.5
8.	Ap	8.7	0.4	1.9	0.8	0.9	1.8	-	0.4	1.8	1.2
9.	Ap	8.4	0.4	1.9	0.8	0.9	1.8	-	-	2.4	1.0
10.	J	9.1	0.4	1.9	0.8	0.9	1.8	-	0.3	1.4	1.3

(Contd...)

11.	J	7.9	0.5	2.2	1.2	0.4	2.0	-	-	2.8	0.8
12.	J	7.8	0.3	2.4	0.9	0.5	2.0	-	-	1.0	1.0
13.	JL	7.3	0.4	1.5	1.1	0.9	1.5	-	-	1.6	1.6
14.	JL	7.6	0.5	1.2	1.5	1.5	1.5	-	-	1.6	1.6
15.	JL	8.0	0.3	1.9	0.8	0.6	1.6	-	-	1.3	1.3
16.	Ja	7.4	0.4	0.9	2.0	0.6	1.0	0.11	0.9	1.0	1.0
17.	JL	7.5	3.5	6.9	9.4	6.2	19.4	-	-	9.2	25.7
	E.X	136.5	9.4	31.6	17.12	15.2	48.1	0.37	4.3	31.42	22.2
	X	8.2	0.63	1.98	1.14	0.95	3.01	0.05	0.48	2.24	1.39
	SD	0.47	0.65	1.18	0.37	0.49	4.44	0.03	0.21	0.87	0.52

1-15: Stagnant 16-17: Well S: September N: November

Table 4.8c: Characteristics of OUSTERI - PLANTS

No	*Species*	*Habi*	*No*	*Species*	*Habit*
1.	Abutilon indicum	Hy	52.	Hydrilla verticillala	H
2.	Acacia auriculiformis	T	53.	Indigolera cordilolia	H
3.	Acanthus ilicifolius	S	54.	Indigofera tinctoria	H
4.	Achyranthes aspera	S	55.	Ipomaea carnea	S
5.	Adhathoda zeylanica	S	56.	Jasminum angustifolium	C
6.	Alternanthera pungens	H	57.	Jatropha curcus	S
7.	Aristida mutabilis	G	58.	Jatropha gossippifolia	S
8.	Aristolochia bracteolate	H	59.	Justicia procumbens	H
9.	Aristolochia indica	C	60.	Justicia simplex	H
10.	Aristida sp.	G	61.	Lantana camara	S
11.	Arundo donax	G	62.	Leucas aspera	H
12.	Azadirachta indica	T	63.	Melia azadirachta	T
13.	Bauhinia tomentosa	T	64.	Merremia tridentata	H
14.	Boerthavia diffusa	H	65.	Mimosa pudica	H
15.	Bombax ceiba	T	66.	Mollugo disticha	H
16.	Borassus flabellifer	T	67.	Mollugo opposilifolia	H
17.	Breynia retusa	S	68.	Morinda corelola	T
18.	Calotropis gigantea	S	69.	Mukia maderaspalana	C
19.	Calycopteris floribunda	Sy	70.	Najas indica	H
20.	Canavalia mollis	C	71.	Nerium oleander	S
21.	Canthium coromandelicum	Sy	72.	Nymphaea pubescens	H
22.	Capparis brevispina	S	73.	Ocimum basilicum	H
23.	Cardiospermum halicacabum	C	74.	Ocimum tenuiflorun	H
24.	Cassia auriculata	S	75.	Oldenlandia umbellata	H
25.	Cassia tistula	T	76.	Opuntia monocantha	S
26.	Chara sp.	Hy	77.	Pandanus canarus	S
27.	Chloroxylon swietenia	T	78.	Passiflora edulis	C
28.	Citrulius colocynthis	C	79.	Peltophorum pterocarpum	T
29.	Cissampelos pareira	C	80.	Phoenix loureirii	S
30.	Cissus quadrangularis	C	81.	Phoenix sylvestis	T
31.	Cleome viscosa	H	82.	Phyla nodiflora	H
32.	Crotolaria pallida	S	83.	Phyllanlhus amarus	H
33.	Croton bonplandianus	H	84.	Polygala javana	H
34.	Cucumis sativus	C	85.	Pongamia pinnata	T

(*Contd...*)

35.	Cynodon dactylon	G	86.	Prosopis juliflora	T
36.	Cyperus arenarius	G	87.	Quisqualis indica	C
37.	Cyperus articulatus	G	88.	Rivea hypocrateriformis	C
38.	Parkinsonia aculeata	T	89.	Samanea saman	T
39.	Delonix regia	T	90.	Sida acuta	H
40.	Dodoneaangustilolia	S	91.	Solanum surrutans	H
41.	Eclipta prostrala	H	92.	Stachytarpheta indica	H
42.	Elephantopusscaber	H	93.	Tamarindus indica	T
43.	Eleusine indica	G	94.	Teclona grandis	T
44.	Eragrosliscilliaris	G	95.	Thespisia populnea	T
45.	Euphorbia hirta	H	96.	Tragia involucrata	C
46.	Ficus benghalensis	T	97.	Tridax procumbens	H
47.	Ficus hispida	S	98.	Typha angusta	G
48.	Fimbristylisaggregata	G	99.	Vernonia cinerea	H
49.	Flueggea leucop	D	100.	Vetiveria zizanoides	G
50.	Gomphrenacelosi	H	101.	Zyziphus xylopyrus	S
51.	Helitropium indi	H	102.	Unidentified	

G: 11 C: 12 H: 28 T: 27 S: 19 Hy: 6

Table 4.8d: Characteristics of OUSTERI - BUTTERFLIES.

No.	*Species*	*Common Name*
1.	Catopsilia crocale	Common Emigrant
2.	Colotis eucharis	Plain Orange Tip
3.	Danais chrysippus	Plain Tiger
4.	Danais limniace	Blue GlassyTiger
5.	Delias eucharis	Common Jazebel
6.	Euploea core	Common Indian Crow
7.	Eurema hecabe	Common Grass Yellow
8.	Hypolimnas missipus	Danaid Eggfly
9.	Mycalesis perseus	Common Bush Brown
10.	Papilio demoleus	Lime Butterfly
11.	Papilio polytes	Common Mormon
12.	Polydorous aristolochiae	Common Rose
13.	Polydorous hector	Crimson Rose
14.	Precis lemonias	Lemon Pansy
15.	Precis niarta	Yellow Pansy
16.	Precis orithya	Blue Pansy
17.	Telchinia violae	Tawny Castor
18.	Vanessa cardui	Painted Lady

Table 4.8e: Characteristics of OUSTERI - FISHES.

No.	*Species*	*Common Name*
1.	Anabas testudineus	Climbing Perch (Panai eri Kendai)
2.	Anguills species	Vilangu
3.	Clarias batrachus	Masaarai Keluthy
4.	Macrones seenghala	Koombu Keluthy
5.	Notopterus	Ambattan Katti
6.	Ophiocephalus marulius	Avuri Viral
7.	Ophiocephalus punctatus	Koravai
8.	Ophiocephalus striatus	Viral
9.	Tilapia mossambica	Tilapi Kandai
10.	Wallago attu	Valai Keluthy

Table 4.8f: Characteristics of OUSTERI - AMPHIBIANS.

No.	*Species*	*Common Name*
1.	Rana cyanophlyctos	Skipping Frog
2.	Rana hexadactyla	South Indian Frog
3.	Rana limnocharis	Paddy field Frog
4.	Rana tigrina	Bull Frog

Table 4.8g: Characteristics of OUSTERI-REPTILES.

No.	*Species*	*Common Name*
1.	Ahaetulla nasutus	Common Green Whip Snake
2.	Atretium schistosum	Olivacious Keel back
3.	Calotes versicolor	Garden Lizard
4.	Dendrelaphis tristis	Common Bronze back
5.	Echis carinalus	Saw-scaled Viper
6.	Eryx johni	John's Earth Boa
7.	Hemidactylus brooki	Brook's Gecko
8.	Hemidactylus frenatus	Southern House Gecko
9.	Hemidactylus leschnaulti	Bark Gecko
10.	Hemidactylus triedrus	Termite Hill Gecko
11.	Lissemys punctata	Indian Mud Turtle
12.	Mabuya carinata	Common Skink
13.	Melanochelys trijuga	Indian Pond Terrapin
14.	Naja naja	Indian Cobra
15.	Plyas mucosus	Common Rat Snake
16.	Sitana ponticeriana	Fan Throated Lizard
17.	Typhlina bramina	Common Worm Snake
18.	Varanus benghalensis	Common Monitor Lizard
19.	Vipera russelli	Russell's Viper
20.	Xenochro phispiscator	Checkered Keel back

Table 4.8h: Characteristics of OUSTERI - BIRDS.

No.	*Species*	*Common Name*	*Migration*	*Nutrition*
1.	Accipiter badius	Shikra	R	T
2.	Acridotheres tristis	Common Myna	R	FI
3.	Alauda gulgula	Eastern Skylark	LM	IAF
4.	Alcedo atthis	Small Blue Kingfisher	R	A
5.	Anans acuta	Pin-tailed Duck	M	A
6.	Anas querquedula	Garganey Teal	M	A
7.	Anthus novaeseelandiae	Paddy field Pipit	R	I
8.	Ardea alba	Large Egret	LM	A
9.	Ardea cinerea	Grey Heron	R	A
10.	Ardeola grayil	Pond Heron	R	A
11.	Artamus fuscus	Ashy Swallow-Shrike	R	I
12.	Athene brama	Spotted Owlet	R	T
13.	Aythya ferina	Common Poachard	M	A
14.	Aythya fuligula	Tufted Poachard	M	A
15.	Aythya nyroca	White Poachard	M	A
16.	Bubulcus ibis	Cattle Egret	R	T
17.	Centropus sinensis	Crow Pheasant	R	T
18.	Ceryte rudis	Lesser Pied Kingfisher	R	A
19.	Chlidonias hybridus	Whiskered Tern	M	A
20.	Circus aaruginosus	Marsh Harrier	M	A
21.	Columba livia	Blue Rock Pigeon	R	TG
22.	Coracias benghalensis	Indian Roller	R	TI
23.	Corvus splendens	House Crow	R	AFI
24.	Cuculus varius	Common Hawk Cuckoo	R	FI
25.	Cypsiurus parvus	Palm Swift	R	I
26.	Dicrurus adsimilis	Black Drongo	R	NI
27.	Dinopium benghalense	L. Golden-backed Woodpecker	R	NI
28.	Egretta garzetta	Little Egret	R	T
29.	Egretta intermedia	Small Egret	R	T
30.	Elanus caeruleus	Black winged Kite	R	T
31.	Eudynamis scolopacea	Koel	R	FI
32.	Halcyon smyrnensis	White Breasted Kingfisher	R	A
33.	Hirundo restica	Swallow	M	I
34.	Merops orientalis	Green Bee-eater	R	I
35.	Merops philippinus	Blue tailed Bee-eater	M	I
36.	Milvus migrans	Pariah Kite	R	T
37.	Nectarinia Iotenia	Loten's Sunbird	R	N
38.	Nectarinia zeylonica	Purplerumped Sunbird	R	IN
39.	Orthotorhus sutorius	Tailor Bird	R	NI
40.	Passer domesticus	House Sparrow	R	ITF
41.	Phalacrocorax niger	Little Cormorant	R	A
42.	Ploceus philippinus	Baya Weaverbird	LM	IF
43.	Prinia socialis	Ashy Wren-Warbler	R	I
44.	Psittacula krameri	Rose-ringed Parakeet	R	FG
45.	Phylloscopus trochiloides	Dull Green Leaf Warbler	R	I
46.	Saxicoloides fulicata	Indian Robin	R	I

R: 40 LM: 3 M: 11 F = 10 N = 6 I = 25 A = 21 T = 18

Table 4.8i: Characteristics of OUSTERI - MAMMALS.

No.	*Species*	*Common Name*
1.	Bandicoota benghalensis	Indian Mole Rat
2.	Bandicoota indica	Bandicoot Rat
3.	Canis aureus	Jackal
4.	Funambulus palmarum	Three-stripped Plam Squirrel
5.	Herpestes edwardsi	Mongoose
6.	Lepus nigricollis	Indian Hare
7.	Paradoxurus hermaphroditus	Palm Civet
8.	Pipistrellus coramandra	Indian Pipistrelle
9.	Rattus raltus	Common Rat
10.	Suncus murinus	Grey Musk Shrew
11.	Vulpus benghalensis	Indian Fox

2. **Figures: 4.2a-d**

   Collection locations of soil, water and plants samples and sites of photography.

3. **Photographs: 4.1-8**

   1. Fallow land in the bed of Ousteri in the north-west. Ipomoea weed can be seen invading this space.
   2. Traditional fish farming in Ousteri when waters are shallow.
   3. An unusual fish catch when the conditions are very favourable.
   4. Tall grass, partly burnt and/cut along with a lone tree of Prosopis Juliflora. A stand of Ipomoea weeds can be seen at the back.
   5. Suthukeny channel. Suthukeny channel brings water to Ousteri from Veedur Dam. The channel is very well engineered and banks are vegetated. The channel opens to Ousted from the south western side. Water retained in tank till March end.
   6. The main shutter at Ousudu which controls the water flow to the ayacut of the tank. The stagnant water here has plenty of fishes. The children are seen fishing in the stagnant water.
   7. The northern most bed of Ousteri land is leased and encroached by locals. Paddy is grown year round. Casuarina plantations are also shown in the photograph. The pump house shown in the picture is used for meeting the water need during summer. Cultivation is legalized in most cases and electricity is supplied at concessional rate in most cases.
   8. Migratory birds in the Ousted Lake. These ducks are migratory winter visitors. Pintail duck and coots are shown in the photograph.
   9. Google Map of Ousteri.

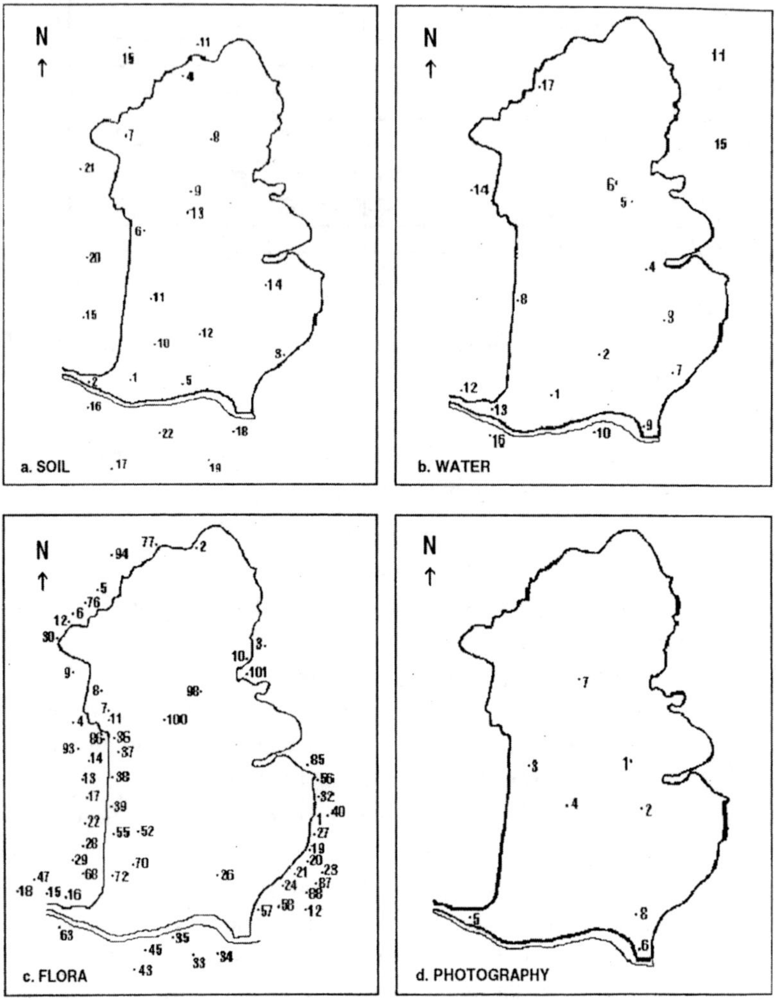

Fig.4.2: Sampling sites at OUSTERI.

1
2
3
4

6
8
5
7

Orochi Mantra Aluvalagam
Mariamman Alayam
Thondamanatham substation
Poothurai Rd
Manaveli
மனவேலி
Poothurai
பூத்துறை
CHARAL FARMHOUSE
India Post
தொண்டமாநத்தம் அஞ்சலகம்
Beach Ground New YScc Pothurai
Shri Amman Temple
ஸ்ரீ அம்மன் கோயில்
Thondamanatham
தொண்டமாநத்தம்
Osudu Lake
Sedarapet Main Road
Poothurai Rd
Sri Draupadi Amman Koil
Amaitheeswarar
Oussudu- Boat Club
Reserve Bank Of India
Indian Bank
இந்தியன் வங்கி
KURUMBAPET
குரும்பபேட்
Amman Koil
Kokilambigai Samedha...
Sri Muthu Mariamman Koil
VIP'S RESIDENTIAL AREA
Koodappakkam
கூடப்பாக்கம்
Poraiyur
பொறையூர்
Konerikuppam
கோனேரிகுப்பம்
Google
Sri Lakshmi Narayana Perumal Temple

9

5. MIRATTUNILAI

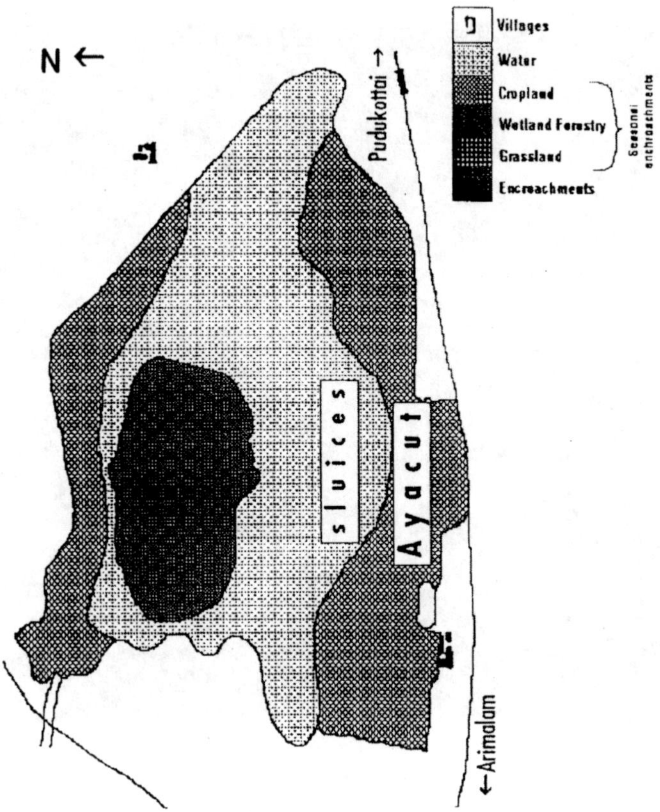

Fig 5.1: Ecography of Mirattunilai Tank.

A. Introduction

Mirattunilai tank in lies at a distance of 10 km from Pudukottai town on way to Arimalam in Mirattunilai village. This tank has been known to exist for nearly 200-300 years and is believed to have been built during King Thondaman's period. This non-system tank belongs to the Upper Vellar Basin and has a total water spread area of 2.8 sq. km, an average depth of 1.75 m. and water holding capacity of 1.55 M.cu.m. The southern side of the tank has an embankment running to a length of 5 km. and a width o12.7 m. Water remains only for 3-5 months after the rainy season. There is an inlet channel called Mirattunilai supply channel which has been encroached upon and is heavily silted and therefore not functional. Water here is thus entirely received from its own catchment comprising about 7 sq. km on the north-western side. This water is sufficient for a single harvest of paddy in an area 012.4 sq. km. south of the tank. The locality is otherwise semi-arid with an annual rainfall of 98 cm. The monsoon is confined to a short period of 75 days/year. Minor crops cultivated during the dry season are groundnut, ragi and maize (Fig. 5.1, Table 5.7).

B. Characteristics

1. Soil (Table 5.1, 5.8a and Fig 5.2a)

The texture of the soil is sandy clayey or sandy loamy. pH varied between 5.9 and 8.9. and electrical conductivity between 0.1 and 2 indicating low salinity. Among macronutrients, Nitrogen and Phosphorus are very low (35-117.5 Kg/Ac and 0.5-73 Kg/Ac respectively). Potassium varied between 27 and 378 Kg/Ac.

Table 5.1: Characteristics of MIRATTUNILAI SOIL@

Parameter		***FS***	***Bed***	***Ayacut***	***WI***	***Mean (SD)***
1.	Texture	SCL	SL	SCL	SC - SL	–
2.	pH	6.5 – 7.9	5.9 – 8.7	6.0 – 8.9	6.9 – 7.6	6.96
3.	E.C*	0.1 – 2.0	0.1 – 0.7	0.2 – 0.3	0.2 – 0.3	0.25
4.	Nutrients#					
	N	43.8 – 117.5	35 – 110	56 – 102		74.51
	P	1.0 – 71.0	0.5 – 73.0	0.8 – 65.0		6.43
	K	54.0 – 378.0	54 – 192	27.0 – 151.0		122.39

@ For more details refer Table 5.8a and Fig.5.3a **mm/cm* # Kg/Acre

2. Water (Table 5.2, 5.8b and Fig. 5.2b)

pH of water is neutral both in the inlet channels and the tank bed. Electrical conductivity varied between 0.2 and 1.3 indicating low salinity. Among cations Calcium varied between 1 and 4 indicating that water belongs to the 'CaCI' geochemical group. The other cations: Magnesium, Sodium and Potassium ranged between 0.8-2.0 Me/l, 0.1-4.1 and 0.02 and 2.8 Me/l respectively. Among anions Chloride varied between 0.7 and 2.6 Me/l and Bicarbonate between 1.6 and 6.2 Me/I.

Table 5.2: Characteristics of MIRATTUNILAI – WATER@

Parameters	*Stagnant*	*Inlet*	*Mean(sd)*
pH	7.2 – 7.8	7.6 – 7.8	7.6 (0.21)
E.C.	0.2 – 1.3	0.3 – 0.3	0.29 (0.05)
S.A.R.	0.1 – 2.3	0.1 – 9.8	0.4 (0.34)
Cations (me/l)			
Ca	1.2 – 4.0	1.0 – 1.4	1.26 (0.17)
Mg	0.8 – 2.0	0.8 – 1.6	1.08 (0.31)
Na	0.1 – 4.1	0.1 – 0.8	0.43 (0.34)
K	0.02 – 2.8	0.02 – 0.04	0.06 (0.05)
Ations (me/l)			
CO_3	–	–	–
HCO_3	1.6 – 6.2	2.2 – 2.6	1.27 (0.42)
Cl	2.2 – 2.6	0.7 – 0.8	0.82 (0.13)

@ For more details refer Tables 5.8b and Fig.5.3a

3. Flora (Table 5.3, 5.8c and Fig 5.2c)

In all 106 species belonging to 91 genera and 52 families are found in and around the tank. These include grasses (13), herbs (45), shrubs (22), climbers (8) and trees (18). These species belong to 5 habit types and 4 habitat guilds. 28 species are found to be of comparative ecological and/or economic importance. The scrub jungle in the tank catchment, though a major contributor to the richness of species has been recently converted into a eucalyptus plantation under the social forestry scheme.

Table 5.3a: Characteristics of MIRATTUNILAI – FLORA@

	Taxonomy				***Habitat***		***Important***	
Habit	***Spp***	***Gen***	***Fam***	***Fs***	***B***	***Ayacut***	***WI***	
Grasses or Sedges	13	12	2	3	11	4	2	4
Herbs	5	35	17	30	13	21 – 25	9	9
Shrubs	22	19	14	20	3	15	6	3
Climbers	8	8	7	8	-	8	3	
Trees	18	17	12	16	3	18	4 – 5	12
Total	91	52	77	30	70	25	28	

@ For more details refer Table 5.8c and Fig. 5.3c.

4. Fauna (Table 5.4a. 5.4b and Fig 5.8d-i)

A total of 99 animal species belonging to 87 genera and 59 families were identified. This comprises of 15 butterflies, eight fishes are a five amphibians, eight reptiles, fifty six birds and seven mammals belonging to 4 habitat guilds. There are 56 species of birds belonging to 53 genera and 36 families. They occupy 5 nutrition classes - frugivores, nectartvores, insectivores, aquatic and terrestrial feeders. It is interesting to note that more insectivorous birds are present in the agricultural fields.

Table 5.4a: Characteristics of MIRATTUNILAI- FAUNA@

Animals	*Taxonomy*			*Habitat*			
	Spp	*Gen*	*Fam*	*TW*	*Hs*	*AF*	*TB*
Butterflies	15	12	5	3	6	9	13
Fishes	8	7	6	8	-	4	-
Amphibians	5	2	1	3	1	3	-
Reptiles	8	8	5	2	4	7	7
Birds	56	51	36	9	22	25	34
Mammals	7	7	6	-	4	5	7
Total	99	87	59	25	37	53	61

@ For more details refer Tables 5.8d-i

Table 5.4b: Characteristics of MIRATTUNILAI – BIRDS@

Migratory Status	*Taxonomy*				*Food Habit*			
	Spp	*Gen*	*Fam*	*F*	*N*	*I*	*A*	*T*
Resident	51	48	31	15	8	28	12	17
Local Migratory	2	2	2	1	-	1	-	1
Migratory	3	3	3	1	1	1	1	-
Total	**56**	**53**	**36**	**17**	**9**	**30**	**13**	**18**

@ For m@ For details refer Tables 5.8h

5. Culture systems

(a) Agriculture: The major crop is paddy. Only a single harvest is obtained per year in an area of about 2.4 sq. km. During summer the land is kept fallow or irrigated with groundwater pumped from wells. Major summer crops are groundnut, ragi and maize (Table 5.5, Fig. 5.1).

(b) Aquaculture: No systematic aquaculture is practiced here. Naturally occurring carps, mullets and catfish are collected freely by the villagers during the rainy season. However when the water level recedes in the tank the fisheries are leased to private parties by the village officials. Rohu and Calla are the two important cultured species. (Table 5.5).

Table 5.5: Characteristics of MIRATTUNILAI - CULTURE SYSTEMS.

Agriculture	*Aquaculture*		*Wetland Forestry*		*Human Settlements*
	Natural	Cultured	Location	Plant	
Paddy	Catfishes	Catla	Inlet Channel	Eucalyptus	Mirattunilai
Pennisetum	Mullets	Rohu	Bund	Acacia	Ottapalampatti
Groundnet	Carps				Pupoipatti
Maize	Anabas				Kattupalampatti
Ragi					Ponampatti

(c) **Wetland forestry:** The tank bed on its north western side was planted with Acacia Arabica a few years ago but these saplings after some initial growth dried off. The eucalyptus plantations raised in the unused inlet channel are *thriving* Villagers depend on these plantations for meeting their firewood needs. A scrub thicket in the tank catchment called Sengeerakkadu was cleared for raising eucalyptus plantations. This has considerably reduced local biodiversity (Table 5.5, Fig. 5.1).

(d) **Settlements:** The tank Mirattunilai is named after the village situated in the eastern banks of the tank. There are five Villages associated with the tank. But only three villages are benefited from the tank water. The tank bed and the catchment area are used as a grazing ground for the livestock from all the villages.

6. Pollution

But for the probable contamination from the pesticides used in Paddy cultivation, there is no other source of pollution in the tank water.

C. Perceptions

People's perceptions about the system vary according to the social status of the respondent. Poor fertility and erosion of the soil are identified as major problems by the locals. The latter is considered as the major factor reducing the water retention period of the tank. The details are given in Table 5.6.

Table 5.6 People's perceptions on MIRATTUNILAI

Soil: Poor fertility and erosion of the soil are identified as major problems by the locals. According to them siltation caused by the eroded soil from the catchment and the bund is the major factor reducing the water retention period of the tank.

Water: Locals consider the highly variable rainfall as the main factor determining the tanks functioning and its utility. The impounded water is just enough for one harvest but not enough to cultivate all the available land. The Oorani system is followed in Mirattunilai village for availing water for domestic purposes. In the peak monsoon the overflow from the tank feeds the Vellaru river. Wells are dug by private parties for extracting water for both irrigation and domestic purposes. Water table is 20-25 meters below the surface. Tail-end farmers depend on well water for irrigation. Disputes among the villages on water distribution are solved through negotiations between elderly citizens of the villages.

Plants: It appears that people are less aware of the changes in the plant cover in the area. Their knowledge of plant utilities such as medicine, load and fodder is limited.

Animals: Local people are well aware of the seasonality and population variations of the animals in the tank surroundings. They have noticed the presence of migratory birds in winter. They attribute the decrease in the number of monkeys, pelicans and peafowl's to the loss of their habitat and poaching by tribals.

Agriculture: Farmers buy bore-well water from private parties on hourly basis. Crop pests are controlled by applying pesticides. Storage pests are controlled by using neem and vitex leaves. But biological control of pests is not known to farmers. Commonly used synthetic pesticides are Sevin, Ecalux, BHC, Dieldrin and Carbaryl. Organic manures like cow-dung and green manure and chemical fertilizers are used.

Aquaculture: People are aware of the existence of edible fauna like crabs, fish's and frogs in the tank. Fishery is accessible to villagers equally when the tank is full, but leased to private parties in March and April when the fishery becomes dense and mature.

Wetland and Social forestry: Acacia arabica is planted on the tank-bed on the North West region. Prosopis occurs on the main bund on the southern side.

Animal Husbandry: Cattle, goats and poultry form the major constituents of the village live stock. According to some villagers buffalo population has declined in recent years.

Others: Farmers feel that the tank bund should be turfed and revegetated with species suitable for grazing. As the Acacia saplings on the bed are becoming inviable due to flooding, the other areas should be dredged to contain all the storable water. The encroached inlet channel should also be reclaimed so as to ensure regular supply of water from Vellar river.

D. Inferences

1. Ecology

Mirattunilai tank is comparatively of recent origin (300 years) belonging to the semi arid rain shadow region of Tamil Nadu. This aspect has a large impact on the vegetation and the ecology of the water body. Pronounced seasonality is one feature of the tank as the water availability is limited to 3-5 months in a year. At other times the tank bed remains slushy in the deeper regions and dry with new vegetation on the *elevated* regions.

(a) **Subsystems** Monitoring of the waterbody and watershed revealed the existence of four major micro habitats associated with the tank system. They are: (a) The Waterbody, (b) The agricultural fields, (c) Shores and bed, (d) Social Forestry.

(i) The waterbody: The waterbody comprises of the water collected in the tank from the catchments. The excess water overflows in to the river. Since it is rainfed, water is available for 3-5 months, until March end. And then a dry season of 4-6 months follows. Many birds feed on aquatic organisms out of which the common sand piper is a winter visitor. A few species of fish, reptiles, molluscans, hydrophytes and semi-aquatic plant species like **Ipomoea**, many algae and phytoplankton occur here. The dried tank bed is in water-logged condition during the initial months of summer, but later there is rapid growth of grasses and herbs. The bed is therefore grazed upon by livestock.

(ii) Agro-ecosystems: The ayacut of the Mirattunilai tank constitutes 2.4 km of chiefly paddy crop area. In summer groundnut, ragi or maize are cultivated. These fields have growth of herbaceous weeds which support many butterflies, provide hideouts for reptiles and mammals. Many insectivorous birds are also observed here.

(iii) Shoreline and bed: Although they are recognisable for the variety of plants and animals found there, they resemble the water body habitat during the drying phase.

(iv) Wetland and Social forestry: Many forest trees like **Strychnos nux-vomica** were reported from the vicinity of Mirattunilai tank. These points towards the biologically rich past of the tank locality. On the north - western side of the tank, eucalyptus plantations at different stages of growth are found. There are also remains of a thicket called 'Sengeerakkadu' which was a rich storehouse of many faunal species like common peafowl and macaques which have considerably depleted due to the clearing of forests. Despite this, the plantations and the remaining patches of thicket support a large number of birds, mammals, reptiles and butterflies. Most plant species occurring in the fringes of Paddy fields, tank embankments, etc. are also reported from Sengeerakkadu. Endangered species are - common pea fowl, Bennet macaque, spot billed pelican and paradise fly catcher.

(b) Habitat Qualities

(i) **Soil:** Soil in general has a sandy loamy texture. pH of the soil varied from 5.9 to 8.9, the mean being 6.96 which is suitable to all crops. Electrical conductivity has a mean value of 0.25 but the actual data shows a distribution from 0.1 to 2. Values of nitrogen varied from 35 to 117.5 kg/ac giving a mean value of 74.51 which is very low. Phosphorus (05-73) and Potassium (27-378) showed variations from very low to very high but mean values indicated adequacy. Thus the soil is only of medium richness in macronutrients.

(ii) **Water:** The mean values of pH (7.2) and E.C (0.29) indicate that the tank is neutral to medium alkaline. Water is suitable for irrigating almost all crops. The high values of Calcium and Magnesium ion concentration compared with low values of Chlorides, Carbonates and bicarbonates indicates mineral saturation probably from weathered rock. High concentration of Potassium is either from inland detritus or from clay.

2. Conservation

(a) Habitats

(i) **Water body:** Water remains for about 3-5months after rains in an area of about 3 sq. km. This is a habitat for a few hydrophytes and 25 animals including fishes and amphibians. Several birds depend on these facultatively or obligately. The security of this habitat depends very much on the drainage from the local catchment and controlled withdrawal through wells.

(ii) **Land:** The banks are barren and susceptible to erosion. Therefore slopes and margins of banks need to be vegetated by grass cover, shrubs and trees-preferably useful to local people. In fact, some places have thickets of past vegetation which should be replicated. The preferences should be for those usable as energy sources, soil binders, humus builders, fodder yielders, etc.

(b) Resources

(i) **Soil:** This is mostly sandy clayey or sandy loamy with neutral pH and low salinity. It is deficient in Nitrogen but rich in Potassium and Phosphorus. Therefore this is useful for pottery and brickwork but needs nitrate inputs for agriculture.

(ii) **Water:** Water resource is available only for a few months, but very useful for all purposes-drinking, washing clothes and cattle bathing.

(iii) **Plants:** Local people have faith in folk medicine and the traditional systems of health management both of which need plants. Fortunately there seem to be no dearth of these plants though they are dwindling systematically. Therefore it is appropriatc to rcstorc all thc spccies of medicinal plants that once existed and are now limited to thickets.

(iv) **Animals:** The animals are poached upon for a variety of purposes. Three of these are prominent as they are becoming extinct-Peafowl, Bonnet Macaque and Spot-billed Pelican. The removal of the Sengeerakkadu remnant forest had a severe effect on animal diversity and population and therefore on resources.

3. Development

(a) **Agriculture** Instead of paddy, people should be encouraged to cultivate less water-needing crops, so that water can be conserved in the wells and underground for longer durations and for potable purposes. Agriculture can be made ecologically friendly by adopting vermiculture and organic fanning.

(b) **Aquaculture:** The tank retains water for three to four months after the monsoon. During this period Catla and Rohu fishes are grown in the tank. The right for terminal harvest is leased out every year. Apart from these, catfishes, mullets, carps and Anabas are also found in the tank. The quantum of fish catch is not known.

(c) **Apiculture:** The availability of water, well vegetated banks and semi-arid climate are suitable for Apiculture. Hence species suitable for the semi-arid zone ought to be identified and introduced. Inputs from Government are essential to local initiatives in the initial stages.

(d) **Sericulture:** Introducing mulberry cultivation of suitable varieties needing less water inputs ought to be explored. This should be possible for a few months atleast, giving a new source of income generation to the locals. The Chinese experience in this regard, using tank sediments and aqua cultural wastes as mulberry fertilizers can be used. Recently, mulberry varieties suitable to semi-arid conditions have been developed.

E. Summary

Table 5.7: Summary of Characteristics: MIRATTUNILAI.

1. Location	10 Km from Pudukottai town. Upper Vellar Basin 10° 12' N X 78° 52' E
2. History	200 - 300 years old, during King Thondaman period
3. Rainfall	98.3 cm/year, 57.6 days/years
4. Temperature	33°C – 23° C (average of 20 years
5. Ayacut	2.79 Sq. Km
6. Catchment	Free = 7.09 Sq. Km. Intercepted = 21.08 Sq. Km. Combined = 28.17 Sq. Km.
7. Yield	6.75 M. Cu. M.
8. Tank	Area = 2.8 Sq. Km.
9. Tank bund	length = 5.07 Km., Width = 27 mt.
10. Supply channel	Holds with anicut across Upper Vellar Length = 2535 meters Bed width = 4 meters Yield = 5.55 M. Cu. M.
11. Storage capacity	1.55 M. Cu. M.
12. Duration of Water	90 - 120 days / 120 – 150 days
13. Sluices	5 (97.74, 484.85, 92.83, 14.74, 41.46 acres of irrigation)
14. Cultivated area	2.4 Sq. Km.
15. Villages associated	5

16. Soil	pH	5.9 - 8.9	N	35 -117.5 Kg/Ac
	E.C	0.1 - 2.0	P	0.5 – 73.0 Kg/Ac
	Texture	SC - SCL	K	27.0 – 378.0 Kg/Ac
18. Water	pH	7.2 – 7.8	Na+	0.1 – 4.1 Me/I
	E.C.	0.2 – 1.3	K+	0.02 – 2.8 Me/I
	S.A.R	0.1 – 2.3	HCO_3-	1.6 – 6.2 Me/I
	Ca+	1.0 – 4.0	Cl-	0.7 – 2.6 Me/I
	Mg+	0.8 – 2.0		
19. Flora	Grasses	13	Climbers	8
	Herbs	45	Trees	18
20. Fauna	Butterflies	15	Fishes	8
	Amphibians	5	Reptiles	8
	Birds	56	Mammals	7

21. Culture System

(a) Agriculture

1. Major Crops – Paddy
2. Minor Crops – Groundnut, ragi, kambu and maize

(b) Aquaculture

1. Natural : Carps, Mullets and Catfish
2. Cultured : Catla and Rohu

(c) Wetland Forestry

Location : Near inlet channel and bund

Species : Eucalyptus, Acacia arabica

22. Current status

Weak bund, input channels encroached for agricultural and housing, bunds breached due to flooding and heavy siltation

F. Addenda

1. Tables: 5.8a-i

Table 5.8a: Characteristics of MIRATTUNILAI-SOIL

					Nutrients (kg/acre)		
No.		***Texture***	***pH***	***E.C mmh/cm***	***N***	***P***	***K***
1	S	SC	7.9	0.20	117.5	1.9	100.8
2	S	SL	6.8	0.20	48.8	1.0	148.5
3	S	L	6.5	0.20	43.8	1.4	117.0
4	O	SL	6.3	0.32	85.0	71.0	162.0
5	O	SC	6.6	0.20	72.0	17.0	87.0
6	O	SL	6.5	2.00	104.0	11.0	378.0
7	M	-	7.5	0.14	93.0	9.0	147.0
8	JL	-	7.4	0.62	98.0	11.0	60.0
9	JL	-	6.8	0.73	84.0	16.0	54.0
10	JL	-	7.2	0.60	74.0	15.0	60.0
11	S	SL	8.2	0.20	110.0	0.5	101.7
12	S	SL	6.8	0.20	71.2	0.6	139.5
13	S	SL	6.0	0.20	73.7	2.1	67.5
14	S	SL	6.0	0.26	82.5	73.0	162.0
15	O	SL	6.3	0.20	67.0	6.0	150.0
16	O	SL	5.9	0.15	85.0	8.0	90.0
17	M	-	7.5	0.13	46.0	18.0	186.0
18	M	-	8.1	0.10	78.0	10.0	192.0
19	JL	-	8.7	0.21	63.0	9.0	117.0
20	JL	-	10.2	0.66	35.0	10.0	54.0
21	JL	-	8.2	0.54	42.0	8.0	135.0
22	S	SL	8.9	0.20	90.0	2.2	180.0
23	S	SL	6.8	0.20	70.0	0.8	146.7
24	S	SL	6.7	0.26	86.0	65.0	150.0
25	O	SC	6.4	0.20	56.0	9.0	96.0
26	O	SL	6.0	0.19	95.0	11.0	27.0
27	S	L	6.8	0.20	102.5	1.1	151.2
28	M	-	7.3	0.19	74.0	8.0	135.0
29	S	SC	7.6	0.20	72.5	1.6	95.4
30	S	SC	6.9	0.26	74.0	41.0	96.0
		E.X	204.6	10.11	1859.0	230.24	3407.4
		X	7.05	0.33	71.5	8.53	117.50
		SD	0.80	0.35	16.91	8.31	43.18

1-10: Fore Shore 11-21: Bed 22-28: Ayacut 29-30: Waste Land

Table 5.8b: Characteristics of MIRATTUNILAI - WATER

Sample		*pH*	*E.C.*	*S.A.R.*	*Cations (me/l)*			*Anions (me/l)*			
					Ca	*Mg*	*Na*	*K*	*Co_3-*	*Hco_3-*	*Cl-*
1.	S	7.4	0.38	0.9	2.0	0.9	1.0	0.10	-	2.7	1.0
2.	O	7.7	0.26	0.4	1.2	0.8	0.4	0.04	-	1.8	0.7
3.	O	7.7	0.23	0.1	1.2	1.4	0.1	0.02	-	1.8	0.7
4.	S	7.8	0.27	0.1	1.5	1.0	0.2	0.16	-	1.6	1.0
5.	S	7.2	1.3	2.3	4.0	2.0	4.1	2.75	-	6.2	6.7
6.	S	7.8	0.25	0.1	1.0	1.6	0.1	0.02	-	2.6	0.7
7.	O	7.6	0.32	0.8	1.4	0.8	0.8	0.04	-	2.2	0.8
	E.X	53.2	1.71	2.4	6.3	6.5	2.6	0.38	-	4.9	
	X	7.6	0.29	0.4	1.26	1.08	0.43	0.06	-	2.17	0.82
	SD	0.21	0.05	0.34	0.17	0.31	0.34	0.05	-	0.32	0.13

1-5: Stagnant 6-7: Inlet

Table 5.8c: Characteristics of MIRATTUNILAI - PLANTS

No	*Species*	*Habit*	*No*	*Species*	*Habit*
1.	Abutilon indicum	Hy	25.	Borreria hispida	H
2.	Acacia arabica	T	26.	Borreria ocymoides	H
3.	Acacia auriculiformis	T	27.	Borreria stricta	H
4.	Acalypha indica	S	28.	Brachiaria ramosa	G
5.	Achyranthes aspera	S	29.	Cadaba fruticosa	T
6.	Aerva lanata	S	30.	Calotropis gigantia	S
7.	Aeschynomene aspera	S	31.	Calophyllum inophyllum	T
8.	Agave angustifolia	H	32.	Canthium coromandelicum	S
9.	Alangium salvifolium	T	33.	Capparis brevispina	S
10.	Albizia amara	T	34.	Carissa spinarum	S
11.	Aloe vera	H	35.	Cassia alata	S
12.	Alysicarpus vaginalis	H	36.	Cassia auriculata	S
13.	Amaranthus spinosus	H	37.	Cassia fistula	T
14.	Andrographis paniculata	S	38.	Cassia occidentalis	S
15.	Anisomeles indica	S	39.	Celosia argentea	H
16.	Anisomeles malabarica	H	40.	Ceratophyllum demersum	H
17.	Apluda mutica	G	41.	Chloris inflata	G
18.	Aristida mutabilis	G	42.	Chloroxylon swietenia	T
19.	Arundo donax	G	43.	Cissus quadrangularis	C
20.	Azadirachta indica	T	44.	Cleome viscosa	H
21.	Blastania garcini	C	45.	Coccinia grandis	C
22.	Boerhavia diffusa	H	46.	Cocculus sp	C
23.	Bombax ceiba	T	47.	Coldenia procumbens	H
24.	Borassus flabellifer	T	48.	Commelina sp.	C

(*Contd...*)

No	*Species*	*Habit*	*No*	*Species*	*Habit*
49.	Corchorus capsularis	H	87.	Murraya paniculata	T
50.	Croton bonplandianus	H	88.	Nerium odorum	S
51.	Cynodon dactylon	G	89.	Ocimum sanctum	S
52.	Dodonaea angustifolia	S	90.	Oldenlandia alata	H
53.	Digitaria chinensis	G	91.	Oldenlandia umbellata	H
54.	Digitaria sp.	G	92.	Opuntia coccinellifera	S
55.	Eclipta alba	H	93.	Opuntia monacantha	S
56.	Elephantopus scaber	H	94.	Parthenium hysterophorus	H
57.	Eragrostis tenella	G	95.	Passiflora edulis	C
58.	Euphorbia hirta	H	96.	Pavonia zeylanica	S
59.	Euphorbia royalana	T	97.	Perotis indica	G
60.	Evolvulus alsinoides	H	98.	Phoenix humilis	S
61.	Evolvulus marmelos	H	99.	Phoenix sylvestris	T
62.	Ficus bengalensis	T	100.	Phyllanthus amarus	H
63.	Fimbristylis aggregata	G	101.	Physalis minima	H
64.	Flueggea leucopyrus	S	102.	Pongamia glabra	T
65.	Garcinia indica	T	103.	Pongamia pinnata	T
66.	Gomphrena celosioides	T	104.	Prosopis juliflora	T
67.	Heliotropium scabrum	H	105.	Psilotrichum nudum	H
68.	Heteropogon contortus	G	106.	Randia malabarica	S
69.	Hibiscus hirtus	H	107.	Rivea hypocrateriformis	C
70.	Indigofera cordifolia	H	108.	Sesbania grandiflora	T
71.	Ipomoea biloba	H	109.	Sida cordifolia	H
72.	Ipomoea carnea	S	110.	Sida rhombifolia	H
73.	Ipomoea sp.	S	111.	Solanum surattense	H
74.	ipomoea tridentate	H	112.	Solanum sp.	H
75.	Ischaemum angustifolium	G	113.	Solanum torvum	H
76.	Jatropha gossippifolia	S	114.	Strychnos nux-vomica	T
77.	Jatropha heterophylla	S	115.	Stylosanthes fruticosa	S
78.	Justicia diffusa	H	116.	Tacca pinnatida	T
79.	Justicia glabra	H	117.	Tamarindus indica	T
80.	Justicia procumbens	H	118.	Tephrosia purpurea	H
81.	Leucas aspera	H	119.	Thevetia neriifolia	S
82.	Lycopersicum esculentum	H	120.	Tragia involucrata	C
83.	Melothria madraspatana	C	121.	Tridax procumbens	H
84.	Mimosa pudica	H	122.	Vernonia cinerea	H
85.	Mollugo oppositifolia	H	123.	Vitex negunto	S
86.	Morinda coreia	T			

G: 14 T: 26 H: 51 Hy: 2 C: 9 S: 27

Table 5.8d: Characteristics of MIRATTUNILAI - BUTTERFLIES

No.	*Species*	*Common Name*
1.	Catopsilia crocale	Common Emigrant
2.	Danais chrysippus	Plain Tiger
3.	Danais limniace	Blue Glassy Tiger
4.	Danais plexippus	Common Tiger
5.	Delias eucharis	Common Jezebel
6.	Ergolis merione	Common Castor
7.	Euploea core	Common Indian Crow
8.	Eurema hecabe	Common Grass Yellow
9.	Hypolimnas missipus	Danaid Egg fly
10.	Melanitis leda	Common Evening Brown
11.	Papilio polytes	Common Mormon
12.	Polydorous aristolochiae	Common Rose
13.	Polydorous hector	Crimson Rose
14.	Precis lemonias	Lemon Pansy
15.	Telchinia violae	Tawny Castor

Table 5.8e: Characteristics of MIRATTUNILAI - FISHES

No.	*Species*	*Common Name*
1.	Anabas testudineus	Climbing Perch (Panai eri Kendai)
2.	Catla catla	Catla Carp
3.	Cirrhina mrigal	Mrigal Carp
4.	Clarias batrachus	Masaarai Keluthy
5.	Labeo rohita	Rohu Carp (Kendai)
6.	OphiocephaJus marulius	Avuri Viral
7.	Ophiocephalus punctatus	Koravai
8.	Tilapia mossambica	Tilapi Kandai

Table 5.8f: Characteristics of MIRATTUNILAI - AMPHIBIANS

No.	*Species*	*Common Name*
1.	Bufo melanosticus	Common Indian Toad
2.	Rana cyanophlyctos	Skipping Frog
3.	Rana hexadactyla	South Indian Frog
4.	Rana limnocharis	Paddy field Frog
5.	Rana tigrina	Bull Frog

Table 5.8g: Characteristics of MIRATTUNILAI - REPTILES

No.	Species	Common Name
1.	Ahaetulla nasutus	Common Green Whip Snake
2.	Calotes versicolor	Garden Lizard
3.	Hemidactylus frenatus	Southern House Gecko
4.	Melanochelys trijuga	Indian Pond Terrapin
5.	Naja naja	Indian Cobra
6.	Plyas mucosus	Common Rat Snake
7.	Xenochro phispiscator	Checkered Keel back

Table 5.8h: Characteristics of MIRATTUNILAI - BIRDS

No.	Species	Common Name	Migration	Nutrition
1.	Accipiter badius	Shikra	R	T
2.	Acridotheres tristis	Common Myna	R	FI
3.	Alcedo atthis	Small Blue Kingfisher	R	A
4.	Ardea cinerea	Grey Heron	R	A
5.	Ardeola grayil	Pond Heron	R	A
6.	Artamus fuscus	Ashy Swallow-Shrike	R	I
7.	Athene brama	Spotted Owlet	R	T
8.	Bubulcus ibis	Cattle Egret	R	T
9.	Centropus sinensis	Crow Pheasant	R	T
10.	Clamator jacobinus	Pied Crested Cuckoo	M	FI
11.	Copsychus saularis	Magpie Robin	R	I
12.	Coracias benghalensis	Indian Roller	R	TI
13.	Corvus macrorhynchos	Jungle Crow	R	AFI
14.	Corvus splendens	House Crow	R	AFI
15.	Cuculus varius	Common Hawk Cuckoo	R	FI
16.	Cypsiurus parvus	Palm Swift	R	I
17.	Dendrocitla vagabunda	Indian Treepie	R	AF
18.	Dicrurus adsimilis	Black Drongo	R	NI
19.	Dinopium benghalense	L.Golden-backed Woodpecker	R	NI
20.	Egretta garzetta	Little Egret	R	T
21.	Egretta intermedia	Small Egret	R	T
22.	Elanus caeruleus	Black winged Kite	R	T
23.	Eudynamis scolopacea	Koel	R	FI
24.	Francolinus pondicerianus	Grey Patridge	R	T
25.	Halcyon smyrnensis	White Breasted Kingfisher	R	A
26.	Haliastus indus	Brahminy Kite	R	A
27.	Hirundo restica	Swallow	M	I
28.	Lanius vittatus	Baybacked Shrike	R	TI
29.	Lonchura punctulata	Spotted Munia	R	IF
30.	Megalaima haemocephala	Crimson Breasted Barbet	R	I
31.	Merops orientalis	Green Bee-eater	R	I
32.	Milvus migrans govinda	Pariah Kite	R	T
33.	Motacilla madraspatensis	Large Pied Wagtail	R	IA
34.	Nectarinia asiatica	Purple Sunbird	R	N

(Contd...)

35.	Nectarinia zeylonica	Purplerumped Sunbird	R	IN
36.	Nectarinia nycticorax	Night Heron	R	A
37.	Oriolus oriolus	Golden Oriole	R	FI
38.	Orthotorhus sutorius	Tailor Bird	R	NI
39.	Passer domesticus	House Sparrow	R	ITF
40.	Pavo cristatus	Common Peafowl	R	T
41.	Phylloscopus trochiloides	Dull Green Leaf Warbler	R	I
42.	Ploceus philippinus	Baya Weaverbird	LM	IF
43.	Psittacula krameri	Rose-ringed Parakeet	R	FG
44.	Podiceps ruficollis	Little Grebe	R	A
45.	Pycnonotus cafer	Red vented Bulbul	R	FIM
46.	Rhopodytes viridirostris	Small Green-billed Malkoha	R	FI
47.	Saxicoloides fulicata	Indian Robin	R	I
48.	Streptopillia chinensis	Spotted Dove	R	T
49.	Streptopillia senegalensis	Little Brown Dove	R	T
50.	Tephridirnis pondicerianus	Common Wood Shrike	R	TI
51.	Tersiphone paradise	Paradise Flycatcher	R	I
52.	Tourdoides striatus	Jungle Babbler	R	FIM
53.	Tringa hypoleucos	Common Sandpiper	M	A
54.	Turdoides caudatus	Common Babbler	R	FIM
55.	Upupa epops	Hoopoe	R	TI
56.	Vanellus indicus	Redwattled Lapwing	R	T

R: 51 LM: 2 M: 3 F = 17 N = 9 I = 30 A = 13 T = 13

Table 5.8i: Characteristics of MIRATTUNILAI - MAMMALS

No.	*Species*	*Common Name*
1.	Bandicoota indica	Bandicoot Rat
2.	Funambulus palmarum	Three-stripped Plam Squirrel
3.	Herpestes edwardsi	Mongoose
4.	Lepus nigricollis	Indian Hare
5.	Pipistrellus coramandra	Indian Pipistrelle
6.	Rattus raltus	Common Rat
7.	Vulpus benghalensis	Indian Fox
11.	Vulpus benghalensis	Indian Fox

2. Figures: 5.2a-d

Collection locations of soil, water and plants samples and sites of photography

3. Photographs: 5.1-8

1. A Panoramic view of Mirattunilai tank after the onset of monsoon. The northern banks are visible in the background. Some vegetational remains are still visible in the bed.

2. Breaching and erosion of the mud embankments of the tank during the rainy season. Sand bags are kept to support the weak portions. As seen in the photograph this erosion causes considerable siltation in the tank.
3. Mirattunilai tank bund soon after the monsoon. The bund has heavily breached owing to its low vegetation cover. Such breaching large scale results in heavy sin content in the tank water.
4. Mirattunilai tank embankment. Despite tree cover the bunds are barren and prone to erosion. The only way to reduce such erosion is to turf the embankments with grass species having good soil binding qualities
5. The overflow facility of Mirattunilai on its south eastern side. This overflow spills over to the channel leading to Therkar river. This is an old masonry work. The overflow in Mirattunilai is high in recent years as the tank bed has become shallower owing to siltation.
6. Overflow water from Mirattunilai has flooded the road, a common site during the rainy season. This water could have been stored if the embankments were strong.
7. The village and agricultural fields in the ayacut of Mirattunilai tank. Major crop is paddy. Coconut is also grown.
8. Ayacut region to which a supply channel is carrying water.
9. Google Map of Mirattunilai.

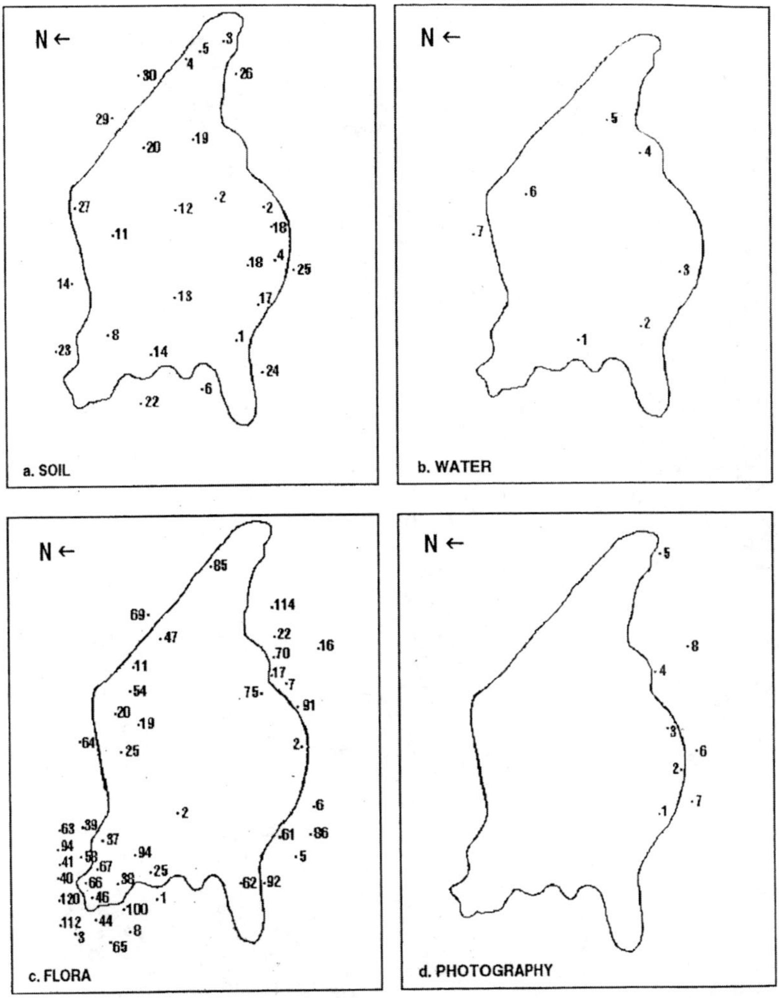

Fig. 5.2: Sampling sites at MIRATTUNILAI.

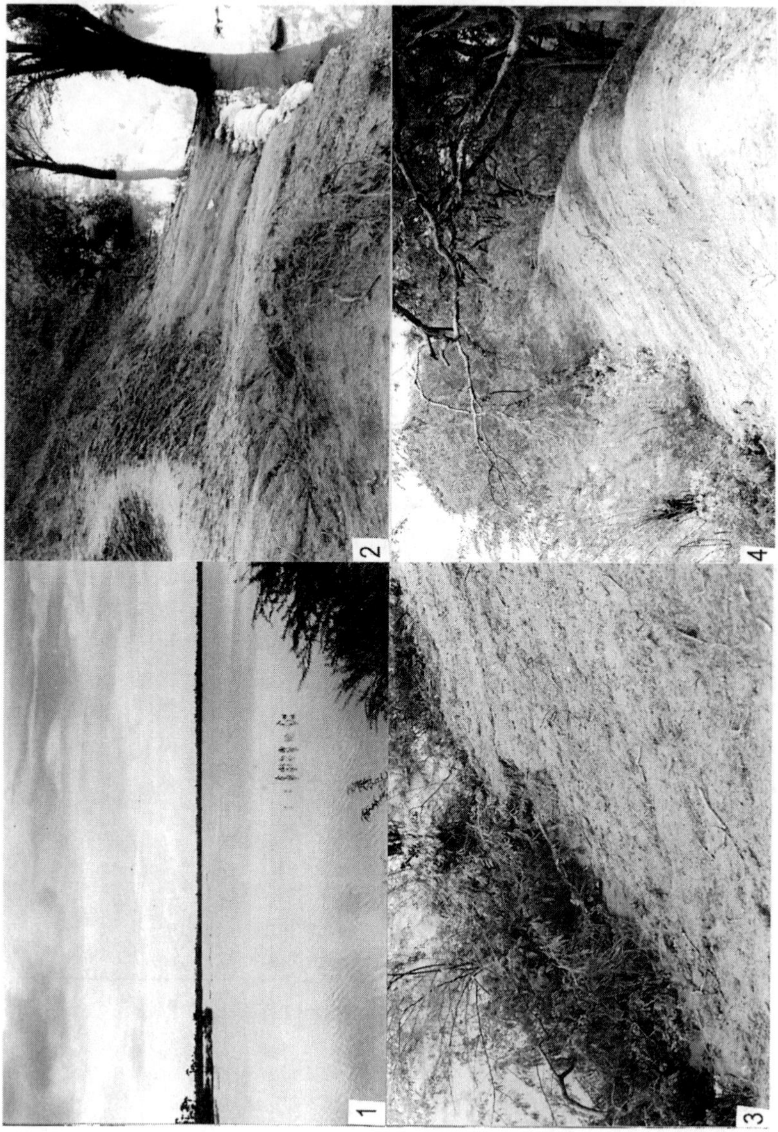

5 6 7 8

Hindu temple
Google
Perumal Kovil
MSA Maligai
Mirattunilai Bus Stop
PSV POLYTECHNIC COLLEGE
663
9

6. KAMBIKUDI

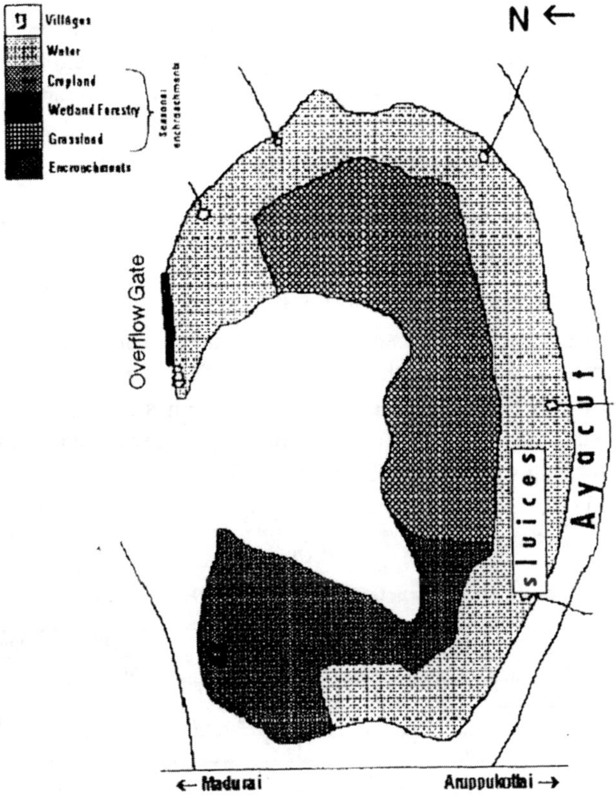

Fig. 6.1: Ecography of Kambikudi Tank.

A. Introduction

Kambikudi tank in Madurai Kamarajar District lies 25 km. east of Madurai town on the Arupukottai road in Kambikudi village. The tank has been known to exist for nearly 800 years. This non-system tank originally belonged to the Upper Gundar basin, receiving water from the Therkar supply channel apart from its own catchment of 5.74 sq. km. The total water spread area of Kambikudi is 5.2 sq. km with an average depth of 1.75 metre and a total water holding capacity of 3.62 M.cu.m. Water is available only for 2-3 months after the rainy season which is inadequate for cultivating 5.4 sq. km. of the Ayacut which was once dependent on this tank for its water requirements. The supply channel is now defunct and the water-spread area is highly silted. Major crop in the region is paddy, cultivated only once in a year. In other months the field is either left fallow or cultivated with cotton, ragi or other millets. The aridity of the region is more pronounced due to low rain fall (80 cm in about 45 days/ year). The mean annual temperature is as high as 38°C. (Table 6.7, Fig. 6.1).

B. Characteristics

1. Soil (Table 6.1, 6.8a and Fig 6.2a)

The texture of the soil is mostly sandy loamy. pH has shown greater variation in the ayacut (5.7-9.1) than in other subsystems. Electrical Conductivity of the soil also has shown considerable variation (0.12-1.2) The macronutrients have also similarly varied for Potassium from 72 to 600 kg/Ac, Nitrogen between 42 and 111.25 kg/Ac, and Phosphorus between 0.51 and 100 Kg/Ac respectively.

Table 6.1: Characteristics of KAMBIKUDI SOIL[@]

	Parameter	*FS*	*Bed*	*Ayacut*	*Wl*	*Mean (SD)*
1.	Texture	SCL	SL	SCL	SL - SC	–
2.	pH	6.5 – 9.0	7.0 – 8.9	5.7 – 9.1	7.4 – 8.9	7.86
3.	E.C*	0.2 – 0.4	0.2 – 1.2	0.12 – 0.7	0.14 – 0.3	0.23
4.	Nutrients#					
	N	42.0 – 106.3	49.0 – 95.0	63 – 113.3	70 – 80	75.09
	P	0.6 – 20.0	1.1 – 23.0	1.4 – 100.0	0.5 – 2.8	8.30
	K	108.9 – 600	72 – 600.0	103.0 – 600	90 – 154	124.51

@ For more details refer Table 6.8a and Fig. 6.2a *mm/cm # Kg/Acre

2. Water (Table 6.2, 6.8b and Fig 6.2b)

The pH value of water varies from 7.6 to 9 and electrical conductivity from 0.2 to 2.50. The cation concentrations also vary: Calcium (1-8), Magnesium (0.4-3), Sodium (0.7-4.2) and Potassium (0.05-13.4). Similar variations are found among anions: Bicarbonate (1.5 - 4.8 Me/l) chloride (0.6-16 Me/I) and Carbonate (0.2-0.3).

Table 6.2: Characteristics of KAMBIKUDI – WATER@

Parameters	*Stagnant*	*Inlet*	*Mean(sd)*
pH	7.7 – 9.0	7.6 – 8.2	7.74 (+/-0.82)
E.C.	0.2 – 2.5	0.9 – 1.9	0.40 (+/-0.34)
S.A.R.	0.8 – 7.2	1.9 – 5.9	1.63 (+/-1.42)
Cations (me/l)			
Ca	1.0 – 8.0	2.3 – 5.9	1.77 (+/-2.39)
Mg	0.4 – 3.0	2.9 – 3.0	1.41 (+/-0.70)
Na	0.7 – 4.2	3.0 – 4.0	0.82 (+/-0.49)
K	0.1 – 13.4	0.04 – 11.0	0.49 (+/-0.49)
Ations (me/l)			
CO_3	0.2 – 0.3	0.2 – -	0.48 (0)
HCO_3	1.5 – 4.0	3.4 – 4.8	1.69 (+/-0.99)
Cl	0.6 – 16.0	3.5 – 13.5	1.41 (+/-1.37)

@ For more details refer Tables 6.8b and Fig. 6.2b *mm/cm #Kg/Acre

3. Flora (Table 6.3, 6.8c and Fig 6.2c)

There are a total of 50 species belonging to 46 genera and 33 families. These include 2 grasses, 28 herbs, 10 shrubs, four climbers, four trees and two hydrophytes found in 4 habitat guilds. Most of them occur in the ayacut (32 species) and foreshore (37 species). About 16 species are found to be of considerable economic and/or ecological importance.

Table 6.3: Characteristics of KAMBIKUDI – FLORA@

Habit	*Taxonomy*				*Habitat*		*Important*	
	Spp	*Gen*	*Fam*	*Fs*	*B*	*Ayacut*	*WI*	
Grasses or Sedges	2	2	1	2	2	1	-	1
Herbs	28	14	22	5	23	6	11	
Shrubs	10	9	6	3	4	3	5	
Climbers	4	4	4	4	-	2	-	3
Trees	4	4	3	3	1	2	2	2
Hydrophytes	2	2	2	-	2	-	-	2
Total	50	48	33	37	13	32	11	16

@ For more details refer Table 6.8c and Fig. 6.2c.

4. Fauna (Table 6.4a. 6.4b and Fig 6.8d-i)

All 112 animal species belonging to 93 genera and 56 families are found in the tank surroundings (17 butterflies, 5 fishes, 6 amphibians, 8 reptiles, 67 birds and 9 mammals). They are distributed in four habitat guilds - tank water, human settlements, agricultural fields and thickets/ bushes. Among the guilds agricultural fields and thickets have the maximum diversity .There are 68 bird species belonging to 61.genera and 45 families. They have varied food habits, most of them however are insectivorous.

Table 6.4a: Characteristics of KAMBIKUDI - FAUNA@

Animals	*Taxonomy*			*Habitat*			
	Spp	*Gen*	*Fam*	*TW*	*Hs*	*AF*	*TB*
Butterflies	17	12	7	3	8	12	15
Fishes	5	3	3	5	-	3	-
Amphibians	6	3	1	4	2	4	-
Reptiles	8	8	5	2	3	5	7
Birds	67	58	34	9	19	32	38
Mammals	9	9	6	-	5	7	9
Total	112	93	56	23	37	63	69

@ For more details refer Tables 6.8d-i

Table 6.4b: Characteristics of KAMBIKUDI - BIRDS@

Migratory Status	*Taxonomy*			*Food Habit*				
	Spp	*Gen*	*Fam*	*F*	*N*	*I*	*A*	*T*
Resident	60	54	38	20	6	26	11	20
Local Migratory	3	3	3	1	-	-	1	1
Migratory	5	4	4	-	-	2	3	-
Total	68	61	45	21	6	28	15	21

@ For more details refer Tables 6.8h

5. Culture systems

(a) **Agriculture**: The major crop in this region is paddy. Only one harvest is possible due to low water availability. The tail end farmers depend on well water for their crops. Most of the land is kept fallow. Cotton is cultivated in the areas with black soil. Other summer crops are millets. The increasing dependence on wells has resulted in the neglect of tank irrigation.

(b) **Aquaculture:** No systematic aquaculture is possible here. Naturally occurring species such as carps, mullets, tilapia and catfish are harvested at the end of the rainy season (Table 6.5, Fig. 6.1).

Table 6.5: Characteristics of KAMBIKUDI - CULTURE SYSTEMS.

Agriculture	*Aquaculture*		*Wetland Forestry*		*Human Settlements*
	Natural	*Cultured*	*Location*	*Plant*	
Paddy	Catfishes	-Nil-	Tank Bed	Acacia	Manthiri Odai
Jasmine	Mullets			Prosopis	Meenachipuram
Cotton	Carps				Kanchamanayakan patti
Maize	Anabas				Kambikudi
Ragi	Tilapia				Pacheri
					Periakambikudi
					Tharachanethali
					Pichampatti

(c) Wetland Forestry: The tank bed and the surrounding wastelands are colonized by Prosopis juliflora growth. Apart from this Acacia arabica plantations are raised on the tank bed. Old plantations on the tank bed have grown and the new ones on the bed have dried up due to drought. The villages around Kambikudi depend on these plantations for their daily fire wood needs.

(d) Settlements: There are about eight villages associated with Kambikudi tank. Reduced efficiency of the tank in meeting the local irrigation needs has resulted in the disappearance of villages from the ayacut, (e.g. Periyakambikudi village) Non-availability of water for a second harvest has forced villagers to migrate to urban areas, in search of jobs.

6. Pollution

There are no polluting industries in the surroundings of the tank. Pollution from other sources are not known. Impact of agricultural run off on the water quality needs investigation.

C. Perceptions

Perceptions of people are one of expectation and hope on the useful role of tanks and their environs in their lives and another of lament and exasperation at the deterioration of tanks and degradation of nature around. Such a psyche assures local participation in any effort to rejuvenate the tank systems on a sustainable basis.

Table 6.6: People's perceptions on KAMBIKUDI.

Soil: People's perception on soil fertility varies. Organic fertilizers used include cattle dung and green manures.

Water: Tank water is used for irrigation. Tail end farmers depend on well water for cultivation. Some farmers even buy water from their neighboring farms at the rate of 20-25 Rs/hour.

Plants: People are not satisfied with the plant cover, though it has improved in recent years. Prosopis is considered a necessary evil - a weed that gives firewood. People use many plants in treating ailments. They feel that more fodder species need to be cultivated and the management of the plantation should be handed over to villagers.

Animals: People are aware of the seasonality shown by he animals. Squirrels and mongooses have increased in number in recent years. Local people are aware of the migratory water fowls. They do not poach them but are unable to check others from doing this. People seem to be unaware of the importance of lizards and amphibians.

Agriculture: Farmers are worried about the increasing cost of cultivation especially when they have to pay even for irrigation water. Cotton cultivation is promising but people feel that more professional input is necessary in this field. Farmers are not aware of the scope of organic farming and the biological control of pests.

Aquaculture: Villagers feel that if the water retention of the tank is increased and some refurbishments are done the lank can be used for aquaculture.

Wetland and Social forestry: people depend on social forestry plantations for firewood and humus: But farmers feel that some fodder crops are immediately needed.

Perspective: People feel that this old tank should be brought back to the condition it was in good olden days through governmental initiative involving local people's participation. The Kambakkal channel should be made functional. They think that the tank is the 'comerstone' of their economy. As the rank dries up, villagers migrate following low yield from agriculture. People fear that if this situation continues more villages will disappear.

D. Inferences

1. Ecology

Kambikudi tank is structurally different from all other tanks under- study. The embankments are not strengthened by boulders; the vegetation cover is poor. Breaching of the bund in rainy season has many implications apart from weakening the embankment and siltation. Its richness in animal and plant diversity is considerable. Though it is ephemeral with alternate harsh climatic extremes of dry and water- logged seasons, three subsystems are identifiable.

(a) Subsystems

(i) **The Waterbody:** The waterbody constitutes the stagnant water collected in the tank bed from its catchments. The excess water from the tank overflows. During the few months of water retention, the waterbody teems with life.

(ii) **Wetland Forestry:** Most of the shoreline is planted with fast growing species. **Prosopis juliflora** grows Wild. For some months these are considerably inundated and for most part remain water starved. Yet they attract many animals. Due to leaf fall and some patches of fertile soil are formed.

(iii) **Agricultural Fields:** The ayacut of Kambikudi tank is mainly cultivated with paddy. In the drier season ragi, cotton and millets are cultivated.

(b) Habitat Qualities

(i) Soil: Soil is sandy loamy or clayey loamy. pH of the soil varies between 5.7 and 9.1 the mean being 7.88 indicating mild alkalinity tolerated by many crops. Electrical Conductivity varies from 0.12 to 1.2, the mean value being 0.23 tolerated by the crops. Value of Nitrogen varies from 42 to 111.25 kg/ac giving a mean value 9f 75.09, Phosphorus and Potassium vary from low to very high levels. But the mean values suggest adequacy. Thus the soil quality vis-a-vis macronutrients is not poor despite drought conditions.

(ii) Water: The pH and E.C values suggest that the water is mildly alkaline and medium saline. High values of Calcium and Magnesium in water may be attributed to the saturation of minerals from weathered rocks. However this aspect needs detailed study. The carbonate saturation and Potassium enrichment could be due to the decay of the shells of molluscans.

2. Conservation

(a) Habitats

(i) Water Body: This is very poor as a habitat because of the ephemeral nature of the water. Yet there are 2 hydrophytes and 23 animals - 5 fishes and 4 amphibians. Birds depend on the aquatic organisms for their nutrition. If the supply channel is renovated and water is made available, it is possible to revive this last dying water body.

(ii) Land: The banks are barren and erosion is common. The bank slopes and margins need to be grassed and vegetated by shrubs and trees- preferably ones useful to local people. The few thickets still surviving should be replicated. The preferences should be for utilities such as energy sources, soil binders, humus builders and fodder yielders.

(b) Resources

(i) Soil: Soil is sandy loamy with low salinity and a neutral pH. Nitrogen inputs are required for agriculture. Phosphorous and potassium content are quite high.

(ii) Water: Water: Low salinity and neutral pH make it suitable for irrigation purposes. Water is also used for drinking, washing and cattle bathing.

(iii) **Plants:** A total of 50 plant species are found around Kambikudi. Of these 16 species are identified as economically or ecologically important. While some of them are already being exploited, the potential utility of others has not yet been realized. The existing plant species contain a few of medicinal value. All these need multiplication.

(iv) **Animals:** A large number of animals and habitats have immense ecological importance as starting points for regenerating a fast degrading habitat.

3. Development

(a) **Engineering Works:** The two most important works are to desilt or deepen the tank bed and strengthen the bund with atleast stone work. These might prevent overflows and help retain water in the tank for longer spells.

(b) **Ecologically Suitable Practices:** As and when the tank water becomes available, rice is planted. Instead, people should be encouraged to cultivate less water-needing crops, so that water can be conserved in the wells and underground for longer durations and for potable purposes. The land should be cultured by Prosopis juliflora, petroplants and Agave on a large scale i.e. on an agricultural scale. Others can follow after some years. Remains of these can be used for developing vermicultural compost. Keeping water for longer durations and using them in a frugal manner are ecological necessities here.

E. Summary

Table 6.7: Summary of Characteristics: KAMBIKUDI.

1. Location		: North of Kambikudi village in Kamarajar (Dist), Upper Gundar Basin 9° 42' N X 78° 7' E			
2. History		: 800 years old, during the period of Sundarapandian			
3. Rainfall		: 76.9 cm/year, 44.1 days/years (average of 50 years)			
4. Temperature		: 38°C			
5. Ayacut		: 541.18 ha (5.41 Sq. Km)			
6. Catchment		: Free: 5.748 Sq. Km. Combined: 80.78 Sq. Km.			
7. Yield		: 6.87 M. Cu. M.			
8. Tank		: Area: 5.2 Sq. Km., Depth: 3.72 m, Capacity: 4.19 M.cum			
9. Tank bund		: length: 5273 m., Width: 2 mt.			
10. Supply channel		: Therkar river Length: 5212 meters Depth: 1 meter			
11. Storage capacity		: 3.52 M. Cu. M.			
12. Duration of Water		: 30 - 60 days / 60 – 90 days			
13. Sluices		: 8			
14. Cultivated area		: 5.4 Sq. Km.			
15. Villages associated		: 5			
16. Soil	pH	: 5.70 - 9.10	N	:	42 -111.25 Kg/Ac
	E.C	: 0.12 - 1.20	P	:	0.48 – 100.0 Kg/Ac
	Texture	: SL - SCL	K	:	72.0 – 600.0 Kg/Ac
18. Water	pH	: 7.60 – 9.00	Na+	:	0.70 – 04.20 Me/I
	E.C.	: 0.23 – 2.50	K+	:	0.05 – 13.40 Me/I
	S.A.R	: 0.83 – 7.18	CO_3-	:	0.20 – 00.30 Me/I
	Ca+	: 1.00 – 8.00 Me/l	HCO_3-	:	1.50 – 04.80 Me/I
	Mg+	: 0.40 – 3.00 Me/l	Cl-	:	0.60 – 16.00 Me/I
19. Flora	Grasses	: 2	Climbers	:	4 Herbs : 28
	Trees	: 4	Shrubs	:	10 Hydrophytes: 02
20. Fauna	Butterflies	: 17	Fishes	:	5
	Amphibians	: 6	Reptiles	:	8
	Birds	: 67	Mammals	:	9

21. Culture System

(a) Agriculture

1. Major Crops – Paddy
2. Minor Crops – Ragi, Cotton and Millets

(b) Aquaculture

1. Natural : Carps, Mullets, Tilapia and Catfish
2. Cultured : Nil

(c) Wetland Forestry

Location : Tank bed

Species : Acacia arabica

22. Current status

Very less inflow, breached bund, reduced depth, encroachments, input channels, monsoon failure.

F. Addenda

1. Tables: 6.8a-i

Table 6.8a: Characteristics of KAMBIKUDI - SOIL.

					Nutrients (kg/acre)		
No.		*Texture*	*pH*	*E.C mmh/cm*	*N*	*P*	*K*
1	S	CL	8.8	0.20	77.5	3.0	108.9
2	O	C	8.0	0.25	106.3	0.6	144.9
3	M	CL	6.5	0.20	103.8	1.3	103.0
4	D	CL	8.2	0.16	46.0	1.4	174.0
5	S	SCL	8.4	0.29	100.0	11.0	204.0
6	M	SCL	8.3	0.38	95.0	20.0	594.0
7	JL	SCL	9.2	0.17	42.0	16.0	540.0
8	JL	SCL	8.7	0.19	57.0	16.0	588.0
9	JL	SCL	9.0	0.14	62.0	16.0	600.0
10	O	CL	8.4	0.20	85.0	2.9	116.1
11	N	C	7.0	1.20	95.0	1.1	148.5
12	D	CL	7.0	0.20	81.3	1.9	108.0
13	D	CL	8.2	0.20	63.0	1.2	300.0
14	S	SL	8.4	0.18	95.0	9.0	72.0
15	M	SCL	8.8	0.21	61.0	11.0	594.0
16	JL	SCL	8.8	0.26	59.0	23.0	600.0
17	JL	SCL	8.2	0.20	56.0	21.0	600.0
18	JL	SCL	8.9	0.22	49.0	16.0	600.0
19	JL	SCL	8.8	0.28	70.0	20.0	588.0
20	S	CL	8.3	0.50	85.0	2.6	103.0
21	O	C	7.2	0.20	111.3	0.5	144.0
22	N	CL	7.7	0.20	77.5	1.4	117.0
23	D	CL	7.8	0.16	64.0	4.8	213.0
24	S	SL	5.7	0.12	109.0	16.0	222.0
25	M	SCL	9.1	0.71	82.0	14.0	486.0
26	M	SCL	8.2	0.31	78.0	100.0	599.0
27	JL	SCL	8.6	0.23	64.0	21.0	600.0
28	JL	SCL	8.0	0.25	63.0	20.0	384.0
29	O	C	7.4	0.20	70.0	0.5	154.8
30	N	CL	7.5	0.14	70.0	3.7	90.0
31	D	SL	8.9	0.30	80.0	02.8	106.0
		E.X	260.9	7.51	235.77	279.7	2628.4
		X	8.15	0.24	76.05	9.32	146.02
		SD	0.80	0.11	18.76	7.92	56.09

1-09: Fore Shore 10-19: Bed 20-29: Ayacut 30-31: Waste Land

Table 6.8b: Characteristics of KAMBIKUDI - WATER.

Sample		*pH*	*E.C.*	*S.A.R.*	*Cations (me/l)*			*Anions (me/l)*			
					Ca	*Mg*	*Na*	*K*	*Co_3-*	*Hco_3-*	*Cl-*
1.	S	7.7	0.2	0.8	1.0	0.4	0.7	0.1	0.3	1.5	0.6
2.	S	9.0	2.1	7.2	7.2	2.8	4.2	13.4	0.3	4.0	16.0
3.	O	8.0	2.5	6.3	8.0	3.0	4.0	12.1	0.2	4.0	15.0

(Contd...)

4.	S	8.2	1.9	5.9	5.9	3.0	4.0	11.0	0.2	3.4	13.5
5.	O	7.6	0.9	1.9	2.3	2.9	3.0	0.1	0.2	4.8	3.5
	E.X	40.5	7.6	22.1	24.4	12.1	15.9	53.5	1.2	17.7	89.9
	X	8.1	1.52	4.42	4.88	2.42	3.18	5.35	0.24	5.9	7.49
	SD	0.50	0.84	2.57	2.75	1.01	1.31	4.70	0.05	4.98	5.91

1-3: Stagnant 4-5: Inlet S: September O: October

Table 6.8c: Characteristics of KAMBIKUDI - PLANTS.

No.	Species	Habit	No.	Species	Habit
1.	Abutilon indicum	Hy	38.	Datura stramonium	S
2.	Abrus precatorius	C	39.	Dodonea angustilolia	S
3.	Acacia arabica	T	40.	Echinops echinatus	G
4.	Acacia auriculiformis	T	41.	Elephantopus scaber	H
5.	Acanthus ilicifolius	S	42.	Eucalypts globulus	T
6.	Achyranthes aspera	S	43.	Euphorbia antiquorum	T
7.	Adathoda zeylanica	S	44.	Ficus bengalensis	T
8.	Aerva lanata	S	45.	Ficus hispida	S
9.	Agave augustifolia	H	46.	Flueggea leucopyrus	S
10.	Amaranthus virdis	H	47.	Gloriosa superba	C
11.	Andrographis paniculata	S	48.	Glycosmis pentaphylla	T
12.	Aristida mutabilis	G	49.	Gomphrena celosioides	H
13.	Aristolochia bracteolata	H	50.	Indigofera cordifolia	H
14.	Aeschenomne aspera	H	51.	Indigofera tinctoria	H
15.	Azadirachta indica	T	52.	Ipomoea carnea	S
16.	Blepharis molluginifolla	H	53.	Ipomoea pes-caprae	H
17.	Boerhavia diffusa	H	54.	Jasminum angustifolium	C
18.	Borassus flabellifer	T	55.	Jatropha gossippifolia	S
19.	Borreria hispida	H	56.	Jatropha glandulifera	S
20.	Borreria stricta	H	57.	Justicia procumbens	H
21.	Breynia refusa	H	58.	Justicia simplex	H
22.	Butia monosperma	T	59.	Leucas aspera	H
23.	Cactus oppuntia	S	60.	Lantana camara	S
24.	Calotropis gigantia	S	61.	Luffa cylindrica	C
25.	Canthium coromandelicum	S	62.	Lycopersicum esculentum	H
26.	Capparis brevispina	S	63.	Mcaranga peltata	T
27.	Carissa spinarum	S	64.	Marsilea sp	Hy
28.	Cassia alata	S	65.	Merremia tridentata	H
29.	Cassia auriculata	S	66.	Mimosa pudica	H
30.	Cissus quadrangularis	C	67.	Mollugo nudicaulis	H
31.	Citrulus colocynthis	C	68.	Mollugo oppositifolia	H
32.	Cleome viscosa	H	69.	Mollugo pentaphylla	H
33.	Cocos nucifera	T	70.	Morinda coreia	T
34.	Coldenia procumbens	H	71.	Moringa olifera	T
35.	Corbichonia decumbens	H	72.	Murraya paniculata	T
36.	Croton bonplandianus	H	73.	Nerium oleander	S
37.	Cynodon dactylon	G	74.	Ocimum sanctum	S

(Contd...)

No.	Species	Habit	No.	Species	Habit
75.	Ocimum basilicum	S	89.	Randia dumatorum	S
76.	Oldenlandia corymbosa	H	90.	Ricinus communis	S
77.	Oldenlandia alata	H	91.	Rivea hypocrateriformis	C
78.	Ottelia alismoides	Hy	92.	Samanea saman	T
79.	Opuntia monocantha	S	93.	Sida acuta	H
80.	Pandanus canarus	S	94.	Sida rhombifolia	H
81.	Phoenix sylvestris	T	95.	Solanum surattense	H
82.	Physalis minima	H	96.	Tamarindus indica	T
83.	Pongamia glabra	T	97.	Tephrosia purpurea	H
84.	Prosopis juliflora	T	98.	Thespisa populnia	T
85.	Parthenium hysterophorus	S	99.	Tridax procumbens	H
86.	Perotis indica	G	100.	Vernonia cinerea	H
87.	Phyla nudiflora	H	101.	Vitex negunto	S
88.	Phyllanthus amarus	H	102.	Ziziphus xylopyrus	S

G: 4 T: 19 H: 39 Hy: 2 C: 7 S: 31

Table 6.8d: Characteristics of KAMBIKUDI - BUTTERFLIES.

No.	*Species*	*Common Name*
1.	Byblia ilithyia	Joker
2.	Catopsilia crocale	Common Emigrant
3.	Colotis eucharis	Plain Orange Tip
4.	Danaus chrysippus	Plain Tiger
5.	Delias eucharis	Common Jazebel
6.	Ergolis merione	Common Castor
7.	Eurema hecabe	Common Grass Yellow
8.	Hypolimnas missipus	Danaid Egg fly
9.	Papilia polymenstor	Blue Mormon
10.	Polydorous aristolochiae	Common Rose
11.	Polydorous hector	Crimson Rose
12.	Precis almana	Peacock Pansy
13.	Precis iphita	Chocolate Pansy
14.	Precis lemonias	Lemon Pansy
15.	Precis nierta	Yellow Pansy
16.	Precis orithya	Blue Pansy

Table 6.8e: characteristics of KAMBIKUDI - FISHES.

No.	*Species*	*Common Name*
1.	Anabas testudineus	Climbing Perch (Panai eri Kendai)
2.	Ophiocephalus marulius	Avuri Viral
3.	Ophiocephalus punctatus	Koravai
4.	Ophiocephalus striatus	Viral
5.	Wallago attu	Valai Keluthy

Table 6.8f: Characteristics of KAMBIKUDI - AMPHIBIANS.

No.	Species	Common Name
1.	Bufo melanosticus	Common Indian Toad
2.	Rana cyanophlyctos	Skipping Frog
3.	Rana hexadactyla	South Indian Frog
4.	Rana limnocharis	Paddy field Frog
5.	Rana tigrina	Bull Frog

Table 6.8g: Characteristics of KAMBIKUDI - REPTILES.

No.	*Species*	*Common Name*
1.	Ahaetulla nasutus	Common Green Whip Snake
2.	Calotes versicolor	Garden Lizard
3.	Hemidactylus frenatus	Southern House Gecko
4.	Mabuya carinata	Common Skink
5.	Melanochelys trijuga	Indian Pond Terrapin
6.	Naja naja	Indian Cobra
7.	Plyas mucosus	Common Rat Snake
8.	Xenochro phispiscator	Checkered Keel back

Table 6.8h: Characteristics of KAMBIKUDI - BIRDS.

No.	*Species*	*Common Name*	*Migration*	*Nutrition*
1.	Accipiter badius	Shikra	R	T
2.	Acridotheres tristis	Common Myna	R	FI
3.	Alauda gulgula	Eastern Skylark	R	IAF
4.	Alcedo atthis	Small Blue Kingfisher	R	A
5.	Ammomanes phoenicurus	Rufous tailed Finch-Lark	R	FI
6.	Anas acuta	Pin-tailed Duck	M	A
7.	Anastomus oscitans	Open billed Stork	LM	A
8.	Ardeola grayil	Pond Heron	R	A
9.	Artamus fuscus	Ashy Swallow-Shrike	R	I
10.	Athene brama	Spotted Owlet	R	T
11.	Bubulcus ibis	Cattle Egret	R	T
12.	Caprimulgas asiaticus	Common Indian Nightjar	R	T
13.	Centropus sinensis	Crow Pheasant	R	T
14.	Clamator jacobinus	Pied Crested Cuckoo	LM	FI
15.	Columba livia	Blue Rock Pigeon	R	TG
16.	Copsychus saularis	Magpie Robin	R	I
17.	Coracias benghalensis	Indian Roller	R	TI
18.	Corvus macrorhynchos	Jungle Crow	R	AFI
19.	Corvus splendens	House Crow	R	AFI
20.	Cuculus varius	Common Hawk Cuckoo	R	FI
21.	Cypsiurus parvus	Palm Swift	R	I
22.	Dendrocitla vagabunda	Indian Treepie	R	AF
23.	Dicrurus adsimilis	Black Drongo	R	NI
24.	Dicrurus leucophaeus	Grey Drongo	R	NI
25.	Dinopium benghalense	L.Golden-backed Woodpecker	R	NI
26.	Egretta garzetta	Little Egret	R	T
27.	Egretta intermedia	Smaller Egret	R	T
28.	Elanus caeruleus	Black winged Kite	R	T

(Contd...)

29.	Eremopterix grisea	Ashycrowned Finch-Lark	R	IF
30.	Eudynamis scolopacea	Koel	R	FI
31.	Francolinus pondicerianus	Grey Patridge	R	T
32.	Halcyon smyrnensis	White Breasted Kingfisher	R	A
33.	Haliastus indus	Brahminy Kite	R	A
34.	Himantopus himantopus	Black winged Stilt	R	A
35.	Hirundo restica	Swallow	M	I
36.	Lanius cristatus	Brown Shrike	R	TI
37.	Locustella naevia	Grass hopper Warbler	R	I
38.	Lonchura malabarica	White throated Munia	R	IF
39.	Lonchura malacca	Black headed Munia	R	IF
40.	Megalaima haemocephala	Crimson Breasted Barbet	R	I
41.	Merops orientalis	Green Bee-eater	R	I
42.	Merops philippinus	Blue tailed Bee-eater	M	I
43.	Milvus migrans	Pariah Kite	R	T
44.	Motacilla flava	Yellow Wagtail	R	I
45.	Nectarinia asiatica	Purple Sunbird	R	N
46.	Oriolus oriolus	Golden Oriole	R	FI
47.	Orthotorhus sutorius	Tailor Bird	R	NI
48.	Passer domesticus	House Sparrow	R	ITF
49.	Pavo cristatus	Common Peafowl	R	T
50.	Phalacrocorax niger	Little Cormorant	R	A
51.	Ploceus philippinus	Baya Weaver bird	R	IF
52.	Podiceps ruficollis	Little Grebe	R	A
53.	Pseudibis papillosa	Black Ibis	R	T
54.	Psittacula krameri	Rose-ringed Parakeet	R	FG
55.	Pycnonotus cafer	Red vented Bulbul	R	FIN
56.	Saxicola caprata	Pied Bush Chat	R	I
57.	Saxicoloides fulicata	Indian Robin	R	I
58.	Streptopillia chinensis	Spotted Dove	R	T
59.	Streptopillia decaocta	Indian Ring Dove	R	T
60.	Streptopillia senegalensis	Little Brown Dove	R	T
61.	Sturnus pagodarum	Black headed Myna	R	FI
62.	Tersiphone paradise	Paradise Flycatcher	R	I
63.	Tringa hypoleucos	Common Sandpiper	M	A
64.	Tringa totanus	Common Redshank	M	A
65.	Turdoides caudatus	Common Babbler	R	FIN
66.	Upupa epops	Hoopoe	R	TI
67.	Vanellus indicus	Red wattled Lapwing	R	T

R: 79 LM: 3 M: 5 F = 21 N = 6 I = 25 A = 15 T = 21

Table 6.8i: Characteristics of KAMBIKUDI - MAMMALS.

No.	***Species***	***Common Name***
1.	Bandicoota indica	Bandicoot Rat
2.	Canis aureus	Jackal
3.	Funambulus palmarum	Three-stripped Palm Squirrel
4.	Herpestes edwardsi	Mongoose
5.	Lepus nigricollis	Indian Hare
6.	Pipistrellus coramandra	Indian Pipistrelle
7.	Rattus raltus	Common Rat
8.	Suncus murinus	Grey Musk Shrew
9.	Vulpus benghalensis	Indian Fox

2. Figures: 6.2a-d

Collection locations of soil, water and plants samples and sites of photography

3. Photographs: 6.1-8

1. **Kambikudi tank:** A view from western bank in the rainy season. In many ways Kambikudi tank resembles Tamil Nadu's numerous disused tanks. Due to the siltation and absence of maintenance the tank has slowly taken the shape of an impounded channel where water is stored only near the bunds since the tank bed has become a fertile agricultural field used by villagers The photograph shows impounded channel and the vegetated tank bed on the left The tank bund is shown on the right side.
2. Another view of Kambikudi tank: The tank bund is vegetated with **Jatropha and Ipomoea**. Black and clayey nature of the soil is visible.
3. This photograph shows the recently planted **Acacia Arabica** saplings. Foreground is the bund of the tank. There exists another old plantation of the same species in the western side of the tank bed.
4. This grown up plantation of Acacia Arabica is a sub system within the tank. It is a roosting site for migratory waterfowls, other birds, reptiles, small mammals like black napped hare etc. The foreground is the tank bund dominated by Ipomoea.
5. The overflow gate of Kambikudi situated on the northern side of the tank. The over flow reaches the near by river. This end is the deepest region of the tank.
6. Agriculture fields on the ayacut of the tank. Major crops are paddy (on foreground) and finger millet (near the bund). A sluice of the tank opening to the agricultural land is seen.
7. Presently the tank is heavily silted and vegetated reducing the water holding capacity. Water is limited to the sides of bund as an impounded channel. Prosopis, Jatropha and Ipomoea form the major components of the vegetation. An unused sluice can be seen on the left.
8. Breached bunds of Kambikudi: The tank bund is made of mud. The vegetation on the bund is poor and inadequate for controlling erosion. The Prosopis growth strengthens the embankment but turfing is needed for stopping the breaching.

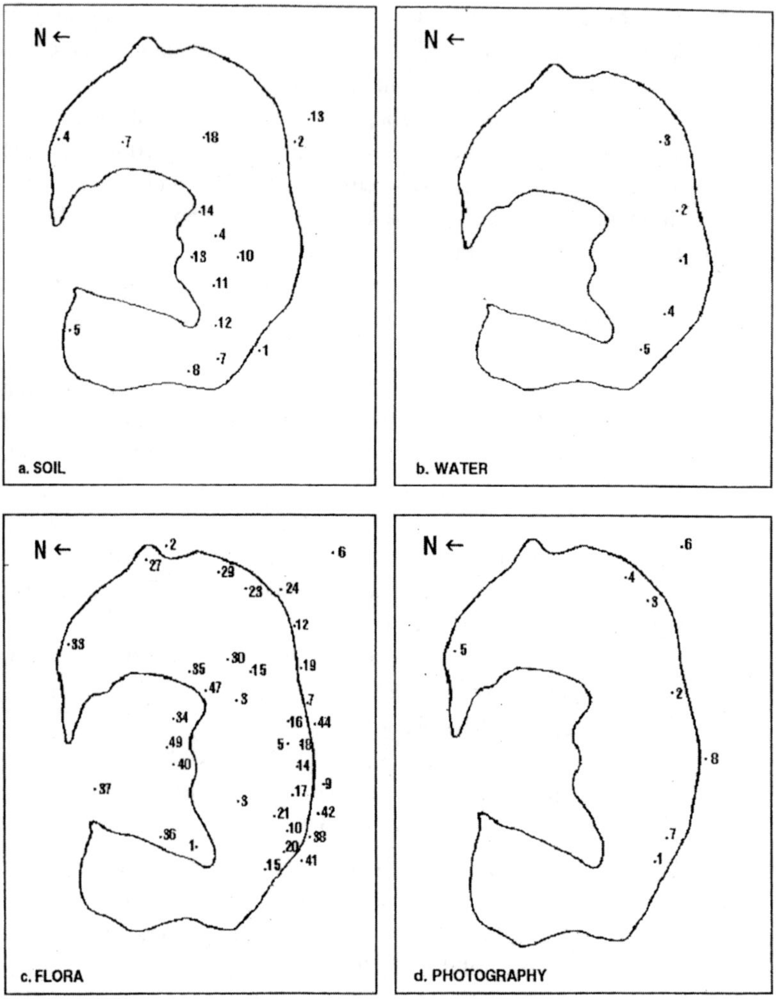

Fig.6.2: Sampling sites at KAMBIKUDI

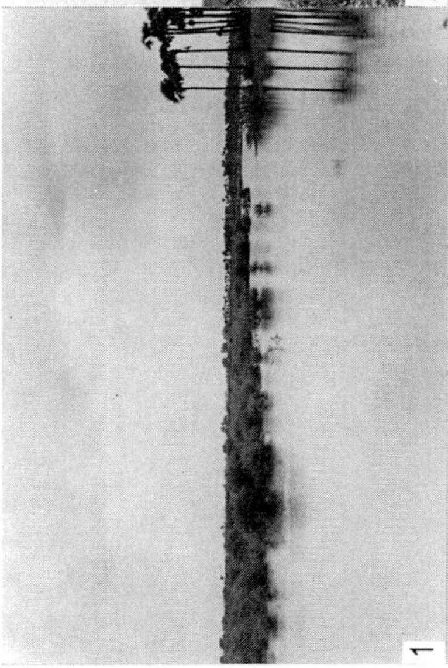

1

2

3

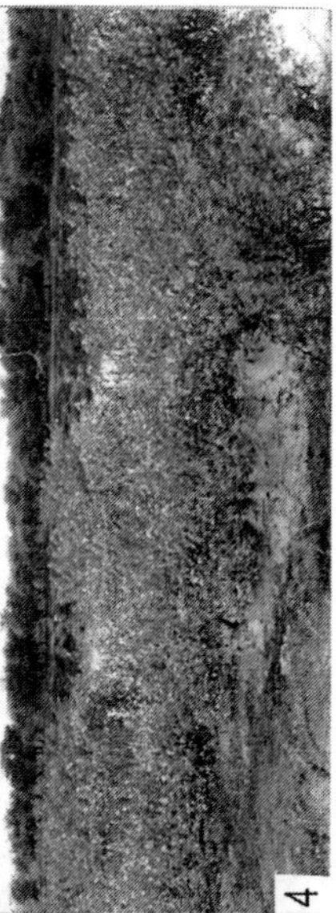

4

5

6

7

8

Chapter - IV

Discussion

The tank ecosystem consists of all the areas and life around the waterbody, such as catchments, ayacut, villages, channels, wells, agriculture, aquaculture, animal husbandry, social forestry along with soil, water, plants, animals and supply channels. These systems have some features of irrigation reservoirs, natural lakes, shallow wetlands, and riverine shorelines. Consequently subsystems vary from one another among tanks. A few may have even micro-habitats as in the case of Kaliveli. But in all, the tank areas, the waterbody functions as a 'cornerstone' component of the region, drawing the surrounding villages for their water, soil, plant and animal needs. In other words, the villages depending on this 'epicenter' appear as a part of the tank ecosystems and not vice versa. Thus, if the tank is not there, many villages will not exist. This is also borne out from history. Human settlements are known to have disappeared along the ancient Mangamma Salai in Southern Tamilnadu because the tanks seem to have run out of water continuously for some years. Such mishaps can be averted through modern science and technology. The current pilot work reveals the inputs each tank needs based on the size and nature of the ecosystem - water, quantity, duration, ayacut, catchment, associated villages, agriculture, aquaculture, flora, fauna and soil.

There are many wells around the tank - conventional and bored, reducing the direct dependence of villages on the tanks. But the wells are dependent on the tanks for their lateral recharge. In this connection it is necessary to study the dynamics of lateral seepage for proper location of wells, the ground water potential, its potability, level of water table and potential for recharge from tank waters. The dynamics of tank-well interactions is a fascinating study in itself.

Water, land and biota of wetlands are common property resources. They are systematically owned up. In case of water, well digging makes groundwater accessible only to the owners. Besides it can also be sold to generate income. As far as land is concerned, foreshore inundated during the rainy season is used for crop rearing. As years pass by "regular ownership pattas" are issued under the right of occupation. Therefore the old statistics are totally invalid especially at Kaliveli, currently the most important. How much is the rainfall? How much goes to sea, to the wetland, to the estuary and to the wells? What is the area of the tank originally and now? How much is encroached and legalized? What is the water spread area and volume of water it can hold? What is the reach of saline waters at high tide and during cyclones? These are the questions, answers to which will go a long way not only in restoring land and water equity among local people but also for initiating proper management inputs.

A. Habitats

1. Soil (Table IV.1)

All tanks have similar pH around the neutral ranges, with only Ousteri recording high value and greater diversity. This may be due to diverse human activities and water inputs both from its own catchment as well as the supply channel. Electrical conductivity is also uniform in all tanks except Kaliveli where it is very high due to sea water intrusion. Nitrogen, phosphorus and potassium are uniformly low in all tanks, except in Ousteri for N and Pillaipakkam for P. Potassium is lowest at Kaliveli and Kaveripakkam. Thus the data collected for this study indicate variations only with respect to a few parameters while most others are rather uniform and needing low inputs, if plant culture has to be widened.

2. Water (Table IV.2)

In all tanks pH and EC are high unlike in their soils. SAR on the other hand is highly variable. Ca, Mg and Na are similarly low excepting at Kaliveli where it is connected to an estuary. In case of K the values are either low or negligible. In case of anions, carbonate and Chloride are high only in Kaliveli. Thus water quality is generally uniform irrespective of its quality and longevity in the tank. The tank habitats are deficient in some aspects and excess in a few others. This perhaps, is the reason why most flora, fauna and cultural activities are similar among the wetland systems.

Table IV.1: SOIL Characteristics of the six Waterbodies.

	Kaveripakkam	*Pillaipakkam*	*Kaliveli*	*Ousteri*	*Mirattunilai*	*Kambikudi*
pH	7.5 (0.88)*	7.04 {0.76}	7.16 (0.41)	7.86 (0.77)	6.96 (0.05)	7.88 (0.62)
	5.90-8.80	5.80-8.10	4.80-8.10	5.60-8.40	5.90-8.90	5.70-9.10
	27 (21)	23 (13)	43 {27)	22 (18)	29 (20)	32 (10)
E.C.	0.23 (0.07)	0.24 {0.08)	0.83 (0.75)	0.3 (0.09)	0.25 (0.14)	0.23 {(0.10)
	0.10-0.60	0.10-1.50	0.09-3.7	0.20-24.0	0.10-2.0	0.12-1.20
	27 (22)	22 (13)	41 (36)	20 (1:8)	29 (28)	31(28)
N	77.65 (17.70)	74.06 (17.78)	76.68 (21.12)	92.31 {23.05)	74.51 (7.99)	75:09 (11.45)
	11.00-148.5	14.0-126.0	30-162.5	95.166.0	35.0-117.5	42.00-111.25
	27 (20)	23 (17)	43 (33)	22 (16)	26 (17)	32 (22)
P	6.56 (4.62)	9.79 (4.91)	8.37 (6.81)	4.97 (1.96)	6.43 (4.76)	8.30 (5.93)
	0.96-55.0	1.4-56.00	0.8-62.0	2.82-30.0	0.5-73.0	0.48-100.0
	27 (22)	22 (20)	42 (29)	20 (17)	26 (24)	31 (17)
K	109.05 (38.00)	131.06 (45.84)	108.71 (41.90)	121.87 (46.1)	122.39 (23.78)	124.51 (24.52)
	17.0-480.0	11.0-633.0	9.0-378.0	72-321.0	27.0-378.0	72.00-600.0
	26 (18)	21 (15)	35 (23)	19 (12)	29 (18)1	8 (13)

* ( ) Standard Deviation

Table IV.2: Water Characteristics of the six Water bodies.

	Kaveripakkam	*Pillaipakkam*	*Kaliveli*	*Ousteri*	*Mirattunilai*	*Kambikudi*
pH	823 (0.53)'*	7.74(0.82)	7.83	8.2 (0.47)	7.6 (0.21)	7.74 (0.82)
	7.9-9.4	6.8-9.0	6.9-9.0	7.3-9.10	7.2-7.8	7.60-9.0
	18	9	8	17	7	5
E.C.	0.78 (0.31)	0.40 (0.34)	2.45 (1.94)	0.63 (0.65)	0.29 (0.05)	0.40 (0.34)
	02-1.5	0.2-1.1	1.3-15.4	0.3-0.80	0.2-1.3	0.20-2.50
	15	9	716	6	5	
SAR	4.03 (1.25)	1.63 (2.39)	7.39 (5.36)	1.98 (1.18)	0.4 (0.34)	1.63 (1.42)
	0.6-5.6	0.3-4.7	2.3-27.0	0.1-3.70	0.1-2.3	0.83-7.18
	14	6	7	16	6	5
Ca	2.82 (1.69)	1.77 (2.39)	2.48 (1.04)	1.14 (0.37)	1.26 (0.17)	1.77 (2.39)
	0.4-3.5	0.3-2.3	2.6-7.80	0.6-2.00	1.0-4.0	1.00-8.00
	18	8	7	16	5	5
Mg+	1.86 (1.12)	1.41 (0.70)	3.78 (2.83)	0.45 (0.49)	1.08 (0.31)	1.41 (0.70)
	0.5-7.5	0.5-2.5	2.0-29.0	0.4-23.0	0.8-2.0	0.40-3.00
	17	9	6	16	6	5
Na+	4.72 (1.10)	0.82 (0.49)	16.29 (15.29)	3.01 (4.44)	0.43 (0.34)	0.82 (0.49)
	2.0-8.5	0.3-6.5	4.1-116.0	0.1-5.10	0.1-4.1	0.70-4.20
	14	6	7	17	6	5
K+	0.07 (0.03)	0.49 (0.49)	0.54 (0.19)	0.05 (0.03)	0.06 (0.05)	0.49 (0.49)
	0.03-0.1	0.03-0.4	0.4-0.90	0.2-0.11	0.2-2.8	0.05-13.40
	4	6	5	7	6	5
CO_3-	0.98 {0.56)	0.48 (0)	2.2 (1.47)	-	0.48 (0.21)	- 0.48 (0)
	0.04-1.6	0.5	0.0-1.20	0.2-0.90	0.20-0.30	
	5	1	3	9	6	5
HCO_3-	3.26 {2.25)	1.69 (0.99)	2.2 (1.46)	2.24 (0.87)	1.27 (0.42)	1.69 (0.99)
	0.6-72	0.8-1.3	0.3-6.20	1.5-4.80	1.6-6.2	1.50-4.80
	18	7	7	16	6	5
Cl-	3.81 {1.99)	1.41 (1.37)	17.24 (4.81)	1.39 (0.52)	0.82 (0.13)	1.41 (1.37)
	0.2-9.0	0.3-8.7	6.7-122.0	0.8-2.70	0.7-2.6	0.60-16.00
	17	7	7	16	6	5

* ( ) Standard Deviation

B. Biodiversity

1. Flora (Tables IV.3 and IV.8a)

The floristic composition varied remarkably with the size of the system or its state of degradation. Thus, Kambikudi supports the least number of flora (50) and Kaliveli the maximum (163). Most species occurred on the foreshore and in the ayacut. Even the low richness of plants in Kambikudi appears enough to support many butterfly species and birds, some of the latter being migratory, probably due to the denseness of forestry plantations around the tank. Or these are mere remnant populations vanishing slowly. If regeneration does not improve Kambikudi tank, many butterflies and other faunal specimens also may gradually disappear - a warning signal to the other tank systems. The richness in Kaliveli and Mirattunilai tally well, as both the tanks had remnants of natural vegetation till recently.

Table IV.3: Floristic Diversity Among Water Bodies.

	KP	PP	KV	OT	MN	KK	TOTAL
Species	95	69	163	101	106	50	273
Genera	81	59	153	95	91	46	
Families	44	37	79	55	52	33	
Habitat specificity							
Foreshore	71	52	131	76	77	37	
Bed	21	15	48	20	30	13	
Ayacut	47	49	130	76	70	32	
Wastelands	28	16	47	45	25	11	
Econ/Ecol	24	19	65	52	28	16	

Table IV. 4: Faunal Diversity among water Bodies.

	KP	*PP*	*KV*	*OT*	*MN*	*KK*	*TOTAL*
Species	110	86	187	153	99	112	223
Genera	92	77	142	123	87	93	
Families	55	47	82	78	59	56	
Habitat Guilds							
Water	37	28	42	39	25	25	
Villages	30	30	52	45	37	37	
Agri, fields	56	52	81	65	53	63	
Thickets	79	53	117	80	61	69	

2. Fauna (Tables IV.4, IV.5 and IV.8b-g)

There is no relationship between the area and the species richness. Though Kaliveli - the largest one - supports nearly 200 species, the smaller ones - Mirattunilai and Kambikudi - have greater richness than Kaveripakkam and Pillaipakkam which are 2-4 times larger. Animal diversity perhaps depends on the plant diversity of past and present. The species richness of the birds is high, suggesting that their nutritive and roosting sources in the habitat are intact - an indication that all is not lost from the ecological foundations of the wetlands. That some of these have 10-30 migratory bird species would itself warrant their protection as bird sanctuaries.

About 273 plant and 223 animal species occur in the six wetland systems, but each water body harbours only 50 - 163 plant species and 86 - 187 animal species. Since the habitat conditions of the wetlands are not very different from each other, there is a possibility that each tank can be enriched biologically.

Table IV.5: Composition of Animal Taxa in the Water Bodies.

	KP	*PP*	*KV*	*OT*	*MN*	*KK*	*TOTAL*
Butterflies							
Species	15	10	19	18	15	17	26
Genera	13	9	13	13	12	12	
Families	6	5	6	8	5	7	
Fishes							
Species	6	6	11	10	8	5	16
Genera	5	5	8	8	7	3	
Families	3	5	7	7	6	3	
Amphibians							
Species	5	4	6	4	5	6	6
Genera	3	2	3	1	2	3	
Families	1	1	1	1	1	1	
Reptiles							
Species	8	7	16	20	8	8	22
Genera	8	7	15	18	8	8	
Families	5	5	9	8	5	5	
Birds							
Species	70	54	120	90	56	67	138
Genera	59	46	89	74	51	58	
Families	35	27	49	47	36	34	
Mammals							
Species	6	5	15	11	7	9	16
Genera	6	5	14	10	7	9	
Families	5	4	10	7	6	6	
Total	110	86	187	153	99	112	223

C. Resources

1. **Land and Soil:** The geomorphology and the geochemistry of the land mass determine the characteristics of the soil and its utility for various purposes such as agriculture, aquaculture, forestry and

Table IV.6: Major Characteristics of the water Bodies.

Parameter	*KP*	*PP*	*KV*	*OT*	*MN*	*KK*
Abiotic Factors						
Area of the water body (sq. km.)	16	9.90	70.5	15.8	2.8	5.2
Water retention period (months)	6-8	6-8	3-4	6-8	3-5	2-3
Average annual rainfall (c.m.)	107.8	106	127	125	98.3	76.9
Plant species	95	69	166	101	127	50
Availability of refugia	No	No	Yes	No	Yes	No
Butterfly species	15	10	19	18	15	17
Bird species	70	54	120	90	56	67
Migratory	10	11	29	18	3	5

construction. The soil qualities are alterable in the long run by human interventions as well as natural biological forces. The current pattern of land use in the wetlands suggest under use, overuse, and wrong use. Bird and animal excreta are useful as fertilizers and as energy sources. Most land must be earmarked for agricultural purposes either with or without water. Only an appropriate part can be left for use as construction material. All the wetland systems have potential to combine traditional practices and modem science. This blending is absolutely warranted as it involves restoration of a million acres of land.

2. **Water:** Water availability from rains, supplies and ground, their qualities and patterns of rainfall variations, runoff, catchment, storage and seepage from the tank, groundwater recharging and irrigation efficiency and finally the economics of irrigation are to be estimated. The present work could assess only a few of these. These data, once available, will enable better stock taking of water resource facilitating appropriate inputs. It is a pity that the coastal wetland is not facilitated to rescue the rain falls that is otherwise allowed to flow in to the sea. This may be the case with most coastal tanks and wetlands else where.

3. **Plants:** Of primary interest is the diversity of cultivated plants. Traditional cultivars carry special importance, because, many of them possess special characteristics such as resistance to pests and drought. Germplasm of such cultivars of all crop plants should be collected for further use. Many medicinal plants occur around the waterbodies. The traditional systems of health management using plants need documentation. There are other plants useful as hedges, soil binders, fuel, food, fodder and

fertilizer, for thatching and weaving, etc. In fact there cannot be a plant without some economic value and some relationship with animals. These are dwindling, sometimes giving way to firewood monocultures. Kambikudi has already become alarmingly deficient in plant resources.

4. **Animals:** There are many domesticated animals such as cattle and sheep. These are consumers of water and plant resources but are resources to man and land. Fish is a source occurring naturally, exploited locally and sold out when water recedes - this happens in all the waterbodies. Some wild animals are hunted for food or trade. This seems to be going on unabated in all the wetlands, though some animals are predators and pests. Some species have already become endangered. Special mention must be made of the guano excretions of birds, especially during October – February adding great fertility to soil. Animal richness is greatest in Kaliveli and considerable every where else.

   Being the most important of the currently studied wetlands, Kaliveli deserves special mention. Species richness here is at stake due to threats from poaching, siltation, saline water intrusion, etc. People utilise the tank bed for different purposes in summer. Hence protecting Kaliveli will be achieved only with their participation and without affecting biodiversity. Clearly stated laws and basic awareness development are essential for this. As most valuable migratory birds are present only in winter, special laws can be enforced. The migratory birds start arriving at the lake by the last week of September and return by the first week of February. Though annual water fowl counts have been made, bird ringing or recapture has not been tried. Therefore there is great scope for a more detailed study on the birds.

D. Human Ecology

1. **Culture Systems:** No sooner do rains set in; rice is planted in all the wetlands using channeled water or groundwater. Fertilizers and pesticides follow. This scenario of deltaic culture is unsuitable to these basically semi-arid areas where the accent should be on water economy, soil conservation and equal opportunity in using the common facility and common resource of water. In these water scarce societies, water should be retained for a long time in the tank and/or community wells but not privatized through tubewells. There should be dry land farming needing minimum

water per unit area which alone increases the arability of land, both by increasing the area available and facilitating double cropping. In such cases it will be easier to develop long-term fertility strategies like composting and bio-fertilizers and pest control through biological means - plants, birds and others.

The water body should be fully utilised for aquaculture by natural means with only inputs of seed and plank tonic cultures. The existing scenario is a reversal of the ideal! Wells take away the tank's resourcefulness. Selfishness of the pirate common properties and their ecological health through the wells.

As for the much flaunted social forestry, it should be differentiated into plantations within the tank and outside it. Those within are inundated by water for various durations and serve as animal habitats. Those outside are plantations on wastelands receiving only natural rainfall. The former must be regulated because they yield greater biomass, enrich soil fertility and provide habitat for animals; but cause gradual reduction in tank area which however can be taken care of through engineering works.

There are 5 - 14 villages around the waterbodies with about 2000 to 5000 inhabitants comprising landowners, daily wage earners and the unemployed. Some of them encroach upon common lands. Consequently the current tanks are only a part of their past stature in every respect.

Table IV. 7: Culture Systems of the Water Bodies.

Systems	*Kaveripakkam*	*Pillaipakkam*	*Kaliveli*	*Ousteri*	*Mirattunilai*	*Kambikudi*
Agriculture						
Major	Plantain	Paddy	Paddy	Sugarcan e	Paddy	Paddy
	Paddy		Millet	Paddy		
	Sugarcane		Groundnut	Millet		
			Coconut			
Minor	Mulberry	Plantain	-Nil-	Plantain	Pennisetum	Jasmine
	Brinjal	Brinjal		Maize	Groundnut	Cotton
	Groundnut	Groundnut			Maize	Maize
	Ragi	Ragi			Ragi	Ragi
	Castor	Kambu				
		Sugarcane				
Aquaculture						
Natural	Catfish	Catfish	Prawn	Catfish	Catfishes	Catfishes
	Mullet	Mullet	Mullet	Tilapia	Mullets	Mullets
	Tilapia	Tilapia	Tilapia	Carps	Carps	Carps

(Contd...)

	Carps	Carps	Carps		Anabas	Anabas
			Anabas			Tilapia
Cultured	-Nil-	-Nil-	-Nil-	-Nil-	Catla	-Nil-
					Rohu	
Wetland Forestry						
Location	Bank Bed	Bank Bed	Foreshore	Bank	Inlet Channel	Tank Bed
	Bund Outer Slope		Bed	(north)	Bund	
Plant	Acacia	Eucalyptus	Eucalyptus	Acacia	Eucalyptus	Acacia
	Prosopis	Acacia	Acacia	Casuarina	Acacia	
		Prosopis	Casuarina	Eucalypt us		
			Prosopis			
Villages	14	5	14+	11	5	8

2. **Socio-economy:** The socio-economic status of the local people and their perceptions on the tanks need to be studied to evolve an ecologically sound management strategy for the waterbody. Such surveys of tank related activities can help understand the impacts of tank irrigation, forestry plantations, dryland agriculture and land use patterns etc. on the local economy. These understandings lead to the emergence of a perspective for longterm restoration of the tanks. However the present study was limited to a sample gathering of local perceptions. This has revealed enough on the degraded state of tanks. What they were, should be and what is the common scenario, are discussed in the report. It is a sad tale of neglect and grabbing.

E. Conservation

Conservation has two facets - firstly the resourcefulness of soil, water, biodiversity and enrichment. The second is to conserve the diversity of the habitats - waterbody, inlet channels, catchments, agriculture, aquaculture, wetland forestry, animal husbandry along with soil, water, plants and animals and above all the villages.

Villages draw sustenance from tank connected resources, which therefore need greater care, so that the human settlements enjoy a longer and richer balance in the resource bank. Unfortunately there are no conservation efforts, leave alone restorative exercises in any of the waterbodies. Even the sluices, regulators, supply channels and bunds remain unattended and in disrepair. Biologically rich thickets are removed in favour of monocultures. But everywhere people want more plants, more water for longer periods and more fertile soil. However fortunately, wetland forestry has turned out to be conservative. The water that normally goes to private properties through the tube wells is consumed by the common forestry which in turn become habitats for animals. Together, they gradually enrich the soil. This being the present state in several tanks, conservation of what is still left and restoration of whatever that is lost can be achieved only under the reign of the local people and their Panchayats.

1. **Land:** Identification and quantification of the land use classes should be carried out so that crops for summer and winter, quality soil suitable for construction purposes, can be selected.
2. **Water:** Existing data appear unreliable. Data on rainfall and variations in the runoff, catchment and storage capacity, seepage, ground water recharging, irrigation efficiency and finally the economics of the well and channel irrigation should be obtained afresh before conservation measures are taken.
3. **Plants:** Varieties of cultivated and other plants of ecological and economic significance are the objectives. Locally used cultivars carry special importance. The traditional varieties may have been lost, but chances of their occurrence in some pockets cannot be ruled out. Germplasm of such cultivars should be collected. Many dwindling medicinal species need conservation.
4. **Animals:** Both domesticated and wild animals call for efforts to increase wild life populations. These have ecological uses. This is possible only by declaring the waterbodies as **Sanctuaries of biodiversity**.

F. Development

For development planning, stock taking of all the resources in the wetland ecosystem is a prerequisite. Water dynamics have to be estimated first. The rainfall, evaporation, ground water and surface water have to be quantified. A qualitative assessment, whether potable or not, etc., need to be made for a few years on a monthly basis.

1. Resource Inventory

Physical and chemical nature of the soil has to be documented for all the microhabitats along with variations in space and time. All plants, prima facie, are to be considered resources. Some of these are parts of local wisdom, but some are still in books only; such as **Gloriosa and Abrus. Plankton**, worms, insects, molluscans, vertebrates and avians need to be explored from a resource angle. Total biological richness of the wetland needs to be quantified. Conservation and improvement of all resources are essential for their subsequent usage for development.

Surveys of land, water, plants, animals and human ecologies around the tanks presented here constitute a resource inventory. When these are integrated with other data already available from the national and regional agencies, one gets a composite and reliable data base. There is not much data yet for any single wetland. And there are 35000+wetlands of different sizes, constituents and characteristics. And these are associated with thousands of villages and several million rural people. This is no small matter but still remains neglected.

2. **People and government**

From their history, experiences and expectations, the perennial desire of people is development through the government - not by their involvement. The governmental activities are mostly confined to so called social forestry, allowing borewells, making available fertilizers and pesticides and extending the services of the agriculture agencies. Thus some development is seen around every tank.

The villages around the waterbodies have been practicing agriculture, aquaculture and social forestry. If permaculture, sericulture, apiculture, vermiculture are added to these involving grasses and forbes of perennial nature on a large scale, keeping in mind the low water requirements of plants, the sustainable development will have been achieved. How? Everything will be protected, conserved and yet economic development will be achieved. This should be the ideal for wetlands.

G. Imperatives

Having arrived at the conclusion that both conservation and development are to go hand in hand, a theoretical framework has to be developed on the action programme, the agents of change and the catalysts. We believe that most development programmes fail to achieve their goals because of the non-cooperation of people and bad coordination of the governmental bodies. We therefore feel that for the success of ecologically oriented development, governmental bodies, Non-governmental agencies, local people and academicians have to provide complementary inputs.

1. **Government**

(a) **Empowerment of the beneficiary:** As well irrigation increased, the importance of public tanks decreased. Major reason for such a change is poor water management strategy, replacing the age old customs. Tank irrigation thrived till a few decades ago because water distribution was carried out by local bodies of farmers in the ayacut or the Zamindars. In some tanks farmers do not have any say. Tail-end farmers had to shift to groundwater irrigation. People are not involved in tank maintenance. This can be reversed only by handing over the tanks back to the village Panchayats. Traditional water management bodies should be rejuvenated and modernised for better results.

(b) **Policy Inputs:** Policies should be based on sound philosophies as governmental programmes and their implementation have long-lasting and indirect effects on agriculture, land use and through them on the daily lives of people. Therefore all decisions have to be based on ecological wisdom of sustainable growth.

Agricultural policies are the most important, as they regulate land use through revenue subsidies, extension, training, expert guidance, irrigation policies, etc. Ecological suitability of a crop should be evaluated. For example, Kaveripakkam tank is capable of supplying irrigation water directly and indirectly for a long duration. So water-demanding and commercial craps such as mulberry and sugarcane can be cultivated. In drier areas drought resistant plants can be introduced through agriculture and social forestry polities. Unhealthy cropping patterns should be prevented through fiscal policies. Arable lands should be brought under cultivation on a priority basis and social forestry given lesser priority. Regulation of deep bore wells in tank vicinity; choice of crop species and crop variety are also crucial from the point of view of resource conservation. Alternative agricultural methods like rotation of crops, organic farming and biological control of the pests should be encouraged. Disincentives to intensive agriculture are needed in the longterm interests of people. Legal inputs in declaring these waterbodies as protected areas are an urgent need.

(c) **Action on the Ground:** Management strategies for restoration and conservation of non-system tanks and system tanks vary because they differ in water retention periods. The villagers are aware of the importance of tanks in their economy but not their ecology. Only when this is achieved, effective participation from locals in sustainable utilisation of the tank resources can be ensured. Sound policies and result-oriented action on the ground are the inputs necessary through various agencies of the government. Some of them may be as follows:

(1) Strengthening of embankments and repairing regulators, sluices, supply and feeder channels, desiltation of the waterbody.

(2) Transfer of the nearby Tamil Nadu areas to Pondicherry legally, so that Ousteri tank can be taken better care of.

(3) Protecting the tank from poaching, giving fishing and grazing rights, removal of encroachments.

(4) Regulating the land use in the surrounding areas of tanks so that all rain water drains into the tank and increases its water holding capacity.

(5) Educating the local people on all the aspects of the tank system so as to motivate them to look after their common property.

(6) Providing financial support to the NGO's involved in the developmental and / or conservational activities in the areas around the tanks.

(7) Establishing initiatives in favour of organic farming, medicinal plant gardens, ecotourism, wetland forestry, aquaculture, etc.

2. Non-Governmental Agencies

Non-Governmental Agencies (NGOs) are recognized as major agents of change. These voluntary bodies have motivated people, built bridges of understanding, achieved goals and most are ecology conscious. Therefore it is appropriate to draw them into tank welfare.

(a) Informal education for awareness development: Success of any development programme depends on the participation of the local people. Therefore the people should be clearly explained, the values and need for resources, importance of restoration. This is crucial for two reasons; firstly local people's involvement in each stage of the project can make them feel proud about the success of project. Secondly, human resources needed for executing the project can be drawn from local people. Informal education should be aimed at helping even the illiterate farmer to grasp the issues of the tank systems.

Public awareness campaigns are another useful way to make locals conscious of their fragile resources and environment.

(b) Specific Projects: NGOS can be encouraged to take up tank related conservation and development projects with actual participation of local people and cooperation of governmental agencies.

3. People

Perceptions of people are two fold. The first is one of expectation and hope on the useful role of tanks and their environs in their lives. The second is one of lament and exasperation at the deterioration of tanks. Such a psyche assures local participation in any effort to rejuvenate tank systems which in turn ensures their sustainability on a long term basis.

(a) Co-operatives and Panchayats: Most of the governmental efforts go in vain as they fail to win the co-operation of locals. Therefore people should be helped to form co-operatives to centralise all operations, especially social/wetland forestry. Thus villagers get cheap fire-wood and a regular income. Later on, such co-operation can be extended to other areas such as dairying, vermiculture, sericulture, apiculture, floriculture, plant and animal refugia, gardens and above all water sharing. On one hand, people can take up developmental activities yielding produce and income. To sustain this for long, on the other hand, conservation measures of water, soil, plants and animals can be taken up. However villages around the tanks cannot do all these. Even these need inputs from trained extension workers and experts.

4. Academics

Inputs are needed in all the areas of concern and relevance to tanks from academicians for conserving, as well as exploiting them, so that the tank remains vibrant while people slowly develop. A few aspects which need immediate attention of researchers are dealt with here under.

(a) Charging the Wells: There are many wells around the tanks - conventional and bored, reducing the direct dependence of villages on the tanks. But the wells are dependent on the tanks for their lateral recharge. In this connection it is necessary to study the dynamics of lateral seepage - direction and distance for proper location of wells. The quality of these waters needs to be analysed for their potability, for, many villagers travel long distances to fetch water. The ground water potential, level of water-table and the potential for recharge from the tank waters are to be assessed. Tank-well interactions are a fascinating study in itself.

(b) **Plankton and Pesticides in water:** Though water remains only for a few months, animal and plant life are supported and agriculture is practiced. Therefore it is apparent that the habitat will harbour both pesticides as well as plankton. While the pesticides could be toxic depending on their degradability and residual nature, the latter are primary producers with starting roles in the food chains. Further, these could be indicators of many events in the system and therefore contribute to a correct understanding of wetland ecology.

(c) **Soil Ecology:** Soil appears greatly exhausted, probably due to aridity and comparatively low biological activity. Yet crops are cultivated whenever water is available, supplemented by fertilizer inputs. Research efforts appear necessary to study the soil exhaustion dynamics in the tank ecosystems. Otherwise the entire land may become useless for cultivation. For both these purposes, a long term surveying and experimentation becomes necessary. Studies of soil fauna and seed banks can give more information on eco-restoration of fields.

(d) **Palynology:** Palynology is a very useful tool for tracing the environmental history of the water bodies such as past vegetation, climatic changes and trends in land use. All these help better management and decision making.

(e) **Soil seed banks and natural regeneration:** Seed stocks in the soil are called the evolutionary memory of vegetation. They lie dormant in the soil till the chance to germinate comes. Studies on seed-banks have a crucial role in the regeneration of habitats. Mirattunilai tank has a forested past but cleared due to recent short-sightedness. Yet these areas can be regenerated if efforts are made to stop the erosion of top soil and litter and along with hem, seed banks and seed germination niches.

(f) **Bird Migration:** More than a score of migratory bird species visit water bodies, especially Kaliveli and Ousteri. The exact populations of each species, their nutritional ethology, seasonality, conservation status are to be monitored. This information can give not only a general ecological profile of the region but also information on the endangered and threatened species.

(g) **Agriculture Ornithology:** Many birds of waterbodies feed on insects. Some of these insects are pests of crops. Birds can help in reducing populations of insects and mammalian pests like mice and bandicoots. A survey of the nutritional patterns and their nesting habitats can give information necessary for deciding the role of birds in pest control. Impacts of pesticides on populations and breeding patterns of birds is another area of agricultural ornithology needing in-depth study.

(h) **Socio Economic Survey:** Socio-economic survey of the tank related activities, as an adjunct to ecological studies, help in developing an integrated picture of the wetland ecosystem with all its strengths and weaknesses. This may lead to the ushering in of a correct mix of conservation and development inputs in a truly holistic fashion.

5. Combined Efforts - Revision of Records

The background data on the waterbodies given by the Revenue, Irrigation and Agriculture Departments differ from each other and the ground realities for a variety of reasons - natural degradation (siltation, aridity) man-made degradation (misuse, encroachments), accent on alternatives (wells), wrong policies and practices (reclamation, poaching, deforestation). Therefore updating the records on the characteristics of the tanks is a prerequisite for an understanding of the inputs required. Such a revision by the departments of revenue, agriculture and public works, is therefore very urgently needed involving local people, academicians and non-governmental organisations.

Table IV.8a: FLORA around the Waterbodies.

Habit	*Species*	*Kp*	*Pp*	*Kv*	*Ot*	*Mn*	*Kk*
Climbers							
1.	Abrus precatorius	-	-	+	-	-	+
2.	Aristolochia indica	-	-	+	+-	-	-
3.	Asparagus racemosus	-	-	+	-	-	-
4.	Blastania garcini	+	+	-	-	+	-
5.	Canavalia mollis	-	-	-	+	-	-
6.	Cardiospermum halicacabum	-	-	+	+	-	-
7.	Cassytha filiformis	-	-	+	-	-	-
8.	Cephalandra indica	-	-	+	-	-	-
9.	Ceropegia elegans	-	-	+	-	-	-
10.	Cissampelos pareira	-	-	+	+	-	-
11.	Cissus quadrangularis	-	+	+	+	+	+

(Contd...)

12.	Citrullus colocynthis	+	+	+	+	+	+
13.	Citrullus lanatus	+	-	-	-	-	-
14.	Coccinia grandis	-	+	-	-	+	-
15.	Cocculus sp.	-	+	-	-	-	-
16,	Combretum albidum	-	-	+	-	-	-
17.	Cucumis sativus	-	-	+	+	-	-
18.	Gloriosa superba	-	-	+	-	-	+
19.	Hemidesmus indicus	-	-	+	-	-	-
20.	Jasminum angustifolium	+	+	+	+	+	+
21.	Luffa cylindrica	+	+	+	+	+	+
22.	Melothria maderaspatana	+	+	-	-	+	-
23.	Mukia maderaspatana	-	-	+	+	-	-
24.	Parthenocissus sp.	+	-	-	-	-	-
25.	Passiflora edulis	+	-	-	+	+	-
26.	Quisqualis indica	-	-	-	+	-	-
27.	Rivea hypocrateriformis	+	+	+	+	+	+
28.	Sarcostemma intermedium	-	-	+	-	-	-
29.	Tragia involucrata	+	+	-	+	-	+
30.	Tylophora indica	-	-	+	-	-	-
31.	Wattakaka volubilis	-	-	+	-	-	-
GRASSES							
32.	Andropis paniculata	+	-	-	-	-	-
33.	Apluda mutica	+	-	-	-	+	-
34.	Apuda sp.	-	-	-	-	+	-
35.	Aristida mutabilis	-	-	+	+	-	-
36.	Aristida sp.	-	-	-	+	-	+
37.	Aristida sp.	-	-	-	-	+	-
38.	Arundo donax	+	+	+	+	+	-
39.	Brachiaria ramosa	-	-	+	-	+	-
40.	Bulbostylis barbata	-	-	-	-	+	-
41.	Chloris inflata	+	+	+	-	-	-
42.	Chloris virgata	+	-	-	-	-	-
43.	Coleus barbatus	+	-	-	-	-	-
44.	Cynodon dactylon	+	+	+	+	+	+
45.	Cyperus arenarius	-	-	-	+	-	-
46,	Cyperus articulatus	+	-	+	+	-	-
47.	Dactyloctenium aegyptium	-	-	+	-	-	-
48.	Digitaria chinensis	+	+	+	-	+	-
49.	Echinops echinatus	-	-	-	+	-	+
50.	Eleusine indica	+	-	-	+	-	-
51.	Eragrostis ciliaris	-	-	+	-	-	-
52.	Eragrostis riparia	-	-	+	-	-	-
53.	Eragrostis tenella	-	-	+	-	+	-
54.	Fimbristylis aggregata	+	+	-	+	+	-
55.	Fimbristylis sp.	-	-	+	-	-	-
56.	Heteropogon contortus	-	+	-	-	+	-
57.	Ischaemum angustifolium	+	-	-	-	+	-
58.	Kyllinga bulbosa	-	-	+	-	-	-
59.	Kyllinga nemoralis	-	-	+	-	-	-

(*Contd...*)

60.	Perotis indica	+	+	+	+	+	+
61.	Saccharum officinarum	+	+	+	+	-	-
62.	Typha angusta	-	-	-	+	-	-
63.	Vetiveria zizanioides	-	-	+	+	-	-
HERBS							
64.	Abutilon indicum	+	+	+	+	+	+
65.	Aerva lanata	+	+	+	+	+	+
66.	Aeschynomene aspera	-	-	-	-	+	+
67.	Agave angustifolia	-	+	-	-	+	+
68.	Aloe vera	-	-	+	-	+	-
69.	Alternanthera pungens	-	-	-	+	-	-
70.	Alysicarpus vaginalis	+	-	-	+	-	-
71.	Amaranthus spinosus	-	+	+	-	+	-
72.	Amaranthus viridis	+	+	+	+	+	+
73.	Ammania baccifera	+	-	-	-	-	-
74.	Argemone mexicana	-	+	-	-	-	-
75.	Aristolochia bracteolata	-	-	+	+	-	+
76.	Aeschynomene aspera	-	-	-	-	-	-
77.	Asystasia gangetica	-	-	+	-	-	-
78.	Blepharis molluginifolia	-	+	-	-	-	+
79.	Boerhavia diffusa	+	+	+	+	+	+
80.	Borreria hispida	+	+	+	+	+	+
81.	Borreria ocymoides	-	-	-	-	+	-
82.	Borreria stricta	-	-	-	-	+	+
83.	Caralluma adscesionist	-	-	+	-	-	-
84.	Celosia argentea	+	-	-	-	+	-
85.	Celosia polygonoides	-	+	+	-	-	-
86.	Ceratophyllum demersum	-	+	-	-	+	-
87.	Cleome viscosa	+	+	+	+	+	+
88.	Coldenia procumbens	+	+	+	-	+	-
89.	Commelina clavata	-	-	+	-	-	-
90.	Commelina ensifolia	-	-	+	-	-	-
91.	Commelina persicariaefolia	+	+	-	-	-	-
92.	Commelina sp.	-	-	-	-	+	-
93.	Corbichonia decumbens	-	+	+	-	-	+
94.	Corchorus capsularis	-	-	-	-	+	-
95.	Croton bonplandianus	+	+	+	+	+	+
96.	Dendrophthoe falcata	-	-	+	-	-	-
97.	Digera muricata	-	-	+	-	-	-
98.	Echinops echinatus	+	-	-	-	-	-
99.	Eclipta prostrata	+	-	+	+	+	-
100.	Elephantopus scaber	+	+	+	+	+	+
101.	Euphorbia hirta	+	+	+	+	+	+
102.	Evolvulus alsinoides	+	+	+	-	+	-
103.	Evolvulus marmelos	-	-	-	-	+	-
104.	Gomphrena celosioides	+	-	+	+	-	-
105.	Gomphrena decumbens	-	-	-	+	-	-
106.	Heliotropium indicum	-	-	+	+	-	-
107.	Heliotropium scabrum	+	+	-	-	+	-
108.	Hibiscus hirtus	+	-	-	-	-	-

(*Contd...*)

109.	Indigofera cordifolia	+	+	-	+	+	+
110.	Indigofera tinctoria	+	+	+	+	+	+
111.	Ipomoea pes-caprae	+	+	+	+	+	+
112.	Justicia diffusa	-	-	-	-	+	-
113.	Justicia glabra	+	-	-	-	+	-
114.	Justicia glauca	+	+	-	-	-	-
115.	Justicia procumbens	-	-	-	+	+	+
116.	Justicia simplex	+	+	+	+	+	+
117.	Leucas aspera	+	+	+	+	+	+
118.	Lycopersicon esculentum	+	+	+	+	+	+
119.	Merremia tridentata	-	+	-	+	-	+
120.	Micrococca mercurialis	-	-	+	-	-	-
121.	Mimosa pudica	+	+	+	+	+	+
122.	Mollugo cerviana	-	-	+	-	-	-
123.	Mollugo disticha	-	-	+	+	-	-
124.	Mollugo nudicaulis	-	-	-	-	-	+
125.	Mollugo oppositifolia	+	+	+	+	+	+
126.	Mollugo pentaphylla	+	+	+	+	+	+
127.	Nelumbo nucifera	-	-	+	-	-	-
128.	Nymphaea pubescens	-	-	+	+	-	-
129.	Ocimum basilicum	+	+	+	+	+	+
130.	Ocimum tenuiflorum	-	-	+	+	-	-
131.	Ocimum canum	+	+	-	-	-	-
132.	Ocimum sanctum	+	+	+	+	+	+
133.	Ocimum tenuiflorum	-	-	+	+	+	-
134.	Oldenlandia alata	+	+	+	+	+	+
135.	Oldenlandia corymbosa	+	+	+	+	+	+
136.	Oldenlandia umbellata	+	+	+	+	+	-
137.	Parthenium hysterophorus	+	+	+	+	+	+
138.	Pedalium murex	-	-	+	-	-	-
139.	Peristrophe paniculata	-	-	+	-	-	-
140.	Phyla nodiflora	+	+	+	+	+	+
141.	Phyllanthus amarus	+	+	+	+	+	+
142.	Physalis minima	+	+	+	-	-	+
143.	Polygala javana	-	-	-	+	-	-
144.	Portulaca oleracea	-	-	+	-	-	-
145.	Psilotrichum nudum	+	-	-	-	-	-
146.	Sida acuta	+	+	+	+	+	+
147.	Sida cordifolia	+	+	+	+	+	+
148.	Sida rhombifolia	+	-	+	-	+	+
149.	Sida spinosa	-	-	-	-	-	+
150.	Solanum amplexicaulis	-	-	+	-	-	-
151.	Solanum surattense	-	-	+	+	+	+
152.	Solanum torvum	+	+	-	-	+	-
153.	Stachytarpheta indica	+	+	+	+	+	+
154.	Suaeda maritima	-	-	+	-	-	-
155.	Tacca pinnatifida	+	-	-	-	-	-
156.	Tephrosia purpurea	+	+	+	+	+	+
157.	Tribulus terrestris	+	+	+	+	+	+
158.	Tridax procumbens	+	+	+	+	+	+

(*Contd...*)

159.	Vallisneria natans	-	-	+	-	-	-
160.	Vernonia cinerea	+	+	+	+	+	+
HYDROPHYTES							
161.	Chara sp.-	-	+	+	-	-	-
162.	Hydrilla verticillata	-	-	-	+	-	-
163.	Hydrolea zeylanica	-	+	-	-	-	-
164.	Marsilea sp.	-	-	+	+	-	+
165.	Najas indica	-	-	+	+	-	-
166.	Ottelia alismoides	-	-	+	-	-	+
SHRUBS							
167.	Acalypha indica	+	-	+	-	-	-
168.	Acanthus ilicifolius	-	-	-	+	-	+
169.	Achyranthes aspera	+	+	+	+	+	+
170.	Adhatoda zeylanica	+	+	+	+	+	+
171.	Aeschynomene indica	-	-	+	-	-	-
172.	Alangium sp	+	+	-	-	-	-
173.	Anisomeles indica	+	+	+	-	+	-
174.	Anisomeles malabarica	-	-	-	-	+	-
175.	Breynia retusa	+	+	+	+	+	+
176.	Cactus opuntia	+	+	+	+	+	+
177.	Cadaba fruticosa	+	-	+	-	-	-
178.	Calotropis gigantea	+	+	+	+	+	+
179.	Calycopteris floribunda	-	-	-	+	-	-
180.	Canthium coromandelicum	+	+	+	+	+	+
181.	Canthium parviflorum	+	-	-	-	+	-
182.	Capparis brevispina	+	+	+	+	+	+
183.	Capparis stylosa	-	-	+	-	-	-
184.	Carissa spinarum	+	+	+	+	+	+
185.	Cassia alata	-	-	-	-	+	+
186.	Cassia auriculata	+	+	+	+	+	+
187.	Cassia occidentalis	-	-	-	-	+	-
188.	Crotalaria pallida	-	-	+	+	-	-
189.	Datura stramonium	+	+	+	+	+	+
190.	Dodonaea angustifolia	+	+	+	+	+	+
191.	Euphorbia thirukalli	-	-	+	-	-	-
192.	Ficus hispida	+	+	+	+	+	+
193.	Flueggea leucopyrus	+	+	+	+	+	+
194.	Gmelina asiatica	-	+	+	-	-	-
195.	Gomphrena celosioides	-	-	-	-	-	+
196.	Hibiscus esculentus	+	-	-	-	-	-
197.	Ichnocarpus frutescens	-	-	+	-	-	-
198.	Ipomoea carnea	+	+	+	+	+	+
199.	Ipomoea sps	-	-	-	-	+	-
200.	Jatropha curcas	-	-	+	+	-	-
201.	Jatropha glandulifera	+	+	+	+	+	+
202.	Jatropha gossypifolia	+	+	+	+	+	+
203.	Jatropha heterophylla	+	+	-	-	+	-
204.	Lantana camara	+	+	+	+	+	+
205.	Leonotis nepetifolia	-	-	+	-	-	-

(*Contd...*)

206.	Lepidagathis cristata	-	-	+	-	-	-
207.	Nerium odorum	+	-	-	-	+	-
208.	Nerium oleander	+	+	+	+	+	+
209.	Opuntia coccinellifera	+	+	-	-	+	-
210.	Opuntia monacantha	+	+	+	+	+	+
211.	Pandanus canarus	+	+	+	+	+	+
212.	Pavonia odorata	-	+	-	-	-	-
213.	Pavonia zeylanica	+	+	+	-	+	-
214.	Phoenix loureirii	+	-	+	-	+	-
215.	Phyllanthus pinnatus	-	-	+	-	-	-
216.	Premna corymbosa	-	-	+	-	-	-
217.	Randia dumetorum	+	+	+	+	+	+
218.	Randia malabarica	+	-	-	-	-	-
219.	Ricinus communis	+	+	+	+	+	+
220.	Secraniga leucopyrus	-	-	-	+	-	-
221.	Solanum nigrum	+	-	-	-	-	-
222.	Stylosanthes fruticosa	-	-	-	-	-	-
223.	Thevetia neriifolia	+	+	+	+	+	+
224.	Vitex negundo	+	+	+	+	+	+
225.	Ziziphus xylopyrus	+	+	+	+	+	+
TREES							
226.	Acacia arabica	+	+	+	+	+	+
227.	Acacia auriculiformis	+	+	+	+	+	+
228.	Acacia nilotica	-	-	+	-	-	-
229.	Ailanthus excelsa	-	-	+	-	-	-
230.	Alangium salvifolium	-	-	+	-	-	-
231.	Albizia amara	+	-	+	-	-	-
232.	Anacardium occidentale	+	-	+	-	+	-
233.	Andrographis paniculata	+	+	+	+	+	+
234.	Azadirachta indica	+	+	+	+	+	+
235.	Bauhinia tomentosa	-	-	-	+	-	-
236.	Bombax ceiba	+	-	+	+	+	-
237.	Borassus flabellifer	+	+	+	+	+	+
238.	Butea monosperma	+	+	+	+	+	+
239.	Calophyllum inophyllum	-	+	+	-	+	-
240.	Cassia fistula	-	-	+	-	+	-
241.	Chloroxylon swietenia	-	-	+	+	+	-
242.	Cocos nucifera	+	+	+	+	+	+
243.	Delonix regia	-	-	-	+	-	-
244.	Eucalyptus globulus	+	+	+	+	+	+
245.	Eugenia bracteata	-	-	+	-	-	-
246.	Euphorbia antiquorum	-	-	+	-	+	+
247.	Euphorbia royalana	-	-	-	-	+	-
248.	Ficus benghalensis	+	+	+	+	+	+
249.	Flacourtia indica	-	-	+	-	-	-
250.	Garcinia indica	-	+	-	-	+	-
251.	Garcinia spicata	-	-	+	-	-	-
252.	Glycosmis pentaphylla	-	-	+	-	-	+
253.	Macaranga peltata	+	+	+	+	+	+
254.	Melia azadirachta	-	-	-	+	-	-

(Contd...)

255.	Memecylon umbellatum	-	-	+	-	-	-
256.	Morinda coreia	+	-	+	+	+	+
257.	Moringa oleifera	+	+	+	+	+	+
258.	Murraya paniculata	+	+	+	+	+	+
259.	Olea sp	-	-	+	-	-	-
260.	Parkinsonia aculeata	-	-	-	+	-	-
261.	Peltophorum pterocarpum	-	-	-	+	-	-
262.	Phoenix sylvestris	+	+	+	+	+	+
263.	Pongamia glabra	+	+	+	+	+	+
264.	Pongamia pinnata	+	-	+	+	-	-
265.	Prosopis juliflora	+	+	+	+	+	+
266.	Samanea saman	+	+	+	+	+	+
267.	Sesbania grandiflora	-	-	+	-	-	+
268.	Strychnos nux-vomica	-	-	-	-	+	-
269.	Syzygium cumini	+	-	+	-	-	-
270.	Tamarindus indica	+	+	+	+	+	+
271.	Tectona grandis	-	-	+	+	+	+
272.	Thespesia populnea	+	+	+	+	+	+

Table IV.8b: Butterflies around the water bodies.

Scientific Name	***Common Name***	***Kp***	***Pp***	***Kv***	***Ot***	***Mn***	***Kk***
1. Ariadne merione	Common castor	+	+	+	-	+	+
2. Biblio ilthya	Jacker	+	+	-	-	-	+
3 Catopsilia crocale	Common emigrant	+	+	+	+	+	+
4. Danaus chrysippus	Plain tiger	+	+	+	+	+	+
5. Danaus genutia	Blue glassy tiger	-	-	+	+	+	-
6. Danais plexippus	Common tiger	-	+	-	-	+	-
7. Delias eucharis	Common Jezbel	+	+	+	+	+	+
8. Euploea core	Common Indian crow	+	+	+	+	+	-
9. Eurema hecabe	Common grass yellow	-	+	+	+	+	+
10. Hebomoia glaucippe	Great orange tip	-	-	-	+	+	+
11. Hypolimnas bolina	Great egg fly	-	-	+	-	-	-
12. Hypolimnas misippus	Danaid egg fly	+	-	+	+	+	+
13. Junonia almanac	Peacock pansy	-	-	+	-	-	+
14. Junonia hierta	Yellow pansy	+	+	+	+	-	+
15. Junonia lemonias	Lemon pansy	+	-	+	+	+	+
16. Junonia orithya	Blue pansy	-	-	+	+	-	+
17. Melanitis leda	Common evening brown	-	-	-	-	+	-
18. Mycalesis perseus	Common bush brown	+	-	+	+	-	-
19. Papilio demoleus	Lime butterfly	-	-	+	+	-	-
20. Papilio polytes	Common Mormon	+	+	+	+	+	+
21. Papilio polymnestor	Blue Mormon	-	-	-	-	-	+
22. Pachliopta aristolochiae	Common rose	+	-	+	+	+	+
23. Pachliopta hector	Crimson rose	+	+	+	+	+	+
24. Precis iphita	Chocolate pansy	-	-	-	-	-	+
25. Telechinia violae	Tawinq castor	+	-	+	+	+	-
26. Vanessa cardui	Painted lady	-	-	-	+	-	-

Table IV.8e: Fishes around the Waterbodies

Scientific Name	*Common Name*	*Kp*	*Pp*	*Kv*	*Ot*	*Mn*	*Kk*
1. Anabas testudineus	Climbing perch	-	-	+	+	+	+
2. Anguilla sp.	Vilangu	-	-	+	+	-	-
3. Catla catla	Catla Carp	+	+	-	-	+	-
4. Cirrhina mrigal	Mrigal Carp	+	+	-	-	+	-
5. Clarias batrachus	Masaarai Keluthy	-	-	+	+	+	-
6. Labeo rohita	Rohu Carp (Kendai)	+	-	-	+	-	-
7. Macrones seenghala	Koombu keluthy	-	-	+	-	-	-
8. Mugil cephalus	Periya Madavai	-	-	+	-	-	-
9. Mugil macrolepis	Madavai	-	-	+	-	-	-
10. Mugil parsia	Pachai Madavai	-	-	+	-	-	-
11. Notopterus notopterus	Ambattan Katti	-	-	-	+	-	-
12. Ophiocephalus marulius	Avuri viral	+	+	+	+	+	+
13. Ophiocephalus punctatus	Koravai	+	+	-	+	+	+
14. Ophiocephalus striatus	Viral	-	-	+	+	-	-
15. Tilapia mossambica	Tilapi Kendai	+	+	+	+	+	-
16. Wallago attu	Valai Keluthy	-	-	+	+	-	+

Table IV.8d: Amphibians around the Water bodies

Scientific Name	*Common Name*	*Kp*	*Pp*	*Kv*	*Ot*	*Mn*	*Kk*
1. Bufo melanostictus	Common Indian toad	+	+	+	+	+	+
2. Rana cyanophlyctis	Skipping Frog	-	-	+	+	+	+
3. Rana hexadactyla	South Indian Frog	+	+	+	+	+	+
4. Rana limnocharis	Paddy field Frog	+	+	+	+	+	+
5. Rana tigrina	Bull Frog	+	+	+	+	+	+
6. Rhacophorus sp.	Tree Frog	+	-	+	+	-	+

Table IV.8e: Reptiles around the water bodies

Scientific Name	*Common Name*	*KP*	*PP*	*KV*	*OT*	*MN*	*KK*
1. Ahaetulla naxetus	Common green whip snake	+	+	+	+	+	+
2. Amphiesma stolata	Buff striped keel back	+	-	-	+	-	-
3. Atretium schistosum	Olivaceous keel back	-	-	-	+	-	-
4. Bungarus caeruleus	Common Indian Krait	+	+	+	+	+	+
5. Calotes versicolor	Garden Lizard	+	+	+	+	+	+
6. Dendrelaphis tristis	Common Bronze back	-	-	+	+	-	-
7. Echis carinatus	Saw scaled viper	-	-	+	+	-	-
8. Eryx johni	John's Earth Boa	-	-	+	+	-	-
9. Hemidactylus brookii	Brook's Gecko	-	-	-	+	-	-
10. Hemidactylus frenatus	Southern House Gecko	+	+	+	+	+	+
11. Hemidactylus leschenaultii	Bark Gecko	-	-	+	+	-	-
12. Hemidactylus triedrus	Termite Hill Gecko	-	-	-	+	-	-
13. Lissemys punctata	Indian mud turtle	-	-	+	+	-	-
14. Mabuya carinata	Common skink	+	+	+	+	+	+
15. Melanochelys trijuga	Indian pond terrapin	+	+	+	+	+	+
16. Naja naja	Indian cobra	-	-	+	+	+	+
17. Ptyas mucosus	Common Rat Snake	+	+	+	+	+	+
18. Snana ponticeriana	Fan throated Lizard	-	-	+	+	-	-
19. Typhlina bramina	Common warm snake	-	-	+	+	-	-
20. Varanus benghalensis	Common Monitor Lizard	-	-	-	+	-	-
21. VipeJa russelli	RusseiliviiJer	-	-	+	+	-	-
22. Xenochrophis piscator	Checkered keel back	+	+	+	+	+	+

Table IV.8f: Birds around the waterbodies

Scientific Name	*Common Name*	*Kp*	*Pp*	*Kv*	*Ot*	*Mn*	*Kk*
1. Accipiter badius	Shikra	+	+	+	+	+	+
2. Acridotheres tristis	Common Myna	+	+	+	+	+	+
3. Acrocephalus dumetorum	Blyth's reed warbler	-	-	+	+	-	-
4. Aegithina tiphia	Common iora	-	-	+	+	-	-
5. Alauda gulgula	Eastern sky lark	+	+	+	+	-	+
6. Alcedo atthis	Small blue kingfisher	+	+	-	+	+	-
7. Amaurornis phoenicurus	White-breasted water hen	+	-	-	+	+	+
8. Ammomanes phoenicura	Rufous-tailed lark	-	-	-	-	-	+
9. Anas acuta	Pintail duck	+	+	+	+	-	+
10. Anas clypeata	Shoveler	+	-	+	+	-	-
11. Anas penelope	Wigeon	+	-	+	+	-	-
12. Anas poecilorhyncha	Spot billed duck	-	-	+	-	-	-
13. Anas querquedula	Garganey	+	+	+	+	-	-
14. Anastomus oscitans	Open billed stork	-	-	+	+	-	+
15. Anthus novaeseelandiae	Paddy field pipit	-	+	+	+	-	-
16. Ardea aba	Large egret	-	+	+	-	-	-
17. Ardea cinerea	*Grey* heron	+	+	+	+	+	+
18. Ardeola grayii	Pond heron	+	+	+	+	+	+
19. Artamus fuscus	Ashy swallow shrike	+	+	+	+	-	-
20. Athene brama	Spotted owlet	+	+	+	+	+	+
21. Aythya ferina	Common pochard	+	+	-	-	-	-
22. Aythya fuligula	Tufted pochard	-	+	-	+	-	-
23. Aythya nyroca	White-eyed pochard	+	+	+	+	-	-
24. Bubulcus ibis	Cattle egret	+	+	+	+	+	+
25. Calidris minuta	little stint	-	-	+	-	-	-
26. Caprimulgus asiaticus	Indian nightjar	-	-	+	-	-	-
27. Centropus sinensis	Crow pheasant	+	+	+	+	+	+
26. Ceryle rudis	Pied Kingfisher	+	+	+	+	-	-
29. Charadrius alexandrinus	Kentish plover	-	-	-	+	-	-
30. Charadrius dubius	Little ringed plover	-	-	-	+	-	-
31. Charadrius mongolus	Lesser sand plover	-	-	+	-	-	-
32. Chlidonias hybrida	Whiskered turn	+	+	+	+	-	-
33. Ciconia ciconia	White stork	-	-	+	-	-	-
34. Circus macrourus	Pale harrier	-	-	+	-	-	-
35. Circus aeruginosus	Marsh harrier	-	+	+	+	-	-
36. Cisticola Juncidis	Streaked fantail warbler	+	-	-	+	-	-
37. Clamator jacobinus	Pied crested cuckoo	+	-	+	+	+	+
38. Columba livia	Blue rock pigeon	+	+	+	+	+	+
39. Copsychus saularis	Magpie-robin	+	-	+	+	+	-
40. Coracias benghalensis	Indian Roller	+	+	+	+	-	-
41. Coracina novaehollandiae	Large cuckoo shrike	+	-	-	-	-	-
42. Corvus macrorhynchos	Jungle crow	-	-	+	-	+	+
43. Corvus splendens	House crow	+	+	+	+	+	+
44. Cuculus varius	Common hawk cuckoo	+	+	+	+	+	-
45. Cursorius coromandelicus	Indian courser	-	-	+	-	-	-
46. Dendrocitta vagabunda	Indian treepie	+	-	+	+	+	+
47. Dicaeum erythrorhynchos	Tiekell's flower-pecker	-	-	+	+	-	-
48. Dicrurus adsimilis	Black drongo	+	+	+	+	+	+
49. Dicrurus leucophaeus	Grey drongo	+	-	+	-	-	+

(Contd...)

50. Dinopium benghalense	L. golden-backed woodpecker	+	+	+	+	+	+
51. Egretta garzetta	Little egret	+	+	+	+	+	+
52. Egretta intermedia	Smaller egret	+	+	+	+	+	+
53. Elanus caeruleus	Black winged kite	-	+	+	+	+	+
54. Eremopterix grisea	Ashy crowned finch lark	-	-	+	-	-	+
55. Escalus magnirostris	Great stone plover	-	-	+	-	-	-
56. Eudynamys scolopacea	Koel	+	+	+	+	+	+
57. Falco peregrinus	Peregrine falcon	-	-	+	-	-	-
58. Falco tinnunculus	Common Kestrel	-	-	+	-	-	-
59. Francolinus pondicerianus	Grey partridge	+	-	+	+	+	+
60. Fulica atra	Coot	+	-	-	+	-	-
61. Gallinago gallinago	Fantail snipe	-	-	+	-	-	-
62. Gallinago stenura	Pintail snipe	-	-	+	-	-	-
63. Gelochelidon nilotica	Gun billed turn	-	-	+	-	-	-
64. Halcyons myrnensis	White breasted kingfisher	+	+	+	+	+	+
65. Haliastur Indus	Brahminy kite	+	+	+	+	+	+
66. Himantopus himantopus	Black winged stiff	+	-	+	+	-	+
67. Hirundo daurica	Striated swallow	-	-	+	-	-	-
68. Hirundo rustica	Swallow	+	+	+	+	+	+
69. Lanius vittatus	Bay-backed shrike	-	-	-	-	+	-
70. Lanius cristatus	Brown shrike	-	-	+	+	-	+
71. Larius ichthyaetus	Black-headed gull	-	-	+	-	-	-
72. Limosa limosa	Black-tailed godwit	-	-	-	+	-	-
73. Lonchura malabarica	White throated Munia	-	-	+	+	-	+
74. Lonchura malacca	Black throated Munia	-	-	+	-	-	+
75. Lonchura Punctulata	Spotted Munia	-	-	-	-	+	-
76. Locustella naevia	Grass hopper warbler	-	-	-	-	-	+
77. Megalaima haemacephala	Crimson-breasted barbet	+	-	+	+	+	-
78. Merops orientalis	Green bee eater	+	+	+	+	+	+
79. Merops philippinus	Blue tailed bee eater	-	+	+	+	-	-
80. Milvus migrans govinda	Pariah kite	+	+	+	+	+	+
81. Motacilla cinerea	Grey wagtail	-	-	+	-	-	-
82. Motacilla citreola	Yellow headed wagtail	-	-	+	+	-	-
83. Motacilla flava	Yellow wagtail	-	-	+	-	+	+
84. Motacilla maderaspatensis	Large pied wagtail	+	-	+	+	+	-
85. Mycteria leucocephala	Painted stork	-	-	+	+	-	-
86. Nectarinia asiatica	Purple sunbird	-	-	-	-	+	+
87. Nectarinia hotenia	Loten's sunbird	+	+	+	-	-	-
88. Nectarinia zeylonica	Purple rumped sunbird	+	+	+	+	+	-
89. Nettapus coromandelianus	Cotton teal	-	-	+	+	-	-
90. Netta rufina	Red crested pochard	+	-	+	+	-	-
91. Numenius arquata	Curlew	-	-	+	-	-	-
92. Nycticorax nycticorax	Night heron	-	-	+	+	+	-
93. Oriolus oriolus	Golden oriole	+	-	+	+	+	-
94. Orthotomus sutorius	Tailor bird	+	+	+	+	+	-
95. Pandion haliaetus	Osprey	-	-	+	-	-	-
96. Passer domesticus	House sparrow	-	+	+	+	-	+
97. Pavo cristatus	Common peafowl	-	-	-	-	+	+
98. Pelecanus philippensis	Spot billed pelican	-	-	+	-	-	-

(*Contd...*)

99. Phalacrocorax niger	Little cormorant	+	+	-	+	-	-
100. Phoenicopterus roseus	Greater flamingo	-	-	+	-	-	-
101. Phylloscopus trochiloides	Dull green leaf warbler	+	+	+	+	+	-
102. Ploceus philippinus	Baya weaver bird	+	+	+	+	-	+
103. Podiceps ruficollis	Little Grebe	+	-	+	+	+	+
104. Prinia socialis	Ashy wren warbler	-	-	+	-	-	-
105. Prinia subflava	Plain wren warbler	-	-	-	+	-	-
106. Pseudibis papillosa	Black Ibis	-	-	-	-	-	+
107. Psittacula krameri	Rose-ringed parakeet	+	+	+	+	+	+
108. Pycnonotus cafer	Red-vented bulbul	+	-	+	+	+	+
109. Pycnonotus jocosus	Red-whiskered bulbul	-	-	+	-	-	-
110. Pycnonotus luteolus	White-browed bulbul	+	-	+	+	-	-
111. Saxicola caprata	Pied bush chat	+	-	+	+	-	-
112. Saxicoloides fulicatus	Indian robin	+	+	+	+	+	-
113. Sterna bengalensis	Indian lesser crested tern	-	-	+	-	-	-
114. Sterna hirundo	Common tern	-	-	+	+	-	-
115. Streptopelia chinensis	Spotted dove	+	-	+	+	+	+
116. Streptopelia decaocto	Indian Ring dove	-	-	-	-	-	+
117. Streptopelia senegalensis	Little brown dove	+	+	+	-	+	-
118. Sturnus pagodarum	Black headed Myna	+	+	+	+	-	+
119. Sypsirurs parvus	Palm swift	+	+	+	+	+	+
120. Tadorna ferruginea	Ruddy shelduck	-	-	+	-	-	-
121. Tephrodornis pondicerianus	Common woodshrike	-	-	-	-	+	-
122. Terpsiphone paradisi	Paradise flycatcher	-	-	+	-	-	-
123. Threskiornis aethiopicus	Sacred Ibis	-	-	+	+	-	-
124. Turdoides affinis	Yellow-billed babbler	+	+	+	+	-	-
125. Turdoides striatus	Jungle babbler	-	-	-	-	+	-
126. Turdoides caudatus	Common babbler	-	-	+	+	-	+
127. Turdoides malcolmi	Large grey babbler	+	-	-	-	-	-
128. Tringa glareola	Wood sandpiper	-	+	+	+	-	-
129. Tringa ochropus	Green sandpiper	-	-	+	-	-	-
130. Tringa stagnatilis	Marsh sandpiper	+	-	-	-	-	-
131. Tringa totanus	Common redshank	-	+	+	-	-	+
132. Tringa lypolencos	Common sandpiper	+	+	+	+	+	+
133. Tumix sylvatica	Little bastard Quail	-	-	+	+	-	-
134. Tyto alba	Bam owl	-	-	+	+	-	-
135. IJpupa epopes	Hoopoe	+	+	+	+	-	+
136. Vanellus indicus	Red wattled lapwing	+	+	+	+	+	+
137. Vanellus malabaricus	Yellow wattled lapwing	-	-	+	-	-	-

Table IV.8g: Mammals around the waterbodies

Scientific Name	*Common Name*	*KP*	*PP*	*KV*	*OT*	*MN*	*KK*
1. Bandicota bengalensis	Indian Mole Rat	-	-	+	-	-	-
2. Bandicota indica	Bandicoot rat	+	+	+	+	+	+
3. Canis aureus (Linnaeus)	Golden Jackal	-	-	+	+	-	+
4. Felis chaus	Jungle cat	-	-	+	-	-	-
5. Funambulus palmarum	Three stripped palm squirrel	+	+	+	+	+	+
6. Herpestes edwardsii	Common Mongoose	+	+	+	+	+	+
7. Tatera indica	Indian Gerbil	-	-	+	-	-	-
8. Lepus nigricollis	Indian hare	-	-	+	+	+	+
9. Macaca radiata	Bonnet macaque	+	-	-	-	-	-

(Contd...)

10. Mus booduga	Little Field mouse	-	-	+	-	-	-
11. Paradoxurus hermaphroditus	Palm civet	-	-	+	+	-	-
12. Pipistrellus coromandra	Indian pipistrelle	-	-	+	+	+	+
13. Rattus rattus	Common rat	+	+	+	+	+	+
14. Suncus murinus	Grey musk shrew	-	-	+	+	-	+
15. Viverricula indica	Small Indian civet	-	-	+	-	-	-
16. Vulpes bengalensis	Indian fox	+	+	+	+	+	+

Chapter - V

Perspectives

Waterbodies are features of nature made mostly by human societies for their economic well being through traditional wisdom. Currently they are not only enmeshed in political expediencies but fortunately have become subjects of scientific insights. The analyses of the current status of the tanks carried out hitherto lead to the development of perspectives on the future of the waterbodies from a holistic point of view.

A. Tragedy of the Commons

1. Socio-ecology

It has been seen that all resources of a wetland are interconnected among themselves and with the rural society as a whole. The tank land and its water are the most important of these common property resources. With the decline in tank rights, duties and managements for reasons of planning and politics, water and land were gradually and systematically owned up.

(a) Water markets

Many wells and tube wells sprang up around tanks, privatising the common surface water as groundwater which is extracted mechanically and sold to neighbouring farmers. And the electrical charges to privately extract this common water for a profit, is subsidized! The water residence in tanks, which is anyway ephemeral, is further reduced due to such extractions and the excessive opportunity usage, etc. The rates of water vary with the diameter of the borewell, depth of water table, duration and quantity of supply and from tank to tank. This may be paid in cash or kind. In some cases a third of the crop is paid. The borewells are sometimes in the tank bed encroached by powerful people or far away from the waterbody itself. In such cases the water is locally stored in small ponds. Water owner has emerged as the new feudal lord.

(b) Land grabbing

In the absence of managerial systems replacing the traditional ones, tank lands are encroached by the neighbouring land owners, local landlords and political forces. Consequently many tanks are mere apologies, as they appear no more than temporary ponds and puddles. This anarchy is beneficial to a few and detrimental for most. However there is an interesting variation to this common trend. In Kaliveli, of South Arcot district the offshore is encroached by a large number of small farmers from the lower economic order. And the government has gradually been legitimizing these by awarding 'pattas'. But these new owners loose 1/4 to 1/3 of the crop as price for water supply from water-lords far away from the wetland. This is expected to be inconsequential due to the vastness of the wetland. But for how long? Socialism through such land 'reforms' at the cost of ecology may also dwindle in the face of the fast completing East Coast Road.

(c) Urban wetlands

While dealing with the rural tank systems it is difficult not to bump into their cousins in the urban systems. Urban wetlands have become the easiest and popularly justified victims of land hunger and speculative profiteering. There are a myriad instances of "converting water into soil" in many towns by dumping solid wastes for "reclaimation". This owned up land is used for raising concrete jungles. Consequently drainage of rain water was reduced and charging the underground aquifer hampered. The sociology, economics and politics of these developments are worth investigating. But can the wetland resources lost during the last 50 years be accounted for, leave alone restored?

B. Accounting Resources

1. Valuing wetlands

Accounting all resources harboured in the tank ecosystem and valuing them on relative and absolute terms may give us an ecological and economic perspective for development options. An attempt is currently being made in this direction as can be seen in the Table V.1.

The sum of accounts for thirteen items are converted to a fraction of 1, the intrinsic value. The present tanks obtained values from 0.9 to 0.6 which means that those in the descending order need correspondingly more conservation inputs. Otherwise they gradually loose ecological resilience and economic utility to the villages. If the value goes down 0.5 either the tank has to be abandoned or restoration efforts are warranted. The tanks obtaining higher values, on the other hand can usher in developmental activities taking care to hold the ecological balances.

Table V.1: Value ranking of the tanks based on the resource potential.

	KP	*PP*	*KV*	*OT*	*MN*	*KK*
A. Habitat						
1. Area	0.5	0.2	1.0	0.3	0.2	0.25
2. Yield	0.9	0.7	1.0	1.0	0.8	0.5
3. Water retention period	1.0	0.8	0.8	1.0	0.6	0.4
B. Resources						
1. Soil	0.8	0.9	0.7	0.8	1.0	0.6
2. Water	0.8	1.0	0.6	1.0	1.0	1.0
3. Plants	0.8	0.6	1.0	0.8	0.8	0.4
4. Animals	0.8	0.6	1.0	0.8	0.6	0.6
C. Cultures						
1. Agriculture	1.0	0.8	1.0	1.0	0.8	0.6
2. Aquaculture	0.8	0.7	1.0	1.0	0.6	0.5
3. Forestry	1.0	1.0	0.8	0.8	0.8	0.8
D. Human Ecology						
1. Pollution	0.8	1.0	0.8	0.8	1.0	1.0
2. People	0.8	1.0	0.8	0.8	1.0	1.0
3. Villages	0.8	0.5	1.0	0.8	0.6	0.5
Total	10.8	9.8	11.5	10.9	9.8	8.15
VALUE	0.83	0.75	0.88	0.83	0.75	0.62

C. Diagnosis Through Expert Systems

1. State of wetland

Marginal inputs will be made only after a policy input. This will be based on the full knowledge on all the tanks. Current methods are highly time consuming. Therefore to assess the current status or diagnise all tanks a fast method has to be adapted. This is called the expert system. Expert system is a kind of software which is expected to simulate an expert's knowledge. The technique belongs to the field of artificial intelligence of advanced logistics and computing. Scarcity of experts, expertise in very restricted and specified areas are some of the problems one has to face in areas like irrigation management where a multidisciplinary approach is necessary. In such situations expert systems can playa important role even in the decision making process. Thus an expert system is expected to work like a pointer of the problems associated with the given tank, the possible remedial measures and management strategies. But to develop such a system which compiles the intelligence, common sense, knowledge and experience of an expert and the data base of enormous diversity and magnitude has to have stores which are hierarchically arranged.

The process of developing an expert system basically involves the following three steps:

(a) First, elicit the knowledge that experts use.
  - When and how they apply it (cases assumed, patterns recognised, tests made)
  - The categories evolved from their experience that they utilize to understand the situation
  - The hypothesis, rules, thumb measurements and parameters they take into account

(b) When these concepts, rules and operations have been elicited from the human experts, they have to be reformulated and transferred into a customized software package designed to reduce the expert's method of diagnosis.

(c) Then comes a third phase in order to test and validate the consistency of computerized knowledge base with what the expert actually does, and try to implement any required modifications. The validation of experts knowledge that has thus been computerized is limited to the particular type of case for which the analysis has been made Developing an expert system for diagnosing all the irrigation tanks in semi-arid India is thus a project with enormous significance in the present context. Further this exercise will result in the compilation of all available data and knowledge base on the tanks for further research.

D. Rapid Evaluation System

1. The Model

There exist more than 35000 irrigation tanks in Tamil Nadu. They are situated in different agro-climatic zones and are managed by a variety of cultural / traditional practices. But most of these tanks are now dysfunctional owing to various reasons. In recent years tanks have attracted the attention of planners and agriculture economists as low investment and locally manageable irrigation systems. Various projects are now operational for tank renovation. Age of the tanks vary from 300 - 800 years. In order to facilitate efficient use of the scarce funding, setting priority is very important. Developing a rapid evaluation system for diagnosis of tanks are thus relevant. An attempt is currently being made, incorporating the features of accounting, valuing and diagnosis leading to development and conservation inputs.

Rapid evaluation system is a tool which can be used by any trained lay man. The data available on various aspects of tank will be investigated and ranked in the evaluation system to come out with an index which will be helpful in

- Determining the overall health of the tank system
- Identifying the potential resource base
- Gauging the possibility of people's participation
- Determining the options in tank restoration and management
- Comparing the tank with others in order to develop a taxonomy of tank scenarios

The evaluation system restricts itself to three major aspects pertaining to tank. They are 1. The structure 2. The user value 3. Attitude of the people. All three aspects are identified as the function of a number of factors. They are qualitatively categorized into three groups and each group is given a scoring ranging from 0 to 2. The total scoring obtained in each category will help determine the status of the tank. This scoring is ultimately expressed as the percentage of maximum obtainable scoring. A key is provided to assess the status of the tank and its components.

E. Conservation and Development

(1) Making for each other

A natural corollary of the above concerns is to quantify the land and water scenarios and the biotic resources. The imperative is to conserve whatever still exists, restore whatever is possible, so that the system comes to life for future development. The converse of this is to develop the region selectively only in some spheres in such a way that other resources are conserved. In other words, conservation for development and development for conservation shall emerge as the middle path wisdom for wetlands. But this has to be based on accounting, valuing and diagnosis of the system.

(a) Wetland forestry

The government has encroached on the tank shores and bed in the name of social forestry which should actually be called wetland forestry due to long periods of water logging. This practice using leguminous plants improves soil quality and animal populations, especially of birds. This is a rare case of doing the best in the worst of times, by a mistaken assumption that silviculture in the tank is equal to the social forestry outside it.

(b) Eco-agriculture

When water is scarce it is not proper to cultivate water intensive crops. Yet paddy is grown and still worse is the cultivation of sugarcane just because one has owned up the tank water through the borewells. Thus by applying a good technology in a wrong place, a single most unjust policy - both ecologically and economically - has been ushered, privatizing common properties, spoiling ecology, and causing social inequalities. Yet there seem to be no attempts made to study the economics involved. Agriculture and technology should therefore go ecological - no water markets, no subsidies for pump sets or electricity and growing less water needing crops for which alone subsidies should be provided by the government.

(c) Bird Sanctuary

Tanks are a sort of bird sanctuaries already to different degrees and durations. Birds influence every other life through food chains, reproductive necessities, nutritional ethologies etc. some of which are of economic significance to the ecosystem. Their excreta contribute to fertility. They bring in plankton from other water bodies. And some of these predate the insect pests of crops. To ensure a continuity of this it is necessary to re-green the barren areas with permacultures and tank shores with wetland forestry. These result in increased productivity and animal diversity. The aquatic productivity also get accelerated leading to an increase of migratory birds and associated fringe benefits in pest control and guanal inputs in agricultural fields. All these may materials only if waterbodies are declared bird sanctuaries and given for adoption to local educational institutions. Poaching of the birds should be curbed by appointing local people as guards.

F. National Tank Authority

(1) The Recommendation

The subtle interrelationships among agriculture, social forestry, the land and water dynamics, biodiversity, the socio-economic milieu and above all the political undertones running through the entire system of waterbodies have to be realised if they are to be resuscitated. Since these waterbodies are a major group of natural, irrigation and drainage sources, there is a need to change our approach towards their management radically i.e. from an engineering outlook to an Ecosystem Approach. This can be done in the interests of the wetlands and their dependent people by reviving the traditional systems of tank management under the Panchayat Raj system and an establishment of a National Tank Authority [NTA], to oversee all aspects of tank resurrection and management.

(a) Panchayat Raj

Tank irrigation requires a strong local authority to generate collective action for tank building, to efficiently distribute the water by optimally allocating it among beneficiaries and over seasons, and to properly maintain the irrigation system. The water dynamics encompass the entire catchment, supply channels, command area, the wells, impediments and adjuncts to these. The villages are intimately connected with this web as constituent parts. Because of a shift from a direct social control to indirect economic hegemony through subtle ownership of water and soil, tanks have degraded severely. Therefore both conservation and development have to go hand in hand, which is possible only with local participation and involvement.

(b) National Tank Authority

Though we are currently focusing on the tanks of Tamilnadu, the same is relevant to Karnataka, Andhra Pradesh,

Maharashtra etc. The same approach is needed to save the eastern coastal rainfall from loosing out to the Bay of Bengal. Further the wetlands - urban and rural are scattered all over India. Therefore the Authority has to be a national one whose responsibility shall encompass conservation and restoration of resources and development of tank ecosystems on an ecologically sustainable scale.

The NTA is visualised as a body for broad policy making and channeling inputs of scientific, technological and financial nature so as to motivate, monitor and strengthen the local bodies in reviving and modernising the tank systems. The inputs cover rainfall harvesting, storage of water, irrigation usage, potability, recharging ground water among others. For these purposes networking with major institutions pertinent to these objectives such as ICAR, ICSSR, DOEF, as well as local bodies and regional institutions is a natural corollary. Since all these have to be mandated to be carried out on ecological bases, biodiversity will be naturally preserved and utilised by local people gradually. Therefore development for conservation and conservation for development will result. Considerable NGO activity is also envisaged. All these may prevent migrations of people to urban areas to a great extent.

Such an Authority or Commission shall encompass system and non-system tanks of Tamil Nadu, Andhra Pradesh, Karnataka, Maharashtra, Uttar Pradesh, Bihar etc. lakes, fresh water aqua cultural systems, urban wetlands, coastal ponds, rural temple tanks, special water harvesting systems in other places such as Rajasthan, Gujarat, Hilly regions and foot hills. The NTA in short has to revive, enhance and maintain an ecological bank of stored water for the greater use of maximum people by strengthening local people from the usurping ethos of dark forces. In this connection it may be stressed that attempts to modernise tanks for which huge financial inputs are incoming should take into consideration the ecological aspects covered in this report.

As a recapitulation, it may be concluded that nucleating each tank along with the dependent villages into a unit - An Eco-political unit - is a necessity. Empowering this unit with the responsibility to regenerate the waterbodies, catalysed by political power, social consciousness and academic inputs is the chief imperative emerging from the present study. If this happens a progressive chapter, a turnaround, will have begun with far reaching positive consequences all around the 50,000 villages and 10-20 million people associated with the tank systems. The concept of values responsible for human progress for so many millennia seem to be sadly out of our dictionaries!

Fig. V.1 A Model for Rapid Evaluation

Name of the tank	:	Date
Name of the Investigator	:	Location of the tank
Agro climatic region	:	Authority of the tank
Age of the tank	:	System/Non system tank

1.0 Health of the Tank

1.1 Status of the catchment area

1.1.1. Ground cover	:	>60%	60-40%	<40%
1.1.2. Siltation	:	Negligible	Moderate	High
1.1.3. Encroachments in the tank area	:	No		Yes
1.1.4. Cattle grazing intensity	:	Negligible	Moderate	High
1.1.5. Fire wood collection	:	Low	Moderate	High
WEIGHTAGE	:	2	1	0

Total Not to Exceed : 10 Scoring Expresseo As The % of The Total:

1.2 Status of the structure

1.2.1. Sluices	:	Good	Satisfactory	Dysfunctional
1.2.2. Embankment	:	Strong	Weak	Eroded
1.2.3. Overflow facility	:	Strong	Weak	Dysfunctional
1.2.4. Supply channel	:	Good	Satisfactory	Dysfunctional
1.2.5. Feeder channel	:	Good	Satisfactory	Dysfunctional
WEIGHTAGE	:	4	2	0

Total Not to Exceed : 20 Scoring Expressed As The % of the Total

1.3 Status of the Ayacut

1.3.1. Irrigated area reduced	:	Nil	10% Over	10%
1.3.2. Cropping pattern intensity	:	Nil	Moderate	High
1.3.3. Water supply at the tail-end	:	Satisfactory	Unsatisfactory	Nil

1.3.4. Dug wells / Borewells	:	Many	A few	Nil
1.3.5. Water markets	:	Many	A few	Nil
WEIGHTAGE	:	2	1	0

Total Not to Exceed : 10 SCORING EXPRESSED AS THE % OF THE TOTAL

1.4 Functional status

1.4.1. Water retention	:	12 Months	6 Months	<6 Months
1.4.2. Maximum water level attained in the last 5 yrs	:	5	Last 2-3	First 2-3
1.4.3. Lateral seepage	:	Minimum	Low	High
1.4.4. Inflow into the tank	:	Good	Low	Nil
1.4.5. Siltation of the bed	:	Minimum	Low	High
WEIGHTAGE	:	4	2	0

Total Not to Exceed : 20 SCORING EXPRESSED AS THE % OF THE TOTAL

2.0 IMPORTANCE AS A RESOURCE BASE

2.1. Forestry	:	Healthy	Stunted	Poor
2.2. Fishery	:	For all	Leased	Nil
2.3. Fodder	:	Increasing	Enough	Declining
2.4. Groundwater	:	Abundant	Depleting	Poor
2.5. Vegetation	:	Increasing	Steady	Declining
2.6. Flowering plants	:	High	Medium	Low
2.7. Useful plants from tank	:	Above 10	Less than 10	Nil
2.8. Butterflies	:	High	Medium	Low
2.9. Migratory Birds	:	Increasing	Declining	Poor
2.10. Users of tank	:	Very high	Moderate	Poor
WEIGHTAGE	:	2	1	0

Total Not to Exceed : 20 SCORING EXPRESSED AS THE % OF THE TOTAL:

3.0 PEOPLES PERCEPTIONS ON THE TANK

3.1. Faith in tanks	:	High	Low	Nil
3.2. Prefers borewell irrigation	:	No	Not certain	Yes
3.3. Favour local management	:	Yes	Not certain	No
3.4. Favour governmental management	:	Yes	Not certain	No
3.5. Favour removal of encroachment	:	Yes	Not certain	No
WEIGHTAGE	:	4	2	0

Total Not to Exceed : 20 SCORING EXPRESSED AS THE % OF THE TOTAL

KEY for evaluation

Category : 1.1 Status of the Catchment area

100-80% : Catchment is healthy. Utilization of catchments for various purposes has not affected the sustainability.

60·79% : The catchment is subjected to degradation needing immediate attention. The factor(s) which contributed 1/0 points will need immediate attention.

60% : Catchments is already degraded. Needs immediate remedial work

Category : 1.2 Status of the structure

100-80% : All the components / structure of the tank is satisfactory condition but the factor (s) which contributed less scoring should need attention.

79·60% : One or the two structural components of the tanks need immediate refurbishments.

60% : The tank structural components need immediate repair / refurbishments

Category : 1.3 Status of the ayacut

100-80% : Ayacut is the healthy. This should be maintained.

60·79% : Ayacut is degrading. Either water supply is less or consumption is more.

60% : Ayacut is already degraded. Water supply, cropping pattern, water markets need urgent modification.

Category : 1.4 Functional status

100-80% : Tank is functionally healthy but the factor(s) which contributed less scoring may need further attention.

79-60% : Users are not getting the best out the tank. To improve the performance of the tank - Those factor(s) which contributed less should be helped.

60% : Improper functioning of the tanks contributed by a number of factors, which need immediate attention.

Category : 2.0 Importance as a resource base

100-80% : The value of tank as a resource base for local community is very high, most resource basis are strong.

79-60% : Some resources basis are depleted or degraded which need immediate attention. Enrichment of which may beneficial to community.

60% : Most resources are depleted. An immediate action plan for resource development should be implemented.

Category : 3.0 Peoples perceptions on tanks

100-80% : Chances of forming a local body for effective water distribution.

79-60% : An awareness development campaign is imminent to educate people on the need for tanks and traditional systems of water management.

60% : There are chances that the present tank will vanish under the veil of neglect.

Chapter - VI

Summary

A. Diagnosis and Taxonomy

The present study reveals the status of six waterbodies spread out from the north east to the south central part of Tamil Nadu. Two of them are Coastal the others are Inland. They are in the low, medium and high rainfall areas. Some are small, others large. One is a natural wetland while others are either system or non-system tanks. All these are in different stages of degradation. The urgent need therefore is to assess the status of all tanks in the Semi Arid Tropics which are estimated to be around 35,000 in Tamil Nadu alone. Diagnosis of some more waterbodies may enable a classification of these thousands of tanks-small, medium, big, system, non-system, wetland categories -in the different rainfall zones with different soil types, human settlements and histories.

B. Summary of Features of Water bodies

A summary of all the features of the water bodies and the managerial inputs required by each of them are given in Tables VI.1 and VI.2 and Figure VI.1. These are self explanatory.

C. Managerial Inputs

Managerial inputs needed by the tanks for their revival as useful wetlands can be made only with the support of governmental infrastructures and extension services, autonomous bodies such as Khadi and Village Industries Board, in association with local Panchayats, NGOs and academia of the region. Formal and informal education of the local people on every aspect of the waterbody is a prerequisite. Meanwhile declaring these water bodies as protected areas under a National Tank.

Authority and reforming the Panchayat Raj Institutions around these wetland systems is an urgent political imperative in our semi-arid tropical region, or else Tamil Nadu's dependence for water on the neighbouring states may become unbearably perennial. This could lead to dangerous geopolitical tensions of which we are already familiar in post independent India.

Table - VI.1: Managerial Inputs For the Six Waterbodies.

		Kp	*Pp*	*Kv*	*Ot*	*Mn*	*Kk*
A. Development and Conservation							
1.	Turfing the embankment	-	-	-	-	+	+
2.	Vegetating the banks	-	+	-	-	+	+
3.	Medicinal plant garden	-	+	+	-	+	-
4.	Leguminous forestry	+	+	+	+	+	+
5.	Zoological park	+	-	+	-	-	-
6.	Bird Sanctuary	+	+	+	+	-	+
7.	Non-formal education	+	+	+	+	+	+
8.	Ecotourism	+	-	+	+	-	-
9.	Ecological agriculture	+	+	+	+	+	+
10.	Apiculture	+	+	+	+	-	-
11.	Sericulture	+	+	-	+	-	-
B. Policy inputs							
1.	Empower Beneficiary	+	+	-	+	-	-
2.	Agricultural policies	+	+	+	+	+	+
3.	Participatory forestry	+	+	+	+	+	+
4.	Land use regulation	+	+	+	+	+	+
5.	Resource inventory	+	+	+	+	+	+
6.	Agriculture	+	+	+	+	+	+
7.	Aquaculture	+	+	+	+	-	-
8.	Socio-economy	+	+	+	+	+	+
9.	Irrigation	+	+	-	+	-	-
C. Research inputs							
1.	Bird migration	+	-	+	+	-	+
2.	Agriculture omithology	+	-	+	-	-	-
3.	Soil Ecology	+	-	+	+	-	-
4.	Palynology	-	-	+	-	-	-
5.	Soil seed banks	-	-	+	-	-	-
6.	Tank-well interations	+	+	+	+	+	+

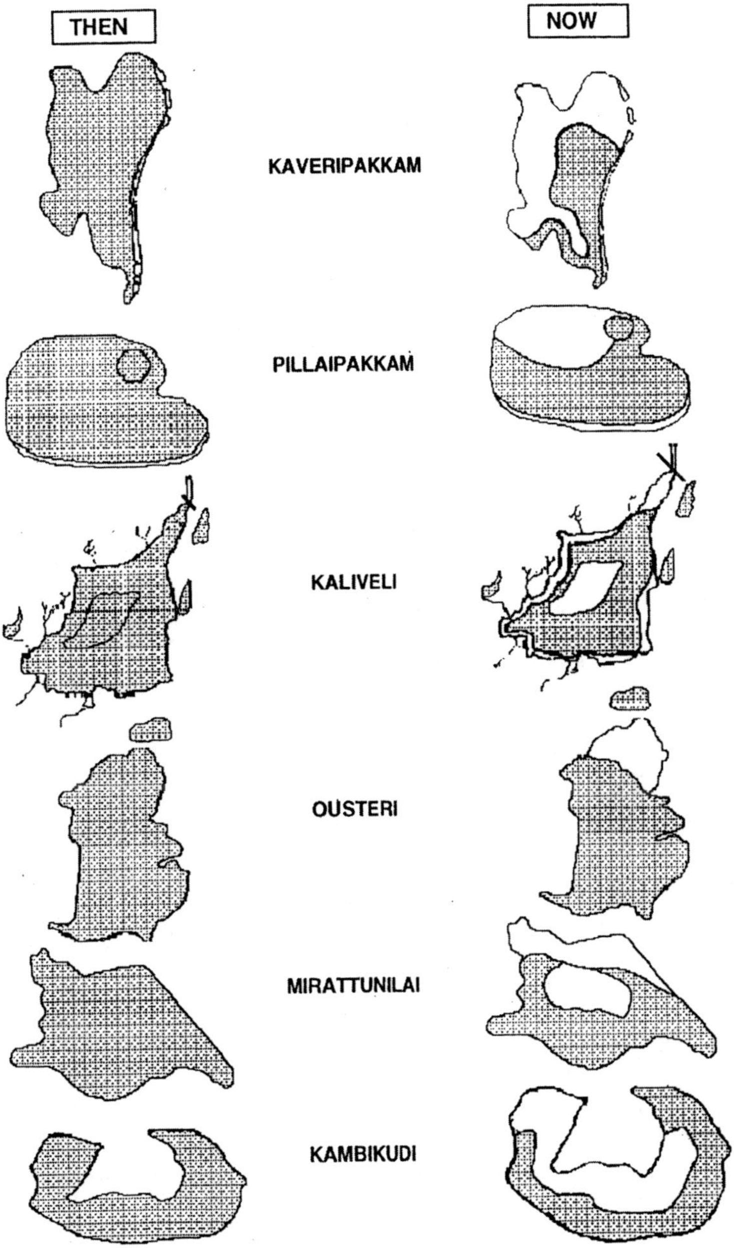

Fig. VI.1: Water Retention Areas of Tanks

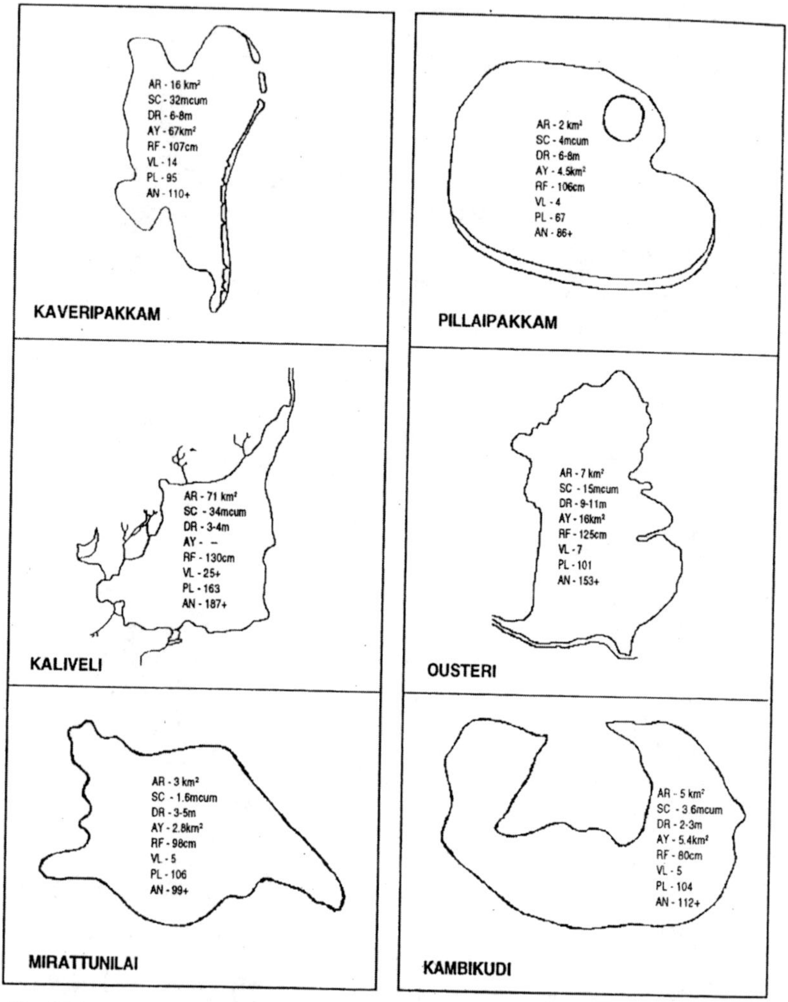

AR – AREA　DR – DURATION OF RETENTION　RF – RAINFALL　PL – PLANTS
SC – STORAGE CAPACITY　AY – AYACUT　VL – VILLAGES　AN - ANIMALS

Fig. VI.2: Characteristics of Six Water Bodies - A Summary.

Table - VI.2: Summary of Characteristics of the Six Waterbodies.

Particulars	*Kaveripakkam*	*Pillaipakkam*	*Kaliveli*	*Ousteri*	*Mirattunilai*	*Kambikudi*
1. Location						
	13°50'N X 79°22'E	12°57'N X 79°57'E	12°08'N X 79°55'E	11°57'N X 79°45'E	10°12'N X 78°52'E	09°42'N X 78°07'E
	Palar river basin	Palar river basin	---	Ousudu village west of ondicherry	Upper vellar basin	Upper Gundar basin
	North Arcot Dt.	Chengeloattu Dt.	South Arcot Dt.		Pudukittai Dt.	Kamarajar Dt.
2. Structure						
Tank type:	System tank	System tank	Natural lake	System tank	Non System tank	Non System tank
Age:	600 yrs.	600 yrs.	---	500 yrs.	300 yrs.	800 yrs.
Area:	16.05 sq. km	5 sq. km(app)	70.47 sq. km	7 sq. km	2.8 sq. km	5.2 sq. km
Depth:	9.3 m	3-5 m	1-2 m	2-3 m	---	3.7 m
Bunds						
Length:	8.25 Km	3.66 Km	No bunds	7.275 Km	5.07 Km	5.27 Km
Width:	3.6 m	---	Sloping banks	3 m	2.7 m	2.00 m
Supply-channel:	Kaveripakkam	Kambakkal	---	Suthukeny	Mirattunilai supply	Therkar river
Sluices:	10	6	---	7	5	8
3. Hydrology						
Catchment:	31.08 sq. km	9.89 sq. km	116.40 sq. km	10.36 sq. km	7.09 sq. km	5.748 sq. km
Intercepted:	---	---	636.28 sq. km	---	21.08 sq. km	---
Combined:	126.91 sq. km	11.19 sq. miles	754.69 sq. km	15.54 sq. km	28.17 sq. km	80.78 sq. km
Equivalent:	---	---	244.0 sq. km	11.4 sq. km	---	---
Yield:	214 M.cu.m	7.12 M.cu.m	34.32 M.cu.m	15.5 M.cu.m	6.75 M.cu.m	6.87 M.cu.m
Storage						
Capacity:	32.9 M.cu.m	3.77 M.cu.m	33.82 M.cu.m	15.29 M.cu.m	1.55 M.cu.m	3.62 M.cu.m
Duration:	6-8 months	6-8 months	3-4 months	6-8 months	3-5 months	2-3 months
4. Climatology						
Rainfall:	107.8 cm/Year	106.2 cm/Year	127 cm/Year	125 cm/Year	98.3 cm/Year	79.6 cm/Year
Rainy Days:	53 days/year	52.8 days/year	65 days/year	---	57.6 days/year	44.1 days/year
Mean temp.:	32°C	32°C	30°C	30°C	36°C	38°C
5. Culture systems						
Ayacut:	67.72 Sq.Km	4.45 Sq.Km	Not known	15.68 Sq.Km	2.79 Sq.Km	5.41 Sq.Km
Double crop:	25.42 Sq.Km	659.48 Ac.	---	---	---	---
Single crop:	42.31 Sq.Km	437.85 Ac.	Not known	---	2.4 Sq.Km	5.4 Sq.Km
Major crops:	Plantain, Paddy and Sugarcane	Paddy	Paddy, Groundnut	Paddy, Sugarcane	Paddy	Paddy
Minor crops:	Mulberry, Brinjal, Groundnut, Ragi and Castor	Ragi, Cotton and Millet	Millets, Cashew	Millets, Ragi	Groundnut, Ragi, Maize	Ragi, Cotton, Millet
Wetland forestry:	Acacia, Prosopis	Eucalyptus and Acacia, Prosopis	Acacia, Prosopis, Casuarina	Acacia, Casuarina	Eucalyptus, Acacia arabica	Acacia, Prosopis
Aquaculture:	Catfish, Mullets and Tilapia	Catfish, Tilapia and Carps	Tilapia, Mughil, Shrimp	Tilapia, Catfish, Carps	Catfish, Carps, Mullets	Catfish, Carps, Mullets

Chapter - VII

References

Ali, S. and S.D. Ripley. 1987. Compact Hand book of Birds of India and Pakistan. Bombay Natural History Society. Oxford University Press, Bombay.

Anonymous. 1973. 'Sad Tale of Irrigation'. Econ. Pol. Weekly, 7, 659-90.

Baliga, B.S. 1960. "Irrigation tanks and their problems". In: Studies in Madras administration, vol.2, 199-208, Government of Madras, India.

Baliga, B.S. 1962. District Gazetteers -South Arcot, Government of Madras.

Bhumbla. D.R 1978. Small Reservoirs: A Programme for Improving Rain-fed Agriculture, Society for the Promotion of Waste-land Development.

Centre for Science and Environment, 1985. The State of India's Environment, 1984-85. The Second Citizen's Report, New Delhi, pp.393.

Chandy. M. 1970. Fishes, National Book Trust, India, New Delhi, 183pp.

Chaturvedi. B.V. 1968. The origin and development of Tank irrigation in peninsular India, Deccan Geographer Vol. VI.

Conservation of Wetlands in India, 1989, Ministry of Environment and Forests, Government of India, New Delhi.

Cook. C.D.K., 1996, Aquatic and Wetland Plants of India, Oxford University Press, pp.385.

Daniel. J.C, 1983, The Book of Indian Reptiles, Bombay Natural History Society, Oxford Univ. Press, Bombay.

Derek. A.S. and Colin. M.P. 1989, A status overview of Asian Wetlands, Asian Wetlands Bureau, Malaysia.

Dugan. P, 1990, Wetland Conservation, A review of Current issues and Required Action, IUCN.

Francis. W, 1906, Madras District Gazetteers - South Arcot, Government Press, Madras.

Gartin. J.H, 1878, Manual of South Arcot District, Lawrence Asylum Press.

Government of India, 1989, Conservation of Wetlands in India, Ministry of Environment .and Forests, pp. 67.

Government of Pondicherry, 1989, Modernisation of Tank Irrigation Systems in Pondicherry Region of Union Territory of Pondicherry, Public Works Department. Vol-1: 125. pp.

Guhan. S, 1984, Irrigation in Tamil Nadu: A survey, Madras Institute of Development Studies, Madras. 75 p.

Indian Standards Institution, 1964, Methods of sampling and test (physical and chemical) for water and soil, Indian Standards Institution, New Delhi.

Janakarajan. S, 1991, In search of Tanks: Some Hidden Facts, Madras Institute of Development Studies, Madras, 38 pp.

Ludden. D, 1979, Patronage and irrigation in Tamil Nadu: A longterm view, In: The Indian Economic and Social History Review, 16 (3).

Maltby. E. and Turner. R.E. 1983, 'Wetlands of the world', Geographical Magazine, 55 (1), 12-17.

Matthew. K.M. 1991, An Excursion Flora of Central Tamil Nadu, India. Oxford & IBH Publishing co. Pvt. Ltd., New Delhi. 183 pp.

Ministry of Environment and Forestry, 1992, Conservation of Wetlands in India, GOI, New Delhi pp. 48.

Mukundan. T. M. 1988, The Ery Systems of South India. PPST Bulletin No.16 Madras.

Nadkarni. M.V. et al 1979, Impact of irrigation: Canal, Well and Tank irrigation in Karnataka, Himalaya Publishing House, Bombay.

Oswald. O. 1991, An expert system for the diagnosis of tank irrigated systems. Institute François de Pondicherry. pp. 157+

Palanisami. K. and Easter. K.W. 1983. The Tanks of South India, University of Minnesota, Minnesota, U.S.A.

Palanisami. K. and Easter. K.W. 1984. Irrigation tanks of south India: Management strategies and investment alternatives, Ind. Journal of Agri. Econ. 39: 214-223.

Ramaswamy. G. K. 1987. Evaluation of tank rehabilitation (Valuthani tank), ME thesis, CWR, Madras, India.

Rao. KL. 1979. India's Water Wealth. Orient Longman, pp. 267.

Scott. DA 1989. A Directory of Asian Wetlands. pp. 367-505, WWF, IUCN, ICBP, IWRB.

Scott. D.A. & Poole. C.M. 1989. A status overview of Asian Wetlands, NO.53. AWB, Kualalumpur.

Subramanian. S. 1985. "Some Features of Tank Irrigation in Tami Nadu. A Note", In; July development seminar, 397-402. MIDS, Madras.

Von. M and Subba Rao. K. V. 1980. Tank irrigation in semiarid tropical India, Part II: Technical features and economic performance, Economics Prog., Progress rep. no.8. ICRISAT, Patancheru, Andhra Pradesh, India, 52 p.

Whittaker. R. Common Indian Snakes. Macmillan India Ltd.

World Wide Fund, India's Wetlands, Mangroves & Coral Reefs India.

Chapter - VIII

Appendices

A. QUESTIONNAIRE
B. BIODIVERSITY
C. BIBLIOGRAPHIES
D. DOCUMENT FROM PWD, TN
E. THREE PUBLICATIONS
F. CONFESSIONS

1. QUESTIONNAIRE

Monitoring Ecosystem Perceptions of the Villagers around the Water Bodies

I. Background Information

1. Name of the Reservoir and its History:
2. Number of villages and their names associated with the Reservoir:
3. Area:
4. Water holding capacity

   (a) *Original* (b) *At present*

5. Catchment area

   Free: *Combined:*

6. Ayacut *I* Command area:
7. Crops

   Types: *Acreage:*

8. Level of underground water in three seasons:

   Dug wells *Bore wells* *Others*

   Season I Season II Season III

9. No. of sluices:

   Name of sluice *Sill level*

10. Do the following exist or not? Details

    (a) *Kudimaramathu:* (d) *Nattanmaikaran:*

    (b) *Neerkatti:* (e) *Kalvai maniyam:*

    (c) *Kanmaikatti:*

11. Where are the records maintained?
12. **Mamunama** document for your tank water distribution exists or not? If so, give details.
13. If there is no such document? How maintenance of channels and distribution of tank water are managed?
14. Maintenance details regarding: (within village and outside)

    (a) *Inlet channel* (c) *Branch channel*

    (b) *Main channel* (d) *Field channel*

15. Conditions of Tank Water Supply

    (a) *Adequate/regular* (b) *Adequate/irregular*

    (c) *Inadequate/regular* (d) *Inadequate/irregular*

    (e) *No supply* (f) *If adequate, by how much?*

    (g) *If regular, when?*

    (h) *Delay in supply; drainage and others*

    (i) *Any other specific problems faced*

16. How *many* additional sources of irrigation?
    (a) *Borewells:* (b) *Wells:*
    (c) *Smaller tanks:*
17. How many borewells are there in your village?
    (a) *Government:* (b) *Private Owned:*
    (c) *Depth:* (d) *Utility:*
18. How many canals are present in your area?
    (a) *How long are they usable?*
    (b) *What for do you use?*
19. Land holdings
    Major: *Minor:*
20. Longevity of water in the tank:
21. Rainfall: average for 10, 50 or 100 years.
    (a) *Annual:* (b) *Monthly:*
22. Temperature
    Yearly mean:
    Maximum: *Minimum:*
23. Wind velocity
    Yearly mean:
    Maximum: *Minimum:*
24. Others:

II. Identification of the Respondent

1. Village: 2. Name:
3. Age: 4. Sex:
5. Education: 6. Caste:
7. Distance from the tank: 8. Utility from the tank:
9. Land holding in the ayacut: 10. Relevance to the tank:

III. Socio-political Status of the Respondent

1. ex - Karnam 2. ex - Maniakarar 3. Sarpanch
4. Panchayat Board President / Member
5. Delegate of Farmers Association
6. Cooperative Society President
7. Political Functionary
8. MLA / ex-MLA / MP / ex-MP
9. Landlord / Small Farmer / Labourer
10. Irrigation owner / Irrigation labourer
11. Literate / Illiterate / employed / unemployed
12. Oldest citizenry: woman / Man

13. Government officer - Irrigation / Agriculture / Health / Public Works / Revenue / Education / Others

IV. Perceptions of the Respondent on the Following:

A. Plants

1. Is the plant cover satisfactory? Yes / No
   - (a) *Foreshore -* (b) *Tank bed -*
   - (e) *Inward slope -* (d) *Surrounding area of bund*
   - (e) *Outward slope of bund*
2. If not, what are your needs?
   - (a) *More trees* (b) *More shrubs*
   - (e) *More hems* (d) *More grass*
3. Was it better or worse than before?
4. What are the reasons?
   - (a) *Natural causes -* (b) *Human causes -*
5. What are the plants used for the following purposes?
   - (a) *Medicines -* (b) *Fuel -*
   - (e) Food - (d) *Fodder -*
   - (e) *Others -*
6. Are these plants monopolized or accessible for all?
7. Do you notice any changes in the plant cover? If yes, what are the changes?
8. What are the weeds in your lank?
9. Are they useful? How?
10. If harmful how do you deal with them?

B. Animals

1. What are the common animals in your region?
   - (a) *Mammals* (b) *Birds* (c) *Reptiles*
   - (d) *Insec1s* (e) *Others*
2. Name the uses of animals in your place?
   - (a) *Food* (b) *Medicine*
   - (c) *Hide* (d) *Others*
3. What are the harmful animals in your place? What are the remedies?
4. Are there recent changes of animals or their populations?
   - (a) *Increase* (b) *Decrease*
   - (c) *Disappearance*
5. What are the likely reasons for the above changes?
6. What are the types of animals in the local waters? Fishes, molluscans, frogs, etc.,
   - (a) *Paddy field* (b) *Channels* (c) *Tank*

7. What are their uses?
8. How much quantity of food animals you get?
   (a) *At a time* (b) *Per year*
9. Are they monopolised or common property or *someone* has rights over them?
10. Do you find anything interesting with any of the animals?
11. Do you get any new birds to your tank during any season of the year?
12. Where do you think they come from?'
13. Why do they come to your tank? Any idea
14. Do they nest *I* roost around your tank? If so, where?
15. Do you poach the birds and other animals?
16. If so, for what?
   (a) *Food* - (b) *Sale* - (c) *Medicine* -
   (d) *Other materials*- (e) *Fun* -
17. How do you poach them?
   (a) Guns (b) *Nets* (c) *Others*
18. Do the outsiders come and poach them?
19. Do you know that you should not poach them?
20. Do you know about their ecological roles?

C. Soil

1. What types of soils are generally found in the command area?
2. Is the soil fertile? Yes / No. What are the reasons?
   (a) *Legumes* (b) *Microbes*
   (c) *Animal wastes* (d) *Others*
3. Do you use local soil for any purpose?
   (a) *Agriculture* (b) *Household purpose*
   (c) *Pottery* (d) *Brickworks*
   (e) *Others*
4. What are the problems associated with soil?

Erosion / pests I infertility

5. What are the effects of these problems?
6. How do you solve the above?
7. What improvements *I* inputs do you need?
8. Have you noticed any change in the soil quality? What are the changes?
9. Do you lose soil during flooding? From where to where?
10. Does it get replenished? How?
11. How much is the encroached area?
12. How is the encroached area used?

D. Water

1. For how long in a year you have water in the tank?
2. What are the sources of water to your tank?
3. When does the tank reach Full Tank Level storage (FTL)?
4. How do you use the tank water?
   Drinking I irrigation I washing I cattle bathing
5. For how long in a year do you use the tank water for irrigation?
6. Is the water enough for your needs?
7. When did you get most satisfactory water supply? How long?
8. When did you experience the worst water scarcity? How long? Why?
   Monsoon failure I Urbanisation I Improper management
9. How many wells in your village?
   (a) *Usual depth* (b) *Ownership* (c) *Utility*
10. Which water do *you* use for drinking and cooking?
11. What is the energy used for water lifting?
    Manpower / Electric or Diesel Engine / Animal
12. What are the uses of these wells?
13. Are the above available for all people or not?
14. When do *you* have excess or enough well water? Why?
15. When do you experience shortages in *your* wells? What are the reasons?
16. Do you get enough rainfall?
17. Where does it go ultimately?
18. Do the tail-end lands get water?
19. Do you face disputes in respect of
    (i) maintenance of channels
    (ii) *distribution d water*
    (iii) *any other incidents*
20. How are the problems resolved?
21. What do you feel about the functioning of village level institution/ organisation regarding maintenance of channels; distribution of tank water and resolving of conflicts among the members?
22. Do you get diseases from the waters of canals, tank, borewells and wells?
23. Which water do you feel most healthy?
24. Do you experience flooding? How frequent is it?
25. Are the bunds of your lank strong enough to withstand flooding?
26. Were there overflows from the tank in the past?
27. Were there cases of bund breaching in the past?
28. What are the rates of water sale?
29. How much do you spend for water?

30. How many borewells exist in the ayacut?
31. Are there borewells in the tank bed?

E. Agriculture

1. Do all the crops depend on tank water?
2. Is the water enough for crops?
3. What are the other sources of supply?
4. Did you suffer drought and crop loss anytime?
   (a) How many times?
   (b) What measures have been taken to face them?
5. Do you adopt crop rotation?
6. What are the pests affecting your crops?
   (a) *Insects* (b) *Fungi* (c) *Bacteria*
   (d) Worms (e) *Others*
7. How do you control pests in the
   (a) *Field* (b) *Storage*
8. Are you applying any biological control measures? What type of biological control?
9. If pesticides are used, what are they? How much quantity?
10. What is the major group of pesticides used?
    Organochlorines / Organophosphates / Carbamates
11. Are they effective
    (a) *Temporarily*? (b) *Permanently*?
12. If not, why?
13. What type of fertilizers do you use?
    (a) *Chemical* (b) *Compost* (c) *Others*
14. Do you adopt organic farming methods?
15. Did you discontinue any old crops?
    For what reason?
    Where are the seed stocks?
16. Are there any changes in the yield?
17. How frequently you change the variety of the crops?
    10, 20, 30 years?
18. Did you introduce any new crop recently? Where from you get the Germplasm?
19. Which crops - old or new - need more water?
20. What are the weeds in your field?
21. Do you practice agriculture in the tank premises?
    (a) *Shoreline* (b) *Tank-bed* (c) *Part of tank*
    (d) *All over*

F. Aquaculture

1. What are the animals in your water bodies?
   (a) *Crabs* (b) *Fishes* (c) *Prawns*
   (d) *Frogs* (e) *Others*
2. What are used for food purposes? If so by whom? How long in a year?
3. Whether aquaculture is practised?
4. What are the types of fishes cultured?
5. Are fishes continuously cultured?
6. Who owns them or are they common property?
7. Are there any traditional rights for any community over the fisheries?
8. Do you get edible animals in the channels and paddies?
9. Do people get any diseases from eating these animals? Any instance?
10. How were the above cured?

G. Animal Husbandry

1. What are the domesticated animals in your village? What are their uses?
   (a) *Milk* (b) *Meat* (c) *Energy*
   (d) *Skin* (e) *Eggs*
   Types *Numbers* *Uses*
2. Where from do they drink water?
3. Do you feed them on local produce?
4. How do you use animal wastes?
   (a) *Manure* (b) *Energy*
5. Where do the cattle graze-inside/outside the tank?
6. If inside,
   (a) *how much area is useful for this purpose*
   (b) *for how long*

H. Social / Wetland Forestry

1. Is there social forestry? If so, what are the species planted?
2. Where do you grow them? In side or out side the tank what is the acreage?
3. What is the yield of each species?
4. What products do they yield?
   (a) *Fire wood* (b) *Fodder* (c) *Others*
5. Who uses them?
6. Do you have forestry in the tank?
7. If so,
   (a) *only in the shoreline,*
   (b) *one section of the tank*
   (c) *most of the tank*

I. Pollution and Health

1. Are your waters polluted? How?
2. What are the reasons for pollution?
3. Are there industries in the neighbourhood? Name them
   Large I Small / Medium / Cottage
4. Do they cause pollution of air?
5. How many of your villagers are employed there?
6. What are the major diseases you suffer from? How long? Reasons?
7. How do you get treated *I* cured?

J. People

1. How many are tail-end farmers?
2. Do they get "common" waters?
3. Or do they buy?
4. Do they depend on rainfall?
5. Do people migrate to other places - *temporarily or permanently*?
6. Are there part-time *I* seasonal workers sentence here? How many?
7. What do they do otherwise?
8. How many are totally unemployed?
9. How is the general awareness of people on the state of the tank?
10. Are there child labourers in the farms?
11. What is the rate of literacy in your village?

K. Others

1. Do you use the tank banks and in what ways?
2. How do you utilise tank beds when there is no water?
3. Who does the following? Since how long?
   (a) *Kudimaramathu* (b) *Neerkatti*
   (c) *Nattanmaikaram* (d) *kalvai maniyam*
   (e) *Kanmaikatti* (f) *Thotti*
4. Do you agree with the official version on the tank fully? If not, in what respects do you disagree?
5. Are there encroachments into the tank area? By whom? Any deterrent action taken or not?
6. Do you need the tank?
7. If not, why?
8. If yes, are you happy with it or need inputs?
9. What are the improvements you suggest?
10. Do you feel any problem due to social forestry of land?
    If yes, what are they?
11. What are the reasons for these problems?
12. Do you have any suggestions to over-come or solve these problems?

13. Is there any increase or decrease in the animal and plant species in the forestland?
    If yes, what are the reasons?
14. Do you have any agreement with the neighbouring village to get over flooded and drainage water from their tanks?
15. Do you have any agreement with the neighbouring village for supply of water from your tank?
16. Who takes the charge of releasing and blocking of water through outlet channel?
17. Is there any traditional method to conserve water through agricultural operations? If so, what are they?
18. Have you experienced *any* difference between tank irrigation and well irrigation with reference to growth, yield, pests of crops and fertilizers and pesticide inputs to crops ?
19. Is there *any* contribution by the tank in recharging the groundwater? What is your opinion regarding this?
20. Do you get seepage from the tank to your well?
21. Does your village have 'Oorani'? Is it maintained well?
22. How many number of labourers are employed per acre starting from nursery to harvesting?
23. What is the normal rate of daily wages?
    Male- *Female -* *Child labourers -*
24. Are there any NGOs assisting you?
25. Are the government officials helpful?

2. BIODIVERSITY

1. TAXONOMY

A. Plants

1. **Acanthaceae**
   Acanthus
   Adhatoda
   Andrographis
   Asystasia
   Blastania
   Blepharis
   Justicia
   Lepidagathis
   Peristrophe
2. **Agavaceae**
   Agave
3. **Aizoaceae**
   Corbichonia
   Mollugo
4. **Alangiaceae**
   Alangium
5. **Amaranthaceae**
   Achyranthes
   Aerva
   Alternanthera
   Amaranthus
   Celosia
   Digera
   Gomphrena
   Psilotrichum
   Stachytarpheta
6. **Anacardiaceae**
   Anacardium
7. **Apocyanaceae**
   Carissa
   Ichnocarpus
   Nerium
   Nymphaea
   Thevetia
8. **Arecaceae**
   Borassus
   Cocos
   Phoenix
9. **Aristolochiaceae**
   Aristolochia
10. **Asclepiadaceae**
    Calotropis
    Caralluma
    Ceropegia
    Sarcostemma
    Secraniga
    Tylophora
11. **Asperaceae**
    Elephantopus
12. **Asteraceae**
    Echinops
    Eclipta
    Parthenium
    Tridax
    Vernonia
13. **Boraginaceae**
    Coldenia
    Coleus
    Heliotropium
14. **Cactaceae**
    Opuntia
15. **Capparaceae**
    Cadaba
    Capparis
    Cleome
16. **Caryophyllaceae**
    Polygala
17. **Ceratophyllaceae**
    Ceratophyllum
18. **Chenopodiaceae**
    Suaeda
    Chloroxylon
19. **Clusiaceae**
    Calophyllum
    Garcinia
20. **Combretaceae**
    Calycopteris
    Combretum
    Quisqualis

21. **Commelinaceae**
Commelina
22. **Convolvulaceae**
Evolvulus
Ipomoea
Merremia
Rivea
23. **Cucurbitaceae**
Cephalandra
Citronella
Coccinia
Cucumis
Luffa
Melothria
Mukia
24. **Cyperaceae**
Cyperus
Typha
Kyllinga
25. **Euphorbiaceae**
Acalypha
Breynia
Croton
Euphorbia
Flueggea
Jatropha
Macaranga
Micrococca
Phyllanthus
Tragia
26. **Fabaceae**
Abrus
Acacia
Aeschynomene
Albizia
Alysicarpus
Bauhinia
Butea
Canavalia
Cassia
Crotalaria
Delonix
Indigofera
Mimosa
Parkinsonia
Peltophorum
Pongamia
Prosopis
Samanea
Sesbania
Stylosanthes
Tamarindus
Tephrosia
Wattakaka
27. **Flacourtiaceae**
Flacourtia
28. **Hydrocharitaceae**
Hydrilla
Ottelia
Vallisneria
29. **Hydrophyllaceae**
Hydrolea
30. **Lamiaceae**
Anisomeles
31. **Lauraceae**
Cassytha
32. **Liliaceae**
Aloe
Asparagus
Gloriosa
33. **Loganiaceae**
Strychnos
34. **Loranthaceae**
Dendrophthoe
35. **Lythraceae**
Ammania
36. **Malvaceae**
Abutilon
Bombax
Hibiscus
Pavonia
Sida
Thespesia
37. **Marsiliaceae**
Marsilea

38. **Melastomataceae**
    Memecylon
39. **Meliaceae**
    Azadirachta Indica
    Melia
40. **Menispermaceae**
    Cissampelos
    Cocculus
41. **Moraceae**
    Ficus
    Moringa
42. **Myrtceae**
    Syzygium
    Eucalyptus
    Eugenia
    Murraya
43. **Najadaceae**
    Najas
44. **Nyctaginaceae**
    Boerhavia
45. **Nympheaceae**
    Nelumbo
46. **0leaceae**
    Jasminum
    Olea
47. **Pandanaceae**
    Pandanus
48. **Papaveraceae**
    Argemone
49. **Passifloraceae**
    Passiflora
50. **Pedaliaceae**
    Pedalium
51. **Poaceae**
    Apluda
    Aristida
    Arundo
    Brachiaria
    Bulbostylis
    Chloris
    Cynodon
    Dactyloctenium
    Digitaria
    Eleusine
    Eragrostis
    Fimbristylis
    Heteropogon
    Ischaemum
    Perotis
    Saccharum
    Vetiveria
52. **Portulaceae**
    Portulaca
53. **Rabiaceae**
    Canthium
54. **Rhamnaceae**
    Ziziphus
55. **Rubiaceae**
    Borreria
    Morinda
    Oldenlandia
    Randia
56. **Rutaceae**
    Glycosmis
57. **Sapindaceae**
    Cardiospermum Dodonaea
58. **Simaroubaceae**
    Ailanthus
59. **Solanaceae**
    Datura
    Lycopersicon
    Physalis
    Ricinus
    Solanum
60. **Stercuiliaceae**
    Corchorus
61. **Taccaceae**
    Tacca
62. **Verbenaceae**
    Gmelina
    Ocimum
    Phyla
    Premna
    Tectona
    Vitex
    Lantana

Leonotis

63. **Vitaceae**
Cissus
Parthenocissus

64. **Zygophyllaceae**
Tribulus

B. Butterflies

1. **Papiliodae**
Papilio
Polidorous

2. **Pieridae**
Catopsilia
Delias
Eurema
Hebomoia

3. **Danaidae**
Danaus
Euploea

4. **Satyridae**
Ariadne
Biblio
Hypolimnas
Junonia
Melanitis
Mycalesis
Telechinia
Vanesia

C. Fishes

1. **Siluridae**
Wallago

2. **Bagridae**
Aorichthys

3. **Clariidae**
Clarias

4. **Channidae**
Channa

5. **Anabantidae**
Anabas

6. **Notopteridae**
Notopterus

7. **Mugilidae**
Liza

8. **Cichlidae**
Oreochromis

9. **Anguillidae**
Anguilla

10. **Cyprinidae**
Catla
Cirrhinus
Labeo

D. Amphibians

1. **Ranidae**
Rana

2. **Bufonidae**
Bufo

3. **Rhacophoridae**
Rhacophorus

E. Reptiles

1. **Emydidae**
Melanochelys

2. **Trionychidae**
Lissemys

3. **Geckonidae**
Hemidactylus

4. **Agamidae**
Calotes
Setana

5. **Scincidae**
Mabuya

6. **Varanidae**
Varanus

7. **Typhlopidae**
Typhlina

8. **Boinae**
Eryx

9. **Colubridae**
Ahaetulla
Amphiesma
Atretium
Dendrelaphis
Ptyas
Xenochrophis

10. **Elapidae**
Bungarus
Naja

11. **Viperidae**
    Vipera
    Echis

F. Birds

1. **Podicipitidae**
   Podiceps
2. **Pelecanioae**
   Pelecanus
3. **Phalacrocoracidae**
   Phalacrocorax
4. **Ardeidae**
   Ardea
   Ardeola
   Bubulcus
   Egretta
   Nycticorax
5. **Ciconidae**
   Anastomus
   Ciconia
   Mycteria
6. **Threskiornithidae**
   Threskiornis
7. **Phoenicopteridae**
   Phoenicopterus
8. **Anatidae**
   Anas
   Aythya
   Netta
   Nettapus
   Tadorna
9. **Accipitridae**
   Accipiter
   Circus
   Elanus
   Haliastur
   Milvus
   Pandien
10. **Falconidae**
    Falcon
11. **Phasianidae**
    Francolinus
12. **Turnicidae**
    Turnix
13. **Rallidae**
    Amaurornis
    Fulica
14. **Charadriidae**
    Calidris
    Charadrius
    Gallinago
    Limosa
    Numanius
    Trianga
    Vanellus
15. **Charadriae**
    Escalus
16. **Recurvirostridae**
    Himantopus
17. **Glarioledae**
    Cursorius
18. **Laridae**
    Chlidonias
    Gelochelidon
    Larus
    Sterna
19. **Columbidae**
    Columba
    Streptopelia
20. **Psittacidae**
    Psittacula
21. **Cucueidae**
    Clamator
    Cuculus
22. **Strigidae**
    Athene
23. **Caprimulgidae**
    Caprimulgus
24. **Apodidae**
    Cypsiurus
25. **Alcedinidae**
    Alcedo
    Carlyle
    Halcyon
26. **Meropidae**
    Merops

27. Upupidae
Upupa
28. Coraciidae
Coracias
29. Capitonidae
Megalaima
30. Picidae
Dinopium
31. Pittidae
Pitta
32. Alaudidae
Alauda
Ammomanes
Eremopterix
33. Hirundinidae
Hirundo
34. Laniidae
Lanius
Tephrodornis
35. Oriolidae
Oriolus
36. Dicruridae
Dicrurus
37. Artamidae
Artamus
38. Sturnidae
Acridotheres
Sturnus
39. Corvidae
Corvus
Dendrocitta
40. Campephagidae
Coracina
Lamius
Tephrodornis
41. Irenidae
Aegithina
42. Pycononotidae
Pycnonotus
43. Muscicapidae
Acrocephalus
Copsychus
Cisticola
Orthotomus
Prinia
Phylloscopus
Locustella
Saxicida
Saxicoloides
Terpsiphone
Turdoides
44. Motacillidae
Anthus
Motacilla
45. Dicaeidae
Dicaeum
46. Nectariniidae
Nectarinia
47. Ploceidae
Passer
Ploceus
Lonchura

G. Mammals

1. Leporidae
Lepus
2. Canidae
Canis
Vulpes
3. Herpestidae
Herpestes
4. Muridae
Bandicoot
Mus
Rattus
Tatera
5. Felidae
Felis
6. Viverridae
Paradoxurus
Viverricula

2. NOTES

A. Plants

1. **Abrus precatorius (Kuntumani):** A conspicuous wiry climber having scarlet seeds with black bottom. Seeds are used as Jeweller's weights, for necklaces and other ornaments. Occurs in the southern and western banks of Kaliveli. An indicator of dry evergreen forests.
2. **Acacia arabica (Karuvelam):** A moderate sized tree reported from all the tanks. Cultivated for fire wood. The wood is also used for agricultural purposes. Acacia plantations in the tanks provide very good roosting site for many migratory and resident avifauna. The nitrogen fixing ability contributes to the increased nutrient quality of the soil.
3. **Adhatoda zeylanica (Adhatoda):** A dense shrub with a foetid scent used as a live fence in villages. Leaves and roots are used by locals to treat respiratory problems especially asthma. An infusion is used as an insecticide.
4. **Aerva lanata:** A many branched under shrub and weed in agricultural fields. It is used in native medicine to cure poisoning. Also used in some religious rituals.
5. **Agave americana:** A typical agave reported from Kambikudi usually cultivated as a source of fiber. Also used as a hedge plant. Provides hiding place for many reptiles and lizards.
6. **Ailanthus excelsa:** A large evergreen tree species. Cultivated for ornamental purposes. The hard wood is suitable for making sea-oing boats, the catamarans.
7. **Alangium salvifolium (Azhinjil):** A small deciduous tree of semi-arid localities. Wood is live brown, hard, scented and useful for ornamental work. In the foreshore of Mirattunilai. Alangium is found abundantly indicating that a forest existed in the locality in the past.
8. **Albizia amara (Usil):** A moderate sized deciduous tree an indicator of dry evergreen formations. The bark is strong and used in making building materials and agricultural tools.
9. **Aloe vera (Kathazhai):** A gregarious shrub. Used as a medicine in treating the bone fracture. Also cultivated for fiber and as a hedge.
10. **Anacardium occidentale (Munthri):** A small tree cultivated in dry, barren lands for its Kernel of high nutritional value. Abundant in the catchments of Kaliveli.
11. **Andrographis paniculata (Nila-Vembu):** An erect herb common in the agricultural fields. This annual herb maintains its population with the help of persistent soil seed banks. The whole plant is used in local medicine.
12. **Apluda mutica (Manda pilla):** A very common grass found in the tank bed and foreshore, often seen scrambling over bushes. It is a fairly good fodder species when young.

13. **Argemone mexicana (Prema thandu):** A strong branched prickly annual reported from Kambikudi. Regeneration is effected by persistent seed banks in the soil. Seeds and oil are used for adulteration.
14. **Aristolochia bracteata (Aadutheenda palai):** A perennial herb seen in almost all tanks. The plant is bitter due to the accumulation of secondary metabolites. Many butterflies lay eggs on it. They accumulate toxic substances in their bodies after feeding on this plant which helps them to deter predators.
15. **Asparagus racemosus (Thannir-vittan):** A common wiry climber occurring in the forested areas; Very important in traditional medicine. Tubers are collected in wild.
16. **Azadirachta indica (Vempu):** A very important and useful tree. Very common in human settlements, tank bonds and surrounding thickets. It is a source of food, medicine and pesticides. Large scale cultivation of this tree in the barren lands of the catchment of tanks is essential.
17. **Bombax ceiba (Ilava):** A very conspicuous tree of gigantic size in some areas. Wood is more durable under water therefore used for making boats. It gives a gum, used in medicine. The cotton surrounding the seeds is used for stuffing pillows and beds. It is also a good refuge for toddy cat, squirrels, bats and many birds. If exploited properly this tree can play a major role in local economy.
18. **Borassus flabellifer (Panai):** A commonly found palm on the tank embankments and surroundings. Every part of this palm is used. Trunk is used for rafters, water pipes, troughs etc. the leaves are used for thatching, fans, hats, basket work etc. the pulp of the fruit is edible. The peduncle yields a toddy which is fermented to arrack or boiled down into Jaggerry. This tree is often seen in clusters. Such palm country supports considerable faunal diversity especially birds like Palm swift and Baya are inextricably attached to Palmyra trees.
19. **Boerhavia diffusa (Mukkurttai koti):** A diffuse herb common in the wastelands and cultivated fields. This herb has medicinal properties and is used in Ayurvedic preparations.
20. **Butea monosperma (Poarasu):** Another deciduous tree species typical to the native type of vegetation. This trees attracts considerable number of birds when in bloom. The wood is durable and a resin is extracted from the tree.
21. **Calophyllum inophyllum (Punnai):** A moderate sized ornamental tree. The wood and seeds are economically important. Oil extracted from the seeds is used in Ayurvedic preparations. This lush green tree with thick foliage is a good roosting ground and hiding place for various animals.
22. **Canavalia mollis:** A prostrate climber found in the thickets and scrub jungles. This plant is often seen in association with Ipomoea. The plant is valuable as a sand binder because of its nodal, roots.

23. **Calotropis gigantea (Erakku):** This is a common shrub seen in the coast lands and embankments of all tanks. Many butterflies have been found laying their eggs on this plant. Some of them accumulate toxins from the leaves. The bark of this shrub gives strong fiber and the silky filore obtained from fruit is used to stuff pillows.

24. **Canthium coromandelicum (Karag chedi):** This thorny shrub is very common in the thickets and scrubs near tanks. This plant shows considerable variation in physiognomy depending on water availability. It bears abundant fleshy fruits which are usually eaten by avian frugivores. The stems and branches are largely used for dry fencing by villagers.

25. **Cephalandra indica (Kovai):** A pretty climber with large white flowers and oblong scarlet fruit with velvety seeds. This is reported from the thickets on the banks of Kaliveli and vicinity of agricultural fields. Fruit is eaten by locals, raw and cooked. This plant can be cultivated in large scale for its fruits which have good market value. A number of birds are seen feeding on these fruits.

26. **Cissampelos pareira (Vatta-t-tiruppi):** A more or less tomentosa climber with rotund leaves common at Ousteri and Kaliveli. This climber is seen only in undisturbed patches of vegetation. So this can be considered as a very good indicator of natural forest vegetation.

27. **Cocos nucifera (Tenga):** The coconut palm, seen cultivated on the vicinity of most tanks. Various parts of the tree are used by villagers. Wood is used for bridges. Leaves are plaited into mats, and used for thatching, fencing, partitions etc. Toddy is obtained by tapping the peduncles and is convertible into arrack, 'Jaggeri'. Kernel of the fruit is edible and yields edible oil. Fibers of the pericarp are used for cordage, matting etc.

28. **Cynodon dactylon (Arugam pillu):** A prostrate grass reported from the vicinity of perennial tanks and fallow agriculture lands. This grass is a very good soil binder and a highly nutritious fodder. Villagers use it as a herbal medicine for treating stomach ailments.

29. **Datura stramonium (Umathai):** The thorn apple, reported from the banks of Kaliveli, Kambikudi and Mirattunilai. Seeds of this plant are medicinal in small amounts and poisonous in excess. The large white flower attracts a number of insects.

30. **Delonix regia (Padenarayan):** This introduced tree besides being ornamental is a host to a number of resident birds, for roosting and nesting, on ~s thickly foliaged crown.

31. **Dendrophthoe falcata (Pulluruvi):** A woody parasitic shrub occurring in the forest patches around Kaliveli. It is seen parasitic on Memecylon. The long fused corolla tube and bright purple color is an adaptation for bird pollination. In neotropics it is a good example for long-term-coevolution and special plant-animal interactions.

32. **Dodonaea angustifolia (Virali):** A shrub noted from vicinity of Kaliveli and Ousteri. This plant is more or less gregarious especially seen dominating the eroded landscapes. Wood is used for tool-handles. A good soil binder useful in land reclamation. This plant is also used as live fencing.
33. **Eucalyptus globulus:** Eucalyptus is widely planted for raising social forestry plantations. This tree grows faster and is economically viable. But as its leaves are rich in secondary metabolic products decomposition rate is much delayed. The foliage is not palatable for cattle. During field surveys our team has observed conversion of arable land to Eucalyptus plantations. This practice is unsustainable.
34. **Ficus sps. (F. bengalensis, F. religiosa, F. hispida):** This forms a special group of plant species, widely distributed and Ecologically important. They are pivotal species in many communities as they provide rewards to the animals when other food sources are not available.
35. **Flacourtia indica:** This plant is typical of dry evergreen patches of Coromandel Coast reported from the banks of Kaliveli an indicator species of past vegetation type of the area and the associated fauna.
36. **Garcinia indica:** This tree is reported from the thickets around Kaliveli. Another typical element of the original flora of the region.
37. **Hydrilla verticillata:** A typical hydrophyte reported from Kaliveli in rainy season.
38. **Ipomoea cornea:** A scandent shrub very common in the seasonally water logged areas of all the tanks. It is able to survive in terrestrial and aquatic habitat and harbours a number of birds-mostly aquatic. Ipomoea islands are seen in almost all tanks when they are flooded.
39. **Jasminum angustifolium:** This climber is reported from the thickets on the banks of most tanks. It is a wild counterpart of common Jasmine. Thus a Germplasm for breeding the commercially important Jasmine. It is also used in traditional health care system.
40. **Lantana camara:** A weak stemmed shrub introduced as an ornamental plant but has invaded the natural plant communities in the tank vicinity. The plant attracts a number of butterflies.
41. **Leucas aspera:** A common weed in the crop fields. The white flowers attract many insects. This herbs has an important role in traditional health management. Reputedly it has mosquito repellent properties.
42. **Pandanus sps:** This shrubby, gregarious plant is seen in the moist tracts near tanks. This is a good soil binder and usually planted as a live fence on the banks of the streams passing through the agricultural fields and on the banks of irrigation channels. These thickets usually harbour a number of animal species like birds, reptiles and small mammals. Leaves are used for making mats.

43. **Phoenix loureirii:** This palm has a shrub like appearance as it does not grow more than three feet. But it is an important component of the thorn forest vegetation. This plant is utilized by locals in a number of ways. Leaves are used for making fences and fiber is extracted from the rachis. The stem is burnt to charcoal. The nuts are relished by birds and bats.

44. **Phyllanthus spp.:** Two species of Phyllanthus are reported from the banks of Kaliveli. One is a herb (P. amarus) the other a shrub (P. pinnatus). The former is used against liver diseases. The latter's fruits are used in the Ayurvedic preparations. These two plants are found occurring only in wild conditions. If their Germplasm is not preserved they may disappear from the locality very soon.

45. **Prosopis juliflora:** This fast growing coppicing plant is very productive and meets the firewood requirements of the rural population. Apart from enriching the soil with nitrogen, Prosopis provides *very* good roosting sites for local and migratory birds and other animals.

46. **Strychnos nux-vomica:** This large tree occurs near Mirattunilai tank, perhaps as a remnant of the forest once existed in this place. The wood of this tree is very hard and thus used for that making handles for various agricultural and other tools.

47. **Suaeda maritima:** A prostrate succulent herb occurring in the tank bed of Kaliveli indicating the salinity of the soil; a typical halophyte. It is interesting to note that the reeds are seen growing at the same place, very unexpectedly.

48. **Tamarindus indica:** This, large tree is commonly seen growing in all villages and plays an important role in the village Economy. The fruits are collected and sold and form is an important Ingredient of many Indian culinary preparations. The wood is very hard and durable. Perhaps in vegetating the wastelands of villages. Tamarind should be a permacultural component.

49. **Tectona grandis:** This deciduous tree is cultivated in large scale for timber production. It is profitable due to many factors like high demand and profit margin on the wood and high survival rate of the saplings.

50. **Tylophora indica:** This climber is reported from the thickets of Kaliveli's banks and known as a medicine for asthma Germplasm of the plant should be preserved and the chances of commercial cultivation of the species needs exploration.

52. **Typha angusta:** The only reed present in the seasonal water bodies under study has significant role in local economy and ecology. Reeds are used for thatching houses by locals and the half burned portions as manure in the field. It is breeding ground for many aquatic organisms and migratory birds.

53. **Vetiveria zizanioides:** A tall grass reported from water logged beds of Kaliveli and Ousteri. This grass is a nutritious fodder. Roots are

medicinally important. Cultivation of these in large scale may benefit cattle. The underground parts can be used for ayurvedic preparations.

54. **Vitex negundo:** A tall shrub. It is a medicinal plant of immense significance. This shrub is used in various ayurvedic preparations. Crushed plant parts are found effective as mosquito repellent. This shrub is used for live fencing by villagers, as it is insecticidal.

B. Butterflies

1. **Ariadne merione (Jocker):** Occurs in almost all tanks; prefers over-ripened fruits; caterpillars remain on the under sides of leaves; generally feeds on Passiflora plants.
2. **Catopsilia crocale (Common emigrant):** Present in all tanks; powerful flier; feeds on nectar of flowers; mud puddling in large numbers on tank bed; main food plants of caterpillars: Cassia fistula, Butea monosperma, Bauhinia.
3. **Danaus chrysippus (Plain tiger):** Present in all tanks; Feeds on Calotropis gigantea. The caterpillars accumulate toxic chemicals which helps the adults to deter predators. For this reason, this butterfly is mimicked by the, female Danaid egg fly.
4. **Danaus genutia (Blue Glossy tiger):** Present in Kaliveli, Ousteri and Mirattunilai; prefers scrub jungles, Main food plants of caterpillars are Calotropis gigantea, Wattakaka volubilis etc.
5. **Delias eucharis (Common Jezebel):** Sighted in all tanks. One of the most common butterflies in the tank environment. This butterfly is distasteful due to the presence of poisons derived from its food plants, especially from Dendrophthoe falcata.
6. **Euploea core (Common Crow):** Observed in all tanks except Kambikudi; a local migrant; its caterpillars teed on a wide range of plants including all species of Ficus, and Nerium Sp.
7. **Eurema hecabe (Common Grass Yellow):** Present in Kaliveli, Ousteri, Mirattunilai and Kambikudi. Very common species through out the year. They are often seen mud puddling on damp patches adjacent to the tank or agricultural fields. The main food plants of caterpillars are the common trees found in tank surroundings, like Cassia fistula, Pithecellobium dulce, Albizia lebbeck, Caesalpinia spp. Perhaps this is the reason for the wide geographical distribution of this species.
8. **Hebomoia glaucippe (Great orange tip):** Occurs in Ousteri, Mirattunilai and Kambikudi. Largest butterfly among the whites. The camouflage pattern of its underside makes it almost invisible among fallen leaves and stones. Eggs are laid singly on Capparis. When alarmed its caterpillar mimics the snake in appearance.
9. **Hypolimnas bolina (Great egg fly):** Present only in Kaliveli. Male fly is highly territorial, Female is a perfect mimic of the Common crow. They lay eggs on Portulaca which is abundant in the tank bed.

10. **Hypolimnas misippus (Danaid egg fly):** Absent only in Pillaipakkam. Prefers open country; most abundant during rains; The male is highly territorial; lays eggs on Abutilon sp.
11. **Precis almana (peacock pansy):** Sighted only in Kaliveli. Prefers dry and arid tracts of wetlands. Shows considerable morphological variation in dry and wet seasons. Usually attracted by marigold flowers.
12. **Precis hierta (Yellow pansy):** Observed in all tanks except Mirattunilai; Prefers dry open plains; very territorial.
13. **Precis lemonias (Lemon pansy):** Absent in Pillaipakkam; more frequent in thickets; fond of flowers and can be seen basking on the ground or on low foliage Lepidagathis.
14. **Mycalesis perseus (Common bush Brown):** Occurs in Kaveripakkam, Kaliveli and Ousteri. These drab colored medium sized butterflies generally prefer wetter and wooded places. They lay eggs on grasses, especially on bamboos and are attracted by overripe fruits, but not by flowers.
15. **Papilio demoleus (Lime butterfly):** These swallow tails are found in Kaliveli and Ousteri One of the favorite food plants of its caterpillars is Aegle marmelos.
16. **Papilio polytes (Common mormon):** This is the most common swallow tail that occurs near human habitations. Prefers curry leaf and citrus plants for laying eggs. Females mimic poisonous 'rose' butterflies.
17. **Pachliopta aristolochiae (Common rose):** Present in all tanks except Pillaipakkam. Red bodied, preferring Aristolochiae for laying eggs. Inedible due to the presence of toxic substances.
18. **Pachliopta hector (Crimson rose):** Common butterfly in all the wetlands containing toxins as deterrents against predators. Migratory; feeds on nectar. Lays eggs on the growing shoots of food plants. Eggs are yellowish green; Instar larvae resemble bird droppings. Eats Annona and Aristolochia Reported as endangered in oriental region.
19. **Telechinia violae (Tawny castor):** Occurs In four tanks. The habitat requirements and the life history strategy are little known.
20. **Vanessa cardui (Painted lady):** One of the widely acclaimed migrant present only in Ousteri during monsoon. This butterfly prefers open moist places generally found associated with the plants like Blumea etc.

C. Fishes

1. **Anabas testudineus:** This fish is capable of tolerating high degree of salinity. Present only in Ousteri and Kaliveli. In Kaliveli this is noted even near the Yedayanthittu estuary. Known to have medicinal properties it is widely consumed by villagers.
2. **Aorichthys seenghala (Koombu keluthy):** A fish capable of tolerating brackish waters. Like *Wallago attu* this fish also uses *ooranis* and satellite ponds as summer refuges.

3. **Clarias batrachus (Masaarai keluthy):** It is mostly a freshwater fish but tolerates salinity, and capable of surviving with atmospheric oxygen for considerable time. The fish is edible and believed to have medicinal properties.
4. **Liza cephalus (Periya madavai):** An edible fish seen in the brackish water affected areas of Kaliveli. They migrate to the less saline areas of the lake during the breeding season.
5. **Notopterus notopterus (Ambattan katti):** This fish prefers only freshwater not edible. More information on its habitat requirements are not available.
6. **Channa marulius (Avun viral):** One of the most common and edible fishes, tolerates salinity; feeds on aquatic plants, insects and tadpoles. This fish is capable of surviving on atmospheric oxygen when removed from water. This enables them to live in slushy habitat and connecting channels of the Ooranis.
7. **Channa punctatus (Koravai):** This species is less tolerant to saline water. This may be the reason why it is absent in Kaliveli, but can also survive in slushy and muddy water.
8. **Channa striatus (Viral):** Reported from Kaliveli, Ousteri and Kambikudi. This fish resembles O. punctatus, in habitat requirements.
9. **Oreochromis mossambica (Tilapi Kendai):** Occurs in all tanks except Kambikudi. This is introduced to the freshwater bodies for commercial fishery. Fish is capable of tolerating slight amount of salinity.
10. **Wallago attu (Valai keluthy):** A freshwater fish capable of tolerating low salinity. Viable populations of this fish are maintained in the perennial satellite ponds during the dry season. These enter Kaliveli during North East monsoon. This edible fish is caught by villagers.

D. Amphibians

1. **Rana cyanophlyctis (Skipping Frog):** Occurs in Kaliveli, Mirattunilai and Ousteri; is adapted to relatively dry conditions such as the barks of the trees in wild. They mainly feed on small flying insects. The eggs are laid in moist areas and November to January is the reproductive period.
2. **Rana hexadactyla (South Indian Frog):** A common frog found in the moist and water logged areas of all the tanks. Principally feeds on insects. Breeds in stagnant water near the tank banks.
3. **Rana limnocharis (Paddy field Frog):** This is a relatively smaller species which is seen in thick undergrowths. The frog feeds on mites and such small preys. Not much is known about its life history.
4. **Rana tigrina (Bull Frog):** A Slight, greenish common species found during monsoons. Once heavily hunted for the flesh from its leg muscles and for export. It feeds mainly on larger insects like grasshoppers. Eggs are laid in stagnant pools of water.

E. Reptiles

1. **Ahaetulla naxetus (Common Green Whip snake):** These are seen on low bushes, scrub jungles and gardens. Diurnal, Feed on small mammals. birds, lizards and frogs This snake is ovoviviparous.
2. **Amphiesma stolata (Butter striped keel back):** Commonly inhabits grasslands and cultivated areas rich in frogs and toads. Diurnal.
3. **Atretium schistosum (Olivaceous keelback):** Usually lives near water or the nearby vegetation. Diurnal. Feeds largely on frog, fish and crab.
4. **Bungarus caeruleus (Common Indian Krait, Kattu viriyan):** It is nocturnal and placid. Feeds mainly on snakes including other kraits, on blind snakes, frogs and lizards.
5. **Calotes versicolor (Common Garden Lizard, Ohnan):** This is the commonest lizard. Largely arboreal, and diurnal. Prefer shrub and under growth. They are camouflaged by immobility and color. Primarily insectivorous.
6. **Dendrelaphis tristis (Common Bronze back, Komberi Mooken):** They live on trees and shrubs rarely coming to the ground. Diurnal, Feeds largely on lizards, tree frogs, snakes and nestlings of small birds. Though this snake is harmless. They are usually killed by man suspecting them to be poisonous.
7. **Echis carinatus (Saw scaled viper, Viriyan Pamboo):** Inhabits dry scrub areas. Largely diurnal. In hot climate it hides under rocks and relies on moisture of the animal it eats. Feeds largely on centipedes, scorpions, insects, mice, geckos and frogs.
8. **Eryx conicus (Russell's Earth Boa, Mannooly):** It is dull with uncertain temper. It burrows into loose soil easily. Feeds on small rodents, frogs, ground feeding birds like mynas and hoopoes.
9. **Eryx johni (John's Earth Boa, Iruthalai Pamboo):** Mostly diurnal and burrowing in nature. The movements are slow and clumsy. Feeds on rats and mice. Very little is known of its breeding habits.
10. **Hemidactylus brookii (Brooks Gecko):** It lives in a variety of habitats-trees, rocks, under stones and on buildings. Mainly an insect eater. The hard shelled eggs are sticky and remain attached to each other and to the substratum.
11. **Hemidactylus frenatus (Southern House Gecko):** Very common Gecko mostly seen in houses and occasionally on trees, Insectivorous
12. **Hemidactylus leschenaultii (Bark Gecko):** Prefers banyan and tamarind trees which have numerous nooks and crevices on the trunk. Very territorial and insectivorous.
13. **Hemidactylus triedrus (Termite Hill Gecko):** This is spotted only at Ousteri, as a ground dwelling form associated with termite hills. Usually stays inside the termite hill during day time. Termite and ants

make the major part of the food. Breeds in hot weather. When termite hills are destroyed this species is threatened.

14. **Lissemys punctata (Indian Mud Turtle):** This is found only in the shallow swamps of Kaliveli nearly half buried in the mud. The turtle is able to withstand prolonged drought conditions, when they retreat into shrub cover. Omnivorous in nature, feeds both on aquatic plants and small animals such as frogs, fishes, crustaceans and snails, but withstands prolonged starvation. Eggs are eaten by man.
15. **Mabuya carinata (Common Skink):** Prefers areas of normal to heavy rain fall. Primarily a ground dweller and diurnal. Largely feeds on insects and small invertebrates. The young are seen in May - June.
16. **Melanochelys trijuga (Indian pond Terrapin, Neer amai):** This common fresh water tortoise prefers sedentary water. Young ones are aquatic and adults, semi-terrestrial. Usually they live in a group in hide out in the bank of the water body. Largely herbivorous and detritivorous. They are nocturnal in habit and forage on land. Tortoises and their eggs are hunted by people for food. This is a major threat for the tortoise population.
17. **Naja naja (Indian cobra, Nalla pamboo, Naga pamboo):** It is found almost anywhere in thickets, as well as open and cultivated fields in and around tanks. Occupy White ant, hills on the ground or on the tangle of roots at the base of trees. Feeds on rats, frogs, toads, birds, lizards and eggs of birds.
18. **Ptyas mucosus (Common rat snake, Sarai pamboo):** Usually diurnal in nature. Takes off readily to water and swims with the head above the water. This is capable of climbing trees. Feeds on almost anything that chance brings within its reach, but prefer, frogs and toads.
19. **Sitana ponticeriana (Fan throated lizard, Veeseri Ohnan):** A ground dwelling, diurnal agamid, common in open sandy scrub country of Kaliveli. Mostly insectivorous. Re production commences in April-May when the throat fan of the male attains brilliant coloration.
20. **Typhlina bramina (Common worm or Blind snake, Sevi pamboo):** It usually lives beneath the soil, stones or debris. These are seen solitary. It has highly polished scales to help passage through soil. It is often upon on by other snakes. Feeds on larvae, pupae, ants and other small insects. Oviparous.
21. **Varanus benghalensis (Common monitor lizard, Udumbu):** It is a diurnal lizard spotted only around Ousteri. More active in the mornings and evenings. Lives in cracks and crevices in the ground. It flicks its tongue in and out like a snake. Carnivorous, eats any animal it can over come.
22. **Vipera russelli (E: Russell's viper, T: Retha aunali, kannadi virian):** It is common in and around the villages, the attraction being the rodents in human settlements. Largely nocturnal and feeds on rodents, squirrels, shrews, kitten, birds and lizards. Usually killed by man.

23. **Xenochrophis piscator (Checkered Keel back, Thaneer pamboo):** This is the commonest one found in tanks and paddy fields. It feeds mainly on frogs, fish and tadpoles.

F. Birds

1. **Accipiter badius (Shikra):** This bird is a lightly built hawk and prefers open wooded plains. Shikra mainly feeds on lizards, mice, squirrels etc. It is fond of village groves. Nests on large trees.
2. **Acridotheres tristis (Indian Myna):** A very common bird seen around human habitations. Mainly feeds on insects, seen attending to grazing, cattle. Nest is a collection of twigs, roots, paper etc.
3. **Aegithina tiphia (Common iora):** A common arboreal bird usually seen in pairs. This resident bird feeds on Insects, their eggs and larvae. Nest is a compact cup of grasses plastered with cob webs.
4. **Alauda gulgula (Indian small skylark):** Occurs in the grassy meadows and cultivated fields. It usually prefers water pools near the bank, local migratory. Nest is a cup like depression on the ground lined with grass.
5. **Alcedo atthis (Small blue kingfisher):** The bird is less water dependent yet a chief proportion of food is constituted by small fishes, tadpoles and aquatic insects. Nesting season varies from March to June. Nest is similar to that of lesser pied kingfisher.
6. **Amaurornis phoenicurus (White breasted Waterhen):** This bird is a resident in wetlands. It feeds on insects, worms, mollusks. Grains and shoots of paddy and marsh plants. It wanders considerably when low lying tracts become water logged. It needs thickets and bushes in the banks for nesting.
7. **Anas acuta (Pintail Duck):** These birds constitute a major part of bird population in all water bodies. During summer when the tank dries up these birds migrate to nearby perennial water bodies. They grub in mud of inundated cultivations and on grassy tank margins. Nest is a depression in grass in open marshy grass land.
8. **Anas clypeata (Shoveler):** Like the other ducks shovelers also are winter visitors from the northern hemisphere. If is the last one to leave at the break of spring. The peculiar spatulate bill of this bird is adapted to its special mode of feeding. Food largely is animal matter. It is not exacting in its food preferences. Nesting season in Southern region is from July-November.
9. **Anas penelope (Wigeon):** The birds are winter visitors from northern pale arctic region. They are mixed surface feeders, largely vegetarian and need continuous water supply as in Ousteri and Kaliveli.
10. **Anas poecilorhyncha (Spot bill or Grey duck):** Reported only from Kaliveli. This bird is locally migratory. Breeding season is from August to November, during Southwest monsoon. A surface feeder on vegetable matter obtained in shallow waters.

11. **Anas querquedula (Blue winged teal / Garganey teal):** This bird is a winter visitor from colder north, one of the earliest migrants to arrive by August. They breed during September to November; basically a vegetarian.
12. **Anastomus oscitans (Open billed stork):** A typical wetland bird and local migratory; this bird mostly feeds on the molluscans and breed in colonies amongst mixed heronries of cormorants, egrets etc. Nest is just a circular platform of twigs with central depression lined with leaves.
13. **Anthus novaeseelandiae (Indian Pipit):** A very familiar resident in the agricultural fields of Kaliveli and Ousteri. A natural predator of the insect pests of crops. Mainly feeds on weevils and small insects. Nesting season lasts from February to October. Nest is a shallow cup of grass, rootlets and hair.
14. **Ardea alba (Large Egret):** Habitat requirement is same as the cattle egret but needs more wilder areas for breeding. Probably this is the reason why large egret is not very common.
15. **Ardea cinerea (Grey Heron):** This bird is a common visitor to all tanks. This feeds mainly on fishes and crustaceans. But nesting requirements do not demand presence of any water body nearby. This species is gregarious in nesting habits. Usually found among heronries. Social forestry plantations and Prosopis growth in wastelands near the water bodies provide excellent roosting sites for these birds.
16. **Ardeola grayii (Pond Heron):** A very common water bird of all tanks. If feeds on various aquatic crustaceans and fishes. This bird is well adapted to its feeding habitats. The brownish appearance makes it unnoticeable among reeds and plant growths. During rainy season they are seen in wastelands feeding on locusts and other insects. Usually pond herons roost in a group. This bird prefers to nest on palm trees but also seen nesting on Tamarind and Jackfruit trees.
17. **Artamus fuscus (Ashy-swallow-shrike):** A familiar bird in the tank. Food mainly consists of moths, butterflies etc. Nest is a loosely built cup of grass roots and fibers upon the base of leaf stalks on a palm tree.
18. **Athene brama (Spotted owlet):** A very common gregarious bird in all tanks. Smaller in size compared to barn owl, and nocturnal. Particularly abundant near human settlements surrounding tanks. This bird's diet chiefly consists of insects, lizards, and mice. Owlet plays a crucial role in controlling the population of mice in agro-ecosystems. Nest is an untidy pad of fibers in tree-hollows.
19. **Aythya fuligula (Tufted pochard):** This is one of the most common winter, migratory diving ducks, Prefers reed fringed satellite ponds and grassy banks. (In case of Kaliveli the perennial waterbodies surrounding the Kaliveli tanks are the main habitat). The bird is suited for diving and swimming both above and below the surface and not walking.

They feed in deep water by diving, hence often seen in open expanses in the middle of tanks. It can remain submerged for considerable time. Main food constitutes mollusks, crustaceans, water insects and hydrophytes.

20. **Aythya nyroca (White eyed Pochard):** This is perhaps the most abundant of the migratory ducks to these waterbodies. Rests during the day in the middle of the tank and flies inland after dusk to feed in inundated paddy fields and on grassy tank margins. Food is mainly vegetable matter, insects, mollusks, small fishes etc.

21. **Bubulcus ibis (Cattle Egret):** These resident birds are mainly seen in grasslands in and around the tanks. Attending grazing cattle and feeding on the insects disturbed by the cattle. Food consists of grasshoppers, butterflies, other insects, frogs and lizards. Mainly roosts on palm tree. Nesting site not necessarily near water.

22. **Calidris minuta (Little stint):** A diminutive winter visitor to Kaliveli. This wader is sociable and gregarious and often mix with other smaller waders. Mainly visits mud flats and marshes on the northern side of Kaliveli. This bird feeds on insects, crustaceans and mollusks. Nest is a cup shaped depression lined with leaves on grassy marsh land.

23. **Caprimulgus asiaticus (Common Indian night jar):** A nocturnal bird from scrubs, groves, agricultural fields and villages surrounding the tanks. Mainly feeds on insects like beetles and moths. The bird nests during. Eggs are laid on bare ground in bush jungle.

24. **Ceryle rudis (lesser pied king fisher):** A bird which is much dependent on the water bodies for its food. The characteristic mode of fishing is spectacular. Largely feeds on fishes, tadpoles, frogs and aquatic insects. Nest is a horizontal tunnel dug in precipitous mud-bank of streams.

25. **Charadrius alexandrinus (Kentish plover):** This bird largely feeds on insects, grasshoppers, tiny crabs etc., gregarious in their feeding habits. Eggs which are broad at one end and abruptly pointed at the end are laid on sand banks.

26. **Charadrius dubius (Little ringed plover):** A resident bird seen mainly on tank beds and reed grounds of Kaliveli and Ousteri. Usually feeds on insects, tiny crabs etc. It nests during March to May. Eggs are laid on the bare shingles on the sand banks.

27. **Charadrius mongolus (lesser sand plover):** Lesser sand plovers occurs only in Kaliveli. These birds are very similar to Kentish plover in habitat requirements and breeding habits.

28. **Chlidonias hybrida (Indian whiskered tern):** Another common winter visitor to south Indian Inland waters and tidal creeks. Food materials include tiny fishes, tadpoles, crabs, grasshoppers and insects obtained from the Reed beds and agricultural fields. Nest is a rough circular pad of Reeds.

29. **Ciconia ciconia (White stork):** White storks are trans-Himalayan migratory winter visitors to Kaliveli. They come in small groups during November and leave soon after the breeding. Their food constitutes frogs, lizards and large insects. 340 individuals of white storks were reported from Kaliveli and Ousteri in 1986 winter.
30. **Circus macrourus (Pale harrier):** A common winter visitor found in wooded scrub, cultivated fields and grasslands; mainly feeds on lizard, frogs, grasshoppers and nestlings. Adapted for continuous flight and fast darting to catch the prey. Breeds in central Asia during April to June. Kaliveli lake especially northern side Yedayanthittu estuary region is a very good winter refuge for these birds.
31. **Circus aeruginosus (Marsh harrier):** Sighted at Pillaipakkam. Kaliveli and Ouster!. Habitat requirements and breeding pattern is almost similar to that of pale harrier.
32. **Cisticola Juncidis (Streaked fantail warbler):** The bird is locally migratory. Food consists of small insect and caterpillars. Nest is a deep oblong pouch of grasses with its mouth at the top lived with to blades of grass.
33. **Clamator jacobinus (pied crested cuckoo):** The bird is a typical Resident visitor. The bird also migrates locally. Main food items are insects including hairy and noxious caterpillars. This bird is a brood parasite, laying the eggs in other bird's nests generally in craw's or babblers.
34. **Columba livia (Blue rock pigeon):** The bird is an occasional visitor to the wetland from surrounding wooded regions. Mainly feeds on cereals, pulses, ground nuts etc. Birds are seen in abundance during harvest seasons in the agricultural fields and in the margins of tanks. The nest is a flimsy collection of a few sticks on a hedge or in a fissure of cliffs and ceilings of dwelling houses.
35. **Copsychus saularis (Magpie-Robin):** A familiar bird in tanks and surroundings; feeds mainly on insects. A ground forager feeding also on nectar. Nest is a pad of grass in a hole on a wall or on tree trunk.
36. **Coracias bengalensis (Indian Roller):** A very common bird of tank surroundings; a resident but locally migratory in winter; Prefers open wooded country; mainly feeds on large insects, frogs, lizards and small rodents. The bird is beneficial to agriculture since it feeds on vast quantities of insect pests. Nest is just a collection of straw rags and rubbish in a natural tree hollow.
37. **Coracina novaehollandiae (large Cuckoo-shrike):** A resident arboreal bird from the evergreen thickets around Kaveripakkam. Feeds also in cultivated fields. Food constitutes large insects captured in the foliage as well as berries of banyan, peepal and other wild figs.
38. **Corvus macrorhynchos (Jungle crow):** The Jungle crow is seen only in small numbers. Like the house crow it does not have any particular food habits. Nests singly or in community.

39. **Cuculus varius (Common hawk cuckoo):** A common resident; mainly feed on insects, caterpillars, lizards and the wild figs. Like pied crusted cuckoo this bird also is a brood parasite on the babblers. Usually single egg is laid in each nest. Hatchlings are reared to maturity by foster parents.
40. **Cursorius coromandelicus (Indian cursor):** A resident bird of Kaliveli especially on the sand banks of southern and northern sides, also on waste and fallow land adjoining the cultivated and ploughed fields. Bird is insectivorous and of great help in controlling the paddy insect pests. Nesting season is March to August 2-3 eggs are laid in shallow scrape or on bare ground in open arid country where they are perfectly camouflaged.
41. **Dendrocitta vagabunda (Tree pie):** Commonly found in the thickets and on trees on the banks of water bodies, feeding on fruits, insects, lizards, frogs etc. The nesting season is from March to May. Nest is deeper than crows, made of thorny twigs and rootlets.
42. **Dicaeum erythrorhynchos (Tickell's flower pecker):** A very common resident bird in the Puttupet sacred groves of Kaliveli and bank thickets of Ousteri. Mainly feeds on the berries of mistletoe. Nesting season lasts from February to June.
43. **Dicrurus adsimilis (Black Drongo):** It is seen very commonly in the agricultural fields, feeding on insects. The nest is made up of fine twigs and fibers woven with cob webs. Nesting season varies from April to August.
44. **Dicrurus leucophaeus (Grey Drongo):** This bird prefers the well wooded inlet channels of Kaliveli, very dexterous in foraging insects. Feeds also on Butea and Erythrina nectar; nesting season lasts from March to June.
45. **Dinopium benghalense (Lesser Golden backed wood pecker):** The bird prefers dry or mixed deciduous forests. The bird works on the bark of trees, chiseling away rotten wood for beetles and insects hiding. Black ants from the ground form a considerable amount of diet. Pulp of ripe fruit as well as flower nectar are also eaten. Nesting season ranges from March to August. Nest is an unlined hollow in a tree trunk.
46. **Egretta garzetta (Little Egret):** This bird prefers wet areas in and around the lakes. It feeds on amphibians, crustaceans, crabs and fishes. The bird is gregarious in nature; nests on trees along with smaller egret and other water birds, often near villages.
47. **Egretta intermedia (Smaller Egret):** This bird is similar to the little egret in its habitat requirements and feeding habits.
48. **Elanus caeruleus (Black winged kite):** A common resident bird of cultivated fields and grasslands. Food constitutes locusts, crickets, mice, lizards etc. This bird breeds through out the year.
49. **Eremopterix grisea (Ashy crowned finch lark):** This lark is a small resident bird. The bird prefers to forage on open scrub, semi cultivated

areas, fallow inlet basins and the tank-bed. Its coloration makes it difficult to spot. Mainly feeds on grass seeds and tiny insects. Nesting season is variable and nest is like a cup like depression in the ground lined with grass.

50. **Escalus magnirostris (Great stone plover):** A resident bird reported only from Kaliveli. It is nocturnal, a fast runner and swimmer. Food mainly consists of crabs from stone bottoms raised up with the specially adapted bill. Feeds also on other small Animals found in the habitat. Nesting is done mainly during February to July. Nest is a shallow scrape in any exposed sandy bed.
51. **Falco peregrinus japonensis (peregrine falcon):** A bird of prey at Kaliveli. Winter visitor to South India; nesting season lasts from March to May. The bird is adapted to its way of life with sharp wings and fast movements; preys largely on ducks, partridges, pigeons, parakeets by stooping on them with tremendous velocity. Open wooded country is preferred by this bird since it helps easy location of prey.
52. **Falco tinnunculus (Kestrel):** Another bird of prey to Kaliveli from Himalayas. This bird also prefers open wooded country as it facilitates hunting of prey. It nests on large trees often inlands, during July-October.
53. **Francolinus pondicerianus (Grey partridge):** Grey partridge is a resident bird of grasslands, thorny scrubs and cultivated fields. The bird is highly camouflaged, runs very fast and hides dexterously to escape from enemy. Mainly feeds near village granaries and cultivated fields on grains, termites, beetles, larvae etc. Breeds round the year.
54. **Fulica atra (Coot):** Coot is reported both as a resident and winter visitor Kaveripakkam and Ousteri and is much dependent on water bodies. In winter, their numbers increase due to migrants from central and western Asia. They mainly feed on grasses, paddy shoots, aquatic weeds, insects, molluscs etc. Nesting season is from July to January.
55. **Gallinago gallinago (Fantail snipe):** This is another wader winter visitor to from Himalayas. Pintail snipe and Fantail snipe are very much alike and their descriptions and nutritional-habitat requirements are more or less same.
56. **Gallinago stenura (Pintail snipe):** An obliteratively colored winter visitor from Himalayas. A typical marsh bird preferring moist soils and mud flats of Kaliveli and its connecting channel to Yedayanthittu. This bird comes in September in large groups and leaves by April. It goes inland to water logged agricultural fields for feeding on worms, insect larvae etc. by probing into soft mud with the tong slender bill. Nest is a shallow grass lined depression in grassy marsh land.
57. **Gelochelidon nilotica (Gull billed tern):** Unlike other terns Gull billed tern has great affinity to coastal water bodies. Kaliveli gives a special habitat for these birds. It feeds on fish, crustaceans, tadpoles

and water insects. Nesting season lasts from March to May. These birds are gregarious in nature and lay eggs on bare ground or on sand banks of Kaliveli near Uppukkali region.

58. **Halcyon smyrnensis (White breasted kingfisher):** One of the most familiar birds of wetlands least dependent on water. The main food consists of fish, tadpoles, lizards, grasshoppers and other insects and occasionally mice. Nesting season ranges from March to July. Nest is a horizontal tunnel dug into the side of a dry tank bed.

59. **Haliastur indus (Brahminy kite):** One of the very common birds feeding on aquatic organisms like crabs, frogs and fishes. This bird is of great help to farmer by feeding on crabs and locusts. Breeding season lasts from December to April.

60. **Himantopus himantopus (Black winged stilt):** This bird is a resident as well as a winter visitor. It is a wader in the seasonal waters where it probes into the squelchy bottom mud for worms, molluscs and insects. The nesting season falls in April to August months. Nest is nearly a depression in the ground or in the margin of the tank.

61. **Hirundo daurica (Striated swallow):** Occurs at Kaliveli alone hawking on winged insects in association with common swallow. Nesting season lasts from April to August.

62. **Hirundo rustica (Common swallow):** A very common gregarious bird seen especially in marshy regions. The bird is a winter visitor for about six months from September onwards. It hawks winged insects high in the sky and near the ground. Roosts in large congregations in reed beds and thickets near water; chiefly feeds on flies and midgets. Breeds in the months of April to June.

63. **Lanius cristatus (Brown shrike):** A common visitor to the tank bed, noted from both Kaliveli and Ousteri. Typical habitat is lightly wooded and scrub country. Mainly feeds on grasshoppers, locusts and small lizards. Nesting season lasts from February to July. Nest is a deep compact cup of twigs, grass, wool etc.

64. **Larus ichthyaetus (Great Black headed Gulf):** A winter visitor to Kaliveli, rarely seen in inland waters. The bird arrives to Kaliveli by September-October and departs by April. In Kaliveli this bird feeds on insects, grub, and shoots of various crops, competes with pariah kite and Brahminy kite for food. Breeding is reported only from Himalayan ranges in summer months.

65. **Limosa limosa (Black tailed godwit):** A winter visitor to Ousteri and Kaliveli A typical wader. This bird also feeds on worms, molluscs, crabs, insects from the water body and the nearby water logged agricultural fields. Poaching though legally banned, is common.

66. **Lonchura malabarica (White throated Munia):** A visitor to the dry tank beds; feeds on the grass seeds on the ground. Nest is a large globular structure of coarse grasses, lined with thin grasses.

67. **Lonchura malacca (Black headed Munia):** Occurs in the moist grasslands, reed beds and wet paddy fields. Feeds on grains and grass seeds; nesting season lasts from June to October.

68. **Lonchura punctulata (Spotted Munia):** A resident bird of Mirattunilai, preferring damp localities, feeds on winged termites and grass seeds. Nesting requirements and habits are very little known.

69. **Locustella naevia (Grasshopper Warbler):** A local migratory bird species reported from Kambikudi. Prefers wooded thorny thickets. Mainly feeds on caterpillars, insects and nectar. Probably affects cross pollination. Nests in May/June months.

70. **Megalaima haemacephala (Crimson breasted barbet (or) Copper smith):** A heavy billed resident; mainly feeds on fruits and berries especially of Banyan and Peepal figs. Sometimes eats termites and insects too. Nesting season varies from January to June. Nest usually is a hole excavated in a snag of a dead soft wood.

71. **Merops orientalis (Small green bee eater):** Reported from all tanks. A grass green bird very common to the tanks and cultivated surroundings. Mainly feeds on dipterans and hymenopteran insects. Nesting season mainly falls from February to May. Nest is a horizontal oblique tunnel ending in a widened egg chamber, dug in the sides of an earth cutting, burrow pit or uneven sandy ground.

72. **Merops philippinus (Blue tailed bee eater):** A bee eater found near water bodies and wetlands. Prefers open country and cultivated fields. As the name indicates food is chiefly winged insects and a confirmed nuisance for honey industry. The bird nests during March-June. Nests usually in a tunnel on tank banks or inlet channels.

73. **Milvus migrans govinda (Pariah kite):** Reported from all tanks. One of the commonest raptor. Usually found near villages surrounding the tank. Nesting season is from September to April. Usually feeds on village wastes, earth worms, winged termites, lizards and mice.

74. **Motacilla cinerea (Grey wagtail):** Another winter visitor to Kaliveli grasslands seen in plenty during the morning hours. The food requirements overlap with that of M.citreola.

75. **Motacilla citreola (Yellow headed wagtail):** A winter visitor to Kaliveli and Ousteri; essentially a water wagtail; feeding on tiny insects on the moist and wet grasslands. The bird is gregarious in nature. Breeding requirements not known.

76. **Motacilla flava (Yellow wagtail):** A winter visitor seen feeding on insects in wet grasslands and fallow lands. Roosts in Reed beds and in the agricultural fields. Not much is known about its breeding habits.

77. **Motacilla maderaspatensis (Grey Wagtail):** This is a very common bird found in village water bodies; feeds mainly on aquatic insects and flies. Nesting season spreads usually through out the year. Nest is a cup shaped pad of rootlets, hair, wool and dry algae.

78. **Mycteria leucocephala (Painted Stork):** This focal migrant depends on the water bodies only for breeding during September and January. Plantations of Prosopis form a very good roosting place for these birds. Nest is a large stick platform with shallow depression in the middle, lined with leaves, straw etc. They feed on molluscans, crustaceans and fishes. More than 250 individuals were reported from Kaliveli during breeding season. The significance of Kaliveli and Ousteri as a water bird habitat increases manifold because of the presence of this rare species.
79. **Nectarinia asiatica (Purple Sunbird):** A common bird in Kambikudi and Mirattunilai. Seen in cultivated and scrub patches feeding on insects, spiders and flower nectar. Its slender curved bill and tubular tongue are adapted for sucking nectar. In doing so this bird helps cross pollination of plants. Nest is an oblong pendulous pouch made of soft grasses and cob web.
80. **Nectarinia lotenia (Loten's sunbird):** Present in the thickets on the banks of tanks; feeds on the nectar of large flowers and tiny insects. Breeding season lasts from March to May. Nest is typical of sunbirds (Oblong pendular pouch of soft grasses)
81. **Nectarinia zeylonica (Purple rumped sunbird):** Commonly seen in the thickets around waterbodies feeding on insects in the prosopis plantations. Main food is nectar of Loranthus and similar parasitic plants. This bird is a known cross pollinator in many plants. Nesting season is not well defined.
82. **Nettapus coromandelianus (Cotton teal):** Well adapted for diving mode of nutrition. Food is chiefly vegetable matter, insects, crustaceans etc. Breeding season is around September-November. Usually nests on tree trunks near the water such as Peepal, Banyan and Tamarind.
83. **Netta rufina (Red crested Pochard):** A winter breeding visitor during September-February living on the shoots and roots of water plants, molluscs, crustaceans, insects etc.
84. **Numenius arquata (Curlew):** This is another winter visitor to Kaliveli lake noted for stalking along the water edge probing into soft soil for food: molluscs, crustaceans, insects, larvae, berries of marsh plants, grassy shoots and other vegetable matter. This bird is poached by locals for its delicious flesh.
85. **Nycticorax nycticorax (Night Heron):** The bird is usually found in the fringes of tanks and agricultural fields. Herons are nocturnal spending the day on some leafy trees-often far from water. Main foods are crabs, fish, frogs and aquatic insects. Nesting is from December to February.

    Generally Herons and Egrets constitute the majority of the water birds present in the inland waters. Water fowl census of Kaliveli, in 1987, counted 1400 individuals of various egrets and 325 individuals of night heron. Some of these are completely water dependent but some are only facultative. Most of these egrets and herons are residents or locally migrating. It can be stated that these water bodies have successfully developed into natural habitats alter long-term evolutionary interaction of floral and faunal components. The population size of these heronries is very important in assessing the importance of these water bodies for long term conservation.

86. **Oriolus oriolus (Golden oriole):** A common bird in tank premises; prefers to feed on insects and figs on trees; rarely a visitor to tank bed. These birds are seen mostly in pairs. Nesting season is from April to July. Nest is a cup shaped formation woven up with cob webs.
87. **Orthotomus sutorius (Tailor bird):** A very common bird in the scrub thickets on the banks of Kaliveli and Ousteri. These birds mainly feed on flying insects, their eggs, grubs, flower nectar of Erythrina etc. Nesting season lasts from April to September
88. **Pandion haliaetus (Osprey):** This is a fish eating hawk visiting Kaliveli during winter months. It is seen flying up and down over the water scanning the surface for any fish coming up within striking depth. During the time of cyclones and depressions in Bay of Bengal many fishes migrate to Kaliveli through Yedayanthrttu estuary. These fishes form the main food of Osprey. Since water depth rarely exceed two meters in Kaliveli this is an ideal habitat for this wader.
89. **Passer domesticus (House sparrow):** A common resident bird in human settlements feeding on grains, small insects, fruit buds, nectar etc.
90. **Pelecanus philippensis (Spot-billed pelican):** A locally migrating water bird important from conservation point of view. During the 1987 water fowl census more than 200 pelicans were noted from Kaliveli. Presence of spot-billed pelican at the Kaliveli is a good indication for its significance as a water fowl habitat. These birds fish by cooperative effort by swimming in a semi-circle. By doing this they drive the fish before them into the shallow area. The birds arrive in Kaliveli from other pelicaneries (e.g. point calimer) in November. Principal nesting season lasts from November to April. These birds nest on the same tree; such aggregations (pelicaneries) are seen on the western banks of Kaliveli.
91. **Phalacrocorax niger (Little Cormorant):** This bird is completely dependent on waterbodies for its feeding and breeding. They always maintain large flock size. These birds live exclusively on fishes, which they chase and capture under water. It is because of this dependence on the aquatic habitats, they are not seen in Kaliveli - which is a seasonal water body. Moreover availability of nesting site i.e. trees around the waterbody is also a determining factor for choosing the habitat, Nesting season is from November to February. These birds are facing severe threat from poachers. The excreta of birds are considered *very*

nutritious especially for paddy cultivation. Nesting in fields is encouraged by the locals as the Guano is a good manure.

92. **Phoenicopterus roseus (Greater Flamingo):** This is a bird of great conservation value. Though reported from Kaliveli during September-January their breeding season is not yet confirmed. Greater flamingo usually visits the lake for feeding in shallow waters with the slender neck bent down between the legs and head completely submerged. The curious bill is inverted so that the ridge of the culman scrapes the ground. Food consists of crustaceans, worms, insects, larvae, seeds of plants etc. 1986-87 winter water fowl census gave an estimate of 800 of flamingos from Kaliveli alone.
93. **Pitta brachyura (Indian pitta):** A common bird found in the ravines and dry nullahs on the banks of Kaliveli. The bird is a resident and migrates locally. Mainly feeds on grubs and insects. Usually seen turning over dead leaves and digging into damp earth for insects and grubs. Nesting season is from May to August. Nest is a large globule made of twigs, grass and roots, under a bush or more commonly up on the forks of low trees.
94. **Ploceus philippinus (Baya weaver bird):** A locally migrating bird roosting in reed beds and wet grasslands. Its local movements are mainly governed by cereal cultivation which provides both nesting materials and food. This bird also feeds on insects. Nesting season lasts from May to September. The pendulous nests are weaved with leaves of rough edged grass. Prefers Palmyra palms. Annual removal of the palm leaves by villagers greatly reduces nesting opportunities.
95. **Podiceps ruficollis (Little Grebe or Dabchick):** This bird is purely aquatic. Since it is slow in taking off from water surface. It escapes from enemies by diving into the water with astounding rapidity. The bird mainly feeds on aquatic insects, tadpoles, frogs and crustaceans, by diving or pursuit. Breeding season is between April and October. The bird prefers to nest on floating vegetation or a raft of debris, often half submerged. Little Grebes are locally migratory. As soon as water is available in tanks after the onset of monsoon they arrive in large flocks, the size of water body determining the flock size.
96. **Prinia socialis (Wren warbler):** Prefer the moist grass lands and reed beds in Kaliveli. Mainly feeds on insects. Nesting season lasts from March to September.
97. **Prinia subflava (Indian-wren-warbler):** A locally migratory gregarious bird mainly preferring the grasslands and scrub jungles found in and around Ousteri. Nesting season is between March and September. Nest is a longish pear shaped pouch of woven grass strips, open or with lateral entrance hole near the top.
98. **Pseudibis papillosa (Black Ibis):** A large black bird reported only from Kambikudi tank. Unlike the white Ibis, this prefers drier tracts

and fallow land; roosts in the social forestry plantations of Acacia arabica on tank beds. The bird mainly feeds on insects, grain and small reptiles. Nesting is reported during the months of November to January. Nest is made up of twigs lined with straw, generally away from water.

99. **Psittacula krameri (Rose ringed parakeet):** One of the common visitors to the wetlands. The food consists of fruits and cereals. Due to the flocking nature and the over consumption of the cereals, farmers consider them as a nuisance in agricultural fields. Nesting season falls chiefly from February to April. Nest usually is a hollow on the tree trunk.

100. **Pycnonotus cafer (Red vented Bulbul):** A very familiar bird in the thickets of waterbodies under study. Seen feeding on peepal and banyan figs besides insects. Nesting season lasts between February and May. Nest is a cup of rootlets plastered outside with cob webs.

101. **Pycnonotus jocosus (Red whiskered Bulbul):** This bird is found around Kaliveli. It is rarely seen along with red vented Bulbul and prefers wilderness. Feed on insects and flower nectar. Nesting season is from February to August.

102. **Pycnonotus luteolus (White browed bulbul):** Usually common in dry-open scrub and bush on the banks. Mainly feeds on banyan and peepal figs, berries of Lantana and Ziziphus and insects. This bird is also identified as a good dispersing agent of seeds .of the above plants. Nesting season lasts from March to September.

103. **Rhopodytes viridirostris (Small Green billed malkoha):** A resident non-parasitic cuckoo reported from the ·wild tracts near the Mirattunilai tank. Prefers the thorny thickets common in these dry tracts. The bird is seen creeping through thickets rarely feeding on ground. Feeds on caterpillar's, large insects, lizards and also on berries. Nests between March and June. Nest is an untidy platform in the thorny thickets.

104. **Saxicoloides fulicata (Indian Robin):** A common bird in tank premises; Seen in thorny scrub thickets on the bank; feeds on insects and their eggs. Usually seen on the termite mounds feeding on termites. Nest is a pad *of* grass lined with rootlets and feather.

105. **Sterna bengalensis (Indian lesser crested tern):** This is a winter visitor during September to November to Kaliveli, the semi coastal wetland. This bird locally migrates from Yedayanthittu to Kaliveli depending on the food availability and compete with other birds like pariah and Brahminy kites for food. This bird mainly feeds on fishes, prawns and other such crustaceans.

106. **Sterna hirundo (Common tern):** A native Indian tern reported only from Kaliveli and Ousteri mainly feeding on fish, tadpoles and water insects. This bird is seen in and around the vegetated inlet channels and the satellite ponds on the margins of Kaliveli. Breeding season falls in between March and June.

107. **Streptopelia chinensis (Spoiled dove):** Another very common bird found in all the tank premises. Like the ring dove and spotted doves this bird is highly dependent on the tank and its surrounding agricultural fields because its major food is cereal grain. Breeds practically round the year.

108. **Streptopelia decaocto (Indian Ring dove):** This resident visitor to Kambikudi is mainly dependent on shoreline agricultural fields for cereal grain food. Acacia arabica plantation is an excellent nesting place for these birds. Nest is a typical scanty twig platform on a bush or on a small tree.

109. **Streptopelia senegalensis (Little brown dove):** A resident visitor to the tanks and wetlands from its typical habitats like wooded country. Like other columbids this bird also depends on the agricultural fields for its food grains. The nest is a flimsy twig platform in Euphorbia clumps.

110. **Sturnus pagodarum (Black headed Myna):** A local migrant to the tank beds when it is moist. Usually seen attending grazing cattle on the tank bed feeding on grasshoppers and insects. The bird also feeds on fruits but is largely omnivorous. Nesting season is from May to July. Nest is a pad of grass, rags etc.

111. **Cypsiurus parvus (Palm swift):** Reported from all tanks. This bird is seen flying about gregariously over open tank bed dotted with Palmyra palms from which it is inseparable. It provides the bird with excellent roosting site. The bird is a flight forager on winged insects; nesting season is undefined.

112. **Tadorna ferruginea (Ruddy shelduck):** This bird is a winter migrant to Kaliveli reaching in September and leaving by February. 30 individuals were reported from Kaliveli during 1986-87 water fowl census. Unlike other ducks these are often seen on the sandy banks than in water. They walk well and with ease and grazes like a goose at the water's edge. Food mainly consists of vegetable matter, molluscs, crustaceans, aquatic insects, fishes and reptiles.

113. **Tephrodornis pondicerianus (Common Wood Shrike):** A resident bird from Mirattunilai tank and the surrounding cultivated fields and trees. Mainly feeds on moths, beetles, caterpillars captured on trees. Nesting season is between February and September.

114. **Terpsiphone paradisi (Paradise flycatcher):** A local migratory bird found in the thick wilderness patches on the banks of Kaliveli especially in Pudupet sacred grove. Feeds on flies and dipterans. Nesting season is in between February and July.

115. **Threskiornis aethiopica (White Ibis):** This is a local migrant. When Kaliveli dries up during summer these birds migrate to nearby perennial water bodies including Ousteri. Feeds in shallow waters with head momentarily submerged. They nest during November to March and nests

are like a platform of twigs made on trees standing in water. 230 individuals of white Ibis were reported from mixed heroneries of Kaliveli during the 1987 survey.

116. Turdoides affinis (White headed Babbler): A very common bird in the thickets found in and around the waterbodies. Gregarious in nature in a group of 6-7. Only one nest in a group and others nurse the breeding one. They are seen ground foraging on bitter lasting insects and grains. Breeding season lasts from February to May.

117. Turdoides caudatus (Common babbler): This bird prefers the open wooded dry scrubs or thickets on the banks of the water bodies. Mainly feeds on insects, berries, grain and nectar. Nesting season is between March and July.

118. Turdoides malcolmi (Large Grey Babbler): A sociable local migrant from Kaveripakkam and surroundings. This species is identified as endemic to South India. The bird prefers cultivated plains and country dotted with neem trees. This bird mainly feeds on spiders and other insects, wild fig berries, grain and nectar of flowers. Nesting season - irregular, more or less throughout the year. Nest is a loosely built cup of twigs, roots and grass. The nests commonly parasitized by cuckoos.

119. Turdoides striates (Jungle Babbler): This local migrant is seen in Mirattunilai and its surrounding wilderness usually in a group of seven- the so called seven sisters. The bird feeds mainly on insects, wild fig berries and grains. Only one female of the group breeds at a time and others ensure the survival of the nestlings. Nesting season is not rigidly defined.

120. Tringa glareola (Wood sand piper): A snipe-like wader bird visiting the tank during winter. One of the commonest and most gregarious among the wading birds found near inland waters like irrigation tanks, flooded paddy fields, etc. Nesting season mainly falls in July-September months. Nest is a scantily lined - depression on a dry patch in marshy grass-covered localities of these tanks.

121. Tringa ochropus (Green sand piper): Green sand piper is a wader noted from Kaliveli lake premises during winter. These birds are seen singly in flooded paddy fields and mud flats they usually feed on detritus fauna extracted from sediment using their specialized bill. Nest is a scanty lived depression on a dry patch in. reed beds.

122. Tringa totanus (Red shank): A typical sand piper. A winter visitor to some tanks. These birds forage gregariously. They run along the tank banks and muddy flats in tank and probe with their bills for food such as insects, larvae, worms and molluscs. Nesting season lasts from July to November. Nest is a scantily lined depression on a dry patch in marshy grass covered localities.

123. Tringa hypoleucos (Common sand piper): A very common winter visiting wader found in Kaliveli and Ousteri. These birds are one of the earliest immigrants and also one of the last to leave, mostly seen after April. They feed on insects, worms, molluscs etc. Nesting season varies from year to year as it depends on the North West monsoon. Nest is a slight depression sparsely lined with leaves and rubbish.

124. **Turnix sylvatica (Little bustard Quail):** A resident bird of scrubs and cultivated fields of Kaliveli and Ousteri. Feeds on grain, seeds, termites, larvae etc. Breeds throughout the year. Nest is just a grass lined scrape or depression in scrub jungle.

125. **Upupa epops (Hoopoe):** A very common bird in tank surroundings; a resident as well as a local migratory. Mainly feeds on insects, grubs and pupa; hence beneficial to agriculture. Nesting season is principally from February to May; nest being a natural tree hollow or hole in a wall untidily lined with straw, rags and rubbish.

126. **Vanellus indicus (Red wattled lapwing):** A very common resident preferring moist land; usually seen in the ploughed fields and tank beds and in the satellite ponds. Food consists of insects, grubs, molluscs etc. Nesting season lasts from March to August. Eggs are laid on bare ground in open waste lands. This bird is very common and easily recognizable by its peculiar alarming call.

127. **Vanallus malabaricus (yellow-wattled lapwing):** Occurs mainly in the western banks of Kaliveli. This bird is another resident lapwing closely related to previously mentioned Red-wattled lapwing; but prefers dry lands. Nesting season is April to July. In summer many lapwings from tank surroundings migrate for filling the available niche on dry bank beds. In winter when tank is flooded, they migrate back to banks.

G. Mammals

1. **Bandicota bengalensis (Indian Mole Rat):** Surroundings of Kaliveli form a typical habitat of Indian mole rat, with moist alluvial tracts. Its presence always made known by a pile of fresh earth resembling a large molehill (hence the name mole rat). The tunnels are planned with emergency exists, grain storage and other facilities. Usually one mole rat is found in each burrow. Young mother lives with her nursery made of straw and leaves. This animal is one of the most destructive pest to the crops. Their populations are regulated by predators like Jackal, Mongoose and Jungle cats.

2. **Bandicota Indica (Bandicoot rat):** Larger than the mole rat, this is present around the human settlements surrounding the tanks; usually feeds on vegetable garbage. From their burrowing habits they do much damage to the grounds, floors, brick works and masonry.

3. **Canis aureus (Jackal, Nari):** The plain land around the tanks, low human populations and abundant hide-outs in agricultural fields, help them thrive hunting smaller mammals, birds and reptiles. Sometimes the turn to poultry lambs, sickly goats and sheep. Little is known about

jackal's family life since they are very secretive in habits. They usually live alone or in pairs. Lack of hunting ground, dense human settlements, habitat destruction are the main reasons for their dwindling populations.

4. **Felis chaus (Jungle Cat, Kaattu poonai):** The Jungle cat is found only in the Kaliveli and its surroundings. It preys on many rodents and raids on village poultry. It is very swift and exceedingly strong for its size. The jungle Cat of Kaliveli is mainly an indicator of the habitat diversity in Kaliveli. This ecosystem has a number of microhabitats like Grassland, Reed swamps, dry evergreen forest tracts, scrubs and man made plantations.

5. **Herpestes edwardsii (The common mongoose, Keeree):** It lives in burrows and holes made by them in termite mound, under trees. They feed on rats, crabs, frogs, reptiles and ground foraging birds like partridges. During monsoon snakes and frogs in the fields and tanks provide a ready .food supply for mongoose. During the dry season with the harvesting of the crops of the 'Porambokku' fields rats and mice find less ample shelter and therefore are more easily hunted. Their role in the economy of Nature is to keep prolific animals such as rats and snakes in check.

6. **Tatera indica (Indian Gerbil):** Noted only in Kaliveli - in the tank bed as well as the fields on the banks. It builds burrows usually under bushes and thickets on the banks. Male burrows have only one entrance and females more. Food consists mainly of fruits, grain, roots, leaves, grass. They also eat insects, eggs and nestlings of small ground birds. During the harvest season they collect grains in plenty and store in underground 'store houses'. It can be exceedingly destructive to crops at every stage of growth. But Gerbil burrows increases the aeration and percolation of water in soil. Usual predators are Jungle cat, Jackal and large birds.

7. **Lepus nigricollis (Indian hare, Musal):** All tanks support good populations of Indian hare due to vast stretches of social forestry and agricultural fields. Faxes, Jackals and Jungle cats are the usual predators. Villagers also hunt them for flesh and skin using traps and Gun. Apart from hunting and predation competitions for food from grazing cattle and goats also threaten the hare populations.

8. **Mus booduga (Indian field Mouse):** Present only around Kaliveli tank. In the Agricultural fields and villages. They live in burrows. Field mouse has almost similar food habits that of Indian gerbil. Its populations are checked by many predators.

9. **Paradoxurus paradoxurus hermaphroditus (Common palm civet):** The common palm civet has unique habitat requirements conditioned by the food habits. The coloration of the fur coat prevents it noticed by enemies mainly man. Open wooded landscapes with abundant fruiting plants are needed for these largely herbivorous animals. They are

nocturnal and also kill birds and small mammals. Civets are also known to climb palm trees to steel the sweet juice which collects overnight in the pots. Being largely frugivorous many tree seeds are dispersed by civets through its excreta. Baya weaver birds and civets usually have fights as the later invade palm trees on which birds have nested. In human settlements civets create havoc killing poultry and feeding on blood. But civets are capable of controlling mice and rats in the Agricultural fields and its surroundings.

10. **Rattus rattus (Common house rat, Veetteli):** Reported from all tanks. One of the very common small mammal in and around the tanks. This has adapted to almost every habitat except water. It prefers warm place beneath roofs, barns and granaries. It is omnivorous and nocturnal. These rats creates major economic and health problems because it destroys food stuffs and transmits infectious diseases like plague and typhus to humans. Main predators dogs, owls, snakes and cats.
11. **Viverricula indica (Small Indian Civet):** This civet is noticed only from the scrub thickets and grassy grounds of Kaliveli. Like the toddy cat, it hunts mice, rats, squirrels, lizards, small birds and insects at night.
12. **Vulpes bengalensis (The Indian Fox, Kulla nari):** Prosopis and Acacia bushes in the tanks form a very ideal place for them to trap their prey. Cultivated fields with irrigation channels provide good hide-out and ensure water availability. They dig their own burrows. These animals hunt small rodents like palm squirrel, common rat, bandicoots and mice. They even feed on insignificant creatures such as insects, crabs, molluscs and small lizards. It does ideal service to the farmer by predating on large number of rats and crabs. It also feeds on vegetables like melons, shoots and pods of Cicer arietinum.

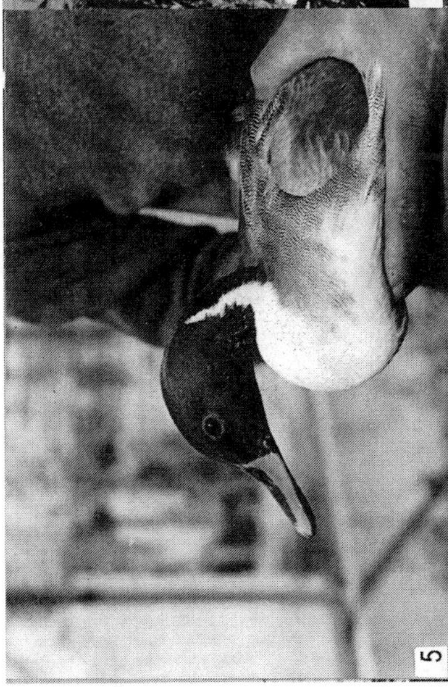
5

6

7

8

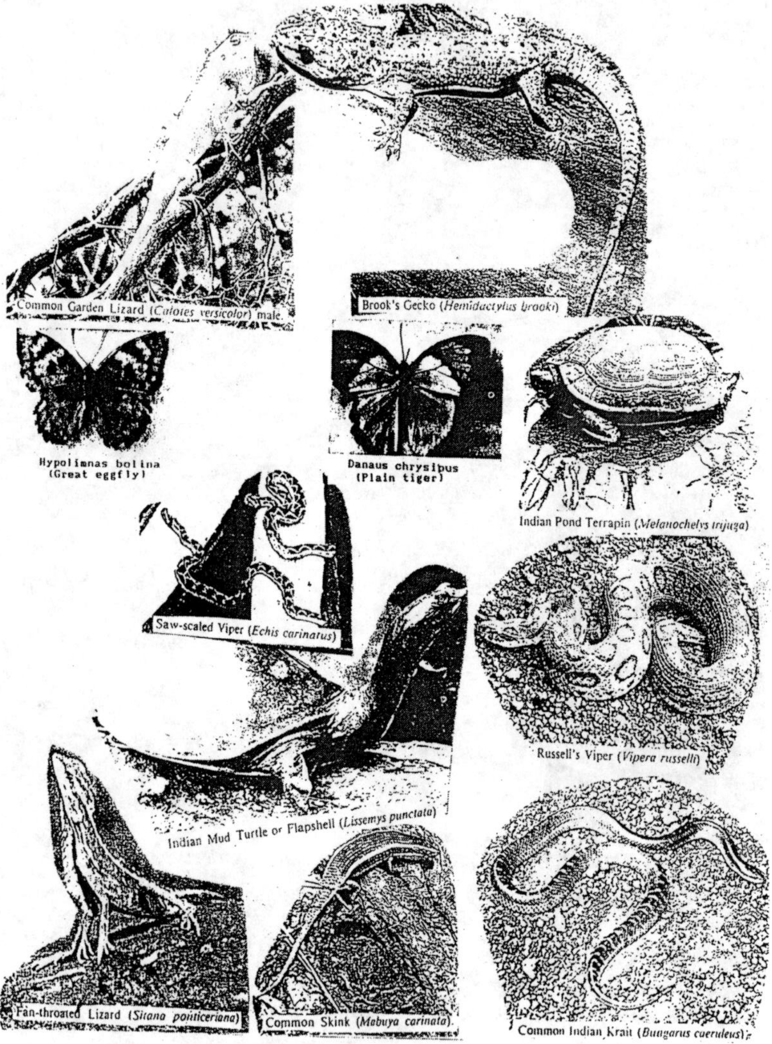

Common Garden Lizard (*Calotes versicolor*) male.

Brook's Gecko (*Hemidactylus brooki*)

Hypolimnas bolina (Great eggfly)

Danaus chrysipus (Plain tiger)

Indian Pond Terrapin (*Melanochelys trijuga*)

Saw-scaled Viper (*Echis carinatus*)

Russell's Viper (*Vipera russelli*)

Indian Mud Turtle or Flapshell (*Lissemys punctata*)

Fan-throated Lizard (*Sitana ponticeriana*)

Common Skink (*Mabuya carinata*)

Common Indian Krait (*Bungarus caeruleus*)

Recurvirostra avosetta
(avocet)
Tringa glareola
(Spotted sandpiper
Anas acuta
(Pintail duck)
Tringa hypoleucos
(Common sandpiper)
Dendrocitta vagabunda
(Tree pie)
Phoenicopterus roseus
(Flamingo)
Ardeola grayii
(Pond heron)
Vanellus indicus
(Redwattled lapwing)
Haliastur indus
(The brahminy Kite)
Pycnonotus cafer
(Redvented Bulbul)
Pitta brachyura
(Indian Pitta)
Dicrurus adsimilis
(Black drongo)
Pelicanus Philippensis
(Spottedbilled Pelican)
Halcyon smyrnensis
Whitebreasted Kingfisher
Francolinus pondicerianus
(Grey patridge)

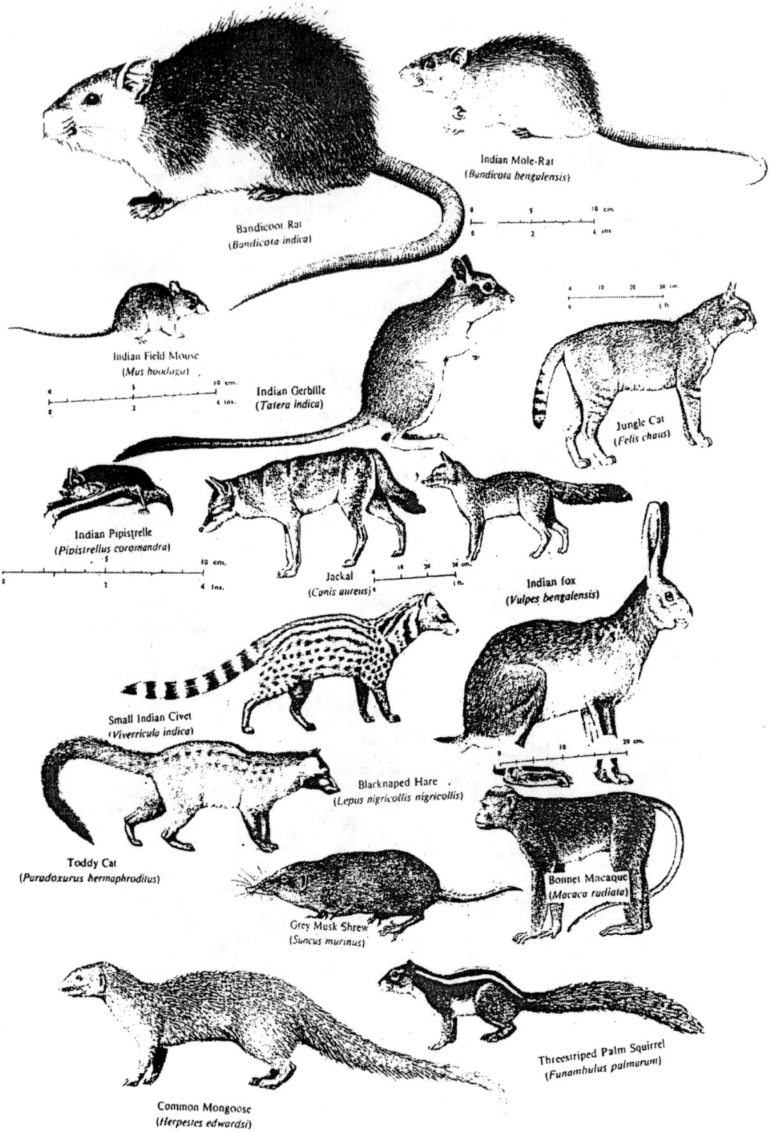
Indian Mole-Rat
(Bandicota bengalensis)
Bandicoot Rat
(Bandicota indica)
Indian Field Mouse
(Mus booduga)
Indian Gerbille
(Tatera indica)
Jungle Cat
(Felis chaus)
Indian Pipistrelle
(Pipistrellus coromandra)
Jackal
(Canis aureus)
Indian fox
(Vulpes bengalensis)
Small Indian Civet
(Viverricula indica)
Blacknaped Hare
(Lepus nigricollis nigricollis)
Toddy Cat
(Paradoxurus hermaphroditus)
Bonnet Macaque
(Macaca radiata)
Grey Musk Shrew
(Suncus murinus)
Threestriped Palm Squirrel
(Funambulus palmarum)
Common Mongoose
(Herpestes edwardsi)

Ipomoea cornea
Cynodon dactylon
Abrus precatorius
Hydrilla verticillata
Marselia

Heliotropium scabrum
Najas sp.
Vitex negundo
Secruningo leucopyrus
Gloriosa superba

Cleome viscosa
Indigofera sp.
Ammania baccifera
Coldenia procumbens
Blepharis molluginifolia
Gomphrena celosioides
Capparis brevispina
Chara sp.

3. BIBLIOGRAPHIES

1. Wetlands

Aakerlund, I.1980. Water resources legislation and forestry policy Forskningsstiftelsen Skogsarbeten, Stockholm (Sweden). 9(11) 63-64.

Adamus, P.R and Stockwell, LT.1983. A method for wetland functional Assessment. Report No.FHWA-1 US. Department of Transportation, Federal Highway Administration, Washington. D.C.

Allanson, B. R. 1990. Inland waters of Southern Africa; an ecological perspective. Monographiae biologicae.64, 458 p.

Allen, S.E.1974 (Ed). Chemical analysis of ecological materials. John Wiley & Sons, New York,565p.

Almberger, P.1989. Environmental effects. Forskningsstiftelsen Skogsarbeten, Stockholm (Sweden). Wetland forestry 8(11) 59·62.

Amador, J.A, Richany, G.H and Jones, R.D. 1992. Factors affecting phosphate uptake by peat soils of the Florida Everglades. Soil Sci. 153 (6)463-470.

Anderson, R.C and Brown, LE. 1991. Establishment of a wetland plant community in a limestone quarry. Castanea. Morgantown, Southern Appalachian Botanical Club 56 (3) 168-175.

Andrews, C.B and Anderson, M.P. 1978. Impact of a power plant on the ground water system of a wetland. Ground Water (USA), 16 (2) 105-111.

APHA, AWWA and WPCF.1981. Standard methods for examination of water and waste water. 16th edition.

Aronson, T.A.1984. Economic Halophytes, A global review. Economic plants for arid lands. Conference of Royal Botanical Gardens. Kew, 23-27.

Aselmann, Iand Crutzen, P.J. 1989. Global distribution of natural freshwater wetlands and rice paddies, their net primary productivity, seasonality and possible methane emissions, J. Aim. Chem.(8) 307·358.

Auclair, A.N.D, Bouchard, A and Pajaczkowski, J. 1976. Plant standing crop and productivity relations in a Scirpus-Equisetum wetland [Canada] Ecology (USA), 57 (5) 941-952.

Aust, W.M. and Lea, and Gregory, J.D. 1991. Removal of flood sediments by a clear-cut. Tupelo-Cypress wetland. Water Res. Bull. 27(1) 111-116.

Bachoon, D and Jones, R.D. 1992. Potential rates of methanogenesis in sea grass marshes with peat and marsh soils in the Everglades. Soil Biol. Biochem. 24 (1) 21- 27.

Baldock, D. 1984. Wetland drainage in Europe IIED/IEEP. London.

Baltezore, J.F.1991. Status of wetlands in North Dakota. Agricultural Experiment station, North Dakota state University, 73p.

Batzer, D.P and Resh, V.H. 1992. Wetland management strategies that enhance waterfowl habitats can also control mosquitoes. J. Am. Mosq. Control Assoc. 8 (2) 117-125.

Bellamy, O.J and Pritchard, T. 1984. 'Project Telma', a scientific framework for conserving the world's peat lands. Biological conservation. 33-40.

Berezkin, D.I. Klimkov, V.T. Nesterenko, I.M and Kvet, J. 1990. Wetland reclamation in the Byelorussian SSR. Tasks, Veg.Sci. 25: 45-54.

Bemaldez, F.G. Rey Benayas, J.M and Martinez, A. 1993. Ecological impact of groundwater extraction on wetlands (Douro Basin, Spain). J.Hydrol. 141 (1/4), 219-238.

Bernard, J.M and Hankinson, G. 1979. Seasonal changes in standing crop, primary production and nutrient levels in a Carex rostrata wetland [USA]. Oikos 32 (3) 328-336.

Berry, B.J.L 1962. Sampling, coding, and storing Hood plain data Farm Economics Division, Economic Research Service, U.S. Dept. of Agriculture, 27p.

Bjoerk, S and Graneli, W. 1978. Energy needs and the environment [Phragmites australis, heating fuel, management of wetland ecosystems] Ambio 7 (4) 150-156.

Blacke, N.M. 1980. Land into water - water into land. Florida state University, Tallahassee, U.S.

Blakely, D. R and Christopher, T .1985. Inland aquaculture development handbook. Oxford: Fishing News, 184p.

Bontadelli, P.F. 1992. U.S wetland protection programs: direction and outlook of steward--ship agencies. Trans. North Am. Wildl. Nat. Resour. Conf., Washington. D.C. Wildlife Management Institute.38-240.

Boutin, C and Keddy, P.A. 1993. A functional classification of wetland plants. J. Veg.Sci4 (5) 591-600.

Boyce, D.R.1987. Rood plain management's effect on surface drainage. Am. Soc. Agric. Eng. Microfiche. Collect. St. Joseph, MI.

Boyt, F.L Bayley, S.E and Zoltek, J. Jr. 1977. Removal of nutrients from treated municipal wastewater by wetland vegetation. J. Water Pollution Control Federation (USA).49(5) 789-799.

Brackhekke, W.G and Drijver, C.A. 1984. Wetlands Importance, Threats and protection. Dutch society for protection of Birds, Netherlands.

Bricker, K.S. Ladda, W and Gannon, J.E. 1978.Composrtion and distribution of crustacean plankton in twelve inland water bodies of Thailand. Bangkok (Thailand). 14p.

Bridges, C. 1989.Waterfowl habitat management on public lands a strategy for the future. Dept. of the Interior, Bureau of Land Management, Washington, D.C 43p.

Bridgham, S.D, Faulkner, S.P and Richardson, C.J. 1991. Steel rod oxidation as a hydrologic indicator in wetland soils. J. Soil Sci. Soc. Am.55 (3) 856-862.

Brinkman, R. 1977. Land suitability evaluation for wetland rice: criteria and required standards. Rome. FAO. 10p.

Brinson, M.M. Lago, A.E and Brown, S. 1981. Primary productivity, decomposition and consumer activity in freshwater wetlands. Annual Review of Ecology and Systematics. 12:123-162.

Brown, W.W. 1978. Wetland mapping in New Jersey and New York Photogram metric Engineering and Remote Sensing (USA). 45(3). 303-314.

Bryant, M.D. 1991. The Copper River Dena pulse study: an interdisciplinary survey of the aquatic habitats. Portland, Or.: U.S. Dept. of Agriculture, Forest Service, Pacific North-west Research Station, 43p.

Campbell, W.A. 1979. Legal aspects of flood plain management. Raleigh (USA). North Carolina State University. 49p.

Carp, E. 1980. A dictionary of western pale arctic wetlands. IUCN-UNEP. Gland, Switzer-land.

Chapman, V.J. 1977. Wet-coastal ecosystems. Elsevier, Amsterdam.

Chescheir, G.M, Skaggs, R.W and Gilliam, J.W. 1992.Evaluationof wetland buffer areas for treatment of pumped agricultural drainage water. Trans. Am. Soc. Agric. Eng. St. Joseph, 35 (1) 175-182.

Childers, D.L. and Gosselink, J.G.1990. Assessment of cumulative impacts to water quality in a forested wetland landscape. J.Environ. Qual. 19(3) 455-464.

Civco, D.L, Kennard, W.C and Lefor, M.W. 1978.A technique for evaluating inland wetland photo-interpretation: The Cell Analytical Method (CAM) [Soil surveys]. Photogram metric Engineering and Remote Sensing (USA). 44(8)1045-1052.

Cooksey, K.E and Cooksey, B. 1978. Growth-influencing substances in sediment extracts from a subtropical wetland: investigation using a diatom bioassay Amphora coffeaeformis, Algae, mangrove communities. Journal of Phycology 14(3) 347-352.

Corniere, P. 1979. The accounts of nature patrimony, inland water, seas, atmosphere, land and soil, vegetal and animal life, natural resources; France. Futuribles-2000, 25: 89-99.

Cowardin, LM, Carter, V, Golet, F.C and La Roe, E.T.1979. "Classification of wetlands and deep water habitats of united States" FW3/OBS-79/31. Office of Biological service, Fish and Wild life Service, U.S. Department of Interior, Washington D.C.

Cowling, S.J. 1977. Classification of the wetland habitats of water-birds Australian Marine Science Bulletin 58, 15 -16.

Craft, C.B and Richardson, C.J. 1993. Peat accretion and N, P, and organic C accumulation in nutrient - enriched and un-enriched everglades peat lands. Ecol. Appl. 3 (3) 446 - 458.

Cramer, T.A. 1993. Limnological and habitat influences on wetland bird communities in the Nebraska Sand hills. 94 pp.

Crance, J. H. 1988. Relationships between Palustrine wetlands of forested riparian floodplains and fishery resources: a review. Washington, DC: U.S. Fish and Wildlife Service, 27p.

Craswell, E.T and Vleck, P.L. 1978. Fate of fertilizer nitrogen applied to wetland rice fields of the United States of America. International Rice Research Inst., College, Laguna (Philippines). Proceedings of the Nitrogen and Rice Symposium. College, Laguna (Philippines).(l) 297-332.

Crawford, P. 1990. Application of the new Timbco Feller Buncher to wetland, steep terrain and selective cutting. PAP. AMER. SOC AGRIC. ENG. St. Joseph, Michigan. 3pp.

Crites, R.W. and Tchobanoglous, G.1992. Discussion of: Nitrogen removal in experimental wetland treatment systems: evidence for the role of aquatic plants. Water. Environ. Res. 64 (7), 920-921.

Crow, J.H and Mac Donald, K.B. 1979. Wetland values secondary production. In: wetland functions and values: The state of our understanding. Greason, P.E et al (eds). American water resources Association, 146 - 161.

Crumpacker, D.W, Hodge, S.W, Friedley, D and Gregg, W.P. Jr. 1988. A preliminary assessment of the status of major terrestrial and wetland ecosystems on federal and Indian lands in the United States. J.Soc. Conserv. Biol. Cambridge, 2 (1) 103-115.

Cubbage, F.W and Flather, C.H. 1993. Forested wetland area and distribution: a detailed look at the South. J.For. 91 (5) 35-40.

Dahl, T.E. 1990. Wetland losses in United States 1780 to 1980s. U.S. Department of Interior, Fish and Wild life service, Washington D.C.

Davidson, T. 1975. Soil organic matter fluctuations in some tropical wetland soils in Turrialba, Costa Rica. IICA, 25(2), 183-190.

Davis, A.F. 1993. Rare wetland plants and their habitats in Pennsylvania. Proc. Acad. Nat. Sci. Phila. Philadelphia, 144, 254-262.

Davis, A.M. 1979. Wetland succession, fire and the pollen record: a mid-western example [in Tamarack Creek, Wisconsin]. American Midland Naturalist (USA), 102(1) 86-94.

De Steven, D and Franke, W, 1990. Germination and growth of Ranunculus cymbalaria, an endangered wetland plant. Mich. Bot. 29 (3) 83-87.

De la Cruz, A.A 1980. Economic evaluations and Ecological implications of Alternative uses of mangrove swamps in S. E. Asia Proceedings of Asian symposium on mangrove evaluation; Kulalumpur, Malaysia. 25 - 29.

De la Cruz, A.A. 1982. Wetland uses in tropics and their implications on the world carbon cycle unpublished message to Edward maltby Quoted In 'water logged wealth'. 1986. Published as an Earth scan paper back by International institute for Environment and Development.

Diggelen, J.van.1991. Effects of inundation stress on salt marsh halophytes. Tasks. Veg. Sci. 22, 62-73.

Diggelen, R. van, Grootjans, A.P, Kemmers, R.H, Kooijman, A.M, Succow, M, Vries, N. P. J. de and Wirdum, G.van. 1991. Hydro-Ecological analysis of the fen system Lieper Posse, Eastern Germany. J.Veg. Sci., 2(4), 465-476.

Domingo, A.A and Hagerman, H.H. 1982. Sorjan cropping system trial in irrigated wet land conditions. Philipp.J. Crop Sci. 7 (3), 154-161.

Drake, B.G. 1992..A field study of the effects of elevated CO_2 on ecosystem processes in a Chesapeake Bay wetland. Aust. Bot. 40 (4/5), 579-595.

Drijver, C. A. and Rodenbarg, W.F. 1988. Water management at cross roads: the case of the Sahelian wetlands. Paper presented at the International symposium on Hydrology of wetlands in Semi-Arid and Arid regions. Seville. Spain.

Dubensky, M,M, Berg, R.S and Berry, W.S. 1993. Forested wetland area and distribution: a forest and paper industry policy. J.For. 91(5), 20-24.

Dugan, P.J. (Ed) 1990. Wetland conservation a review of current issues and required action. IUCN, Gland, Switzerland.

Dykyjova, D and Kvet, J.1978. Primary productivity of freshwater wetlands in: M.Smart (Ed.) Proc. Internat. Conf. on wetlands and wild fowl. International waterfowl resource bureau, Slimbridge, England.

Earthscan 1984. Cropland or wasteland - The problems and promises :of Irrigation. Earth scan press Briefing document 38.

Etherington, J.R. 1983. Wetland ecology. Edward Arnold, London.

Finlayson, M and Moser, M (eds) I991. Wetlands. Facts on File Limited, Oxford.

Finlayson, C.M, Hollis, Ted, Dacis, Tim and Crivelli, Alain. 1992. Managing Mediterranean wetlands and their birds: proceedings of a symposium on managing Mediterranean wetlands and their birds for the year 2000 and beyond. Slimbridge, UK: International Waterfowl and Wetlands Research Bureau; Ozzano Emilia, Italy: Istituto Nazionale di Biologia della Selvaggia. 285p.

Florida Cooperative Fish and Wildlife Research Unit. 1990. Savannah Coastal Refuges. Development and application of a habitat succession model for the wetland complex of the Savannah National Wildlife Refuge.

Folke, C.1991. The societal value of wetland life-support. Ecol. Econ. Environ. 1, 141·171.

Frayer, W.E and Hefner, J.M. 1991. Florida wetlands: status and trends, 1970's to 1980's. U.S. Fish and Wild life Service, Southeast Region, 31 p.

Gallagher, J.L. 1978. Decomposition Process: Summary and recommendations, In: Fresh-water wetlands: Ecological process and management potential. Good, R.E. et al (eds). Academic Press, New York. 145 -151.

Garber, M.P and Moorhead, O.J. 1992. Selection, production and establishment of wetland trees and shrubs. Bull. Coop. Ext. Serv. Univ. Ga. Coil. Agric. 1082, 12.

Gebhardt, K.A. 1990-1991. Riparian area management: Riparian and wetland classification review. U.S. Dept. of the Interior, Bureau of Land Management, Service Center, 56p.

George, M. 1992. The land use, ecology and conservation of Broad land. 558bp.

Ghosh, D.1983. Sewage treatment fisheries in East Calcutta wetlands; Low cost resource - conserving option in environment repair. Project report utilization of Calcutta's sewage, Government of west Bengal, Calcutta, India 1983.

Godfrey, R.K and Wooten, J.W. 1979. Aquatic and wetland plants of southeastern United States: monocotyledons. 712 p.

Golubev, G.N. 1988. Sustainable management of water resources: a basin wise approach. Int. J. Water Resour. Dev. 4 (4) 219-223.

Good, R.E. Whigham, D.F and Simpson, R.E. 1978. Freshwater wetlands. New York.

Goode, D. 1983. Conservation of wetland habitat in Britain; An assessment of priorities. Paper presented at Meeting at institute of Biology on 'Wetlands under threat?' Natural history Museum.

Goode, B.N and Pierce, R. J.1990. Federal wetland regulation Reference manual, Wetland Training Institute, 283p.

Gore, A.J.P. 1983. Introduction In: Gore, AJ.P. (Ed) Ecosystems of the world (4A) Mires, Swamp, bog, fen and moor. 1. Elsevier, Amsterdam. 1-34.

Gosselink, J.G and Baumann, R.H. 1980. Wetland Inventories: Wetland loss along the United States Coast. Z. Geomorph. 34,173-187.

Gosselink, J.G and Turner, R.E. 1978. The role of hydrology in fresh water wetland Ecosystems, In: Freshwater wetlands: Ecological process and management potential. Good, R.E. et a! (eds) Academic Press, New York. 63-78.

Green, F.H.W. 1980. Reid under-drainage before and after 1940. The Agricultural History review. (128), 120-123.

Growns, J.E, Davis, J.A, Cheal, F, Schmidt, LG, Rosich, R.S and Bradley, S.J. 1992. Multivariate pattern analysis of wetland invertebrate communities and environmental variables in Western Australia Aust. J. Ecol, 17 (3) 275-288.

Gupta, T,R and Foster, J.H. 1975. Economic criteria for freshwater wetland policy in Massachusetts. Amer. Jour. Agric. Econ. 57(1), 40-45.

Gustafsson, J.1980. Drainage techniques [wetland forestry]. Forsknings stiftelsen Skogsarbeten, Stockholm (Sweden). 6(9) 26-36.

Hackney, C.T and Yelverton, G.F. 1990. Effects of human activities and sea level rise on wetland ecosystems in the Gape Fear River estuary, North Carolina, USA. Tasks. Veg. Sci. 25, 55-61.

Hamilton, L.S. and Snedaker, S.C. (Eds) 1984. Handbook for Mangrove area management. UNEP - East West Centre - IUCN.

Hansen, P.L. 1984. Classification and management of riparian-wetland Shrub sites in Montana Gen. Tech. Rep. INT. U.S. Dep. Agric. For Serv. Intermt. Res. Stn. 289, 68 - 78.

Harbell, S and Lines, I.1991. Aquaculture development permits for wetland areas. Ext. Bull. Wash. State Univ. Coop. Ext. Serv. 1620, 2.

Heitmeyer, M.E. 1980. Characteristics of wetland habitats and waterfowl populations in Oklahoma. 263p.

Higgins, K.F. 1992. Waterfowl production on the Woodworth Station in south-central North Dakota, 1965 - 1981. Washington D.C. : U.S. Dept. of the Interior, Fish and Wildlife Service, 79p.

Hoagland, B.W and Jones, R.L 1992. Wetland and riparian flora of the Upper Green River Basin, South Central Kentucky. Trans. Ky. Acad. Sci. Louisville, 53 (3/4), 141 - 153.

Hollis, G.E., Agnew, C.T and Sterenson, A.C 1985. Water fowl damned. Geographical Magazine, 7, 564.

Hubbard, D.E. 1988. Glaciated prairie wetland functions and values a synthesis of the literature. Washington, D.C.: Fish and Wildlife Service, U.S. Dept. of the Interior, 50p.

Hunter, J.M., Rey, L and Scott, D. 1982. Man made lakes; Man made diseases. Social Science and Medicine 1(1) 34.

Hupp, C.R and Bazemore, D.E. 1993. Temporal and spatial patterns of wetland sedimentation, West Tennessee. J.Hydrol.141 (114),179 - 196.

Inter agency Committee on Wetlands Restoration and Creation (U.S.).1992. A national program for wetlands restoration and creation: report of the Inter agency Committee on Wetlands Restoration and Creation to the Policy Coordinating Group, Interagency Task Force on Wetlands, 47p.

International Workshop on Modernisation of Tank Irrigation System 1982. Proceedings of the International Workshop on Modernisation of Tank Irrigation System: problems and issues. Madras: Centre for Water Resources, Anna University, 223p.

IUCN-UNEP-WWF. 19800. World conservation strategy. IUCN. Gland, Switzerland.

IUCN.1984. A tale of two wetlands, IUCN Bulietin.5,15.

Jacobson, Jr.G.K, Almquist, Jacobson, H and Winne, J.C. 1991. Conservation of rare plant habitat: insights from the recent history of vegetation and fire at Crystal Fen, northern Maine, USA. Bioi. Conserv. 57 (3), 287-314.

Jauron, L and Labonte, D.1981. Inland Waters Directorate. Quebec Region. Summary study of the macrophytes of the La flamme Lake (Quebec): Direction generale des eaux interieures, Environment Canada, Region du Quebec.

Jeyapalan, B.A. 1978. Water management of tank irrigation system in Tamilnadu, India. International Commission on Irrigation and Drainage. Philippine National Committee, Manila ICID Second Regional Afro. Asian Conference technical papers. Manila (Philippines). 1, 77-87.

Johansson, C.E. 1979. Survey of wetland objects in Sweden. Solna (Sweden). SNV. 362 p.

John, D.M. 1966. The inland waters of tropical West Africa: ban introduction and botanical review. Schweizerbartsche Verlag., 244p.

Johnson, R.L 1960. Timber harvest from wetlands, in: Greeson, et al (Eds) Wetland functions and values; the state of our understanding. 598-605, American water resources Association, Minneapolis, Minn.

Jolley, J.W. 1962. The efficiency of constructed wetland-pond systems in the reduction of sediment and nutrient discharges from agricultural watersheds. Orono, Me., 180p.

Kana, T.W, Baca, B.J and Williams, M.L. 1986. Potential impacts of sea level rise on wetlands around Charleston, South Carolina Washington, D.C.: U.S. Environmental Protection Agency, Office of Policy Planning and Evaluation, 65p.

Keete, C.W. 1972. Marsh production: A survey of the literature contribution to Marine Sciences (t6), 163 - 183.

Kentula, M.E and Hairston, A.J.1992. Wetlands: an approach to improving decision making in wetland restoration and creation. 151 p.

Kienitz, G. 1979. Hydrological regime as influenced by drainage of wetlands. UNESCO, Paris.

Kirali, S.J, Cross, F.A and Buffington, J.D. 1990. Federal coastal wetland mapping programs: a report by the National Ocean Pollution Policy Board's Habitat Loss and Modification Working Group. Washington, D.C. U.S. Dept. of the Interior, Fish and Wildlife Service. 174p.

Kirby, R.E, Lewis, S.J, Sexson, T.N. 1988. Fire in North American wetland ecosystems and fire-wildlife relations: an annotated bibliography Washington, DC: Fish and Wildlife Service, U.S. Dept. of the Interior, 146p.

Kogawa, H. 1932. The men who created varieties of wetland rice. Shinchosha, Tokyo, Heisei 289p.

Koonlin, T. 1980. Logging the swamp for food. in: Stanton, W.R. and Flach, W. (Eds) The equatorial swamp as a natural resource, 13-34.

Kuether, D.O. 1977. Soil compaction and wetland rice tillage systems [in Asian countries]. College, Laguna (Philippines). 14p.

Kusler, J.A. 1983. Our national wetland heritage. A protection Guidebook Environmental Law institute, Washington. D.C.

Kusler, J.A. 1992. Wetlands delineation. Environment. 34 (2) 6-11, 29-37.

Kusler, J.A and Daly, Sally. 1989. Proceedings of an International Symposium: Wetlands and river corridor management, July 5-9, 1989, Charleston, South Carolina USA. Berne, N.Y.: Association of Wetland Managers, 520p.

Kusler, J,A and Hamann, Richard G. 1985. Wetland protection: strengthening the role of the states: proceedings of a national symposium. 711 p.

Kuzila, M.S, Rundquist, D.C and Green, J.A. 1991. Methods for estimating wetland loss: the Rain basin region of Nebraska, 1927-1981. J. Soil Water Conserv. 46 (6), 441-446.

La Baugh, J.W, Witer, T.C, Adomitis, V.A and Swanson, G.A. 1987. Hydrology and chemistry of selected prairie wetlands in cotton wood lake area, Stutsman country, North Dakota 1979-82. US Geological survey Professional paper 1431, 26p.

Lacki, M.J, Hummer, J.W and Webster, H.J. 1992. Mine-drainage treatment wetland as habitat for herpetofaunal wildlife. Environ. Manage. 16(4), 513-520.

Laclaire, L.V. 1992. Ecology of temporary ponds in North-Central Florida. 175p.

Lammers, R, 1977. Sampling insects with a wetland emergence trap: design and evaluation of the trap with preliminary results. American Midland Naturalist (USA). 97(2) .381-389.

Lammers, T.G and Van Der Vak, A.G. 1977. A checklist of the aquatic and wetland vascular plants of Iowa I. Ferns, fern allies, and dicotyledons 41-88.

Larson. J.S. 1983. Wetland value assessment: A review. paper read at SCOPE - UNEP. Work shop on Ecosystems dynamics in Wetlands and shallow water bodies. Tallinn. Estonian. SSR. 3-13.

Latip, M.A and Harith, Z.H. 1991. Pre-survey of aquatic weeds in wetland rice cultivation in Sabah. Malays. Appl. Biol. 20 (1)113-116.

Le Doux, C.B and Baumgras, J.E. 1990. Cost of wetland protection using a Christy cable yarder. PAP. AMER. SOC. AGRIC. ENG. St. Joseph, (90-7573) 13pp.

Leck, M.A and Simpson, R.L 1993. Seeds and seedlings of the Hamilton Marshes, a Delaware River tidal freshwater wetland. Proc. Acad. Nat. Sci. Phila. 144, 267-281.

Leibowitz, N.C, Squires, L and Baker, J.P. 1991. Research plan for monitoring wetland ecosystems. Corvallis, Or.: Environmental Research Laboratory, U.S. Environmental Protection Agency, 157pp.

Leitch, J.A and Baltezore, J.F. 1992. The status of North Dakota wetlands. J. Soil Water Conserv. 47(3), 216-219.

Ludden,. A.P., Frink, D.L and Johnson, D.H. 1983. Water storage capacity of natural wetland depressions in Devils, Lake Basin of North Dakota. Jour. soil and water conserv. 38, 45-48.

Lugo, A.E and Snedaker, S.C. 1974. The ecology of mangroves. A review of Ecology and systematics. 5p.

Lugo, A.E, Brown, S and Brinson, M.M. 1990. Concepts in wetland ecology. Ecosystems of the World. 15, 53-85.

Lugo, A.E, Brinson, M.M and Brown, S. 1990. Synthesis and search for paradigms in wetland ecology. Ecosystems of the World. (15) 447-460.

Luzar, E.J and Henning, S. A.1989. Alternative perspectives on wetland evaluation and use: proceedings of a regional workshop, Baton Rouge, Louisiana, November 10-11, 1988. 46pp.

Lyon, J.G. 1993. Practical handbook for wetland identification and delineation. Boca Raton, FL : CRC Press, 157pp.

Macartney, C. 1985. These 'Wastelands' are vast store houses. World wide Fund wetlands pack-2 WWF. IUCN, Gland, Switzerland.

Macintosh, D.J. 1983. Riches lie in tropical swamps. Geographical Magazine. 45, 184-188

Maltby, E. 1983. Wetlands for future. Geographical Magazine.45, 626-627.

Marble, Anne D.I992. A guide to wetland functional design. Boca Raton: Lewis Publishers, 222p.

Mathews, E and Fung, I. 1987. Methane emission from natural wetlands; Global distribution, area and environmental characteristics of source. Global Biogeochemical cycles. 1, 61-86.

Mathias, M.E and Moyle, P. 1992. Wetland and aquatic habitats. Agric. Ecosyst. Environ. 42 (112), 165-176.

Mayya, S.G and Prasad, R. 1989. Systems analysis of tank irrigation. I. Crop staggering. J.lrr. Drain. Eng. New York, N.Y.: American Society of Civil Engineers. 115(3), 384-405.

Mclntyre, S.C and Naney, J.W. 1991. Sediment deposition in a forested inland wetland with a steep-farmed watershed. J. Soil Water Conserv. 46 (1), 64-66.

Mc Namara, J.P, Siegel, D.I, Glaser, P.H and Beck; R.M. 1992. Hydrogeologic controls on peat land development in the Malloryville Wetland, New York (USA). J. Hydrol. 140(1/4), 279-296.

Meeks, G and Runyon, L.C. 1990. Wetlands protection and the states. Denver, Colo.: National Conference of State Legislatures, 26p.

Michaelis, F.B. 1984. Possible effects of forestry on inland waters of Tasmania: a review. Environ. Conserv. 11 (4) 331-343.

Mickle, A.M. 1993. Pollution filtration by plants in wetland-littoral zones. Proc. Acad. Nat. Sci. Phila 144, 262-290.

Miller, J.B. I976. Wetland classification in western Canada: a guide to marshes and shallow open water wetlands in the grasslands and parklands of the Prairie Provinces. Can. Wildl. Serv. Rep. Ser.37, 38

Miller, B.A. 1985. Strategy for costal wetland development in Jamaica. International peat symposium, Kingston.

Mitch, W.T and Gosselink. J.G. 1985. Wetlands. Van Rostrand Reinhold Co. New York.

Mitchell, D.S. 1978. Aquatic weeds in Australian inland waters. Australian Government Publishing Service, Canberra, 199p.

Mitsch, W.T, Day, T.W., Jr, Tylor, T.R and Madden, C. 1982. Models of North American Fresh water wetlands· A review. International Journal of Ecology and Environmental Sciences.6, 109-140.

More, N.W. 1984. Ramsar confederation. Groningen.

Moritsugu, M. 1985. A preliminary investigation on chemical quality of inland waters in Kenya Ber. Ohara Inst. Landwirtsch. Bioi. Okayama. Univ. 19 (1), 25-34.

Morris, J.T. 1991. Effects of nitrogen loading on wetland ecosystems with particular reference to atmospheric deposition .. Palo Alto, Calif.: Annual Reviews, 22, 257-279.

Morton, J.F. 1976. Craft industries from coastal wetland vegetation. In: Wiley, M.L. (Ed.) Estuarine products. Academic press. New York, 254-226.

Moss, B. 1980. Ecology of freshwaters. Blackwell, Oxford.

Motts, W.S and Heely, R.H. 1973. Wetlands and ground water in Larson, J.S. (Eds.) a guide to important characteristics and values of fresh water wetlands in the north east water resource. Research centre University of Massachusetts, Amherest. 1973, 5-8.

Munro, J.W. 1991. Wetland restoration in the mitigation context Restoration and Manage. Notes. Madison, Wis. 9 (2), 80-86.

Murphy, R. A.1992. Problem identification and planning strategies for saline wetland protection in Lancaster County Nebraska.161p.

Mutz, K.M and Lee, L.C. 1987. Wetland and riparian ecosystems of the American West: Eighth Annual Meeting of the Society of Wetland Scientists, May 26-29, 1987, Seattle, Washington.9, 349.

National Association of Conservation Districts.1991. Ducks Unlimited. The Wealth in wetlands. NACD, League City, Tex.

Neue, H.U, Quijano, C and Scharpenseel H.W. 1991. Conservation and enhancement of wetland soils. Evaluation for sustainable land management in the developing world: proceedings of the International Workshop on Evaluation for Sustainable Land Management in the Developing World, Chiang Mai, Thailand, 15-21 September 1991. 279-303.

Nurse, E.A. 1985. Maintaining freshwater and marine biological diversity in LDCs. Reported in wetlands Conservation programme. WWF. IUCN, Gland, Switzerland.

Ogawa, Y and Ichimura, S. 1984. The relationship between phytoplankton diversity and trophic status of inland waters. Jap. J.Ecol.34 (1J 27-33.

Olson, R.K. 1993. Created and natural wetlands for controlling non point source pollution. Boca Raton, Fla. : C.K. Smoley, 216p.

Oppen, M. von and Subba Rao, K.V. 1980. Tank irrigation in semi-arid tropical India. Patancheru, Andhra Pradesh, India: International Crops Research Institute for the Semi-Arid Tropics, 3p.

Oppen, M. von and Subba Rao, K.V. 1987. Tank irrigation in semi-arid tropical India. economic evaluation and alternatives for improvement. Patancheru, Andhra Pradesh. India: International Crops Research Institute for the Semi-Arid Tropics. 38p.

Oresman, S.M. Tiffany, J and Robbins, C.S. 1948. Breeding bird survey: damp deciduous scrub with numerous standing dead trees. Audubon Field Notes 2, 226p.

Owen, C.R and Jacobs, H.M. 1992. Wetland protection as land-use planning: the impact of section 404 in Wisconsin, USA. Environ. Manage. 16(3), 345-353.

Palanisami, K. 1988. Evaluating the performance of tank irrigation systems Agric. Syst. 28(3), 161-177.

Palanisami, K and Easter, K.W. 1987. Small-scale surface (tank) irrigation in Asia. Water Resour. Res. 23 (5), 774-780.

Pannier, R. 1985. Mangroves impacted by human induced disturbance; A case study of Orinoco delta mangrove Ecosystem. Environmental Management 3, 225-237.

Patten, B.C., 1931. Wetlands and shallow continental water bodies. The Hague, the Netherlands: SPB Academic Publishing, 1990.

Payne, J.M and Wentz, W.A. 1992. Private property and wetland conservation. Trans. North Am. Wildl. Nat. Resour. Conf. Washington, D.C., 225-233.

Pehrsson, O. 1979. Wetland management for seed production - important waterfowl food - a literature review. Solna (Sweden). SNV. 84p.

Peterson, M.J. 1991. The vascular flora of Lovets Pond, Jackson County, Illinois. Trans. III. State Acad. Sci. 84 (1/2), 28-41.

Petr, T. 1982. Introduction to types of inland waters [Swamp fisheries, South East Asia]. FAO. Fish Rep. 288, 3-12.

Pettry, D.E. 1991. Wetland delineation. Proc, Annu. Hardwood Symp. 51-56.

Phillips, M.M. 1993. Wetland plant communities and factors influencing plant distributions at the Cedar Creek Natural History Area, Minnesota. 220p.

Podloucky, R. 1976. Wetland campaign in Europe: Consequences of the damming-up of a wetland of international importance. Natur, und. Landschaft. 51(5), 151-152.

Prasad, R and Mayya, S.G. 1989. Systems analysis of tank irrigation. II. Delayed start and water deficit. J. Irr. Drain. Eng. New York, 115(3). 406-420.

Reed, R.M, Salk, M.S and Webb, J.W. 1991. Evaluation of impacts on wetlands: do NEPA analyses integrate wetland protection requirements? 8p.

Reed, S.C and Brown, D.S. 1992. Constructed wetland design - the first generation. Water Environ. Res. Alexandria, Va. 64(6), 776-781.

Reinecke, K.J. 1992. DUCKDATA: a bibliographic data base for North American waterfowl (Anatidae) and their wetland habitats. Washington, D.C.: U.S. Dept. of the Interior, Fish and Wildlife Service, 7p.

Reppert, R.T. 1992. Wetlands mitigation banking concepts. Fort Belvoir, VA: U.S. Army Corps of Engineers, Water Resources Support Center, Institute for Water Resources, Policy and Special Studies Division, 25p.

Richardson, C.J. 1979. Primary productivity values in freshwater wetlands, In: Wetland functions and values: The state of our understanding. Greason, P.E. et al (eds) 131-145.

Richardson, C.J, Kadlec, J.A, Wentz, W.A, Chamie, J.P.M and Kadlec, R.H. 1975. Background ecology and the effects of nutrient additions on a central Michigan wetland, 52p.

Richardson, C.J. 1983. Pocosins; Vanishing wastelands or valuable wetlands. Bioscience. (33), 626-633.

Roberts; M.L. and Stuckey, R.L. 1992. Distribution patterns of selected aquatic arid wetland vascular plants in relation to the Ohio canal system, Bartonia. Proc. Phila. Bot. Club. 57, 50-74.

Romanowski, N. 1992, Water and wetland plants for southern Australia. Port Melbourne, Vic.: Lothian Book, 168 pp.

Ruelle, R. 1991. A pesticide and toxicity evaluation of wetland waters and sediments on national wildlife refuges in South Dakota. Pierre, S.D.: U.S. Fish and Wildlife Service, Fish and Wildlife Enhancement, South Dakota State Office, 11p.

SWCS, 1992. SWCS adopts wetland policy statement. J. Soil Water. Conserv. 47 (6), 438-440.

Sadlon, N.P. 1992. On course with nature working within the quagmire of wetland regulation. U.S.G.A. Green Sect. Rec. 30(2), 21-23.

Saenger, P., Hegrel, E.J and Davie, J.D.S. 1983. Global status of mangrove ecosystems. IUCN, WWF, Gland, Switzerland.

Sather, J.H. and Smith, R.D. 1984. An overview of major wetland functions. US. Fish and Wild life service FWS/OBS 84/18. US Department of Interior, Washington, D.C.

Sather, J.H. (ed.) 1976. Proceedings of the National Wetland Classification and Inventory Workshop. [Washington]. Fish and Wildlife Service, U.S. Dept. of the Interior. 110p.

Schneller-McDonald, K, Ischinger, L.S and Auble, G.T. 1990. Wetland creation and restoration: description and summary of the literature. Washington, D.C. U.S. Dept. of the Interior, Fish and Wildlife Service, 198p.

Schuhart, A. 1978. Where the wetlands are [National Wetland Inventory, land use, USA]. Soil Conservation (USA). 44(4) 17-20.

Schulz, M, Beardsell, C and Sandiford, K. 1991. Sites of faunal significance in the western wetlands of Melbourne. Melbourne: Wildlife Branch, Dept. of Conservation and Environment, 284p.

Scott, D.A and Carbonall, M. (Eds.) 1986. A dictionary of neotropical wetlands IUCN, Cambridge and IWRS, Slim bridge.

Scott, D.A and Carbonnell, M. 1985. A directory of Neotropical wetlands. IUCN, Gland, Switzerland.

Scott, D.A and Poole, C.M. 1989. A status overview of Asian wetlands. AWB. Kulalampur, Malaysia.

Segelquist C. 1990. Synthesis of soil-plant correspondence data from twelve wetland studies throughout the United States Washington, D.C.: U.S. Dept. of the Interior, Fish and Wildlife Service, 24p.

Shanmugham. C.R, Sakthivadivel.R and Savadamuthu.S. 1984. Performance appraisal of tank irrigation system - a micro level study. Productivity and equity in irrigation systems *I* edited by Niranjan Pant. New Delhi: Ashish, 179-197.

Sharma. K.P. 1982. Use of water resources in relation to the inland fisheries of India. FAO. Fish. Rep. 288,150-166.

Sheail. J. 1992. The re-establishment of wetland habitats - a search for guidelines. Agric. Eng. 47 (3), 71-73.

Shepard. J.P, Lucier. A.A and Haines. L.W. 1993. Industry and forest wetlands: cooperative research initiatives. J. For. 91(5), 29-31, 33.

Siegel.W.C. 1992. Forestry implications of water quality and wetland law Outlook. Proc. Agric. Outlook Conf.U.S.Dep.Agric.172-179.

Sipple, W.s. 1987. Wetland identification and delineation manual. Washington, D.C.: Office of Wetlands Protection, Office of Water, U.S. Environmental Protection Agency.

Skinner, J and Smart, M. 1984. The El Kala Wetlands of Algeria and their use by water fowl. Wild life, 106-118.

Squires, L and Preston, E. 1992. A research strategy to develop ecological indicators of wetland condition: presented at the Society of Wetlands Scientists 13th Annual Meeting, June 1-5, 1992, New Orleans, Louisiana 28p.

Stevens, K and Ehrle, E.B. 1990. The Hampton Creek wetland complex in southwestern Michigan. VI. Transect survey of bryophyte populations. Mich. Bot. 29(2). 55-64.

Stewart, R.E and Kantrud, H.A. 1971. Classification of natural ponds and lakes in the glaciated prairie region. U.S. Fish Wildl, Serv, m Resour, Publ. 92, 57p.

Stewart, R.E and Knatrud, H.A. 1972. Vegetation of prairie potholes, North Dakota, in relation to quality of water and other environmental factors. U.S. Geol. Surv. Prof. Pap. 585-D,36p.

Still, D.A and Shih, S.F. 1991. Using Land sat data and Geographic Information System for wetland assessment in water-quality management. Proc. Soil Crop Sci. Soc. Fla. 50, 98-102.

Symoens, J.J. 1988. Vegetation of inland waters. Handbook of vegetation science Academic Publishers.

Thompson, K.1977. Primary productivity of African wetlands with particular reference to the Okavango delta. In: A Campbell (Ed). The Okavango delta and its future utilization, 67-69.

Thunhorst, G.A. 1968. Wetland planting guide for the northeastern Untied Stales: plants for wetland creation, restoration and enhancement. St. Michaels, Md.: Environmental Concern, 179p.

Tilton, D.L. 1977. Seasonal growth and foliar nutrients of Larix laricina in three wetland ecosystems. Canadian Journal of Botany (Canada). 55(10) 1291-1298.

Tiner, R.W. 1993. Using plants as indicators of wetland. Proc. Acad. Nat. Sci. Phila. 144, 240-253.

Tubpun, Y. 1966.The economics of small tank irrigation in northeast Thailand. in: Irrigation investment, technology and management strategies for development. ed: K.W. Easter. West view Press, 129-146.

Turner, R.E. and Maltby, E. 1093. Lousiana is the wetland state. Geographical magazine. 45,92-97.

Turner, K and Jones, T. 1991 Wetlands: market and intervention failures. London: Earthscan, 202p.

Tydeman, C. 1984. General value of man made wetlands for wild life in Europe, WWF, wetland pack-1, WWF-IUCN, Gland, Switzerland.

Uhler, F.M. 1956. New habitats for waterfowl. Trans. N.Am. Wildl. Conf. 21, 454.

Vyskot, M. 1985. The tree layer. Dev. Agric. Manage. for Ecol. (15A) 81-120.

WWF-IUCN. 1985. Wetlands conservation programme 1985-87.Life at the water's edge. WWF - IUCN, Gland, Switzerland.

Waddington, J.M, Roulet, N.T and Hill, A.R. 1993. Runoff mechanisms in a forested groundwater discharge wetland. J. Hydrol 147 (1/4), 37-60.

Wagner, Joel. 1989. Wetland regulatory compliance: a guidance manual for the National Park Service, Mid-Atlantic Region. National Park Service], 1p.

Weinmann, F. 1992. Wetland plants of the Pacific Northwest. US Army Corps of Engineers, Seattle District, 85p.

Weller, M.W. 1981. Fresh water marshes: Ecology and Wildlife management – University Minnessota Press, Minneapolis. 146p.

Weller, M.W. 1978. Management of freshwater marshes for wildlife in Freshwater wetlands: Ecological process and Management Potential. Good, R.E., Wligham, D.F., Simpson, R.L., (eds) Academic Press, New York. 267-284.

Whigham. D. 1983.The long wetland. Geographical magazine.45, 240-244.

Williams, T.D and Dodd Jr, C.K. Importance of wetlands to endangered and threatened species. In: Greeson, P.E. et al (ed) 565-575.

Williams, A.E. 1992. Wetland protection programs: direction and outlook of the U.S. Army Corps of Engineers. Trans. North Am. Wildl. Nat. Resour. Conf. 57, 234-247.

Wisheu, I.C and Keddy, P.A. 1991. Seed banks of a rare wetland plant community: distribution patterns and effects of human-induced disturbance. J. Veg. Sci. 2 (2) 181-188.

World Wildlife Fund, 1992. Statewide wetlands strategies: a guide to protecting and managing the resource. Washington, D.C.: Island Press, 268p.

World Wildlife Fund, 1992. Environmental Defense Fund. How wet is a wetland? : The impacts of the proposed revisions to the Federal Wetlands Delineation manual. New York, NY: Environmental Defense Fund; Washington, DC: World Wildlife Fund, 175p.

Zinn, J.A and Copeland, C. 1982. Wetland management. Congressional research service report. ser. No. 97-11-US Library of congress, Washington. D.C.

2. Irrigation Tanks

Abblie, L., Harrison, J.O and Wall, J.W. 1982. Economic return to investment in irrigation in India. World Bank Staff Working Paper 536. Washington, D.C. : The World Bank.

Ackermann, W.C, White, G.F and Worthington, E.B. (eds) 1973. Man-made lakes; their Problems and Environmental Effects, American Geophysical Union, Washington, DC.

(Monograph 17).

Adams, R, Adams M, Willens, A and Willens, A. 1978. Dry Land Man and Plants, Architectural Press, London.

Agarwal, A. 1981. 'Supplying water: maintenance problems and community participation', Development Digest, 19(4), 74-85.

Agnihotri, A.K and P. K. Joshi. 1985. Regional disparities and soil degradation vis-a-vis canal irrigation Problem and appraisal. Proceedings of the formulation and appraisal of irrigation projects meeting. Water Resources Studies Program, Patna University, Patna.

Aurora, G.S. 1986. The sociological dimension of the composite watershed management, ICRISAT, Patancheru, India.

Anonymous. 1979. The Social Response to Irrigation: An Indian Case Study. J. Develop. Stud. 16, 3-26.

Antony C.F(Ed) 1982. Gazateer of India, Union territory of Pondicherry. Pondicherry Vol.1.

Bharadwaj, K.1990. Irrigation In India - Alternative perspectives. Indian Council of Social Sciences Research, New Delhi, 73 p.

Bottrall, A.F. 1981. 'Water, land and conflict management', ODI Review, No.1, 73-83.

Bottrall, A.F. 1981 Comparative study of the management and organization of irrigation projects. World Bank Staff working Paper 458. Washington, D.C.: World Bank.

Bottrall, A. 1985. Management issues related to the main system .In Irrigation management: Research from Southeast Asia, ed. T. Wickham. New York: Agricultural Development Council.

Bowonder. R and others. 1987. Land use, water logging, and irrigation management. Land Use Policy 4 (November).

Burt, O.R. 1964. Optimal resource use over time with an application to ground water. Management Science 2 (September).

Bull, D. 1982. A Growing Problem: Pesticides and the Third World Poor, Oxfam (Public Affairs Unit), Oxford.

CBIP (Central Board of Irrigation and Power).1953. Irrigation in India through the Ages, CBIP, New Delhi.

Central Water Commission.1988. Water Resources of India, New Delhi.

Center for Science and Environment.1986. The study of India's environment, 1984/85: The second citizens report. New Delhi.

Chambers, R.1985. In search of a water revolution: Questions for managing canal irrigation in the 1980s. Water Supply and Management 5:5-18.

Charlu, T.G.K and K. Dutt. 1982. Ground water development in India REC Technical Series I. New Delhi: Rural Electrification Corporation.

Chaturvedi, M.C.1975. Water 2000: Second India series. New Delhi.

Chaturvedi, M.C and Rogers, P. 1985. Water Resources System Planning. Some case studies for India, Indian Academy of Sciences, Bangalore.

Chambers R, Saxena N.C and Shah T. 1989. To the Hand of the poor- Water and Trees Oxford & IBH. p.273.

Chopra, K. 1987. Irrigation, fertilizer use and land degradation: Paper E/ 133/88. New Delhi: Institute of Economic Growth.

Coward, Jr.E.W. (ed) 1980. Irrigation and agricultural development in Asia: Perspectives from the social sciences. Ithaca, N.Y.: Cornell University Press.

Dasgupta, Partha. 1986. Control of resources. New Delhi: Oxford University Press.

Dakshina Murti, C et al. 1973. Water Resources of India and their Utilisation in Agriculture. Water Technology Centre, New Delhi 1973.

De Donnea, Fr:X. 1982. 'The role and limits of normative models in water resources planning and management, In: Laconte, P and Haimes, Y.Y. (eds), Water Resources and Land-use Planning: a Systems Approach, Martinus Nijhoff, the Hague, 7-19.

Desai, C.G. 1975. Water resources potential of Union Territories. Planning Commission, New Delhi.

Dhawan, B.D. 1982. Development of tube well irrigation in India. New Delhi: Agricole.

Dhawan, B.D, 1987b. Water resource development: Ground water versus surface irrigation. Institute of Economic Growth. New Delhi. Mimeo.

Dhawan, B.D, 1988. Dry farming: The new hope. The Economic Times, View point column. Bombay. 13 January.

Dikshit, G.S, Kuppuswamy, G.R and Mohan, S.T. 1993. Tank Irrigation in Karnataka – A historical survey. Gandhi Sahitya Sangha, Bangalore, 335p.

Dodge, D.P, Goodchild, G.A, Tilt, J.C and Waldriff, D.G. 1983. Manual of Indstuctions, Aquatic Habitat Inventory Surveys. Fisheries Branch, Ministry of Natural Resources. Ontario. 168 p.

Elumalai, G. 1982. "Modernisation of tank irrigation system. Farmers views". In: Proceedings of the international workshop on modernisation of tank irrigation system, Problems and issues, 10-12 Feb.1982. CWR, Madras, India.

Engelhardt, T. 1984. Economics of traditional small holder irrigation systems in the semi-arid tropics of south India, Doctoral thesis, University Hohenhein, RFA.

FAO. 1977. Conservation Guide I: Guidelines for Watershed Management, FAO, Rome.

Fauchon, J. 1980. 'Oasis agriculture: how pumps divide the peasantry', Ceres, 13 41-5.

Fernando, C.H, 1980. The fishery Potential of Man-made lakes in South East Asia and some strategies for its optimization. Biotrop Aniv. publ.

Government of India. 1987. National Water Policy, New Delhi.

Government of Tamilnadu, 1987. Irrigation Reservoirs in Tamil Nadu, Madras.

Guhan, S. 1993. The Cauvery River Dispute - Towards Conciliation, Frontline publication, Madras, 78 p.

Gopal, B. 1991. Wetland (mis) Management by keeping people out. Two examples from India in Landscape and Urban Planning, 20 Elsevier, Amsterdam.

Hardin G and Baden J. 1971. Managing the commons. Freeman and Co.

Hollaender, A. (ed). 1979. The Biosaline Concept: an Approach to the Utilisation of Underexploited Resources, Plenum Press, New York, (Environmental Science Re· search, Vol. 14)

Hutchinson, C.F, Dutt, G.R and Anaya, G.M.(eds) 1981.Ralnfail Collection for Agriculture in Arid and Semi-Arid Regions, Commonwealth Agricultural Bureaux, Slough.

International Wetlands and Waterfowl Research Bureau. 1989. A directory of Asian Wetlands, Slimbridge, U.K.

International symposium on Water Resources conservation, Pollution and Abatement.Dec.11-13, 1981. Roorkee, Proceedings, Savita Prakashan, New Delhi.

India, Central Water Commission. 1981. Report on the status of irrigation development in India through major, medium, minor. and CAD. schemes. New Delhi.

India, Central Water Commission.1984b. Report of the working group on minor irrigation for formulation of the Seventh Plan proposals, for the years 1985/90. New Delhi.

India, Central Water Commission.1986. Groundwater development in India New Delhi.

Institute for Development studies (IDS). 1980. Who gets the last rural resource? The potential and challenge of lift irrigation for the rural poor. IDS Study Seminar 88 DP 156. Lewes, U.K.:IOS, University of Sussex.

Jakhade, G.S. 1987. Surface water resources of India. Paper presented at the First National Water Convention. New Delhi: Ministry of Water Resources.

Kandaswamy, P. 1987. Agricultural water requirements (2000 A.D.). Water Technology Centre. Tamil Nadu Agricultural University. Coimbatore, India.

Kamath, S.U. 1990. Historical role of tanks in Karnataka March of Karnataka, Vol. 28, February 1990. Bangalore.

Krishnamurty, B.V.1983. Eco-development in Southern Mysore - A Historical Perspective. Env. Serv. Group. WWF. New Delhi.

Laconte, P and Haimes, Y;Y. (eds). 1982. Water Resources and Land-use pianning: a Systems Approach, Martinus Njihoff, The Hague and Kluwer Boston, Hingham, Massachusetts.

Lal, D. 1972. Wells and welfare: An exploratory cost benefits study of the economics of small scale irrigation in Maharashtra Paris: Organization for Economic Corporation and Development.

Lenton, R.L. 1984. A note on monitoring productivity and equity in irrigation systems. In Productivity and equity in irrigation systems, .ed. Niranjan Pant, 51-65. New Delhi: Ashish.

Lenton, R.L. 1987. Lecture notes. Lecture presented at the fifth training of trainers program, Anna University, Madras.

Lawton, H.W and Wilki, P.J. 1979. 'Ancient agricultural systems in dry regions', in Hall, A.E., Cannel, G.H. and Lawton, H.W. (eds), Agriculture in Semi-Arid Environments, Springer· Verlag, Berlin, (Ecological Studies Analysis and Synthesis, Vol.34).

Lipton, M. 1977. Why Poor People Stay Poor: a Study at Urban Bias in World Development, Temple Smith, London.

Ludden, D. 1980. Ecological Zones in the Cultural Economy of Irrigation in Southern Tamil Nadu in Coward (ed)., Irrigation and Agricultural Development in Asia, Cornell University Press. New York.

Merrey, D.J. 1982. 'Reorganizing irrigation: local level management in the Punjab [Pakistan)' in Spooner, B. and Mann, H.S. (eds), Desertification and Development: Dryland Ecology in social Perspective, Academic Press, London and New York, 83·109.

Min. Envi. & For. GOL 1990. Wetlands of India - A Directory.

Moorti, T.V. 1976. Impact of Different Sources of Irrigation on Input - Output Relations, Crop patterns and farm policies. Seminar Series 13, Bombay: Indian Society of Agricultural Economics.

Mohanakrishnan, S.P. 1990. Selected papers on Irrigation, Irrigation Management Training Institute, Tiruchi.

Madras Institute of Development Studies.1986. Tank Irrigation in Tamil Nadu - some Macro and Micro perspectives. Madras Institute of Development studies, Madras, Report submitted to the International Labour Organization, March 1993, 174 pp +Tables, Maps and Figures.

Nadkarni, M.V. et al.1979. Impact of irrigation: Canal, Well and Tank irrigation in Karnataka, Bombay. Himalaya Publishing House.

Nallusamy, M. 1987. Monitoring and evaluation of lank Modernisation project - Visali Tank, ME, thesis, CWR, Madras, India.

National Academy of Sciences. 1974. More Water for Arid lands: Promising Technologies and Research Opportunities, National Academy of Sciences, Washington, DC. (Report of a Panel of the Advisory Committee on Technological Innovation, Board of Science and Technology for International Development Commission on International Relations.

National Academy of Sciences.1975. Underexploited Tropical Plants with Promising Economic Value, National Academy of Sciences, Washington, DC. (Report of the ad hoc Panel of the Advisory Committee on Technology Innovation).

O'Mara, G.T. 1984. Issues in the efficient use of surface and groundwater in irrigation. World Bank Working Paper 707. Washington, D.C: The World Bank.

Pacey, A and Cullis, A. 1986. Rainwater Harvesting: the Collection of Rainfall and Run-off in Rural Areas, Intermediate Technology Publications, 9 King Street, London WC2E8HW.

Palanisamy, K. 1982. Managing tank irrigation systems: basic issues and implications for improvement. Proc. Int. Workshop on Modernising of Tank Irrigation systems, Madras, 149·158.

Palanisami, K and Easter, K.W.1984.Tank irrigation in India and Thailand: Problems and prospects, ODI Irrigation Management Network, 10E, London, UK.

Palanisami, K and Flinn, J.C. 1988. Evaluating the performance of tank irrigation systems. Agricultural Systems 28: 161 177.

Pant, N. 1984a Community tube well: An organizational alternative to small farmers irrigation. Economic and Political Weekly 19 (June Review of Agriculture): A59-A85.

Pant, N and P, Raj.1985. Community tube well and agricultural development. New Delhi: Ashish Publishing House.

Prasad, T, Kumar, B.S and S. Kumar. 1987. Water resources development in India: Its central role in the past and crucial significance for the future. Paper presented at the international symposium on water for the future, April, University of Rome, Italy.

Peter, T. 1978.Tropical man-made lakes-the ecological impact, Archive fur Hydrobiology, 81,368-85.

Postel, S. 1985. Conserving Water: the Untapped Alternative, World watch Institute, NW Washington DC, 20036. (World watch Paper No.67).

Rao, K.L 1979. India's Water Wealth. Orient Longman, p. 267.

Rogers, P. 1983. Irrigation and Economic Development: Some lessons from India, Harward University, Cambridge (Mass). Division of Applied Sciences.

Reddy STS. Status of Tanks in Karnataka. Bangalore (Unpub).

Repetto, R. 1987. Skimming the water: Rent-seeking and the performance of public irrigation systems. World Resources Institute, Washington D.C.

Sathyamurthy, S.T. 1966. Descriptive catalogue of the butterflies. Bulletin of the Madras Govt. Museum. Govt. of Madras.

Sawant, S.D. 1986. Irrigation and water use in Indian agriculture since independence. Bombay: Oxford and IBH Publishing Co.

Schumacher, E.F. 1974. Small is Beautiful: a Study of Economics as if People Mattered, Sphere Books, London.

Sivanappan, R.K.1990. Economic Evaluation of Tanks (in) Seminar on Traditional Water Harvesting Systems of India, New Delhi, Oct. 9-11.

Suseela, R and Meinzen, D. 1964. Local Management of Tank Irrigation in South India -- Organisation and operation. Cornell University. New York.

Sakthivadivel, R, Savadamuthu, S., Shanmugan, C.R., Balakrishnan, P.K and Arputharaj, C. 1982. "A pilot study of modernisation of tank irrigation in Tamilnadu". In: Proceedings of the international workshop on modernisation of tank irrigation system. Problems and issues. 10-12 Feb. 1982. CWR, Madras, India.

Shanmugam, C.R. 1975. Report on the Ford foundation funded tank rehabilitation program, CWR, Madras, India.

Shanmugham, C. R and Sakthivadivel, R. 1986. An action research study on modernizing a tank irrigation system in Tamil Nadu. Center for Water Resources, Anna University, Madras. Mimeo.

Sivanappan, R.K. 1985. "Critical issues concerning irrigation in Tamilnadu". In: July development seminar. 425-433, MIDS, Madras, India.

Srivastava, G.P. 1962. Traditional forms of co-operation in India, Indian Co-operative Union, New Delhi.

Stern, P.H. 1979. Small Scale Irrigation: a Manual of low-cost Water Technology (Intermediate Technology Publication Ltd, and the International Irrigation Information Centre, London), Russell Press, Nottingham.

Subramanian, S. 1985. "Some Features of Tank Irrigation in Tamil Nadu. A Note", In: July development seminar, 397402. MIDS. Madras.

Tamil Nadu, Public Works Department (PWD). 1984. Tank modernization proposals: Srivilliputtur Big Tank. Srivilliputtur, Tamil Nadu.

Tamil Nadu, Public Works Department (PWD).1984b.Tank modernization works: Various papers, Madurai, Tamil Nadu.

U.S. Army Corps of Englneers.1979. Wetland Values, Concepts and Methods for Wetlands Evaluation. Institute for Water Resources, Virginia 109p.

UNEP 1983. Rain and Storm water Harvesting in rural Areas: A Report by the United Nations Environment Programme, Tycooly International Publishing, Dublin, (Water Resources Series, Vol. 5).

Vaidyanathan, A. 1986. Water control institutions and agriculture: A comparative perspective. Indian Economic Review.

Vaidyanathan, A. 1987. Irrigation and agricultural growth. Indian Jour. Agric. Econ. 42: 503-527.

Vohra, B.B. 1982. Land and Water Management Problems in India.

Vohra, B.B. 1985. Towards a national Water Policy. Key-note address delivered at National Seminar on Command Area Development. Bangalore,.

Vohra, B.B.1987. Case of Natural Resources still an area of great neglect. M.C.Rajamannar Memorial Oration on Environment.

Vaidyanathan, A and Jankarajan, S. 1989. Management of Irrigation and its effect on Productivity under different Environmental and Technical Conditions - A study of two surface Irrigation systems in Tamilnadu. Madras Institute of Development Studies, 342 p.

Von oppen, M and Subba Rao, K.V. 1980. Tank Irrigation in Semi Arid Tropical India, Part I: Historical and Spatial Distribution. International Crop Research Institute for the Semi- Arid Tropics (ICRISAT), Hyderabad.

Venkataramani, G. 1974. Minor irrigation in Tamilnadu, Sangam Publishers, Madras, India 120p.

Venkataram, B.R. 1985. Administrative feasibility of a tank irrigation authority, Economics Progress Rep. ICRISAT, Patancheru, India, (72) 125 p.

Von Oppen M and Subba Rao, K.V. 1980. Tank irrigation in semi-arid tropical India, Part II: Technical features and economic performance, Economics Prog., Progress rep. no.8, ICRISAT, Patancheru, Andhra Pradesh, India, 52 p.

Wade R. 1982b. 'Employment, water control, and water supply institutions: South India and South Korea', IDS Discussion Paper; 182, Institute of Development Studies, University of Sussex, Brighton, UK.

Walker, B.H. (ed) 1979. Management of Semi-Arid Ecosystems, Elsevier, Amsterdam (Developments in Agricultural and Managed Forest Ecology, vol.7).

Welchert, W.T and Freeman, B.N. 1973. 'Horizontal wells', Journal of Range Management, 26 253-5.

WWF-India, 1991. The wetlands of Calcutta-sustainable development or real Estate takes over?

Zonn, I.S. 1979. 'Ecological aspects of irrigated agriculture', Water Supply and Management, 3 285-95.

3. Soil Seed Banks

Alm, D.M., Stoller, E.W and Wax, L.M. 1993. An index model for predicting seed germination and Emergence rates. Weed Tech. 7, 560.

Appanah, S. and Nor, S.M. 1990. Natural regeneration and its implications for forest management in the Dipterocarp forest of peninsular Malaysia. In: Gomer-Pompa, A, et al (Eds). Rainforest Regeneration and Management, MAB 6, 361. UNESCO, PARIS.

Archibald, O.W. 1981. Buried viable propagules in native prairee and adjacent agricultural sites in central Saskatchewan. Can. J. Bot. 59, 701.

Archibald, O.W and Hume, L. 1983. A preliminary survey of seed input into fallow fields in Saskatchewan. can. J.Bot. 61, 1216.

Auld, T.D. 1986. Population dynamics of the shrub Acacia suaveolens (Sm.) Wild.: dispersal and the dynamics of the soil seed bank. Aust. J.Ecol. Oxford : Blackwell Scientific Publications. 11 (3) 235-254.

Ball, D.A. 1992. Weed seed bank response to tillage, herbicides and crop rotation sequence. Weed Sci. 40, 654.

Barbour, M.G and Lange, RJ. 1966. Seed populations in some natural Australian top soils. Ecology 48, 153.

Bard, G.E. 1952. Secondary succession on the Pedmont of New Jersey. Eco. Monogr. 22, 195.

Barton, L.V. 1961. "Seed Preservation and Longevity". Wiley (Interscience), New York.

Baskin, J.M and Baskin, C.C.1982. Effects of wetting and drying cycles on the germination of seeds of Cyperus inflexus. Ecology 63, 248.

Baskin, J.M., Baskin, C. and McCormick, J.F. 1987. Seasonal changes in germination responses of buried seeds of Portulaca smallii. Bull. Torrey Bot. Club 114, 169.

Baskin, J.M and Baskin, C.C. 1981. Seasonal changes in germination responses of buried seeds of Verbascum thapsus and V. blattaria and ecological implications. Can. J.Bot. 59,1769.

Baskin, J.M and Baskin, C.C.1994. Role of temperature in regulating timing of germination in soil seed reserves of Lamium purpureum L. Weed Res. 24, 341.

Baskin, J.M and Baskin, C.C. 1987. Temperature requirements for after-ripening in buried seeds of four summer annual weeds. Weed Res. 27, 385.

Baskin, J.M and Baskin, C.C.1985. The annual dormancy cycle in buried weed seeds: A continuum. Bicisci. 35, 492.

Baskin, J.M and Baskin, C.C. 1983. Seasonal changes in the germination responses of buried seeds of Arabidopsis thaliana and ecological interpretation. Bot. Gaz. (Chicago) 144, 540.

Beale, P.E 1974. Regeneration of Trifolium subterraneum cv. Yarloop from seed reserves in soil on Kangaroo Island. J. Aust. Insl. Agric. Sci. 40, 78.

Beauchamp, H, Lang, R and May, M. 1975. Topsoil as a seed source for reseeding strip mine spoils. Res. J.Wyo. Agric. Exp. Stn. 90, 1.

Benit D.L, Derkson, D.A and Panneton, B. 1993. Innovative approaches to seed bank studies. Weed Sci. 40. 650.

Bertiller, M.B and Coronato, F. 1994. Seed bank patterns of Festuca pallescens is semi-arid patagonia (Argentina) - A possible limit to bunch reestablishment. Biod. & Con. 3, 57.

Beuret, E. 1984 Soil seed bank and cultivation: the relation between potential and real flora Eidgenössisches Volkswirtschafts departements. 23 (1/2) 89-96.

Bigwood, D.W and Inouye, D.W. 1988. Spatial pattern analysis of seed banks: An improved method and optimizing sampling. Ecology 69, 497.

Bostock, S.J. 1978. Seed germination strategies of five perennial weeds. Oecologia 36, 113.

Bradshaw, A.D and Chadwick, M.J. 1980. "The Restoration of Land". Blackwell, Oxford.

Brenchley, W.E and Warington, K. 1945. The influence of periodic fallowing on the prevalence of viable weed seeds in arable soil. Ann. Appl. Biol. 32, 285.

Brenchley, W.E. 1918. Buried weed seeds. J.Agric.Sci. 9, 1.

Brown, J.S and Venable, D.L. 1986. Evolutionary ecology of seed banks annuals in temporally varying environments. Am.Nat. 127, 31.

Buhler, D.D and Maxwell, B.D.1993. Seed separation and enumeration from soil using K_2CO_3 centrifugation and image analysis. Weed Sci. 41, 298.

Carey, P.D and Watkinson, A.R. 1993. Dispersal and fate of seeds of Winter annual grass. Vulpia ciliata J.Ecol. 81, 759.

Carroll, E.J and Ashton, D.H. 1965. Seed storage in soils of several Victorian plant communities. Vict. Nat. 82, 102.

Cavers, P.B., Kane, M. and Otode, J.T. 1992. Importance of Seed banks in establishment of newly introduced weeds - A case study of prosomillet (Panicum miliacenm).Weed Sci. 40, 630.

Cavers, P.B. 1983. Seed demography. Can. J.Bol. 61, 3578.

Chaluner, B. 1993. Fate in a seed: dispersion of seeds and other late natural history writings by H.Thoreau. Nature 363, 507.

Chippendale, H.G and Milton, W.E.J. 1934. On the viable seeds present in the soil beneath pastures. J.Ecol. 22, 508.

Colosi, J.C., Cavers, P.B and Bough, M.A. 1988. Dormancy and survival in buried seeds of proso millet. Panicum miliaceum. Can. J. Bot. 60, 161.

Conti, R.S and Gunther, P.P. 1984. Relations of phenology and seed germination to the distribution of dominant plants in Oxkefenokee Swamp. In "The Okefenokee Swarnp: Its Natural History, Geology, and Geochemisuy" (A.D.Cohen, D.J. Casagrande, M.J. Andrejko and G.R. Best, eds.), Wetland Surveys, Los alamos, New Mexico. 144.

Cowling, R.M., Lamom, B. and Pierce, S.M. 1987. Seed bank dynamics of four co-occurring Banksia species. J.Ecol. 75, 289.

Currie, J.A. 1973. The seed-soil system. In "Seed Ecology" (W. Heydecker. ed.) Butterworth, London 463.

Darwin, C. 1857. On the action of sea-water on the germination of seeds. J.Linn. Soc. London 1, 130.

Debaeke, P, 1888 Population dynamics of some broad-leaved weeds in cereals. I. Relation between standing vegetation and soil seed bank. Weed Research Oxford: Blackwell Scientific Publications. 28 (4) 251-263.

Delouche, J.C., Still, T.W., Raspet, M. and Lienhard, M. 1962. The tetrazolium test for seed viability. Mississippi Agricultural experiment station Technical Bulletin 51, 2-59.

Donald, W.W. 1993. Models and sampling for studying seed survival with wild mustard (Sinapis arvensis) as a case study. Can. J.Plant sci.73, 637.

Donelan, M and Thompson, K, 1980. Distribution of buried viable seeds along a successional series. Biol. Conserv. 17, 297.

Dore, W.G and Raymond, LC. 1942. Pasture studies. XXIV. Viable seeds in pasture soil and manure. Sci.Agric. 23, 69.

Dunn, W.J and Best, G.R 1984. Enhancing ecological succession. 5. Seed bank survey of some Florida marshes and role of seed banks in marsh reclamation. In "Surface Mining, Hydrology, Sedimentology and

Reclamation" (D.H. Graves, ed.), Off.Eng.Serv., University of Kentucky, Lexington. 365.

Duvel, J.W.T. 1902. Seeds buried in soil. Science 17, 872.

Egley, G.H. 1986. Stimulation of weed seed germination in soil. Rev. Weed Sci. 2, 67.

Enright, M. 1985. Evidence of a soil seed bank under rainforest in New Guinea. Aust.J.Ecol. 10, 67.

Epp, G.A. 1987. The seed bank of Eupatorium odoratum along a successional gradient in a tropical rain forest in Ghana J.Trop. Ecol. 3, 139.

Evanarl, M. 1980-81l. The history of germination research and the lesson it contains for today. Israel J.Bot. 29, 4.

Ewart, A.J. 1908. On the longevity of seeds, Proc. R.Soc. Victoria [N.S.] 21, 1.

Ewel, J and Conde, L.1979. Seeds in soils of former everglades farmlands. In "Proceedings of the First Conference on Scientific Research in the National Parks" (R.M.Linn, ed.), Trans. Proc. Ser. 1,225. Natl. Park Serv., U.S. Dept. Int., Washington, D.C.

Fenner, M. 1985. "Seed Ecology". Chapman & Hall. London.

Fischer, A. 1987. Studies on the population dynamics at the beginning of secondary succession. Berlin: J. Cramer, 1987.234 p. : 46 ill.

Forcella, F., Eradatoskoul, K and Wagner, S.W. 1993. Application of weed seed bank Ecology to Low input crop management. Ecol. appl. 3, 74

Forcella, F. 1984. A species area curve for buried viable seeds. Aust. J.Agri. Res. 35, 645.

Forcella, F., Wilson, R,J., Renner, K,A., Dekker, J., Harvey, R.G., Alm, D.A., Buhler, D.O and Cardina, T, 1992. Weed seed banks of United States Corn Belt - Magnitude, Variation, Emergence and Application. Weed Sci. 40, 636.

Froud-Williams, R.J., Chancellor, R.J and Drennan, D.S.H. 1983. Influence of cultivation regime upon buried weed seeds in arable cropping systems. J.Appl. Ecol. 21, 629.

Granstrom, A. 1987. Seed viability of fourteen species during five years of storage in a forest soil. J.Ecol. 75. 321.

Gray, P.N and Bolen, E.G. 1987. Seed reserves in the tailwater pits of playa lakes in relation to waterfowl management. Wetlands 7, 11.

Grime, J.P. 1979. Plant strategies and vegetation processes John Wiley and Sons, Chichester.

Grime, J.P. 1981. The role of seed dormancy in vegetation dynamics. Ann. Appl. Siol. 98, 555p.

Gross, KL 1990. A comparison of methods for estimating seed numbers in the soil. J.Ecol. 78, 1079-1090.

Gross, K.L, Renner, K.A 1989. A new method for estimating seed numbers in the soil. Weed Sci. Weed Science Society of America 37. 836-839.

Guariguata, M.R and Azocar, A. 1988. Seed bank dynamics and germination ecology in Espeletia timotensis (Compositae), an Andean giant rosette. Biotropica 20, 54p.

Guevara, S.S and Gomez-Pompa, A. 1972. Seeds from surface soils in a tropical region of veracruz Mexico. J.Arnold Arboretum 53, 312p.

Gunther, P.P., Casagrande, D.J and Cherney, R.R. 1984. The viability and fate of seeds as a function of depth in the peats of Okefenokee Swamp. In "The Okefenokee Swamp: Its Natural History, Geology, and Geochemistry" (A.D. Cohen, D.J. Casagrande, M.J., Andrejko, and G.A. Best, eds.). Wetland Surveys, Los Alamos, New Mexico 168.

Hagg, R.W. 1983. Emergence of seedlings of aquatic macrophytes from lake sediments. Can.J.Bot. 61, 148p.

Harper, J.L, Williams, J.T and Sagar, .R. 1965. The behaviour of seeds in soil. Part I. The heterogeneity of soil surfaces and its role in determining the establishment of plants from seed. J.Ecol. 53, 273p.

Hart, R. 1977. Why are biennials so few? American Naturalist 111, 792p.

Haug, P.T and Dyne, G.M. 1968. Secondary succession in abandoned cultivated fields: An annoted bibliography. Oak Ridge National laboratory-Tennessee.

Haukas, D.A and Smith, L.M. 1993. Seed bank composition and predictive ability of field vegetation in Plaua Lakes. Wetlands 13, 32

Hayashi, I and Numata, M. 1971. Ecological studies on the buried seed population in the soil as related to plant succession. VI viable buried seed population in the Miscanthus and Zoysia type grasslands in Japan. Jap.J. Ecol. 20, 243p.

Hemsley, W.B. 1895. Vitality of seeds, Nature (London) 27, 5p.

Heydecker, W., ed.1973. "Seed Ecology". Pennsylvania State Univ. Press, University Park and London.

Hopkins. D.R and Parker, V.T. 1984. A study of the seed bank of a salt marsh in northern San Francisco bay. Am. J.Bot. 71, 348p.

Howe, H.F and Small Wood, J. 1982. Ecology of seed dispersal Annual Review of Ecological Systematics 13, 201p.

Hume, L and Archibold, O.W. 1966. The influence of a weedy habitat on the seed bank of an adjacent cultivated field. Can.J.Bit. 64, 1879p.

Hutchings, M.L 1986. Plant population biology. In "Methods in Plant Ecology" (P.D. Moore and S.B. Chapman, eds.) Blackwell, Oxford 377p.

Jensen, H.A. 1969. Content of buried seed in arable soil in Denmark and its relation to the weed population. Dan.Bot.Ark. 27, 1.

Jimenez, H.E and Armesto, J.J. 1992. Importance of the soil seed bank of disturbed sites in Chilean matorral in early secondary succession. J.Veg.Sci. 3 (5) 579-586.

Keddy, P.A and Ellis, T.H. I985. Seedling recruitment of 11 wetland plant species along a water level gradient: Share or distinct responses? Can.J.Bot. 63, 1876p.

Keddy, P.A and Reznicek, A.A. 1986. Great Lakes vegetation dynamics: The role of fluctuating water levels and buried seeds. J.Great Lakes Res. 12, 25p.

Keddy, P.A and Reznicek, A.A. 1982. The role of seed banks in the persistence of Ontario's coastal plain flora Am.J.Bot. 69. 13.

Keeley, J.E. 1987. Ten years of change in seed banks of the chaparral shrubs, Arctostaphylos glauca and A,glandulosa. Am.Midl. Nat. 117. 446.

Kellman, M. 1978. Microdistribution of viable weed seed in two tropical soils. J. Biogeogr. 5, 291.

Kellman, M.C. 1974. The viable weed seed content of tropical agricultural soils. J.Appl. Ecol. 11, 669.

Khan, M.A. 1993. Relationship of seed bank to plant distribution in saline arid communities. Pak.J.Bot. 25, 73.

Kiirkki, A. 1883. Seed bank and vegetation succession in a bandoued field in Karkali Nature Reserve, Southern Finland. Ani.Botanics Fennici 30, 139.

King, T.J. 1976. The viable seed contents of ant-hill and pasture soil. New Phytol., 77, 143.

Kinucan, R.J and Smeinbs, F.E. 1992. Soil seed bank of a semiarid Texas grassland under three long-term (36-years) grazing regimes. Am. Midl.Nat. 128 (1) 11-21.

Kivilaan, A and Bandurski, R.S. 1981. The one hundred year period for Dr. Beal's viability experiment. Amer.J.Bot. 68, 1290p.

Lavorel, S., Debussche, M., Lebreton, T.A and Lepart, J. 1993. Seasonal patterns in seed bank of Mediterranean old-fields. Oikos 67, 114p.

Leck, M.A and Graveline, K.J. 1979. The seed bank of a freshwater tidal marsh. Am.J.Bot. 66, 1006.

Leck, M.A and Simpson, R.L 1987. Seed bank of a freshwater tidal wetland: Turnover and relationship to vegetation change. Am.J Bot, 74, 360.

Legere, A.1992. Crop weed management and the dynamics of the weed seed banks. Weed. Sci. 40, 629.

Lerman, J.C and Cingliano, E.M. 1971. New carbon-14 Evidence for six hundred years old Canna compacta seed. Nature 232, 568.

Llech, M.A and Simpson, R.L. 1994. Tidal fresh water wetland zonation: seed and seedling dynamics. Aqua Bot. 47, 61.

Lonsdale, W.M., Haffey, K.L.S and Gillet. J.D. Seed bank dynamics in Mimosa pigra an invasive tropical shrub. J.App. EcoI. 25, 963.

Lonsdale, W.M. 1993. Losses from the seed bank of Mimoso pigra: soil micro organisms Vs. temperature fluctuations. J.Appl. Ecol. 30, 654.

MacArthur; R.H. 1972. "Geographical Ecology" Patterns in the Distribution of Species". Harper & Row, New York.

Madsen. C. 1986. Wetland restoration: A pilot project. J, Soil water Conserv. 41, 159.

Major, J and Pyott; W.T. 1966. Buried viable seeds in two California bunch grass sites and their bearing on the definition of a flora. Vegetati 13, 253.

Manders. P.T. 1990. Soil seed banks and post-fire seed deposition across a forest – fynbos ecotone in the Cape Province. J.Veg. Sci. 1(4) 491-498.

Marks, M.K and Nwachuku, A.C. 1986. Seed bank characteristics in a group of tropical weeds. Weed Res. 26, 151.

Martin, A.C and Barkley, W.D. 1961. "Seed identification Manual". Univ. of California Press, Berkeley.

Maun, M.A and Lapierre. 1986. Effects of burial by sand on germination and seedling emergence of four dune species. Am. J.Bot. 73, 450.

Mayer, A.M. 1980-61. Germination research-the state of the art. Isr.J.Bot. 9, 1.

Mayer, A.M and Poljakoff-Mayber, A. 1975. "The germination of Seeds". Macmillan, New York.

Mc Rill, M and Sagar, G.R. 1973. Earth worms and seeds. Nature 243, 482.

Mc Graw, J.B. 1993. Ecological genetic variation in seed banks. 4 Differentiation of Extant and seed bank derived populations of Eriophorum vaginatum. Arc. & Alp. Res. 25, 45.

Mc Donald, A.W. 1993. The role of seed bank and sown seeds in the restoration of an English flood meadow. J.Veg. Sci. 4, 395.

Mc Graw. J.B. 1987. Seed bank properties of an Appalachian sphagnum bog and a model of the depth distribution of viable seeds. Can.J.Bot. 65, 2028.

Meredith, T.C. 1985. Factors affecting recruitment from the seed bank of sedge (Cladius mariscus) dominated communities at Wicken Fen, Cambridgeshire, England. J.Biogeogr. 12. 463.

Milberg, P. 1993. Seed bank and seedling emerging after soil disturbance in a wet seminatural Grass land in Sweden. Ann.Bot.Fen. 30, 9.

Milton, W.E.J. 1939. The occurrence of buried viable seeds in soils at different elevations and in a salt marsh. J.Ecol. 27, 149.

Mladenoff, D.J. 1990. The relationship of the soil seed bank and under story vegetation in old growth northern hardwood-hemlock tree fall gaps. Can.J.Bot. 68 (12) 2714-2771.

Moore, J.M and Wein, R.W. 1977. Viable seed populations by soil depth and potential site recolonization after disturbance. Can.J.Bot. 55, 2408.

Odum, S. 1965. Germination of Ancient Seeds. Aoristic observations and experiments with Archeologically dated soil samples. Dansk. Bot. Ark. 24, 1.

Ohtsuka, T and Ohsawa, M. 1994. Accumulation of Buried seeds and establishment of ruderal therophytic communities in disturbed habitat central Japan. Vegetatio 110, 83.

Oosting, H.F and Humphreys, M.E. 1940. Buried viable seeds in successional series of old fields and forest soils. Bull. Torrey Bot. Club 67, 253.

Parker, V.T and Leek, M.A. 1985. Relationships of seed banks to plant distribution patterns in a freshwater tidal wetland; Am. J.Bot. 72, 161.

Pederson, R.L. 1981. Seed bank characteristics of the Delta Marsh, Manitoba: Applications for wetland management. In "Seed Proceedings of the Midwest Conference on Wetland Values and Management (B. Richardson, ed.), Freshwater Soc., Navaree, Minnesota. 61.

Perry, J.N and Gonzalez and ujar, J.L. 1993. Dispersal in meta population Neighbourhood Model of an annual plant with a seed bank. J.Ecol. 81, 453.

Pierce, S.M, Cowling, R.M. Dynamics of soil-stored seed blinks of six shrubs in fire-prone dune fynbos. J.Ecol. 79(3) 731-741.

Putz, F.E and Appanah, B. 1987. Buried seeds, Newly dispersed seeds and the dynamics of. a lowland forest in Malaysia Biotropica 19, 326.

Rabinodz., D. 1981. Buried viable seed in a North American tall-grass prairie: The resemblance of their abundance and composition to dispersing seeds. Oikos 36, 191.

Roberts, H.A. 1981. Seed banks in soil. Adv. Appl.Bio, 6, 1-55.

Roberts, H.A and Neilson, J.E. 1982. Seed banks of soils under vegetable cropping in England. Weed Res. 22, 13.

Roberts, H.A and Neilson, J.E. 1982. Changes in the soil seed bank of four longterm crop/herbicide experiments. J.Appl.EcoI. 18, 661.

Russi, L., Cocks, P.S and Roberts, E.H. 1992. Seed bank dynamics in a Mediterranean grassland. J.App.EcoI. 29, 763.

Saulei, S.M and Swaine, M.D. 1988. Rain forest seed dynamics during succession at Gogol. Papua New Guinea J.Ecol. 76, 1133.

Schmidt, K.P and Lawlor, L.R. 1983. Growth rate projection and life history sensitivity for annual plants with a seed bank. Am.Nat. 121, 525.

Schneider, R.L and Sharitz, R.R. 1986. Seed bank dynamics in a southeastern riverine swamp. Am.J.Bot. 73, 1022.

Sharukhan, J. 1974. Studies on plant demography - Ranunculus repans L, R.bulboswi L. and R. acris. L. II. Reproductive strategies and plant population dynamics. J.Ecol. 62, 151.

Slivertown, J.W. 1983. Why biennials sometimes not so few? Amer.Nat. 121, 448.

Sllvertown, J.W and Dickie, J.B. 1981. Seedling survivorship in natural populations of nine perennial chalk grassland plants. New phytologist 88, 555.

Soderstrom, E. 1986. The effect of secondary forest on the soil bank of primary forest. In putz. F.E. (ed.) Tropical biology: An ecological approach. Organisation for tropical studies Durham, North Carolina 97.

Suzuki, W. 1993. Germination of Rubus palmatus var coptophyllus and R.microphyllus seeds buried in soil for 75 years. Ecological Research 8.

Therheedt. G.N.J and Drost, H.J. 1994. Potential for the development of Marsh Vegetation from the seed bank after Drawdown. Biol.Cons. 67, 1.

Thompson, K and Grime, J.P. 1979. Seasonal variation in the seed banks of herbaceous species in ten contrasting habitats. J. Ecol. 67, 893.

Thompson, K. 1987. Seeds and seed banks. New Phytol. 106, Suppl., 23.

U.S. Department of Agriculture. 1948. "Woody-Plant Seed Manual," USDA, Washington, D.C.

Ungar, I.A and Woodell, S.R.J. 1993. The relationship between the seed banks and species composition of plant communities in 2 British salt marshes. J.Veg.Sci. 4, 531.

Van der Valk, A.G. 1981. Succession in wetlands: A Gleasonian approach. Ecology 62, 688.

Van der Valk, A.G and Davis, C.B. 1979. A reconstruction of the recent vegetational history of a prairie marsh, Eagle Lake, Iowa, from its seed bank. Aquat. Bot. 6, 29.

Van der Valk, A.G. 1986. The impact of lilter and annual plants on recruitment from the seed bank of a lacustrine wetland. Aquat. Bot. 24, 13.

Van der valk, A.G and Davis, C.B.1978. The role of seed banks in the vegetation dynamics of praire glacial marshes. Ecology 59, 322-35.

Volodina, I.A, 1993. On the problem of studying soil banks of seeds of near-Caspian Deserts. Investiga Academii Nank 149.

Warwick, M.A 1984. Buried seed in arable soils in Scotland. Weed Research 24, 261-68.

Watkinson. A.R. 1978. The demography of sand dune annual: Vulpinafasciculata II. The dynamics of seed populations. Jour. Ecol. 66, 35-44.

Welling, C.H., Pederson, R.L and Van der Valk, A.G. 1988. Recruitment from the seed bank and the development of emergent zonation during a drawdown in a prairie wetland. J.Ecol. 76, 483.

Wesson, G and Wareing, P.F. 1969. The role of light in the germination of naturally occurring populations of buried weed seeds. Jour.Exp.Bot. 20, 403-13.

William, S.G. 1993. Soil seed banks in 4 Lower Montane forests of Mexico. Jour. Trop. Ecol. 9 (3) 321.

Wilson,·S.D, Moore, D.R.J arid Keddy, P.A. 1993. Relationship of Marsh seed banks of Washington patterns along environmental gradients. Fresh water Biology 29, 361.

WiIson, R.G. 1988. Biology of weed seeds in the soil. Weed management in agro-ecosystems: ecological approaches (eds.) Miguel A. Altieri, Matt Liebman. Boca Raton. Fla.: CRC Press, p. 2S-39.

Young, J.A and Evans, R.A. 1975. Germ inability of seed reserves in a big sagebrush community. Weed Sci. 23, 358.

Zhang, J and Mann, M.A. 1994 ..Potential for seed bank formation in seven lakes sand dune species. Amer.J.Bot. 81, 387-394.

Zhang, J and Mann, M.A. 1990. Effects of sand burial on seed germination, seedling emergences, survival and growth of Agropyron psammophilum. Can.J.Bot. 68, 304-310.

4. DOCUMENT FROM PUBLIC WORK DEPARTMENT, TN:

Irrigations Department

1. Introduction

I have great pleasure in presenting before this august House the Demand under "Irrigation and Buildings" of the Public Works Department, which is one of the oldest and prestigious Departments of the Government of Tamil Nadu.

Public Works Department is in charge of formulating and implementing Major, Medium and Minor Irrigation Schemes, Operation and Maintenance of Irrigation Systems and Construction and Maintenance of Buildings for State Government Departments and Agencies. The Public Works Department has been reorganized to have two wings, viz. Water Resources Organisation and Buildings Organisation, from December 1995. The objective of the Water Resources Organisation is to ensure effective management and distribution of Surface and Ground Water for its optimum utilisation in a rational and scientific manner to maximise agricultural production productivity of all the water using sectors. The objective of the Buildings Organisation is to ensure cost effective methods of building construction and maintenance by using modern technology.

2. Irrigation

Tamil Nadu with a geographical area of 130 lakh hectares is ranked eleventh in size among the Indian States. The net area sown in Tamil Nadu is about 60 lakh hectares of which about 30 lakh hectares or 50% get irrigation facilities from sources as given below:-

Adopted from Policy Note 2003-2004: Demand No. 38

1.	Canals	.. 9.50 lakh hectares
2.	Tanks	.. 9.00 lakh hectares
3.	Wells, Tube wells	.. 11.50 lakh hectares

Development of Irrigation in Tamil Nadu

The National Commission on Agriculture in 1976 assessed the ultimate irrigation potential of Tamilnadu through Major and Medium Irrigation sources as 15.00 lakh hectares. At the commencement of the First Five Year Plan, there were 23 Major and Medium Irrigation Projects benefiting 11.00 lakh hectares. In the IX plan period upto 2001-2002, the area under irrigation has risen to 29.72 lakh hectares.

During 2002-2003, an additional irrigation potential of 4924 hectares is expected to be created. During 2003-2004, additional irrigation potential of 9804 hectares is proposed to be created. Now the World Bank has further extended the project period for one more year i.e. 31-3-2004.

Diversion of Water to Tamil Nadu From Adjacent States

Tamil Nadu is a deficit State in water resources and has almost fully exploited all its surface water potential. The neighbouring States like Karnataka, Kerala and Andhra Pradesh are richly endowed with water resources. For further water resources development, Tamil Nadu has to depend upon inter basin water transfers from the adjoining basins of the neighbouring States or even to Long Distance Transfers. Tamil Nadu has moved the National Water Development Agency set up by the Government of India for diversion of surplus waters available in the adjoining States to augment its water resources.

The National Water Development Agency (N.W.D.A.) has also taken up the Inter Basin Study of the Peninsular Rivers for development which includes diversion of the surplus waters of the west flowing rivers in Pamba and Achankoil of Kerala to benefit arid areas in Madurai, Ramanathapuram, Virudhunagar and Tirunelveli Districts. The matter is being pursued by the State Government with the Government of Kerala and the Government of India.

The National Water Development Agency has also taken up studies for diversion of the surplus waters of Mahanadhi and Godavari via Krishna-Pennar-Palar-Cauvery-Vaigai Link. The pre-feasibility report on these links has been prepared by the N.W.D.A.

Another scheme viz, Pandiar-Punnampuzha Irrigation – cum – Hydro Electric Power Generation scheme is being actively pursued with the Government of Kerala.

Water Resources Organisation

As a first step towards effective implementation of the Water Resources Consolidation Project through improved functional specialisation, Water Resources Organisation was formed with effect from December 1995, in the Public Works Department.

Under the Water Resources Organisation, the Water Management in the State has been decentralised along river basins and the entire State has been divided into four regions, viz. Chennai, Tiruchirappalli, Pollachi and Madurai. A Basin Manager in the rank of Chief Engineer heads each basin.

Water Resources Organisation is functioning with the following Chief Engineers

(1) Engineer-in-Chief, Water Resources Organisation, Chennai.

(2) Chief Engineer, Plan Formulation, Chennai.

(3) Chief Engineer, Design, Research and Construction Support, Chennai.

(4) Chief Engineer, Operation and Maintenance & Inter State Water, Chennai.

(5) Chief Engineer, State Ground and Surface Water Resources Data Centre, Chennai.

(6) Chief Engineer, Chennai Region, Chennai.

(7) Chief Engineer, Tiruchirappalli Region, Tiruchirappalli.

(8) Chief Engineer, Pollachi Region, Coimbatore.

(9) Chief Engineer, Madurai Region, Madurai.

(10) Chief Engineer & Director, Institute for Water Studies, Tharamani, Chennai.

(11) Chief Engineer, Irrigation Management Training Institute, Tiruchirappalli.

Economising the Use of Irrigation Water

Since the surface water potential is almost fully utilised, there is hardly any scope for any new Major or Medium Irrigation Projects in the State. Conserving the available water by modernisation of the existing canal systems and tank irrigation has to be given more attention so that optimum utilisation of water could be ensured and wastage avoided. Water thus saved could be utilised for extending irrigation facilities to new areas or for raising additional crops in the same area.

With the above in view, the work of modernising the Periyar Vaigai Irrigation System was taken up with World Bank assistance. Similarly, the National Water Management Project was also taken up with World Bank assistance to improve the efficiency and productivity of the old irrigation systems in Sathanur, Kodaiyar, Thambaraparani, Cumbum Valley, Amaravathy Old Channels, Sethiathope, Marudhanadhi and other commands through a more reliable, predictable and equitable irrigation service. The Tamil Nadu Water Resources Consolidation Project (WRCP) with the objectives similar to those of National Water Management Project has been taken up for implementation since 1995-96. The World Bank has given approval for extending the period upto 31.3.2003 to complete the balance works.

Now the World Bank has further extended the project period for one more year i.e. upto 31-3-2004.

Budget Provision

The outlay for 2003-2004 is Rs.399.07 crore including a provision of Rs. 16.98 crore for the Water Resources Consolidation Project.

Major Irrigation Projects

Since the surface water potential of the State has already been almost fully exploited, there is no Major Irrigation Project under execution at present.

3. State Plan Schemes

Medium & Minor Irrigation Schemes

At the commencement of the Annual Plan 2003-2004, the following Medium and Minor Irrigation Schemes were in progress:-

(1) Strengthening of Periyar Dam (Peermedu, Kerala State)

(2) Nanganjiar Reservoir (Dindigul District)

(3) Irukkangudi Reservoir (Virudhunagar District)

(4) Shanmughanadhi Reservoir (Theni District)

(5) Malattar Anicut Scheme (Ramanathapuram District)

(6) Providing irrigation facilities to 58 villages (Madurai District)

(7) Andiappanur Odai Reservoir (Vellore District)

(8) Shenbagathope Reservoir (Thiruvannamalai District)

(9) Bathalapalli – Malattar Reservoir Scheme (Vellore District)

(10) Kuppanatham Reservoir Scheme (Thiruvannamalai District)

(11) Varattar – Vallimadurai Reservoir Scheme (Dharmapuri District)

(12) Kalvoi – Sadayaneri Scheme (Thoothukudi District)

(13) Narayana Cauvery channel (Ramanathapuram District)

(14) Formation of new tank across Uppu Odai (Tiruchirappalli District)

(15) Tank across Mudalaimuthuvari (Thanjavur District)

(16) Gadana Extension Scheme (Tirunelveli District)

(17) Tank across Nayodai (Dindigul District)

(18) Tank across Ramakkal Odai and Anaivilundan Odai (Dindigul District)

(19) Nallathangal Odai Tank (Erode District).

(20) Anicut across Andi odai (Tiruchirappalli District).

(21) Reservoir across Nagariar near Sasthakoil (Virudhunagar District).

(22) Reservoir across Vellakalkanar near Vinnamangalam (Vellore District).

(23) Tank across Sirumalaiar (Dindigul District).

(24) Augmentation of water supply to Vellianai and three other tanks from Kodaganar reservoir (Karur District).

(25) Improvements and Beautification of Parks in and around reservoirs

(26) Desilting and Modernisation of Vandiyur tank (Madurai District)

(27) Formation Of 18th Canal In Uthamapalayam Taluk Of Theni District

(28) Strengthening The Existing Upstream And Downstream Cut-Off Walls Of Upper Barrage At Upper Anicut (Mukkombu)

(29) Reservoir Across Mambazhathuraiyar (Kanyakumari District)

(30) Extension Of Nilaiyur Channel (Madurai District)

(31) Ullar Reservoir Across Palaiyar And Valamazhaiyar (Tirunelveli District)

(32) Reservoir Across Mirukandanadhi (Tiruvannamalai District)

(33) Rehabilitation And Modernisation Of The Lower Bhavani Irrigation Systems And Inclusion Of 23,000 Acres Of Land In Lower Bhavani Ayacut.

(34) Additional Funds For Rehabilitation Of 4 Channels In Kumbakonam Town Limit.

(35) Desilting Uyyacondan Channel, Kudamurity River, Ariyar, Koraiyar And Strengthening of Banks For Protecting Flood Damages In Tiruchy Town.

(36) Removal of Jungle And Bushes And Kattamanakku In River Cauvery And Portion From Trichy To Karur.

(37) Construction Of Syphon In Pugalur Channel To Divert The Polluted Noyyal Orathupalayam Water.

(38) Rehabilitation Of Anicut Across Nanganjiar Odai Near Pallapatti In Karur District.

(39) Desilting Kathiriinkulam And Its Channels In Dindigul District.

(40) Balance Works In Canal Channempatti Anicut Scheme.

(41) Balance Works In Periyar Main Canal From Melur To Maravanmangalam Tank.

(42) Rehabilitation of Vilathurai Pumping Scheme In Kuzhithurai River. (WRCP)

(43) Flood Prevention Scheme In Trichirapalli City

(44) Poigaiyar Reservoir (Kanyakumari District) under WRCP

(45) Nambiyar Reservoir (Tirunelveli District) under WRCP

(46) Rajathopekanar Reservoir (Vellore District) under WRCP

(47) Koundinyanadhi (Mordhana) Reservoir (Vellore District) under WRCP

(48) Adavinainarkoil Reservoir (Tirunelveli District) under WRCP

(49) Anicut across Gridhamal near Athikulam (Virudhunagar District) under WRCP

(50) Vadakkupachayar Reservoir Scheme (Tirunelveli District) under WRCP

(51) Kodumudiyar Reservoir (Tirunelveli District) under WRCP

(52) Sothuparai (Varahanadhi) Reservoir (Madurai District) under WRCP.

Note: Out of the 52 schemes, nine schemes (items 45 to 52) are being executed as the Scheme Completion component of the Water Resources Consolidation Project (which has been comprehensively dealt with separately).

Present Stage of the Above Ongoing Schemes

(1) Strengthening of Periyar Dam: (Peerimedu, Kerala State)

Periyar Dam near Thekkady is the main source of Irrigation for an ayacut of 84269 Ha. In Theni, Dindigul, Madurai, Sivagangai and Ramanathapuram Districts.

As per the 999 years lease Agreement executed during 1886, the Periyar Dam was constructed during 1887-1895 to store water upto 152 feet level.

During the year 1979, when some apprehensions about the safety and strength of the dam were raised, the matter was referred to the Central Water Commission for their assessment and advice. After a joint discussion with the officials of both the Government, Central Water Commission suggested the following remedial measures.

A. Emergency Measures

I. Providing RCC Capping and Widening the top of dam by 6 feet.

II. Providing additional spill ways.

B. Medium Term Measures:

Cable Anchoring.

C. Long Term Measures:

Providing concrete backing on the surface of dam.

D. Shutters of the spillway to be raised fully to Lower level in the Reservoir to (+) 136 feet as temporary measure to facilitate carrying out the remedial measures.

Subsequently Strengthening of baby dam, raising Parapet wall and Energy Dissipation arrangement were also suggested by Central Water Commission in addition to the above.

According to the Central Water Commission recommendation, the storage of water could be raised to 145 feet after completing the emergency and medium term measures and to the full level of 152 feet after completing all the strengthening measures.

All the dam strengthening works suggested by Central Water Commission in the first conference in 1979 have been completed except strengthening of Baby Dam.

For Periyar Dam, the final report of the Expert Committee was given to the Ministry of Water Resources in March 2001. The Government of Tamil Nadu has sent the views on the final report to the Central Government. The Ministry of Water Resources has filed the final reply on the final report of the Expert Committee in the Supreme Court. The Supreme Court has called the two Government to file their reply on the final report. The Government of Tamil Nadu has filed in the Supreme Court, its response to the final report of the Expert Committee on 06.02.2002. The Government of Tamil Nadu has also filed its response to the reply affidavit filed by Government of Kerala in respect to the final report on 25.02.2002. The transfer petition is yet to be disposed off by the Honourable Supreme Court.

Proposal for strengthening of Baby Dam had been sent to the Government of Kerala for their concurrence as early as in 1987 and inspite of repeated requests by Tamilnadu, their concurrence is not forthcoming. However in anticipation of Kerala Government concurrence, contract for strengthening of Baby Dam has been settled.

The Contractor has filed petition on 12.09.1999 in the High Court of Kerala praying for direction to the Kerala Government for not obstructing to do the strengthening work. This case is pending in High Court of Kerala. As per Government instructions the site handed over to contractor has been taken back on 13.09.2002 without terminating the agreement, so the Baby Dam work could not be taken up at present.

As directed by the Chief Minister of Tamilnadu, an interstate meeting had been conducted at Chennai on 10.06.2002 with the P.W.D. Minister of Tamilnadu and the Kerala P.W.D. Minister regarding interstate water issues and Periyar Dam issue. However the work will be started only after the concurrence of the Kerala Government.

The Budget Estimate proposed for 2003-2004 is Rs. 0.01 lakh (for Baby Dam).

(2) Anganjiar Reservoir (Dindigul District)

This scheme contemplates the formation of a reservoir across Nanganjiyar, a tributary of river Amaravathy near Idayankottai village in Palani Taluk, Dindigul District to benefit 2,530 hectares of new ayacut with a stabilisation of 24 hectares of old ayacut in Idayankottai, Valayapatti and Chinnakamapatti villages in Vedasandur Taluk of Dindigul District and Sendamangalam village of Karur Taluk of Karur District at an estimated cost of Rs. 20.70 crore.

In this project construction of uncontrolled spillway is in progress. Earth dam works and main canal and spill way works are nearing completion. The Government have approved the reappraisal estimate of this project for Rs. 37.36 crore. The works are in progress. Totally 80% of the work has been completed.

The Budget provision for the year 2003-04 is Rs. 348.35 lakh.

(3) Rukkangudi Reservoir (Virudhunagar District)

This scheme is for the formation of reservoir across Vaippar near Irrukangudi village, Sattur Taluk, Virudhunagar District at a cost of Rs. 28.70 crore. The scheme aims at stabilising an extent of 254 hectares, bridging the gap of 255 hectares and giving new irrigation facilities to 3,705 hectares of dry lands in Rajapatti, Masarpatti, Sakkihapatti, Thappatti, Keelanattukurichi, Melakarandai, Shencottai, Keezhakarandai, Vadamalapuram, Vowal Thotti and Vedapatti villages of Vilathikulam Taluk of Thoothukudi District.

In this scheme, construction of masonry dam across Arjuna and Vaippar rivers are in progress at various stages. 80% of main canal and 95% of Branch Canal have been completed. Cross masonry works in canal are in progress. The revised estimate for Rs.62.20 Crore has been approved by Government.

The Budget provision for the year 2003-04 is Rs. 2000.00 lakh.

(4) Shanmughanadhi Reservoir (Theni District)

This scheme contemplates the formation of a reservoir across Shanmughanadhi (Varattar) near Royappanpatti village in Uthamapalayam Taluk of Theni District.

The scheme aims at irrigating 664 hectares of new dry land in Royappanpatti village of Cumbum Taluk and Mallingapuram, Chinnaovalapuram, Erasakkanaickanur, Kanniservaipatti, Alagapuri, Odaipatti, Seepalakottai villages in Uthamapalayam Taluk.

The Government have sanctioned this scheme at a revised estimate cost of Rs.14.70 crore. The components of the scheme are an earth dam, masonry dam-non overflow section, uncontrolled spillway, head sluice and canals with necessary structures.

In this scheme, all works have been completed except distributaries work which are nearing completion.

The Budget provision for the year 2003-04 is Rs. 100.00 lakh.

(5) Malattar Anicut (Ramanathapuram District)

This scheme is for the construction of an anicut across Malattar river below the existing Kamudhi regulator and just below the confluence point of Gridhamal and Paralayar rivers with Malattar near Sengapadi village in Kamudhi Taluk of Ramanathapuram District.

This scheme will benefit stabilisation of an extent of 1758 hectares besides bridging a gap of 156 hectares under 54 tanks in O.Karisalkulam, Veppankulam (Kamudhi Taluk), Pammanendal, Ariyamangalam, Punavasal, Veppankulam (Kadaladi Taluk), Meenankudi, Orivayal and Kadugusandai villages in Kamudhi and Kadaladi Taluks.

The Government have sanctioned this scheme at an estimated cost of Rs.15.40 crore. The main components of the scheme are a Masonry Anicut, Head Sluice 2 Nos., Right and Left Main Canals with necessary structures.

Construction of body wall of anicut from LS 0m to LS 200m and LS 200m to 385m is completed. Construction of right side head sluice and scouring sluice works and formation of earth dam are in progress. Construction of left side head sluices and scouring sluice agency settled and work to be started.

The Budget provision for the year 2003-04 is Rs. 500.00 lakh.

(6) Providing Irrigation Facilities To 58 Villages In Usilampatti Taluk (Madurai District)

This scheme envisages excavation of a high level canal of 27.26 Km from the proposed head works on the right flank of the Vaigai Dam at LS 2425 m from the spillway to provide irrigation facilities to the 58 villages in Usilampatti Taluk. This canal will be an unlined one for carrying the surplus floodwater from Vaigai River to provide irrigation facilities to 58 villages in Usilampatti Taluk whenever both Vaigai Reservoir and Ramnad Big Tank surplus simultaneously. It includes formation of 3 new tanks to get supply from the above high level canal. The Government have accorded approval for this scheme at an estimated cost of Rs.33.81 crore.

By implementing this scheme, 570 hectares of wet lands will be stabilised besides bridging a gap of 128 hectares of wet lands under 29 existing tanks and 3 existing ponds in Usilampatti Taluk. Further new dry ayacut of 227 hectares will be brought under irrigation through 3 new tanks.

In this scheme, land acquisition work is in progress. Out of 14 works, tenders have been accepted for 12 works and 9 works are in progress at various stages. 3 works are held up due to objection of land owners. Tender proposals for the balance two works have been rejected and re- tenders are to be invited. Building works are completed.

The Budget provision for the year 2003-04 is Rs. 526.25 lakh.

(7) Andiappanur Odai (Vellore District)

This scheme envisages the formation of a reservoir of 112 M.Cft. capacity across Andiappanur Odai near Andiappanur village in Vaniyambadi Taluk of Vellore District.

The Government have sanctioned this scheme at an estimated cost of Rs.18.28 crore. The Government have also accorded Revised Administrative Sanction for Rs.27.38 crores.

By implementing this scheme, an extent of 810 hectares of direct ayacut in Andiappanur and Irunappattu villages in Vaniyambadi Taluk will be benefited for raising double dry crops.

Transfer of 39.69 hectares of forest land, 15 hectares of poromboke land and acquisition of 100.245 hectares of Patta land are involved.

Land acquisition completed except 9.85 Ha. in which court case is pending. Forest land has been handed over to Public Works Department. Preliminary works for forming approach road to dam site and camp colony have been completed. "NABARD" has been approached for loan assistance. Agency settled for the main work and the work is in progress.

The Budget provision for the year 2003-04 is Rs.1292.00 lakh.

(8) Shenbagathope Reservoir (Tiruvannamalai District)

The Shenbagathope Reservoir Scheme contemplates the formation of a reservoir across Kamandalaru in Shenbagathope village of Polur Taluk in Thiruvannamalai District.

The Government have sanctioned this scheme at an estimated cost of Rs.21.33 crore. The Government have accorded the Revised Administrative Sanction for a sum of Rs.34.00 crores for this scheme.

This scheme will benefit 2067 hectares by stabilisation and 642 hectares by bridging the gap in Vallur, Kangaramandal, Santhavasal, Naramangalam, Illuppakkunam, Paravathiagaram, Aliyabad and Enthuvambadi villages in Polur Taluk, Kuppam, Kamakukur, Arni, Mamandur, Kalpoondi, Mullipattu, Paiyur in Arni Taluk, Vazhapanthal, Melpudupakkam, Mampakkam, Melpalandai, Arur, Suraiyur and Ponnambalam villages in Arcot Taluk, Tirumani, Munugapattu, Melpudur and

Melseshamangalam in Cheyyar Taluk and Anmarudhai in Vandavasi Taluk. By implementing this scheme, a long time demand of this backward region for better irrigation facilities will be fulfilled.

Preliminary works such as construction of store shed, fencing at Aliyabad etc. have been completed.

For implementation of this scheme, an extent of 99.62 hectares of forest land, 21.50 hectares of private patta land and 3.25 hectares of poramboke land are required. Land acquisition process and transfer of forest land are completed.

Agency settled for the main work. Work is in progress. "NABARD" has accorded approval for loan assistance.

The Budget provision for the year 2003-04 is Rs.1979.38 lakh.

(9) Bathalapalli–Malattar Reservoir (Vellore District)

The scheme contemplates formation of a reservoir across Malattar river near Bathalapalli village in Gudiyatham Taluk, Vellore District. The Government have sanctioned this scheme at an estimated cost of Rs.29.55 crore.

This scheme will stabilise 1,064 hectares of ayacut and bridge the gap of 61 hectares in Balur, Machampattu, Vasanampalli, Nariyampattu, Reddimankuppam, Sarangal Kailasagiri, Ayithampattu, Sathampakkam, Rajakal, Alingikuppam, Malmurugai, Melpatti, Kulithigai, Chinnathottalam, Ulli, Kothakuppam, Aranganalalur, Olakasi and Chithathur villages of Gudiyatham Taluk. Besides, provision for drinking water facilities to Peranampet town and the way side villages and for industrial purposes has been made in this scheme. Also the wells in the area now affected by pollution from tanneries will become good water sources in course of time.

The components of the scheme are Earth dam, Masonry spillways, River sluices, Pickup anicut and drops.

For implementation of this scheme, an extent of 36.98 hectares of patta land, 17.81 hectares of forest land and 11.32 hectares of poramboke land are required. Land acquisition works are completed. Forest land has been handed over to Public Works Department. NABARD has been approached for loan assistance.

The Budget provision for the year 2003-04 is Rs. 100.00 lakh.

(10) Kuppanatham Reservoir (Tiruvannamalai District)

The scheme contemplates formation of a reservoir across Cheyyar near Kuppanatham village in Chengam Taluk of Thiruvannamalai District. The Government have sanctioned this scheme at an estimated cost of Rs.35.46 crore.

This scheme will stabilise an extent of 2528 hectares and bridge a gap of 580 hectares under 22 tanks fed by 5 anicuts and 2 open off-takes across Cheyyar in Kayampattu, Valaiyampattu, Thandapattu, Kariyamangalam, Vadankuppam, Melvanakkampadi, Melpuluthiyar, Perumpattam, Pakkripalayam, Thukkapettai, Memalur, Kayampatu, Gengaravaran, Sennasamudram, Ponneri, Sinnasamudram, Padiagaram, Narasinganallur, Thorapadi, Munnoormangalam, Nachipattu, Kunjilam, Periyeri, Unnamalai-puram, Puduchengam, Anvarbad, Alaputhur, Tamaraipakkam and

Aridaraimangalam villages in Chengam Taluk, Munnurmangalam, Kariyandal, Anandal, Melpunjai, Vasudevampattu and Kizhithur villages in Tiruvannamalai Taluk and Kadaladi, Kunathur and Kizhathur villages in Polur Taluk.

The components of the scheme are Earth dam, Masonry spillway and River sluice.

For implementing this scheme, an extent of 190.42 hectares of patta dry lands, 103.75 hectares of poromboke lands, and 13.34 hectares of forest lands are required. Acquisition of patta land and transfer of poromboke lands are under way. Forest lands handed over to Public Works Department. NABARD has been approached for loan assistance.

Preliminary works for preparation of design and drawings are in progress. The Budget provision for the year 2003-04 is Rs. 250.00 lakh.

(11) Varattar– Vallimadurai Reservoir (Dharmapuri District)

This scheme contemplates formation of a reservoir across Varattar near Vallimadurai village in Harur Taluk in Dharmapuri District. The Government have sanctioned an amount of Rs.19.20 crore for this scheme. The Government have accorded sanction for the Revised Estimate for an amount of Rs.35.95 Crore.

This scheme will stabilise an extent of 110 hectares of wet lands besides benefiting an extent of 1047 hectares of single crop dry lands under Keeraipatti anicut, Ellappudayampatti anicut and Mankuppam Eri benefiting Vallimadurai, Thathavalasi, Somanathan, Keeraipatty, Kudumiyampatti, Achalvadi and Somanathampudur villages in Harur Taluk.

The components of this scheme are Earth dam, Surplus weir, Head sluices and Canal.

For implementation of this scheme, an extent of 94.31 hectares of patta dry land and 24.87 hectares of reserve forest lands have to be acquired in addition to the transfer of 23.82 hectares of poromboke land. The Government of India has accorded final approval for diversion of forest land on 22-12-2000.

Main works are in progress. "NABARD" has accorded approval for loan assistance. The Budget provision for the year 2003-04 is Rs. 1496.00 lakh.

(12) Kalvoi – Sadayaneri (Thoothukudi District)

The Government have sanctioned an amount of Rs.12.33 crore for this scheme which comprises widening the existing Kalvoi – Sadayaneri Channel upto Kalvoi Tank and widening the existing Sadayaneri Channel, excavation of Sadayaneri Extension Channel, improvements to the existing Mudalur Odai from Karumeniyar to Vairavantharuvai and excavating a link canal from Vairavantharuvai to Puthantharuvai.

This scheme contemplates utilising the Thambaraparani surpluses for filling twelve tanks in Sadayaneri and Thanjaikkulam to irrigate 314 hectares of ayacut. Besides, two Tharuvais (lakes) will also get filled which will help recharge 634 wells in four villages for irrigating coconut cultivation in 875 hectares. This scheme will also benefit Kalvoi, Vellur, Udayarkulam, Vellamadam, Pidaneri, Eluvarimukki, Nangaimazhi, Sathankulam, Sasthan-vinallur, Kumadikottai, Thirupanikkuthan Tharuvai and Pattakurichi villages in Tiruchendur and Sathankulam Taluks.

This work is now taken up under State funds and 98% of works completed. Balance works are in progress at various stages.

The Budget provision for 2003-04 is Rs.0.01 lakh.

(13) Renovation of Narayana Cauvery Channel (Ramanathapuram District)

The Government have sanctioned the scheme for Rehabilitation of Narayana Cauvery Channel and its anicut (Mandalamanickam Anicut) to feed Sayalkudi tank and other 33 tanks in Ramanathapuram District at an estimated cost of Rs.5.75 crore.

This scheme gives irrigation support to 1942.97 hectares of lands in Mandalamanickam, Kamuthi, Mandalnadu, K.Nedungulam, Seemanendal, Kundukulam, K.Veppankulam, O.Karisalkulam, Kovilankulam, Koomboothi, M.Pudukulam and Villanendal villages in Kamuthi Taluk, Kallakari villlage in Tiruchuli Taluk, Sayalkudi, M.Karisalkulam, N.Karisalkulam, A. Usilangulam, S.Vagaikulam, Pillayarkulam, S.Keerandai and Keela Allikulam villages in Kadaladi Taluk of Ramanathapuram District.

90% works completed. Balance works are in progress.

The Budget provision for the year 2003-04 is Rs. 200.00 lakh.

(14) Tank Across Uppu Odai (Tiruchirappalli District)

The Government have sanctioned the scheme for formation of a tank across the Uppu Odai, its confluence with Nandiar near Siruvayalur village Hamlet of Kanakiliyanallur village in Lalgudi Taluk, Tiruchirappalli District at an estimated cost of Rs. 4.18 crore.

This scheme will provide irrigation facilities to a new dry extent of 152 hectares in Kanakiliyanallur village in Lalgudi Taluk.

The components of the scheme are formation of earth bund, surplus weir, three irrigation sluices and three Channels. Nearly 75% of the work has been completed. Further works are in progress.

The Budget provision for the year 2003-04 is Rs. 60.00 lakh.

(15)Tank Across Mudalai Muthu Vari (Thanjavur District)

The Government have sanctioned the scheme for formation of a tank across Mudalai Muthu Vari in Chennampatti village in Thanjavur Taluk and District at an estimated cost of Rs. 9.73 crore.

This scheme will stabilise 110 hectares of existing wet ayacut, bridge a gap of 9 hectares of wet land and provide irrigation facilities to a new dry extent of 364 hectares in Chennampatti and Vallampudur villages in Thanjavur District and Karumpoondi village in Pudukottai District.

The components of this scheme are 2300 metre long earth bund, uncontrolled weir and four sluices. Totally 78.50% of the works has been completed. The remaining works are in progress. Land acquisition process under private negotiations is in progress.

The Budget provision for the year 2003-04 is Rs. 200.00 lakh.

(16) Gadana Extension Scheme (Tirunelveli District)

The Government have sanctioned the scheme for formation of an extension reservoir on the right flank of the existing Gadana Dam in Ambasamudram Taluk of Tirunelveli District at an estimated cost of Rs.18.82 crore.

The scheme will stabilise irrigation in an extent of 511 hectares, bridge a gap in 187 hectares and provide irrigation facilities to a new extent of 67 hectares in Sivasailam, Mela Ambur, Keela Ambur and Mannarkoil villages in Ambasamudram Taluk.

The components of the scheme are earth bund of 930m length with one irrigation sluice, main canal with 3 branch canals for a total length of 18.71 Km and formation of an inter-connecting water way by cutting open the saddle dam for a length of 120m.

About 70% of works are completed and the balance works are in progress. NABARD has accorded sanction for loan assistance for this scheme.

The Budget provision for the year 2003-04 is Rs. 294.20 lakh.

(17) Tank Across Nayodai (Dindigul District)

The Government have sanctioned the scheme for formation of a tank across Nayodai a tributary of Mangariyar in Kannivadi village, Dindigul Taluk and District at an estimated cost of Rs.3.50 crore. Revised Administrative sanction for this scheme has also been accorded for Rs.7.2 Crore.

The scheme will provide irrigation facilities to a new extent of 148 hectares in Kannivadi, Alanthuranpatti, Veerapudaiyanpatti and Thettupatti villages in Dindigul Taluk and District.

The components of the scheme are earth bund of 620-m length, high coefficient weir of 30-m length, one tower head sluice and field canal of 4120 m length.

Construction of surplus weir and forming earthern dam are in progress. The Budget provision for the year 2003-04 is Rs. 200.00 lakh.

(18) Tank Across Ramakkal Odai And Anaivilundan Odai (Dindigul District)

The Government have sanctioned the scheme for the formation of tank across Ramakkal Odai and Anaivilundan Odai, tributaries of Kodaganar river in A.Vellode village and Keelakottai village in Dindigul Taluk and District at an estimated cost of Rs.3.55 crore. Revised Administrative sanction for this scheme has also been accorded for Rs.5.65 Crore.

This scheme will provide irrigation facilities to 107.65 hectares of new dry lands in A. Vellode and Keelakottai villages in Dindigul Taluk and District.

The components of this scheme are earth bund 480m long, weir with a surplus course to connect the weir to Ramakkal Odai, Head sluice, River sluice and Field canals. The High Court, Chennai has ordered not to proceed with the work without settling the land acquisition charges.

The Budget provision for the year 2003-04 is Rs.450.00 lakh.

(19) Reservoir Across Nallathangal Odai (Erode District)

The Government have sanctioned the scheme for the formation of a reservoir across Nallathangal Odai near Eswarankoil in Ponnivadi village of Dharapuram Taluk in Erode District at an estimated cost of Rs.31.01 crore. Revised Administrative sanction for this scheme has also been accorded for Rs.42.70 Crore.

This scheme will provide irrigation facilities to 1,919.87 hectares of new dry extent in Nallanpalayam, Alampalayam, Poramium Thurambadi, Moolanur and Ponnivadi villages of Dharapuram Taluk in Erode District.

The components of this scheme are earth dam 3450m, uncontrolled spillway, one head sluice and one river sluice. Construction of quarters and Sub Division Office Buildings is nearing completion. Formation of Earth Dam and Construction of Spillway are in progress.

The Budget provision for the year 2003-04 is Rs.450.00 lakh.

(20) Anicut Across Andi Odai (Tiruchirappalli District)

The Government have sanctioned the scheme for formation of an Anicut across Andi Odai near Kallagam village in Lalgudi Taluk, Trichichirappalli District at an estimated cost of Rs.1.21 crore.

This scheme will stabilise existing irrigation in an extent of 82 hectares of wet ayacut and provide irrigation facilities to a new dry extent of 84 hectares in Kallagam village of Lalgudi Taluk in Tiruchirappalli District and Poondi village of Ariyalur Taluk in Perambular District.

The components of this scheme are Masonry Anicut of 36m length, one head sluice, main canal (left side) 3,350m long with cross masonry works and flood bank 700m long.

All the works have been completed.

(21) Reservoir Across Nagariyar Near Sasthakoil (Virudhunagar District)

The Government have sanctioned the scheme for formation of a reservoir across the river Nagariar near Sasthakoil in Rajapalayam Taluk of Virudhunagar District at an estimated cost of Rs.7.97 crore.

This scheme will stabilise 1016 hectares of existing ayacut and bridge a gap of 184 hectares under the existing 13 tanks in North Devathanam, South Devathanam, Sethur, Muthusamypuram, Kovilur, Nallamangalam and Chettiarpatti villages in Rajapalayam Taluk.

The components of this scheme are earth bund for a length of 1600m, uncontrolled spillway, river sluice and excavation of new surplus course.

50% work completed. Balance Work is in progress. NABARD has accorded sanction for loan assistance for this scheme.

The Budget provision for this scheme 2003-04 is 493.00 lakh.

(22) Reservoir Across Vellakkal Kanar (Vellore District)

The Government have sanctioned the scheme for formation of a reservoir across Vellakkal Kanar near Vinnamangalam village in Vaniyambadi Taluk of Vellore District at an estimated cost of Rs.7.70 crore.

This scheme will stabilise 431 hectares of existing irrigation besides bridging a gap of 57 hectares in Kannadikuppam, Periyankuppam, Sanarkuppam, Melkrishnapuram, Ambur, Samalapuram, Karunwaram, Vadapudupatti, Kilmurugi, Thottalam, Madumur and Katanpakkam villages in Vaniyambadi Taluk.

The components of this scheme are earth dam 320 m long, surplus weir of 40 m length and construction of River sluice.

For implementation of this scheme, 35.82 hectares of forest land is required. Stage I approval for diversion of forest land is complied by Government of India. Work will be commenced after Land Acquisition.

The Budget provision for the year 2003-04 is Rs. 200.00 lakh.

(23) Tank Across Sirumalaiyar (Dindigul District)

The Government have sanctioned the scheme for formation of a new tank across Sirumalaiyar near Rajadhani Kottai village in Nilakottai Taluk of Dindigul District at an estimated cost of Rs.4.91 crore.

Revised administrative sanction has been accorded for Rs.8.87 Crore.

This scheme will provide irrigation facilities to a new dry extent of 128 hectares in Oruthattu village in Nilakottai Taluk.

The components of this scheme are earth bund of 975-m length including surplus weir of 40m length, one head sluice and surplus course for a length of 60m. Earth bund 0.500m sluice and surplus weir have been completed. Balance works are held up due to land acquisition.

(24) Augmentation of Water Supply to Vellianai and Three Other Tanks From Kodaganar Reservoir (Karur District)

The Government have sanctioned the scheme for augmentation of water supply to Vellianai tank and three other tanks from Kodaganar reservoir in Karur Taluk and District at an estimated cost of Rs.1.00 crore.

This scheme will stabilise 440 hectares of existing wet ayacut besides bridging a gap of 116 hectares in Vellianai, Uppidaman-galam, Veerarakiam and Valayalkaranpudur villages in Karur Taluk and District.

The components of this scheme are rehabilitation and improvements to the Right Main Canal for the length of 53.50 Km, repairs to existing cross masonry works and construction of 5 inlet sluices.

80% of the work has been completed. Balance work is in progress.

(25) Improvements and Beautification of Parks in and Around Reservoirs

The Government have sanctioned the proposal for improvements and beautification of the parks in Krishnagiri, Sathanur, Amaravathi, Vaigai, Aliyar, Bhavanisagar, Manimuthar, Vidur and Mukkombu Dam sites at an estimated cost of Rs. 3.00 crore.

The improvements and beautification works in the Krishnagiri, Aliyar, Bhavanisagar, Amaravathi, Sathanur, Vaigai, Vidur and Mukkombu dam and Manimuthar Dam have been completed.

The Budget provision for the year 2003-04 is 0.01 lakh.

(26) Esilting and Modernisation of Vandiyur Tank (Madurai District)

The Government have sanctioned the scheme of Desilting and Modernisation of Vandiyur Tank and establishing park and beautification at an estimated cost of Rs. 2.50 crore.

Desilting works are completed.

(27) Formation of 18th Canal in Uthamapalayam Taluk of Theni District

The Government have sanctioned the scheme for formation of 18th Canal in Uthamapalayam Taluk in Theni District at an estimated cost of Rs.26.52 crore.

The scheme will stabilise irrigation in an extent of 511.16 hectares bridge a gap in 73.90 hectares and provide irrigation facilities to a new extent of 22.81 hectares in Tempucheri, T.Chindalacheri, Pannaipuram, Kombai, Sankarapuram, Vembakottai, Thevaram, Lakshminaickanpatti, Pothaipuram, Meenakshipuram, Gudalur and Uthamapuram village in Uthamapalayam Taluk.

The components of the scheme are construction of head sluice and excavation of a canal for a length of 38.90 km and formation of 4 numbers of new tanks at an estimated cost of Rs.26.52 Crore. The works have been split up into 3 reaches.Works in all the three reaches are in progress.

(28) Strengthening the Existing Upstream and Downstream Cut-off Walls of Upper Barrage at Upper Anicut (Mukkombu) (Tiruchirapalli District)

The Government have sanctioned the scheme for strengthening the existing Upstream and Downstream cut off walls of Upper barrage at Upper Anicut (Mukkombu) at an estimated cost of Rs.6.00 crore.

Works have been completed.

(29) Reservoir Across Mambazhathuraiyar (Kanyakumari District)

The Government have sanctioned the scheme for formation of a reservoir across Mambazhathuraiyar near Villukuri village in Kalkulam Taluk in Kanyakumari District at an estimated cost of Rs.9.50 crore.

This scheme will stablise 3.57 hectares, bridge a gap of 25.82 hectares in single crop and 18.14 hectares in second crop and provide irrigation facilities to a new extent of 308.98 hectares in Kalkulam and Villukuri villages in Kalkulam Taluk in Kanyakumari District.

The components of the scheme are formation of earth dam of 295 m length, surplus weir of 50m length and construction of sluice and excavation of right and left side channels.

(30) Extension of Nilaiyur Channel (Madurai District)

The Government have sanctioned the scheme for extending the Nilaiyur channel from upstream of Perungudi tank to feed Valankulam and Kambikudi tanks series in Madurai, Virudhunagar and Sivagangai Districts at an estimated cost of Rs.8.94 crore.

The scheme will stabilise irrigation in an extent of 2686.53 hectares and bridge a gap in 1126.03 hectares in Valayapatty, Thothiyapatti, Chinnaulagani, Valayankulam, Nedu Madurai, Kudakovil, Vellarakulam, Periya Alangulam, Sambakulam, Kombadi, Ayyampatti, Eliyarpatti, Mochipatti, Paraipatti, Pulichangulam, Anaikulam, Sangumadai, Chalanguruni, Nallur, Vadakkupeerikulam, Pappanodai, Ramankulam, Kaluvankulam, Virathanur, Muthankulam, Panaikulam, M.Alangulam, Nedunkulam, Sathankulam, Sagadathatti, Chinnaudappu, Kuthiraikutty, Kodal Sengulam, Kosarankundu, Udaikulam, Kosarapatti and Konthakulam villages in Madurai South Taluk, Chinna Ulagani, Virusankulam, Vidathakulam and Keelauppa-likundu villages in Thirumangalam Taluk Kadambankulam, Aviyoor, Pulapatti, Mangulam, Kuraadi, Udaikulam, Arasakulam, Royarpatti, Kambikudi, Pappankulam, S.Alangulam, Anmalpe-rukki, Chatrampulamkulam, Pannaivalathanpatti, Vetrilaimurichan-patti and Allalaperi villages in Kariapatti Taluk, Kancharankulam, Valayankulam, Surampatti, Thiraliyar, Mukkudi, Ilandaikulam, Vadurankulam, Karankalakudi, Rakkankulam, Sengulam, Vadakkur, Paraiyankulam and Usalankulam villages in Manamadurai Taluk.

The components of this scheme are construction of head sluice-cum-regulator, excavation of main canal for a length of 7.850 Km and branch canal for a length of 3.00 Km including cross masonry works.

55% of works completed. Balance works in progress. NABARD has accorded approval for loan assistance. The revised estimate for an amount of Rs.19.49 Crore is approved by Government.

(31) Ullar Reservoir Across Palaiyar and Valamazhaiyar (Tirunelveli District)

The Government have sanctioned the scheme for formation of a reservoir across Palaiyar and Valamazhaiyar near Sivagiri village in Sivagiri taluk, Tirunelveli District at an estimated cost of Rs.39.20 crore.

The scheme will stabilise irrigation in an extent of 971.95 hectares and bridge a gap in 595.18 hectares in Royagiri, Sivagiri, Thenmalai, Thirumelapuram, Naranapuram, Kottaiyar, Chinthamaniperi, Koodaloor and Ramanathapuram villages in Sivagiri Taluk, Panaiyur, Vayali, Marathoni, Thiruvenkadam, Chatrapatti and Karichathan villages in Sankarankoil Taluk.

The components of this scheme are earth dam, spillway, construction of 2 sluices, improvements to Rasingaperiar and Kulasekaraperiar, construction of dividing wall and improvements to the existing anicuts and tanks.

Finalisation of design is under progress.

The Budget provision for the year 2003-04 is Rs.100.00 lakh.

(32) Reservoir Across Mirukandanadhi (Tiruvannamalai District)

The Government have sanctioned the scheme for formation of a reservoir across Mirukandanadhi near Melsolankuppam village in Polur taluk in Tiruvannamalai District at an estimated cost of Rs.16.79 crore.

This scheme will stabilise irrigation in an extent of 778.05 hectares and bridge a gap in 81.10 hectares in Melsolankuppam, Gangavaram, Senandal, Nallanpillai Pettran, Gangamaladevi, Kettavarampalayam, Siruvallur, Ernamangalam and Solavaram in Polur taluk of Tiruvannamalai District.

The components of this scheme are earth dam of 670-m length, uncontrolled spillway, one head sluice and one river sluice.

For implementing of this scheme 80.82 hectares of patta land and 23.37 hectares of poramboke land are required. Government have accorded sanction for acquisition of private patta land under urgency clause. The work will be taken up during the current year. "NABARD" has been approached for loan assistance.

The Budget provision for the year 2003-04 is Rs.440.00 lakh.

(33) Rehabilitation and Modernisation of the Lower Bhavani Irrigation Systems – Estimate Rs. 55 Crore and Inclusion of 23,000 Acres of Land in Lower Bhavani Ayacut.

The Government have issued orders to include 23,000 acres of land in Lower Bhavani ayacut.

During 1999-2000 an amount of Rs.6.84 Crore was allotted and desilting work is carried out in Lower Bhavani Basin System for a total length of 313 KM for Canals, Drains, Channels.

During 2000-2001, an amount of Rs.6.27 Crore was allotted for desilting works in canals, channels, drains in Lower Bhavani Basin System.

During 2001-2002, an amount of Rs.1.62 Crore was allotted.

Desilting works were carried out for a total length of 280 KM, out of 800 KM. length. During the year 2002-03, more work can be done since the closure period is 4 months. Balance works have been programmed to be completed within two years.

(34) Additional Funds For Rehabilitation Of 4 Channels In Kumbakonam Town Limit – Estimate Rs. 1.91 crore.

Three channel work completed. Remaining one channel 50% of work completed.

(35) Desilting Uyyacondan Channel, Kudamurity River, Ariyar, Koraiyar and Strengthening of Banks For Protecting Flood Damages in Tiruchy Town-estimate Rs. 2.50 crore.

Works have been completed.

(36) Removal of Jungle and Bushes and Kattamanakku In River Cauvery and Portion From Trichy to Karur - Estimate Rs. 10.00 lakh.

Works have been completed.

(37) Construction of Syphon In Pugalur Channel to Divert The Polluted Noyyal Orathupalayam Water - Estimate Rs. 35.00 lakh

Tender was accepted but work could not be commenced in view of pendency of a writ petition in High Court, Chennai.

(38) Rehabilitation of Anicut Across Nanganjiar Odai Near Pallapatti in Karur District – Estimate Rs. 33.00 lakh.

65% of works completed. Balance work is in progress.

(39) Desilting Kathiriinkulam and Its Channels in Dindigul District – Estimate Rs. 50.00 lakh

40% of work completed. Balance works are in progress.

(40) Balance Works in Canal Chennempatti Anicut Scheme –Estimate Rs.15.00 Lakh

Work Has Been Completed.

(41) Balance Works in Periyar Main Canal From Melur To Maravanmangalam Tank – Estimate Rs. 1.00 Crore.

62% of Work is Completed. Further Work is in Progress.

(42) Rehabilitation Of Vilathurai Pumping Scheme In Kuzhithurai River – Estimate Rs. 5.00 Lakh. (Taken Up Under W.r.c.p)

Work Has Been Completed.

(43) Flood Prevention Scheme in Trichirapalli City

Government have accorded sanction for implementation of a flood prevention scheme at an estimated cost of Rs.50.00 Crores to avert the recurrence of flood damages occurred during November 1999 in Tiruchirappalli City.

Under the scheme, obstruction at the place where Kudamurutti river joins the Cauvery river will be removed, Ariyaru, Koraiyaru and Kodingal drainage channel will be widened and the embankments of Uyyakondan canal will be strengthened.

The estimate has to be revised for lining the channels both sides and bottom within existing bed width, without any land acquisition and for current schedule of rates.

The scheme will be implemented with HUDCO assistance during 2003-4.

Details of Progress of Minor Irrigation Schemes Sanctioned as Part II Schemes For1999 – 2000

(1) Diversion of Vaigai Flood Water to Feed Rajakambeeram Tank and 15 Other Tanks (Sivagangai District)

The Government have sanctioned the scheme for "Diversion of Vaigai flood waters to feed Rajakambeeram tank and 15 other tanks in Manamadurai taluk of Sivagangai District" at an estimated cost of Rs. 3.09 crore.

This scheme will stabilise irrigation in an extent of 1039.61 hectares, bridge a gap of 198.99 hectares and provide irrigation facilities to a new extent of 8.25 hectares in M.Karisalkulam, Chinnakkannanur, Rajakambeeram, Kilangattur, Annavasal and Arimandapam in Manamadurai taluk Velaneri, Kallikudi and Pidariseri in Paramakudi taluk.

The components of this scheme are head regulator at L.S. 32.050 km. from Vaigai river, lining the bed and sides of right main canal from LS 32,050 m. to 33,900 m., regulator at LS 33,885 m. and head sluice at LS 33,870 m. of right main canal, excavation of supply channel for 2.20 km. and cross-drainage works.

Standardisation of bund for 15 tanks is completed. The works will be completed in 2003-04.

(2) Anicut Across Vellar to Feed Panchatti and Other Tanks (Pudukkottai District)

The Government have sanctioned the scheme for "Construction of an anicut across Vellar to feed Panchatti and other tanks in Alapirandan village in Arantangi taluk of Pudukkottai District" at an estimated cost of Rs. 141.00 lakh.

This scheme will stabilise 672.14 hectares and bridge a gap of 35.11 hectares of wet lands in Panchatti, Amanji, Kundagavayal, Keelachery, Sivanthankadu and Perunavalur villages.

The components of this scheme are construction of anicut, excavation of supply channel, forming of flood bank and standardisation of tanks.

NABARD has accorded sanction for loan assistance for this scheme. The scheme is physically completed.

Progress of Schemes sanctioned during 2001-2002 (Part II Scheme) (1) Minor Irrigation Schemes

Sl. No	*Name of Scheme*	*Details*	*Stage of Work.*
1	Formation of a tank across Mathalappallam river near Ramakondahalli Village in Pennagaram Taluk of Dharmapuri District.	Est. Amount: Rs.1415 Lakhs Benefit I Crop 700 Acres II Crop 400 Acres	Preparation of land plan schedule is in progress. Action is being taken to invite tenders. NABARD has been approached for loan assistance.
2.	Construction of anicut across old Coleroon in Perumpattu Village in Chidambaram Taluk of Cuddalore District.	Est. Amount: Rs.162 Lakhs Benefit 460 Acres	Tender received and it is under process. HUDCO has been approached for loan assistance.
3.	Excavation of new supply channels from Badathalar tank to feed Vennampalli tank and 10 other lower down tanks upto Kashimpur tank of Krishnagiri Taluk in Dharmapuri District.	Est. Amount: Rs.700 Lakhs Benefit 840.74 Acres New 500 Acres	Preparation of land plan schedule is in progress. Action is being taken to invite tenders. NABARD has been approached for loan assistance.
4.	Kadanjeri (Pudukadai) lift irrigation scheme in Vilavancode Taluk of Kanyakumari District.	Est. Amount: Rs.219 Lakhs Benefit 572.50 Acres	Work is proposed to be completed during 2003-04.
5.	Formation of a tank across Vellapparai Odai in Theppampatti Village in Andipatti Taluk of Theni District.	Est. Amount: Rs.119.00 Lakhs Benefit 104.28 Acres	70% of work completed. Further work in progress.

(2) Special Minor Irrigation Programme Scheme

Sl. No.	*Name of Scheme*	*Details*	*Stage of work*
1	Formation of Pond across Kanar near Payappanaikanpet H/o Pachur village of Tirupattur taluk in Vellore District	Estimated Cost : Rs.12.00 Lakh Benefit New : 19.88 Acre Additional F.P :17.36MT	Land acquisition is under progress. Work to be started

(*Contd...*)

2	Formation of a Pond across hillstream in S.F.No.19 in Sempalli village in Gudiyatham Taluk in Vellore District	Estimated Cost : Rs.13.00 Lakh Benefit New : 33.39 Acre Additional F.P :30.88MT	Work is nearing completion.
3	Formation of a new pond in S.F.No.123 of Unanthangal village in Rasipuram Taluk in Namakkal District	Estimated Cost : Rs.25.00 Lakh Benefit Stabilisation : 19.19 Acre New : 37.35 Acre Additional F.P :21.07MT	Scheme dropped in G.O.Ms.No.304 Public Works dated 9.8.02.
4	Restoration of Pudu Eri pond in Periyapanamutu village in Krishnagiri Taluk in Dharmapuri District	Estimated Cost : Rs.15.00 Lakh Benefit New : 65.10 Acre Additional F.P :32.55MT	70% work completed. Further work is in progress.
5	Formation of a new pond in S.F.No.724 of Pillaipalayam village in Musiri Taluk lin Trichy District	Estimated Cost : Rs.23.00 Lakh Benefit New : 51.00 Acre Additional F.P :23.93MT	Work completed.
6	Construction of an anicut across Akasakumuliyar river to supply Mullipadi tank through Mullipadi Channel, Musiri Taluk in Trichy District	Estimated Cost : Rs.32.00 Lakh Benefit Stabilisation : 58.95 Acre Gap : 244.74 Acre Additional F.P:342.42MT	Work in progress.
7	Formation of a new pond across vari near Melmunayanur village, Kulithalai taluk in Karur District	Estimated Cost : Rs.13.00 Lakh Benefit: Stabilisation : 103.00 Acre Additional F.P :44.00 MT	Tender accepted. Work is to be started soon.

(*Contd...*)

8	Construction of an anicut across Koraiyar river to feed Nallamangankulam and other four tanks in Rajagiri Village in Kulathur Taluk in Pudukottai District	Estimated Cost : Rs.47.00 Lakh Benefit: Stabilisation : 87.29 Acre New : 33.11 Acre Gap : 7.83 Acre Additional F.P:109.06MT	Work is in progress
9	Formation of a new tank near Sukkampatti village Vedachandur Taluk in Dindigul District	Estimated Cost : Rs.38.00 Lakh Benefit: New : 37.00 Acre Additional F.P :43.42MT	Work to be taken up and completed during 2003-04.
10	Formation of a pond in S.F.No.73, 74 & 75 in Vadipatti of Oddanchattram Taluk in Dindigul District	Estimated Cost : Rs.14.00 Lakh Benefit: New : 37.50 Acre (Double Crop) Additional F.P:35.82 MT	Work to be taken up and completed during 2003-04.

(3) Anti Sea Erosion works.

Construction of Rubble Mound Wall along the Shore of North Chennai Coast	Estimated Cost : Rs.283.00 Lakhs Work nearing completion.
Protecting the left over portion of coast line from Thiruvattiyur to Thalaukuppam to a total length of 2.38 KM.	Estimate Cost Rs.1057.39 Lakh. Work will be taken up.

2003-2004 New Schemes proposed under Part

Sl. No.	***Name Of Work***	***Details***
	Minor Irrigation Schemes	
1.	Conversion of diversion mud bund into masonry training wall in Palar river at the off take of Athur Vadapathy tank supply channel in Chengleput Taluk, Kancheepuram District	Estimated Amount: Rs.120.00 Lakh Benefits Stabilisation: 398.13 Acres Gap : 293.65 Acres

(Contd...)

2.	Formation of a pond across Sambarpallam Odai in SF No.18 in Alamarathupatty Village and conversion of defunct Sorakkapatti tank to a pond by linking the surplus of Sambarpallam pond in Mettur Taluk in Salem District	Estimated Amount: Rs.125.00 Lakh Benefits New :450.32Acres
3.	Formation of a new tank across Pachilainachiamman Odai (Manthurai Odai) near G.Kallupatty in Periyakulam Taluk of Theni District	Estimated Amount: Rs.127.00 Lakh Benefits New :160.00Acres
4.	Formation of a new tank across Periyaoothu Odai in Chinnaovalapuram Village in Uthamapalayam Taluk of Theni District	Estimated Amount: Rs.202.00 Lakh Benefits New Ayacut : 117.46Acres

Special Minor Irrigation Schemes

1.	Construction of an anicut across Suriyar to feed Pappankulam and other tanks in Kulathur Taluk, Pudukottai District	Estimated Amount: Rs. 70.00 Lakh Benefits Stabilisation: 86.64 Acres Gap:98.34 Acre.
2.	Construction of an anicut across Pungampallam near Godupatti in Vattivanahalli village of Pennagaram taluk of Dharmapuri District	Estimated Amount: Rs. 74.00 Lakh Benefits New Ayacut : 86.05Acres
3.	Improvement to Puliyankulam	Estimated Amount: Rs.36.00
	Supply Channel and excavation of new channel from Puliyankulam to Pennathur Tank in Pennathur village of Manapparai Taluk in Tiruchi District	Lakh Benefits Stabilisation: 102.47 Acres Gap : 83.58 Acres
4.	Formation of a pond across Odai in Palakombai Village in Andipatti Taluk in Theni District	Estimated Amount: Rs.54.00 Lakh Benefits Stabilisation: 78.64 Acres Gap :63.35Acres

Additional Irrigation Potential

During 2003-2004, an additional irrigation potential of 9804 hectares is targetted to be created from Medium and Minor Irrigation Projects (Anicuts/ Reservoirs).

Water Resources Consolidation Project (W.R.C.P)

(i) The Water Resources Consolidation Project at a total cost of Rs.840.84 crore was cleared by the World Bank in 1995. Government of Tamil Nadu accorded sanction for an amount of Rs.807.49 crore as the base cost in September 1995. The Project is to have come to a close on 31.03.2002. Based on the request of the State Government, the World Bank has given approval for extending the scheme upto 31.3.2003. Now the World Bank has further extended the project period for one more year i.e., upto 31.03.2004.

(ii) The project is implemented as a sector investment loan, financing an agreed State-wide programme to improve the productivity and sustainability of Tamil Nadu's irrigation sector, to introduce multi-sectoral water planning, to integrate farmers in irrigation management and to strengthen the State's institutional and technical capability in water development, management and planning.

(iii) The project will enhance agricultural production in about 6 lakh hectares (about 50% of the State's surface irrigated area) directly benefiting some 40 lakh farmers. Irrigation will be put on a sustainable footing through rehabilitation and modernisation of the systems linked with farmer participation and upgraded maintenance and water management.

(iv) The WRCP provides for rehabilitation and modernisation of 16 irrigation systems and 25 Minor Irrigation Schemes in Tamil Nadu (except those in Cauvery Basin) and for completion of the nine on-going irrigation projects, viz., Poigaiyar, Nambiyar, Sothuparai, Mordhana, Rajathopekanar, Kodumudiyar, Vadakkupachayar, Adavinainarkoil and Gridhamal schemes.

(v) The Government is giving high priority to this project. Administrative sanction for 2347 packages at a cost of Rs. 1062.00 crore has been accorded. The details of estimate are as follows.

Sl. No.	*Details of works*	*No. of packages approved (including slices)*	*Value (Rs. in crore)*
1. a) b)	System Improvement and Farmers' Training (SIFT) and scheme Completion Minimum Rehabilitation Works	343 946	744.53
2.	Farmers' Organisation Turnover	15	4.00
3.	Equipment for Operation & Maintenance	3	18.00
4.	Irrigation Management and Training Institute	14	13.00

(*Contd...*)

5.	Water Planning and Research	68	42.00
6.	Environmental Management	12	10.00
7.	Land Acquisition & Economic Rehabilitation	4	17.00
8.	Institutional Strengthening and	311	77.87
	general Such as buildings, computers, vehicles, furniture 's, telephones etc and consultancy.		
9. a)	Additional Schemes Rehabilitation of Non-System Tanks 620 Nos.	620	100.00
b)	Dam Safety spill over works. (Gomukhi, Sathanaur, willington, Vidur and Sethiathope)	5	20.60
c)	Institutional Strengthening (Computerisation of Management information system)	6	15.00
	TOTAL	2347	1062.00

The budget allocation for this project for 2003-2004 is Rs.16.98 crore.

At the commencement of Annual Plan 2003-2004, the following Major and Medium Irrigation Schemes will be continued under W.R.C.P.

(44) Poigaiyar Reservoir - W.R.C.P. (Kanyakumari District)

This scheme contemplates formation of a reservoir across Poigaiyar near Aralvoimozhi village in Thovalai Taluk in Kanyakumari District.

By implementing this scheme, a new ayacut of 202 hectares of dry lands will be benefited and a gap of 57 hectares will be bridged besides stabilising an extent of 192 hectares in Shenbagaraman Pudur and Aralvoimozhi villages of Thovalai Taluk and Palavoor village of Radhapuram Taluk. Besides, 20 Mcft of water will be spared to meet the drinking water needs of four villages in Thovalai Panchayat Union.

A portion of earthdam was executed under State funds. Balance works of earth dam, excavation of new main canal including cross drainage works, excavation of surplus course, excavation of link canal, formation of road, construction of parapet wall, Improvements to Chungan Odai, balance works in surplus weir and formation of approach road have been completed at revised estimate cost of Rs.11.75 crore under Water Resources Consolidation Project.

The Budget provision for the year 2003-04 is Rs. 0.01 lakh.

(45) Nambiyar Reservoir - W.R.C.P. (Tirunelveli District)

This scheme is to form a reservoir across Nambiyar river in Radhapuram Taluk of Tirunelveli District.

The scheme aims at irrigating 152 hectares of new dry lands besides bridging a gap of 185 hectares and stabilising an extent of 369 hectares in Kottaikarunkulam, Urumankulam, Ramanathapuram, Karaichitti -

Puthur, Kasthurirangapuram, Kumarapuram, Muthumothumozhi and Thisayanvilai villages of Radhapuram Taluk.

Earthdam and construction of right side canal sluice and excavation of right main canal have been completed under State fund. The balance works are taken up under Water Resources Consolidation Project at a revised estimated cost of Rs.20.50 crore and completed except 3 additional packages.

The Budget provision for the year 2003-04 is Rs. 0.01 lakh.

(46) Rajathopekanar Reservoir – W.R.C.P. (Vellore District)

This scheme contemplates the formation of a reservoir across Rajathopekanar near Chengi village in Gudiyatham Taluk of Vellore District.

The scheme has been designed to stabilise an extent of 202 hectares of existing ayacut besides bridging a gap of 17 hectares in Chengi, Latteri, Vilundakkal, Oyyathur and Senur villages in Gudiyatham, Vellore and Vaniyambadi Taluks.

In this project earth dam, surplus weir, surplus course and canal sluice and lining works in canal from 0 m to 5000 m including cross drainage works have been completed under State funds.

Balance works in head works, excavation of link canal to feed Latteri, Vilunthakal and Oyyathur tanks and lining of channel for 5000 m including construction of cross drainage works were taken up at an estimated cost of Rs. 2.56 crore under Water Resources Consolidation Project.

The scheme works have been completed on 31.7.2000.

The Budget provision for the year 2003-04 is Rs. 0.01 lakh.

(47) Reservoir Across Koundinyanadhi Near Mordhana Village – W.R.C.P. (Vellore District)

This scheme contemplates formation of a reservoir across Koundinyanadhi near Mordhana village in Gudiyatham Taluk of Vellore District.

This scheme aims at providing an additional ayacut of 1152 hectares stabilising an extent of 2585 hectares and bridging a gap of 285 hectares spread over 34 villages in Gudiyatham and Vellore Taluks.

The construction of masonry dam was originally taken up during 1990-91. Subsequently the work was taken up under World Bank aided WRCP with effect from 01.07.1994. Under WRCP the project was modified to excavate new left and right main canal. The reservoir work was completed.

The balance work of excavation canal is in progress.

The Budget provision for the year 2003-04 is Rs. 17.01 lakh.

(48) Adavinainarkoil Reservoir – Wrcp (Tirunelveli District)

This scheme is to construct a reservoir across Hanumanadhi in Mekkarai village in Shencottah Taluk of Tirunelveli District.

The scheme will stabilise 1562 hectares of existing ayacut and bridge a gap of 616 hectares in addition to providing new irrigation to an extent of 93 hectares in Vadagarai-Kilpidagai, Vadagarai-Melpidagai, Panmozhi, Achanpudur, Neduvayal, Kodikurichi, Nainaragaram, Kilangadu and Ayakudi villages of Shencottah and Tenkasi Taluks.

The Administrative approval for the scheme was accorded for Rs. 37.69 Crore during May 1990. WRCP.

The entire work has been completed for a revised estimate value of Rs. 64.29 Crore under The Budget provision for the year 2003-04 is Rs. 0.01 lakh.

(49) Anicut Across Gridhamal River Near Athikulam Village – Wrcp (Virudhunagar District)

This scheme is for the construction of an anicut, left and right side canals in Gridhamal river near Athikulam village in Virudhunagar District at an estimated cost of Rs. 3.47 crore under Water Resources Consolidation Project.

It aims at stabilising 943 hectares of wet lands in Irunjirai, Ulakudi and six other tanks in Tiruchuli Taluk of Virudhunagar District and to bridge a gap of 323 hectares of ayacut in Athikulam, Manur, Maraiyur, Ulakudi, Narikudi, Irunjirai, Athithanendal and Varisaiyur villages of Tiruchuli Taluk.

All works such as, Construction of anicut and canal works in LMC and RMC have been completed, to an estimated value of Rs. 2.53 Crore.

The Budget provision for the year 2003-04 is Rs. 0.01 lakh.

(50) Vadakkupachayar Reservoir - W.R.C.P. (Tirunelveli District)

This scheme envisages the formation of a reservoir across Vadakkupachayar, a tributary of Pachaiyar near Manjuvilai village in Nanguneri Taluk in Tirunelveli Dt.

This scheme aims at stabilising 574 hectares of existing ayacut, bridging a gap of 464 hectares of existing irrigated area besides providing irrigation facilities to a new extent of 769 hectares under 45 tanks in Kalakadu, Nanguneri, Ullankulam, Illankulam and Parappadi villages of Nanguneri Taluk. Also an extent of the existing single crop area of 1568 hectares will receive irrigation for a second dry crop.

The scheme has been completed in all respects under Water Resources Consolidation Project at a revised estimate cost of Rs. 45.38 Crore.

The Budget provision for the year 2003-04 is Rs. 0.01 lakh.

(51) Kodumudiyar Reservoir – W.R.C.P. (Tirunelveli District)

This scheme contemplates the formation of a reservoir across the jungle stream of Kodumudiyar and Kombaiyar at their confluence point near Tirukurungudi village in Nanguneri Taluk in Tirunelveli District.

This scheme is aimed to stabilise an extent of 791 hectares and bridge a gap of 779 hectares in addition to conversion of 193 hectares of single crop into double crop in Mayiladi, Eruvadi, Nambithalaivanpattiyam, Vadakku-Valliyoor, Therku-Valliyoor, Rajakkamangalam, Achampadu, Anaikulam, Thalaikulam, Therkku-Kallikulam, Shanmugarengapuram, Kumbikulam, Alanginaru Thirumalapuram and Radhapuram villages in Radhapuram and Nanguneri Taluks.

The works on improvements to the existing canals have been completed under State funds. Balance works have been completed at a revised estimate cost of Rs. 30.50 Crore under Water Resources Consolidation Project except four additional packages.

The Budget provision for the year 2003-04 is Rs. 0.01 lakh.

(52) Sothuparai (Varahanadhi) Reservoir – Wrcp (Theni Dt)

This scheme contemplates the formation of a reservoir across Varahanadhi near Tenkarai in Periyakulam Taluk in Theni District.

The scheme aims at stabilising 739 hectares of wet lands and bridging a gap of 27 hectares of wet lands besides irrigating a new extent of 405 hectares of dry land in Thenkarai and Thamaraikulam villages of Periyakulam Taluk.

Construction of masonry dam has been partially completed under State funds. Balance works in masonry dam, canals, distributaries and buildings are implemented at an estimated cost of Rs. 34.72 crore under Water Resources Consolidation Project.

All the works such as masonry dam, building works, road work, Excavation of canal and distributories including construction of cross masonry works were completed, at a revised estimate value of Rs. 34.72 Crore. The proposal for construction of Project House at Dam Site has been dropped.

The Budget provision for the year 2003-04 is Rs. 0.01 lakh.

Progress of various important works included under Water Resources Consolidation Project

Sl. No.	*Name of work*	*Est. amt. in Lakhs*	*Total No. of Pack-ages*	*No. of pack-ages com-pleted*	*No. of pack-ages in pro-gress*	*No. of pack-ages to be taken up.*
1.	**CHENNAI REGION** Cheyyar Anicut	610.63	7	7	--	--
	System Rehabilitation work					
2.	Palar Anicut System Rehabilitation work	1883.45	18	18	--	--
3.	Poiney Anicut System Rehabilitation	651.03	8	8	--	--
4.	Tirukoilur Anicut System Rehabilitation work	938	7	7	--	--
5.	Tholudur and Pelandurai Anicut System Rehabilitation work	480.87	9	9	--	--
6.	Minor Schemes	3576.46	14	14	--	--
7.	Sathanur System Rehabilitation work	1890.00	19	19	--	--
8.	Sethiathope Anicut System Rehabilitation	1016.74	9	9	--	--
9.	Mordhana Reservoir Project	8229.57	11	7	4	--
10.	Rajathopekanar Reservoir Project	131.00	3	3	--	--
	POLLACHI REGION Parambikulam Aliyar Project	15214.00	61	60	1	--
11.	**MADURAI REGION** Chittar Anicut System Improvement Works	705.00	10	10	--	--
12.	Manjalar Reservoir System Rehabilitation work	102.00	5	5	--	--
13.	Vaigai Old Ayacut Rehabili-tation work	5867.00	21	21	--	--

(Contd...)

14.	Minor Schemes	875.00	15	12	3	--
	STAGE – II					
15.	Cumbum Valley System	568.00	11	11	--	--
16.	Kodayar System Rehabilitation work	3552.00	36	36	--	--
17.	Marudhanadhi Reservoir Project Rehabilitation work	106.00	3	3	--	--
18.	Tambaraparani System Modernisation and rehabilitation work	3237.00	23	20	3	--
19.	Periyar Vaigai System Construction and improvement work	1600.00	8	7	1	--
20.	Adavinainar Koil Reservoir Project Scheme Completion work	6428.76	3	3	--	--
21.	Gridhamal Anicut System Construction works	253.20	3	3	--	--
22.	Kodumudiyar Reservoir Project Formation work	3050.00	5	4	1	--
23.	Nambiyar Reservoir Project Scheme completion	2050.00	9	8	1	--
24.	Poigaiyar Reservoir Project Scheme completion	1175.00	9	9	--	--
25.	Sothuparai Reservoir Project Scheme completion	3472.00	4	4	--	--
26.	Vadakkupachai yar Reservoir Project Scheme Completion	4538.00	9	9	--	--
	TOTAL	72200.71	340	326	14	--

Water Resources Consolidation Project - Phase - II

To improve the overall efficiency and the storage capacity of the State's meagre water resources, a follow-on project to Water Resources Consolidation Project, viz., Water Resources Consolidation Project-Phase-II is contemplated for implementation with World Bank assistance at an estimated cost of Rs.2890.00 Crores.

The project proposals include certain left out items of Water Resources Consolidation Project, rehabilitation of system and non-system tanks, irrigation schemes both new and ongoing. Eco-restoration works conjunctive use of Ground and Surface Water Development in Sivaganga and Pudukottai Districts etc. were also proposed.

Basinwise master plans were prepared integrating the needs of all the stakeholders in the Basin, while preparing detailed estimates. The Water balance studies for each basin shall be the basic document.

These project proposals were sent to the Government of India to seek World Bank assistance. The Govt of India has sent the proposal to World Bank. The project is proposed for implementation during 2003-2010.

Farmers Organisation and Turn Over

Under the Water Resources Consolidation Project (W.R.C.P.) being implemented in the State from 1995-96 with necessary financial assistance from the World Bank, Farmers' active participation in deciding on implementation of the rehabilitation works of the main canal and distribution systems as well as in taking over the Operation and Maintenance of the distribution systems were given high priority. About one third of the total ayacut area maintained by the Water Resources Organisation of Public Works Department has been covered under this programme through 1900 Water Users Association formed.

The Tamil Nadu Farmers Management of Irrigation Systems Act already enacted has been brought into force from 1.10.2002 with approval of necessary rules and issue of Notification. Implementation of the Act in an extent of about 7.0 Lakh hectares of command area covered under Water Resources Consolidation Project is in progress. All the needed follow up actions would be initiated during 2003-2004 to consolidate the already established Water Users Association to ensure their sustainability and effective functioning. Ways and means for extending this programme to the balance ayacut areas will also be explored and strategies developed.

The Budget provision for the year 2003-04 is Rs. 0.01 lakh.

Participatory Irrigation Management

The Participatory Irrigation Management is now implemented in about 7.00 Lakh hectares under WRCP and CAD Programmes. It is proposed to extend this programme in the balance 10.00 lakh hectares during 10th Five Year Plan.

Water Service Charges Committee (W.S.C.C.)

For the purpose of rationalizing the rate of water in respect of agriculture, a committee has been constituted under Water Resources Consolidation Project, by Government of Tamilnadu in 1996 with the Commissioner of Revenue Administration as Chairman and secretary to Government of various Departments as Members and a co-opted Consultant Economist as an important member to suggest further restructuring of the water rates so that full maintenance charges would be recovered from the beneficiaries. The Water Service Charges Committee met 15 times. In the last meeting held on 27.06.2002, the committee has decided to enhance the Local Cess (LC) and Local Cess Surcharge (LCS) instead of delinking of water rates from Land Revenue as earlier recommended.

Based on the recommendations of the W.S.C.C., the matter has been considered in detail and placed before the cabinet meeting held on 25.07.2002.

The cabinet approved the imposition of Additional water rates of Rs. 70 per acre (Rs. 175 per ha.) on I and II Class wet crops and Rs.60 per acre (Rs. 150 per ha) for irrigated dry crops. To give effect to the above cabinet decision, necessary amendment to the Act has been issued by the Government on November 11, 2002. Further orders for brining into force of the amendment issued to said Act with effect from 01.07.2003 has been issued on 18.03.2003.

4. Abilitation of 620 Rainfed Minor Irrigation Tanks At An Estimated Cost of Rs.104.29 Crore In Palar, Tambraparani and Vaigai Basins Under Wrcp With World Bank Assistance

The World Bank Tenth Supervision Mission during November 15 to 24, 2000 made field visits to Chennai and Coimbatore Region for finalising the additional schemes involving expenditure of Rs.379.60 crore to utilise the savings in the WRCP project on account of the depreciation in rupees value during the duration of the project.

By considering the capacity of man power and to promote standard of living of the marginal farmers and to solve to some extent the problem of drinking water, the World Bank Mission has considered the additional proposal for rehabilitation / Modernisation of rainfed tanks of 462 tanks in Palar basin with an ayacut of 63002 ha at an estimated cost of Rs. 81.90 crore, 77 tanks in Tambaraparani Basin with an ayacut of 10,140 ha at an estimated cost of Rs. 13.18 crore and 81 tanks of Vaigai basin with an ayacut of 7678 ha at an estimated cost of Rs. 11.18 crore aggregating 620 tanks at an estimated cost of Rs. 104.29 crore.

The Government have accorded administrative approval for the above proposal of Rehabilitation of 620 tanks for Rs. 104.29 crore. All the works have been taken up for execution during 2001-2002. Upto end of November 2002, works in 381 tanks have been completed. Water Users Association are formed and registered for all the 620 tanks and MOU signed.

The Budget provision for the year 2003-04 is Rs. 0.01 lakh.

5. Modernisation and Irrigation Management In Tamilnadu With Loan Assistance Of National Bank For Agricultural And Rural Development (Nabard) Under "Nabard – Rural Infrastructure Development Fund (ridf) V" Nabard Ridf V – Phase I

The project proposal is for modernising 44 minor irrigation tanks spread over in 23 districts of Tamilnadu at an estimated cost of Rs. 14.66 crore, benefiting 5054 hectares was approved by Government with the financial assistance of NABARD under Rural Infrastructure Development Fund (RIDF).

The aim of the project is to modernise, to upgrade the standard of minor irrigation tanks in Tamilnadu for enhancing the irrigation potential by carrying out lining of field channels improvement to sluices, surplus weir, standardisation of bund and streamlining in-flow channel to the tanks.

The Government have accorded sanction to this project for Rs.14.66 crore and allotted the works to Regions of WRO for execution.

The Government issued orders for executing the works through Water Users Association with the involvement of Non Government Organisation. The works are under execution through Water Users Association.

The Budget provision for the year 2003-04 is Rs. 116.41 lakh.

Integrated Water Resources Management In Ramanathapuram Dt

The Government have decided to take up Phase I of Integrated Water Resources Management Project in Ramanathapuram District at a cost of Rs.24.36 Crore with HUDCO Loan Assistance. By implementing the schemes, the tanks and channels and Ramanadhapuram District will get benefited.

6. Desilting and Rehabilitation of Tanks, Channels in Tamilnadu.

Irrigation tanks serve as one of the most important water resources for the rural communities in the State. Most of the tanks are situated in the State where there are no rivers of importance. These water harvesting structures were ingeniously designed by the native rulers and managed by the local communities over the past several centuries.

It is reported that over the past years, the irrigated area by tanks is coming down steadily at an increasing rate. The general deteriorating condition of tanks is characterized by siltation in the tank beds and supply channels, encroachments in the tank bund, foreshore, waterspread and supply channels, repairs in damaged sluices, weirs, bunds.

The State is facing a grave situation through the deteriorating tanks, facing the marginal and small farmers into a cycle of deprivation and debt as also leaving them increasingly at the mercy of the vagaries of monsoon.

In order to improve the storage capacity and irrigation efficiency of the existing tanks, more thrust is given by the Government for optimal utilization of available water. It will also serve the twin objectives (i.e.) Irrigation and drinking water.

Considering the backwardness of the rural people living in Ramanathapuram District and to improve their socio economic condition it has been planned to rehabilitate the rain fed tanks / non- system tanks. A project proposal at an estimated cost of Rs. 24.36 crore has been prepared and posed to HUDCO for loan assistance.

Similarly proposals are being formulated for other Districts to rehabilitate the rainfed tanks, by getting loan from various funding agencies.

7. Modernisation of Cauvery Delta

The Cauvery Delta System is nearly 2000 years old. This system can serve efficiently only if the structural components are modernised. A Master Plan for modernisation of the Cauvery System including Flood Control and Drainage Rehabilitation was first prepared by the Government of Tamil Nadu in 1970 for seeking International Financial Assistance. But the project could not be taken up as an Externally Aided Project for want of clearance (Inter State angle) from the Ministry of Water Resources, Government of India. However, the modernisation work was taken up in piecemeal to meet the urgent needs of irrigation, flood control and drainage with the State funds. But these efforts were inadequate for the requirement of the Delta.

Therefore, the modernisation of the Cauvery Delta is proposed to be taken up in three phases. A project report for Phase I, at an estimated cost of Rs. 460 crore, has been sent to the Government of India for forwarding it to World Bank. This project has the following components.

(1) Modernisation & Rehabilitation of ten rivers in the delta benefiting 70,000 hectares,

(2) Modernisation & Rehabilitation of 323 channels,

(3) Improvements to 109 Drainage works,

(4) Flood Control works to a tune of Rs. 23.02 crore,

(5) Other miscellaneous works.

8. Cauvery Water Dispute

The Interim Orders of the Cauvery Water Disputes Tribunal (CWDT) awarded in 1991, have not been implemented by the State of Karnataka, ever since they have been passed. The State of Karnataka has been impounding all the inflows as the monsoon strated each year in their four major reservoirs viz. KRS, Kabini, Harangi and Hemavathy and withdrawing all the quantities required for their irrigation and only surpluses if any are flowing down, that too belatedly, with the result, the kuruvai cultivation which is to start in the Cauvery Delta in June could not be done in time and the kuruvai area also comes down drastically year after year.

In good years, Mettur inflows even exceeded the quantity of 205 TMC in the normal course. But in subnormal years like 1995, the Tamilnadu irrigation was badly hit and all our pleadings before the Supreme Court did not bring us solace crops grown in more than 2 lakh acres failed that year.

On our suit filed before the Supreme Court for effective implementation of the Interim Order in 1992 (O.S. 1/92), on the insistence of the Court, the Government of India constituted the Cauvery River Authority (CRA) chaired by the Prime Minister with the Chief Ministers of the four basin States as Members, in 1998. A Monitoring Committee consisting of officers was also constituted to assist the CRA but not to take any decision.

The State of Tamilnadu found that even the CRA turned out to be just a Political Committee and could not direct the State of Karnataka unequivocally to implement the Interim Order, with the result, Tamilnadu continued to suffer year after year unpredicted quantities of flow and delayed start of cultivation operation. The State had to therefore file another suit before the Hon'ble Supreme Court in 2001 (O.S.No.3/2001) to get the CRA's structure suitably modified for effective implementation of the Interim Order and thereafter the final order of the Tribunal.

The year 2002-2003, which is a sub-normal year, proved to be a critical year affecting Tamilnadu most. In the previous irrigation year 2001-2002, the State was left with a shortage of 43 TMC in the flows to be ensured at Mettur, at the end of the irrigation season, which was not made good by the State of Karnataka till the end. The freak rainfall in February 2002 also damaged the crops, which were ripe for harvest. The carry-over storage at the end of the last season was poor and stood at only 11 TMC, with the result, the Mettur reservoir could not be opened on the scheduled date of 12th June during the year 2002-2003.

The south west monsoon during this year, though set in on 03.06.2002, did not intensify and it picked up only in the month of July and continued with a few breaks during the months of August and September. On the whole, the south west monsoon in the Cauvery basin was deficient and the inflows into the Karnataka reservoirs were below normal. The State of Karnataka, as usual, did not let water from their reservoirs to ensure flows at the Mettur reservoir as per the Interim Order, not even a part of the inflow they received as a commitment to the downstream States of Tamilnadu and Pondicherry.

The State of Tamilnadu had therefore to approach the Supreme Court again, with a suit (O.S.No.3/2002) filed in July 2002. On the I.A. filed in the suit O.S.No.3/2002, the Supreme Court of India, in its order dated 03.09.2002, directed that the State of Karnataka should release water from its reservoirs in Karnataka so that 1.25 TMC feet of water was ensured at Tamilnadu's Mettur Reservoir daily till a decision on the implementation of the Interim Orders in a deficit year after arriving at an agreed deficit sharing formula was taken by the CRA and their orders will take effect from 04.09.2002.

The Supreme Court's order came as a ray of hope to the farmers of the Cauvery Delta area, who had already lost the Kuruvai crop due to non receipt of supplies from Karnataka. The Tamilnadu Government opened the Mettur reservoir for irrigation on 06.09.2002.

The CRA which met on 08.09.2002 took a decision that Karnataka should make available 9,000 cusecs daily on a weekly average basis to Tamilnadu (about 0.8 TMC feet per day) during the months of September and October as against the 1.25 TMC feet of water per day at Mettur insisted upon by Tamilnadu. The State of Karnataka did not comply with either the orders of the Supreme Court or the directions of the CRA and did not release the waters due to Tamilnadu. The Hon'ble Chief Minister of Tamilnadu led an all party delegation and presented a Memorandum to the Hon'ble Prime Minister on 21st September 2002 seeking his intervention. Nothing happened and the inflow into Mettur continued to be dismally poor.

The State of Tamilnadu was forced to file two contempt petitions in the Supreme Court against the Chief Minister of Karnataka, one in September 2002, when the State of Karnataka failed to implement the directions of the Supreme Court to release 1.25 TMC of water per day and the second in October 2002, when it also failed to implement the CRA's decision, which was later confirmed by the Supreme Court. It is only after the Supreme Court's severe observations made during the hearing of the contempt petition, that the Chief Minister of Karnataka filed an affidavit on 27.10.2002 tendering unconditional apology for not obeying the Court's order and assured the Court that the Government of Karnataka had started releasing 10,000 cusecs of water from that day morning. The Supreme Court did not pass their orders on that affidavit but posed the matter to 1st November to watch the behaviour of Karnataka. The releases also dwindled and at the end of October 2002, counting on the orders of the Supreme Court and the directions of the CRA, the over all deficit in the flows into Mettur reservoir was 23.18 TMC.

When the Supreme Court again met on 01.11.2002, they ordered that the State of Karnataka will continue to release water so as to ensure at Mettur 9000 cusecs daily till 6th midnight and thereafter as per the Interim Orders of the Tribunal. The Supreme Court further ordered that CRA will meet and take further decision including that of making up the deficit of 23.18 TMC as on 31.10.2002 that accrued in the months of September and October, 2002.

During the month of November 2002, the stipulated inflows into Mettur reservoir as per the Supreme Court orders upto 6th and thereafter as per the Interim Orders, was received, but the earlier deficit of 23.18 TMC as on 31.10.2002 was not made up.

In the month of December 2002, the inflows received were only about 6.1 TMC as against the stipulated flow of 10.37 TMC as per the Interim Order.

The CRA meeting which was originally scheduled to be held on 29.11.2002 could not be held for lack of quorum. The apology tendered by the Chief Minister of Karnataka is yet to be accepted by the Hon'ble Supreme Court. The Supreme Court is awaiting the final outcome of the CRA as per their earlier orders which is to decide on the making good of the shortfall.

The situation in the Cauvery Delta irrigation is grim. Having lost kuruvai, farmers who were apprehensive of even starting the samba crop, had to start the samba crop some by transplantation when they could get some water supplemented by rain and some by direct seeding. Yet only in about 8 lakh acres out of 11 lakh acres, samba crop could be raised. With the best of attempts, using the storage available in Mettur most economically and even resorting to release of waters from Mettur in short spells of release and non-release, a practice unheard of in Mettur management so far, the storage cannot last beyond 10th of January 2003. The crops need supply at least upto February end. Unfortunately the north east monsoon has also failed badly this year.

In the 8.00 lakh acres of samba crops planted, except a small area the majority area could not be saved. With the unrelenting and adamant response for the State of Karnataka refusing to share the water they have now beyond their cropping season.

9. Krishna Water Supply Project

The Government of Tamil Nadu entered into an agreement with the Government of Andhra Pradesh on 18.4.1983 according to which the Government of Andhra Pradesh shall deliver 12 TMC of water excluding the transmission loss of 3 TMC at the Tamil Nadu Border over a period of 8 months in a year.

The component of the project falling within Tamil Nadu limit is called "Krishna Water Supply Project" and that in Andhra Pradesh limits is called "Telugu Ganga Project".

The originally sanctioned estimated cost of Krishna Water Supply Project in Tamil Nadu limit was Rs.46.44 Crore. The reappraised cost was Rs.196.04 Crore (as per 1996-97 Schedule of Rates).

The total estimated cost of Telegu Ganga Project comes to Rs.2345 Crore (as per 9/97 Project Report), of which Tamil Nadu's share is Rs.639.40 Crore. So far Andhra Pradesh Government have incurred Rs.1,820.00 Crore towards this project and Rs.512 Crore has been paid to Andhra Pradesh as Tamil Nadu's share.

Kandaleru water was released by Andhra Pradesh for the first time on 29.9.1996. The following are quantum of water released from Kandaleru Dam and quantity realised at Tamil Nadu border.

The 38th meeting of the Liason Committee was held on 5.2.2002 and the Government of Andhra Pradesh was requested to complete the work early.

Sri Sathya Sai Central Trust has come forward to take up improvements to Kandaleru - Poondi Sector in Andhra Pradesh limit to see that 12.00 TMC of water is diverted at Tamilnadu Border to Chennai city for drinking water purpose.

Due to heavy rain in October 2001 and November 2001 in Tamil Nadu the canal from 0 Km to 4 Km at Tamil Nadu border was damaged and the Government have allotted Rs.71.88 Lakh for carrying out repair works in Tamil Nadu limit.

Year	*Water released from kandaleru into K.P. Canal (TMC)*	*Water realized at Tamil Nadu border (in TMC)*	*Percentage of ealization*
1996-97	0.610	0.076	12.50%
1997-98	4.339	2.290	52.80%
1998-99	4.077	2.810	69.00%
1999-2000	3.990	1.830	45.86%
2000-2001	17.790	6.688	37.59%
2001-2002	1.108	0.400	36.10%
2002-2003 till date	9.461	3.262	34.48%

The Government have decided to implement the Chennai City Water Supply augmentation Project II, to augment the Chennai City Water Supply at a cost of Rs. 493 Crore. The objective of this project is to prevent rain water from running off into sea by construction of check dams, reservoir, percolation tanks etc. to store surplus water in Kosasthalayar, Cooum, Adyar and Palar rivers.

This proposal is now proposed to be revised to Rs.340 Crore.

10. New Veeranam Project

The New Veernam Project was originally sanctioned in August 1993 for Rs. 464.00 crore under the caption "Second Madras Water Supply Project, New

Veeranam" as a World Bank aided project. The project envisaged the supply of 190 Mld. of water to the Chennai city.

The sanction included Rs. 60.00 crore for the improvements to source works comprising.

(1) improvements to the Vadavar Channel which brings water from lower Coleroon Anicut to Veeranam Tank,

(2) Removal of shoals in the Veeranam Tank and raising its F.T.L. by 2' to increase the existing capacity of 935 Mcft. to 1485 Mcft. and (3) Strengthening of the foreshore bund.

Subsequently, revised administrative sanction was accorded for the source works for the project including modernisation of the command conveyance system of Vadavar Canal and also Veeranam Tank for Rs. 110.95 crore in April 1996. By improvements to the conveyance system, 56,034 acres of ayacut (11,178 acres under Vadavar and 44,856 acres of ayacut under Veeranam) are expected to receive uninterrupted irrigation facility.

The Government have decided to implement the Chennai City Water Supply Augmentation Project within 18 months. The transmission of water for Chennai City Water Supply has been programmed to be taken up and completed by CMWSSB by 9/2003. For implementation of the projects TUFIDCO has sanctioned a loan of Rs. 35.00 crore for essential item of works.

There are 25 packages of works in this project. The details of estimates and present status of the works are given below:

(1) Improvements to Vadavar Channel Out of the 6 packages, at a cost of 26.39 Crore, 3 packages are completed. In other 3 packages 90% works are completed.

(2) Raising Full Reservoir Level of Veeranam Tank by 2 feet (0.61m) & strengthening Veeranam Main Bund at a cost of 10.68 Crore. Works in all the four packages are in progress.

(3) Improvements to existing foreshore bund & formation of new foreshore bund at a cost of Rs.10.31 Crore. Work completed in all the 4 packages.

(4) Modernisation of command conveyance system of Vadavar 24 Channels, Veeranam 34 Channels in 2 packages is proposed at a cost of 25.00 Crore. 7 channels in Vadavar and 5 channels in Veeranam is proposed to be taken up immediately and the balance works are proposed to be taken up subsequently.

(5) Black topping of Veeranam Tank Main Bund at a cost of Rs.1.50 Crore. It wiill be taken up after the completion of main work subject to availability of fund.

(6) Repairs to Lower Anicut Shutters. Work at a cost of Rs.108.00 Crore is in progress. 17% work is completed.

(7) Improvemtns to Veeranam Byewash, New regulator across Vadavar, Improvements to Godavari drain, Improvements to surplus regulartor and VNSS shutters at a cost of Rs.5.37 Crore. Out of the total number

of 4 packages except Godavari Drain priority will be given for other 3 packages.

(8) Repairs to existing staff quarters and Construction of New Project House at a cost of Rs. 0.55 crore. Repairs to staff quarters completed.

(9) Miscelleneous items with cost escalation - Rs. 30.07 crore.

Total packages 25 for Rs. 110.95 crore.

Due to escalation in cost of construction materials and labour, revised estimate was prepared for Rs. 150 Crores which is under consideration. So far an expenditure of Rs. 54.10 Crores has been incurred.

The Budget Estimate for the year 2003-04 is Rs. 1000.00 lakh.

11. Parambikulam Aliyar Project - Renewal of Agreement

An agreement between the Governments of Tamilnadu and Kerala was entered into on 29-05-1970 with retrospective effect from 09-11-1958 for utilisation of flows in the rivers of Anamalayar, Nirar, Sholayar, Parambikulam, Palar and Aliyar and the streams flowing into them for generation of hydro electric power, irrigation, drinking water supply, industrial use and any other purposes in the two States. The arrangements embodied in the agreement are open for review in the light of the experience gained and to such modifications as may be mutually agreed upon as a result of such review at the expiry of 30 years from 9-11-1958 and once in every 30 years thereafter. The agreement was due for review on 9.11.1988.

Accordingly, both the Governments exchanged the documents for review on 21-09-1989 and held several Ministerial level discussions. An Inter State Committee comprising the Officials of both Tamil Nadu and Kerala was constituted, among others, to present a comprehensive report on the review of the Parambikulam Aliyar Agreement. The Committee meeting was held at Tiruvananthapuram and Attakatti, but no consensus was reached.

The Government of Kerala has to consider the following:

(i) To honour its commitment for permitting diversion of 2.5 TMC from Anamalayar River to PAP System in as much as they have completed the Idamalayar Hydro Electric Project.

(ii) To permit utilisation of the entire yield at Upper Nirar without restriction for the period from October to January in a year in as much as they have completed the projects (Idamalayar and Idukki as per agreement)

(iii) To give its concurrence for the construction of a balancing reservoir above Manacadavu Weir to ensure regulated discharges.

(iv) To accord its concurrence to the new schemes for diverting the flows of Upper Nirar to Nallar through a tunnel by construction of diversion weir and to construct a power house at Nallar and for diverting the flows to Tirumoorthy dam thereby minimising transmission loss.

(v) To supplement their requirements for Chitturpuzha Basin, by diverting either the surplus flows over and above 2.5 TMC. required for Tamil Nadu from Anamalaiar or by diverting flows from Thekkadiar.

A bilateral discussion between the Irrigation Ministers of Kerala and Tamilnadu was held on 28-11-96 at Chennai. As there was no conclusive agreement on any of the issues discussed during the meeting, it was decided to hold further discussions. This subject was again discussed in the Minister Level meeting held between Government of Kerala and Government of Tamilnadu on 10.06.2002 at Chennai. It was decided that a Technical Committee comprising of 3 Engineers viz. two from Water Resources Organisation and one from the State Electricity Board from each states may be constituted to review and submit report on PAP issues for finalizing the review of Parambikulam Aliyar Project Agreement at Minister level meeting initially and at Chief Minister's level meeting finally. Accordingly, Technical Committee was constituted and first meeting held on 11.12.2002 at Parambikulam and discussed the various issues.

12. Pandiyar-punnampuzha Project

Pandiyar-Punnampuzha is an Inter State river with its origin in Tamil Nadu, joining Chaliyar River in Kerala. The west flowing rivers of Pandiyar-Punnampuzha having their origin in high peaks of Nilgiris join at about 5 km west of Guddalore Town and the river beyond the confluence is called Punnampuzha, This joins Chaliyar river in Kerala State near Nilambur. Ultimately, this drains into Arabian Sea near "Baypore". This project area is located in the Udagamandalam-Mysore road.

As per 1965 understanding between Tamil Nadu and Kerala, Pandiyar-Punnampuzha Hydro Electric Project envisages utilisation of the west flowing waters of Pandiyar and Punnampuzha rivers from a total catchment area of 171.38 Sq. Km. (66.20 Sq. Miles) with an average annual yield of 14.

TMC for power generation with a gross head of 500.60 m (1642 ft) and with an installed capacity of 100 MW (2x50 MW) for the first stage and 150 MW as ultimate. The average annual generation would be 409 MU. The Planning Commission approved the proposal in 1969.

Subsequently, on representation from the ryots of Coimbatore district, the possibility of diverting the waters of Pandiar-Punnampuzha lying within Tamil Nadu to Moyar arm of Bhavani river for use by Tamil Nadu was investigated and this was also found feasible. Tamil Nadu wanted diversion of at least 7 TMC of water eastward to Tamil Nadu.

During the bilateral discussion held on 28-11-1996 between the Irrigation Ministers of Kerala and TamilNadu, a request was made for the diversion of at least 7 TMC of tail race waters of Pandiyar-Punnampuzha Scheme to meet the drinking water and irrigation requirements in the drought prone areas of Coimbatore – Erode districts and it was informed by the Kerala Government that they would be in a position to offer their views on examining the project proposal from Tamil Nadu.

The Tamil Nadu Electricity Board has since formulated the Pandiyar-Punnampuzha Project proposal for implementation in two phases at an estimated cost of Rs.904.00 Crore during the year 1998. The first phase, envisages an installed capacity of 2 x 50 MW utilising 7 TMC of water (50% of the total yield of 14 TMC) to be released into Kerala territory after generation of power. Work will also be simultaneously commenced for diversion of 7 TMC of water towards Tamil Nadu. In the 2nd phase 2 x 30 MW power is proposed to be generated in the Sigur Basin of Tamil Nadu utilising the diverted 7 TMC of water. After generation of power, the water will join Moyar river in Tamil Nadu. Both the phases are proposed to be taken up simultaneously.

The Government of Tamil Nadu has sent the project report prepared by the Tamil Nadu Electricity Board to the Kerala Government in September 1998 and requested their concurrence to take up the project. Kerala Government has not readily agreed to the diversion of 7 TMC of water eastward. The State Government is pursuing the matter. The State Government in April 1998 have requested NHPC to take up and execute this project. This subject was discussed in the Minister Level Meeting between Government of Kerala and Government of TN held on 10.06.2002 at Chennai. The officials from Kerala told that they are not in receipt of the Project Report for reacting the proposal. It was decided in the meeting that the Tamilnadu Electricity Board will furnish the Project Report to Kerala State Electricity Board and thereafter a meeting between Chairmans of the Electricity Boards may be held to arrive at a solution. Accordingly a meeting was held at Kerala on 10.07.2002 betrween Engineers of Tamilnadu Electricity Board and Kerala State Electricity Board. Further action is in progress by Tamilnadu Electricity Board.

13. Peninsular River Development Component Of National Perspective Plan Mahanadhi – Godhavari – Krishna – Pennar – Cauvery - Vaigai –Gundar Links

The Peninsular rivers viz. Mahanadhi, Godhavari, Krishna, Pennar, Palar, Cauvery, Vaigai and Gundar are proposed to be inter-linked under the Peninsular River Development component of the National Perspective Plan formulated by the Government of India. The National Water Development Agency is entrusted with the task of investigation and preparation of project proposals for the peninsular river links.

The National Water Development Agency has already prepared pre-feasibility reports on Mahanadhi-Godhavari, Godhavari- Krishna, Krishna-Pennar and Pennar-Cauvery, Cauvery-Vaigai- Gundar links. It has identified the surplus and deficit basins and assessed the surplus available in Mahanadhi and Godhavari for transfer to Krishna, Pennar, Cauvery and Vaigai basins.

According to the proposal, the surplus flows of Mahanadhi and Godhavari rivers would get diverted to Pennar river in Andhra Pradesh. The diversion from Pennar to Cauvery would be through a link canal 534 Km. long to divert about 9,455 mm3 (334 TMC) of Pennar water from Somasila reservoir to the Grand Anicut across river Cauvery via Palar. The link canal would provide irrigation and drinking water supply enroute in Andhra Pradesh and TamilNadu. Further a quantity of 3855 mm3 (136.1 TMC) would be delivered at Grand Anicut for use in Cauvery Delta and also in the areas south of Cauvery basin.

The Cauvery-Vaigai-Gundar link is the last leg in the link. This aims at diversion of 2252 mm^3 (79.5 TMC) from the quantity of 3855 mm^3 (136.1 TMC) to the south of Cauvery upto Gundar for irrigation, water supply etc.,

The State Government is keenly interested in the expeditious execution of the Peninsular Rivers development component.

The Government of Tamilnadu is continuously stressing the Government of India to constitute a high level body under the Chairmanship of Prime Minister to ensure speedy finalisation and time bound implementation of Peninsular river development component.

State Ground and Surface Water Resources Data Centre

Tamil Nadu is the Pioneer State in developing ground water for various purposes. The State Ground and Surface Water Resources Data Centre is assessing the ground water potential periodically by applying various parameters arrived during the field study. As on July 1997, about 63% of the available ground water resources have been utilised. Ground Water, being a dynamic resource, requires continuous exploration, monitoring and assessment, involving multi-disciplinary studies. This data centre under the control of a Chief Engineer undertakes the following:

(1) Monitoring of water level in 1746 control wells in Tamil Nadu. An overall Ground Water quality network was finalised in consultation with DHV Consultants (Delft Hydraulics Von Consultants) for entire Tamilnadu to assess general water quality, on monsoonwise ground water pollution and fertiliser impact on ground water. Ground water samples are being collected once in a year (Pre-monsoon) for general study and once in three months from the problematic areas.

(2) Monitoring of ground water quality in the State (3400 samples)

(3) Watershed study, conducting hydrometeorological observations under different soil conditions. (16 water sheds)

(4) Analysis of rainfall data and establishing relationship between the runoff and seepage. (400 rainfall stations)

(5) Intensive Survey on mini watershed basis for all the districts of Tamilnadu based on Ground Water Resources Estimation Committee Norms - 1997 for the assessment of Ground Water Potential.

(6) Rendering Consultancy Services to farmers, Government departments and Government Undertakings for selection of suitable locations for constructing ground water abstraction structures.

(7) Issuing ground water clearance for implementing Minor Irrigation Schemes.

(8) Special studies for monitoring sea water intrusion into fresh water aquifer. (920 k.m along the coast)

(9) Drilling of exploratory bore holes. (50 bore holes)

(10) Also preparing various artificial recharge schemes to improve Ground Water conditions.

Apart from the above, the other schemes such as science and technology inputs including research and development are being undertaken including Ground Water awareness.

A provision of Rs. 207.33 lakh has been made for the above works in B.E 2003-4.

Hydrology Project

The World Bank came forward in 1995 to assist the Government of India Agencies in the development of Scientific Data Base consisting of all aspects of Hydrological Cycle including Surface Water and Ground Water in terms of quality and quantity under Hydrology Project.

The project period is for 6 years from 1996-2003 (upto 31.03.2003). The cost of project is Rs. 51.149 Crores.

The true objectives of the project is being achieved in full.

In order to consolidate the gains earned from the Hydrology Project - I, the Hydrology Project - II is on the anvil. The main thrust area will be integrated Water Resources Management, conjunctive use of surface and ground water, rain water harvesting etc. for the strengthening of the infrastructure of Ground and Surface Water Resources Data Centre units.

The project consists of two major components namely Surface Water and Ground Water and the project estimate cost works out to Rs.101 Crores.

The Hydrology Project - II will pave way towards better tomorrow for a sustainable HIS expanded to Water Information System (WIS) for the integrated water resources management as stipulated in the National Water Policy 2002.

Programme for 2003-2004

The World Bank have informed the Government that the Bank funding will be limited to expenditures incurred before the current project closing date of March, 31st, 2003 and operation and maintenance cost for the sustenance of the benefits of the project gained beyond 31.03.03 will have to be provided through the State's own budgetary resources.

A provision of Rs. 265.50 lakh has been made in the Budget Estimate 2003-2004

The project closure date has been further extended upto December 2003 by World Bank.

Artificial Recharge Schemes with Central Assistance

Tamil Nadu being an agrarian State, much importance is given for the exploitation of ground water for the development of agriculture as about 95% of the surface water resources have already been harnessed in the State and about 68% of ground water potential is utilized.

Augmentation of ground water resources becomes necessary, when the natural recharge is slow and not upto the expected / required level. In such eventuality, it is high time to go in for artificial recharge of ground water.

This Department is preparing various schemes of Artificial recharge of Ground Water adopting various techniques such as

Subsurface dykes and check dams across

(i) Rivers and streams

(ii) Percolation ponds in pervious zones location of various artificial structures have been evolved in Tamilnadu using - Remote Sensing and Geographical Information System Techniques.

Central Government has come forward for funding the construction of the Artificial structures for augmenting ground water. Various schemes are being formulated for implementation of the same in various districts. State Level Committee has been constituted to monitor the implementation of the above schemes and District Level Coordination Committee is being formed in each District under the Chairmanship of the District Collector to implement the schemes.

Proposal for recharging structures on water shed basis will be prepared by District Level Technical Coordination Committee and will be sent to State Level Technical Coordination Committee for approval and funding the schemes.

Rain Water Harvesting

Government of Tamilnadu is committed to ensure that potable drinking water is available to all habitations in next five years. In certain and semi arid and difficult terrain rain water harvesting may be the only techno-economically viable and sustainable solution.

Rain water harvesting is the deliberate collection of rain water within a catchment and use for the purpose of drinking, irrigation etc.

Rainwater storage is generally done in man made tanks, lined pits and small dams or in the sandy beds of seasonal rivers.

The collection and storage will be done only during rainy season.

The amount of water harvested depends on the frequency and intensity of rainfall.

Rain water harvesting is useful to meet water demand for domestic use especially during summer.

It augments the ground water storage and avert's decline of water levels.

It improves quality of ground water, it reduces soil erosion. Rain Water Harvesting may be done by Roof Water Harvesting and by surface run off harvesting.

The Government of Tamilnadu in the I Phase has programmed to implement the rain water harvesting schemes at top priority.

Ground Water Act – 2003.

There is continuous over-exploitation of ground water in the recent years in Tamil Nadu which leads to alarming lowering of ground water level and deterioration of quality and many existing irrigation and drinking water wells have become dry. This is adversely affecting the small and marginal farmers who mostly depend upon the ground water sources for their livelihood.

To safeguard the small and marginal farmer's rights to use the limited Ground Water resources available and also to control and regulate the indiscriminate extraction of ground water, the Government has passed the Tamil Nadu Ground Water (Development & Management) Act 2003.

14. Dam Safety Assurance and Rehabilitation Project

A Proposal for getting World Bank assistance has been submitted to the Ministry of Water resources, Government of India at an estimated cost of Rs.60.00 crores to carry out Dam Safety Works. This proposal is now under active consideration of the Government of India.

Under this project, it is proposed to carry out Dam Safety Works for the following 10 dams.

1. Sathanur, 2. Ponnaniar, 3. Siddhamali, 4. Sholayar, 5. Perunchani, 6. Manimuktha nadhi, 7. Periyar, 8. Pechiparai, 9. Manimuthar 10. Amaravathy

15. Rehabilitation And Reclamation Of Chennai City Waterways

1. **Desilting and Construction of Flood Defences For Chennai City Water Ways with Hudco Loan Assistance.**

In order to prevent frequent floods damages, Government during 1998 ordered for executing a Rs.300 Crores project "Rehabilitation of Chennai City Water Ways" named as "Millennium Project" with HUDCO loan assistance. The Project is based on the report of international consultant M/s. MOTT Mac Donald of United Kingdom. The main objective of this Scheme is to remove the silt and sludge deposited in the various water ways of Chennai viz., Cooum river, Adayar river, Buckingham Canal, Otteri Nullah, Captain Cotton Canal and other major drains within the boundary of Chennai Metropolitan Area. The project proposes to rehabilitate Slum Dwellers encroached on the banks of the above water ways.

The Scheme is being implemented since October 1999 by dividing it into 4 convenient packages except Covum the work in other 3 packages are in progress.

Package-I: Desilting and Resectioning of Buckingham Canal from Ennore creak to Muttukadu.

Almost 85% works have been completed in this package except for a 4.6 Km. length in South Buckingham Canal which is heavily encroached on both sides. Alternative Technical proposals are under consideration for desilting this reach. Works are expected to be completed shortly.

Package-II: Construction of flood defences and resectioning of Adayar river.

About 40% works have been completed in this package. The culvert works across Velachery drain and Kosasthalaiyar flood banks have been completed. In Adayar river desilting and resectioning works have been completed upstream of Nandambakkam bridge and works are in progress in downstream side. The works are expected to be completed shortly.

Package-III: Construction of flood defences and resectioning of drains in Chennai Metropolitan Area.

The works involve desilting of Ambattur surplus course, Formation of new drains for Red Hills, Chembarambakkam, Madhavaram, Thanikachalam Nagar drainage and Korattur lake.

2. Removal of Sand Bar and Prevention of Sand Bar Formation on the Mouths of Cooum and Adayar Rivers on the Confluence of these Rivers With Bay of Bengal.

The National Institute of Ocean Technology (NIOT) under Government of India, Department of Ocean Development, had given a groyne based solution for the sustained opening of Cooum river mouth as technology demonstration project. A groyne for a length of 170 m has been constructed into the Sea at a cost of Rs. 78.00 lakh. Based on the suggestion of NIOT, it has been decided to raise the height of the groyne by 1.5 m.

The groyne based solution will be extended for Adayar river, after studying the performance of the groyne in Cooum river mouth.

The Budget provision for the year 2003-04 is Rs. 2300.00 lakh.

16. Irrigation Management Training Institute

Irrigation Management Training Institute, Tiruchy is one of the 11 such Institutes in the Country. It was established in 1984 under USAID. It is imparting training to farmers, field level staff and officials of WRO, Agricultural Engineering Department and Agriculture Department. Now the Institute is functioning under the funds provided by the state Government as grant-in-aid.

(1) Training

This Institute is acting as the Nodal Agency for the training component of water resources consolidation project, which is being implemented by WRO with World Bank Aid. At present this Institute is fully engaged in conducting and organising specific trainings recommended by the consultants for the farmers, field Staff and officials of WRO apart from the inter disciplinary trainings being given to WRO, agricultural engineering and agricultural officers under general head.

For the year 2003-2004 it is programmed to conduct 180 national trainings. The above programmes will cover 2500 farmers and 2000 officers in Irrigation management.

Irrigated Agriculture in Tensification Programme –

Tamil Nadu being a tropical State, water while transmitted through canals for irrigation is being lost from 20 to 50% by evaporation and seepage. To prevent such losses and to increase water use efficiency and to increase the production, Irrigated Agriculture Intensification Programme Phase II is programmed by involving Water Resources Organisation, Agricultural Engineering, Department of Agriculture, Tamilnadu Agricultural University and Irrigation Management Training Institute with an outlay of Rs.650 lakhs over a period of three years.

Main strategy of the programme is to transport the water by improving the canal by lining.

Sl. No.	*Training Programme for 2003-04*	*Nos*	*Rs.in laks*
I.	1. National training	180	150
	2. IAIP Training/Demonstration		200
II.	Institutional strengthening		20
III.	Publications		15
IV.	Action Research		
	(a) Research activities approved by research advisory committee	2	10
	(b) Proposal submitted to CWC	2	10
	Total	**184**	**405**

17. Institute For Water Studies

1. **Water Resources Assessment Studies**

   Institute for Water Studies (IWS), Tharamani is the Nodal Agency for Water Planning for Tamil Nadu and it is also the Technical Secretariat for the Water Resources Control and Review Council of the Government of Tamil Nadu. Its main function is to plan, assess and to given suggestions for managing the Water Resources of Tamil Nadu in a scientific manner.

   The river basins of Tamil Nadu have been clubbed into 17 major river basin groups for study purposes. Water Resources Plan for all the river basin groups at macro level has been completed except for Cauvery basin. Based on these studies a report on "State Frame Work Water Resources Plan of Tamil Nadu" with annexures dealing with each river basin of Tamil Nadu has been prepared. This report contains details of both Surface and Ground water resources availability assessed on a scientific manner for all the river basins of Tamil Nadu. It also contains details of water requirement for various sectors such as domestic, industry, agriculture, livestock etc. for the year 1999 and for the future years 2004/2019/2025/2044 and 2050 A.D. From these assessment of water resources potential and water demands during various years the water surplus and deficit basins are identified so that planning for conservation measures could be initiated. Stake holders meetings were conducted in each river basin to obtain the views and suggestions of various local departmental officers, NGOs and farmers and their views were taken into account in finalising the report.

Micro level studies for Palar, Vaippar, Kodaiyar and Vaigai basins have been completed. An integrated river basin simulation model for these basins has been developed.

2. Environment Unit

An Environmental Unit was established in the Institute for Water Studies to advise the Government on policy matters liasoning with the State and Central Government Organisations, to conduct Environmental Impact Assessment of projects and to maintain data bank on environmental issues and carrying out research programmes under Water Resources Consolidation Project.

2.1 Environmental Action Plan

Environment unit was incharge of monitoring environmental aspects in the micro level reports for Palar, Vaippar and Kodaiyar basins prepared by M/s.Tahal Consultancy Ltd. At present, micro level report for Vaigai and Tambiraparani basins are under preparation by this unit.

Supporting the Technical Secretariat for Vaigai and Tambiraparani river basin Board by the way of furnishing necessary environmental data.

The Environmental unit took an active participation with the World Bank team members during their visits to the Institute for Water Studies.

3. Water Resources Research Fund (WRRF)

Under Tamil Nadu Water Resources Consolidation Project, a Water Resources Research Fund was created to support a practical programme on research to assist in the formation, in the water sector funded by the World Bank. A Research Advisory Committee (RAC) was also constituted to advise the Water Resources Organisation (WRO) for identifying the topics of research and to guide the WRRF.

30 research studies on water related and environmental topics amounting to a total value of Rs. 309.34 lakhs has been awarded to the research institutions like IIT, Chennai, Anna University, Agricultural University, Bharathidasan University etc. and these studies are now under the completion stage.

The Budget estimate for 2003-04 is Rs. 0.01 lakh.

4. Expert Committee On "Rain Water Harvesting And Safe Guarding Ground Water"

An Expert Committee was constituted to suggest measures for augmentation and conservation of water resources to meet the future demands. Twenty one meetings were conducted by this committee and relevant data from various departments have been received and completed. The committee also submitted a report suggesting various proposals for augmenting Chennai city domestic water supply. Final draft report was prepared and is circulated to all Expert Committee members for final modifications if any.

5. **Water Resources Control and Review Council**

Water Resources Control and Review Council was established under the Chairmanship of Hon'ble Chief Minister of Tamil Nadu in order to take an integrated view on the utilization, deployment and distribution of scarce water resources of the State with reference to well defined order of priorities to be determined. Under this five sub committees dealing with agriculture / ground water / industries/ environment / domestic water requirements etc. were formed to provide necessary input to the committee for deliberation.

The council in its sitting on 23/11/98 deliberated on the "Farmers participation in irrigation management and functioning of irrigation systems in Tamil Nadu" and on the "Need to enact legislation for regulation and control of ground water". Of these two topics the "Tamil Nadu Farmers Management of Irrigation Systems Bill" has been passed by the legislature and the assent of the President of India has been received and published in the Tamil Nadu Government Gazette as "Tamil Nadu Farmers Management of Irrigation Systems Act".

6. **Institutional Strengthening**

Under the World Bank assisted "Water Resources Consolidation Project" the IWS was strengthened with computers, connected accessories and establishing Management Information Systems.

7. **Remote Sensing**

The Photogeological and Remote Sensing Lab is functioning in the Institute for Water Studies, PWD since 1972.

The Remote Sensing Unit of PWD, Tamil Nadu has successfully carried out the ground water studies in Ponnaiyar & Tamiraparani river basins in co-ordination with the Central Government Agencies, Space Application Centre (SAC), Ahmedabad and National Remote Sensing Agency of Department of Space – Government of India.

Sites had been selected by this Remote Sensing Unit in the drought hit Vellore, Thiruvannamalai, Ramanathapuram, Tirunelveli, Sivagangai and Dindigul districts during the period of 1980 – 1983 for sinking of distress drinking water open wells which are still in good use.

Adopting visual interpretation and computer based digital interpretation, multipurpose thematic maps on geology, soil, geomorphology, land use and lineaments were generated for river basin wise, district wise and taluk wise and they have been field checked and corrected.

For the use of Tahal Consultants in the compilation of water planning reports for Palar, Vaippar & Kodaiyar, basins the following theme maps were generated and supplied.

(i) Sub basin map (ii) Geology map

(iii) Land use map (iv) Geomorphology map

(v) Lineament map (vi) Soil map

(vii) Slope map

(viii) Water level map for pre monsoon and post monsoon seasons

(ix) Water quality map for pre monsoon and post monsoon

Considering the special nature of the work carried out by the Remote Sensing Unit, IWS, the Government have declared this centre as ***"Tamil Nadu State Centre for Remote Sensing Application"***.

This centre is engaged in the generation of maps on geology, geomorphology, structure & lineament, soil, drainage, water potential area, ground water recharge area, water level, water quality and sub basin boundary maps for the use by the Palar and Tamiraparani river basin Boards which have been formed first of its kind in Tamil Nadu. More over the three dimensional Digital Elevation Models also were generated through computer for Palar & Tamiraparani basins.

The changes that have occurred in the forests, lands, irrigation tanks and their command areas over a period of time i.e. what were the areas under forest, tanks and command areas in 1980 and how much they had reduced in 2001 due to environmental degradation have been precisely assessed using the satellite imageries.

The pollution effects caused by the Tannery industries in Palar basin, the extent of the affected agricultural lands and the change in water quality have been studied in detail and identified.

Using the funds provided by the Tamil Nadu State Land Use Board of State Planning Commission, Government of Tamil Nadu special studies were undertaken

1. In the Upper Palar to find out the environmental degradation due to polluting tannery industries and deduction on land use.
2. Thurinjalar minor basin of Ponnaiyar basin using Remote Sensing & GIS techniques for targeting ground water potential and selection of artificial recharge structures.

Using the funds provided by the same organization, a project has been undertaken to identify the ground water potential areas with in the over exploited Chengam block of Thiruvannamalai District using Remote Sensing & GIS techniques. Further the different category of waste lands were also identified in that block and suitable action plan – remediation were proposed to convert them as productive lands.

For World Bank review, the land use pattern in Palar, Tamiraparani, Vaigai, Ponnaiyar, Nambiyar, Kodayar and Gundar were generated for the years 1980 and 1999.

8. Technical Secretariat For River Basin Boards

The Technical Secretariat for the River Basin Management and Development Boards (RBMDB) for Palar and Tambiraparani has been formed at the Institute for Water Studies, Tharamani, Chennai-600 113 from August 2002 with the Chief Engineer, IWS as the Chairman.

River Basin Management and Development Board

The Government of Tamil Nadu have set up River Basin Management and Development Boards (RBMDB) for Palar and Tambiraparani river basins.

The objectives of RBMDB are integrated planning, monitoring, management and development of water and land and to have the active involvement of stakeholders in each river basins.

Hon'ble Minister for Public Works is the Chairman of the RBMDB. Development Commissioner, Secretaries to Government for Finance, Water Resources, Agriculture, MAWS, Rural Development, Industries, Forests and Environment, all MPs and MLAs representing the constituencies in the river basin, Chairman of all the Panchayat Unions, Chairman of Municipal Councils, District Collectors, representatives of the different departments, Chief Engineers and Superintending Engineers concerned of WRO, three representatives of industries and three eminent NGOs in the area and Chief Engineer, Central Water Commission are members of the RBMDB.

The Government have also constituted a Basin Management Committee (BMC) for each of the RBMDB to take decisions on behalf of the RBMDB. The Hon'ble Minister for Water Resources is the Chairman of the BMC. The members of the BMC are the Development Commissioner, Government of Tamil Nadu, Secretaries to Government for Finance, Water Resources, Agriculture, MAWS, Rural Development, Industries, Forests and Environment departments, Chief Engineer, WRO, two MPs and two MLAs nominated by Government, Collectors of concerned districts, District Panchayat Presidents from the basin area, three representatives of the Water Users Associations, one eminent person from the basin area and one representative of NGO.

The Government have also approved the formation of the Technical Secretariat for supporting the RBMDB and BMC with 13 specialists of different disciplines. The Chief Engineer & Director, Institute for Water Studies is the Chairman of the Technical Secretariat. The Technical Secretariat is functioning from August 2002.

The Technical Secretariat has organized three meetings / workshops to identify and assess the environmental and social issues related to the river basins.

1. Brainstorming meeting on Palar river basin environmental and social issues at IWS, Tharamani, Chennai on August 6, 2002.
2. Consultative workshop on "Strategic environmental assessment for Palar river basin" at Chennai on October 18, 2002.
3. Stakeholders' meeting to discuss the environmental issues of Tambiraparani river basin at Tirunelveli on November 23, 2002.

The second meeting of the RBMDB of Palar river basin was held at Tiruvannamalai on November 9, 2002. Hon'ble Minister for Public Works (Water Resources) and Chairman of the Board presided the meeting. The members have discussed the various issues of the basin.

The second meeting of the RBMDB of Tambiraparani river basin was held at Tirunelveli on November 24, 2002. Hon'ble Minister for Public Works (Water Resources) and Chairman of the Board presided the meeting. The members have discussed the various issues of the basin.

3. Gundar Basin

S.No.	*Name of River*	*Name of Anicut*	*Location in (km)*	*No. of tanks benefited*	*Ayacut benefited in acres*
1.	Vellimalai odai	1. Vellimalai	4.5	1	61.00
2.	Therkkar (Aswamanathi)	2. Matharai	8.5	1	50.73
		3. Karukkatanpatti	10	1	96.52
		4. Nallakulam	14	1	112.66
		5. Sathangudi	29	1	288.00
		6. Venkatasamutharam	33	1	318.00
		7. Vadakarai	35	1	478.00
		8. Melakottai	43	1	146.65
		9. Maikkudi	42	1	603.40
		10. Kallanai	45	1	120.00
		11. Kambikudi	48	1	1334.04
		12. Chatram Puliyankulam	53	1	311.99
3.	Goundanadhi	13. Kanakkankulam Sub Survey	3	(D.A)	60.11
		14. Angayarkanni	5	(D.A)	22.90
		15. Chokkanathan	7	1	105.98
		16. Thalai Anikal	8	(D.A)	70.45
		17. Thirumanickam	9	1	299.96
		18. Mochikulam	16.5	1	71.63
		19. Sembarani	18	1	148.61
		20. Madaiyur	19.5	(D.A)	148.61
		21. Soundarpatti	21.5	1	228.00
		22. Kilavaneri	23	1	22.88
		23. Thirali	30	1	374.00
		24. Melanesaneri	35	1	221.00
		25. Arasapatti	37	1	739.00
		26. Sivarakottai	39	1	349.00
		27. Kurayur	45	10	1582.53
		28. Chennampatti	54	21	2432.72
4.	Varattar	29. Karuvattu	4.5	(D.A)	21.00
		30. Kuppammal Samutharam	6	1	146.33
		31. Vandapuli	7	1	82.98
		32. Sennelperi	15	1	110.12
		33. Allappalacheri	17	1	155.01
5.	Malattar	34. Mandalamanickam	22	34	4795.40
		35. Kamudhi regulator	36	71	17928.00
		36. Malattar	43	54	4727.12
		37. Sankarathevan	57	4	105.16
6.	Gridhamal	38. Ambalathadi	23	22	3922.23
		39. Kattanoor	35	16	4055.20
		40. Athikulam	45	9	3098.74
		41. Nallukurichi	57	9	1166.16
		42. Abiramam	68	6	1790.53
7	Paralaiaru	43. Paralai Anicut	23	34	2021.44
		Paralai Directly Fed Tanks	-	20	3003.56
		Total	**336**	**58018.07**	

D.A - Direct Ayacut

5. THREE PUBLICATIONS

Resurrecting a tradition

C B S R Sharma

Once a part of Indian tradition, tanks today are disappearing from the face of the country. The tank system — which was used to store rainwater meant for subsequent use by locals —thrived during the rule of feudal lords and declined with them.

Despite their utility for drainage, storage, charging wells and reducing the havoc caused by floods, tanks were encroached in rural areas while in cities they were filled up. In order to conserve tanks, an 'ecosystem approach of management' is necessary. This can be achieved by setting up a National Tank Authority (nta) which can be entrusted with conservation, restoration, and development of all tanks in India. The jurisdiction of such an authority shall encompass the tanks of Tamil Nadu, Andhra Pradesh, Maharashtra, Uttar Pradesh, Karnataka and Bihar; the coastal ponds of Orissa, West Bengal, and other water harvesting systems like temple tanks, lakes, and urban wetlands.

But, why has the tank system degenerated? Borewells sunk around tanks and operated on subsidised electricity, have greatly reduced the quantity of water in them. As tank beds remained fallow for greater durations they were gradually encroached upon.

The number of borewells, scale of encroachments and the level of siltation all depended on the intensity of the monsoons, the geography of the local catchment area and the statuses of the tank mechanisms. Sometimes, borewells are sunk in tank beds. The owner of the borewells and lands in the *ayacut* (irrigated

[In] Down to Earth Vol. 6 Issue: 30/10/1997.

area under a tank), and the encroacher of tanks is usually the same person. Thus what till then was a common resource has now become private property.

However, even today there are some 200,000 tanks in the country most of which are located in Karnataka, Andhra Pradesh, and Tamil Nadu. Tanks account for 10 per cent of the present irrigated area of the country and therefore need to be conserved by an authority like the NTA.

The requirements for setting up the NTA are academic, financial, and logistic in nature. These cover rainwater harvesting, storage of water, irrigation usage, potability, recharging groundwater; nature of soil, water, plants etc. The other aspects relate to animals, agriculture, aquaculture, social, and wetland forestry. Biodiversity will be naturally preserved and utilised by people residing in the surrounding areas. The history of the tanks and the perception of local people on all these is a necessary starting point.

Therefore, the existing records on tanks should be revised. Rapid evaluation techniques have to be developed. This will lead to the emergence of a value system to classify tanks and earmark them for either development or conservation, and restoration.

Tank irrigation requires a strong local authority to rally collective action. The water dynamics encompass the entire catchment, supply channels, command area and the wells. The destinies of villages are intimately connected with this web. Therefore both conservation and development have to go hand in hand, which is possible only by nucleating each tank along with the dependent villages into an eco-political unit under the local self government.

Although stressing on strong local authority in managing tanks and advocating the need for a body like the NTA in the same breath may appear contradictory, it actually may not be. The NTA is visualised as a body for broad policy making and channeling inputs of a scientific and financial nature so as to motivate, monitor and strengthen the local bodies in reviving tanks.

The first duty of the NTA is to declare tanks as protected ecosystems and the associated groundwater as public property. The next task will be to conduct a tank census based on ground realities. By resurrecting tanks and regulating groundwater, a source for drinking water which is a major rural need will be greatly fulfilled.

C B S R Sharma teaches at the Salim Ali school of ecology and environmental sciences of Pondicherry University, Pondicherry

Tanks of Tamil Nadu: An Ecological Revival
A National Tank Authority is Urgently Needed

Professor C.B.S.R. Sharma Salim Ali School of Ecology and Environmental Sciences Pondicherry University Pondicherry

Introduction

In these times of escalating water scarcity, revival of traditional storage systems such as ponds, tanks, and similar wetlands is necessary for fuller utilisation (jf rainfall. This revival is being achieved through development and conservation practices, about which all available knowledge must be obtained. Most of the tanks are in Tamil Nadu, Andhra Pradesh, Karnataka, Maharashtra, and parts of Uttar Pradesh, Bihar, and Rajasthan. Unfortunately, there is no comprehensive database on them; in fact, there has been no study on the state of tanks in India. Therefore studying these irrigating wetlands on a holistic basis, that is, ecologically, has become an urgent need. We have sought to fulfill this need by means of a two-year field and laboratory study of six water bodies extending from northeast to south central Tamil Nadu and representing different climatic and structural conditions. It constitutes a pioneering study on the ecography of tank systems in India-systems that currently encompass 3.3 Mha.

Tamil Nadu Scenario

There are about 40,000 tanks scattered throughout the state, only 7,400 of which have *ayacuts* of more than 40 ha. The total potential under this minor irrigation system is 1 Mha. Water regulation continues to be under the control of local communities, although practices differ from place to place. Being small, farmer-managed systems, these tanks have moulded the rural societies. The area, the people, and the agroeconomic conditions around the tanks vary only slightly; hindrances from administrative agencies also are limited. Therefore reviving these centuries-old systems will not be difficult. However, these systems are spread all over Tamil Nadu and most of them are in a state of disrepair and decay.

Larger landowners acquire control of more land through encroachment and more water by sinking mechanised wells in command areas.

Although 60 percent of Tamil Nadu is drought prone, only one third of the annual precipitation is utilised. It is therefore imperative to harvest rainfall, which is why the state has traditionally been a land of ponds and tanks. Unfortunately, because many of these systems have been filled in and built on, Tamil Nadu has suffered more than its share of water shortage. Tanks' utility to local people should have been enhanced, for they are no longer merely a part of village structure; each village has become a part of a tank ecosystem.

[In] Proceedings of the Seminar on Conservation & Development of Tank Irrigation for Livelihood Promotion, Madurai, India, 12 July 1996. A Joint Publication of the Conservation and Development Forum (CDF) and the Network of Institutions Engaged in Tank Management (1999)

Ecological Perspective

The International Union for Conservation of Nature (IUCN), the World Wide Fund for Nature (WWF), and the Ramsar Convention (1971-1989)recognised the importance of wetlands reclamation. Therefore the government of India formed a National Commission on Wetlands in 1989. Various management aspects were to be implemented and managed through four Acts of Parliament: the Environment Protection Act (1986), the Forest Conservation Act (1980), the Wetland Conservation Act (1972), and the Water Act (1974). While IUCN has detailed criteria for wetlands identification and management, the government has developed a management plan. Yet no data were collected on the vast number of tanks in India-first among its nine types of wetlands. Thus there is an obvious need for studying smaller water bodies-with an ecological approach directed towards economic sustainability of villages and an economic approach aimed at ecological stability of tank systems-if the tanks are to be used to full capacity forever.

Methodology

The tanks involved in this study are Kaveripakkam, Pillaipakkam, Kaliveli, Ousteri, Mirattunilai, and Kambikudi. A combination of methods has been employed in the collection, analysis, and interpretation of tank system data. These methods include field surveys of tanks to collect soil and water samples, plant specimens, animal observations, and anecdotal, information; analysis of soil and water samples; identification of biota; and interviews with officials concerned with tanks. All data on soil, water, flora, fauna, agriculture, aquaculture, and silviculture have been analysed and summarised for each tank and the results compared.

Habitats

Results of soil data analysis indicate variations with respect to only a few parameters; most others are uniform. Consequently, tank-irrigated lands need limited inputs if the spectrum of crop culture has to be widened. Water quality also is generally uniform irrespective of the length of time water is in the tank. Tank habitats are deficient in some aspects and overabundant in a few others. Perhaps this is the reason most flora, fauna, and cultural activities are similar among the wetlands systems.

Biodiversity

Floristic composition of the tanks was found to vary with the size of the system or its state of degradation. Thus Kambikudi tank supports the least number of flora (50) and Kaliveli tank the maximum (163). Most species occur on the foreshores and in the *ayacuts.* Even the low diversity of plants in Kambikudi tank appears sufficient to support many butterfly and bird species. If Kambikudi tank is not improved, many butterflies and other fauna also may gradually disappear-a warning signal to other tank systems. However, no relationship was observed between tank location and richness of animal species.

Animal diversity may depend on plant diversity. Species richness among birds is high, suggesting that their nutritive and roosting sources in the habitats are intact-an indication that all is not lost from the ecological foundation of these wetlands. That some of these tank systems support 10-30 migratory bird species would itself warrant their protection as bird sanctuaries. Species richness in Kaliveli and Mirattunilai tanks is consistent with the fact that both tanks had remnants of natural vegetation until recently.

Although about 273 plant and 223 animal species occur in the six wetlands systems, each water body harbours only 50-163 plant species and 86-187 animal species. Since habitat conditions among these wetlands systems vary only slightly, it is possible that each tank can be enriched biologically.

Resources Land and Soil

The geomorphology and geochemistry of the land mass, in combination with human intervention and natural biological forces, determine the resourcefulness of the soil and land. The current pattern of land use in these wetlands systems suggests underuse, overuse, and improper use. Bird and animal excreta are used as fertilisers and energy sources. Most land must be earmarked for agriculture, either with or without water, leaving only a limited portion available for use as construction material. All of these wetlands systems have the potential to operate under both traditional and modern practices. Because it could result in restoration of a million acres of land, such a blending is absolutely warranted.

Water

A number of variables must be estimated to improve assessment of water resources. These include water availability from rainfall, supplies, and groundwater sources; qualities and patterns of rainfall, runoff, catchment, tank storage and seepage, and groundwater recharge; irrigation efficiency; and irrigation economics. It is unfortunate that people living in the coastal wetlands lack the means to prevent rainfall from flowing into the sea.

Plants

Of primary interest is the diversity of cultivated plants. Traditional cultivators carry special importance because many of them possess special characteristics such as resistance to pests and drought. Germplasm from cultivators of crop plants should be collected for further use. Many medicinal plants occur around the water bodies as well as other plants useful as hedges, soil binders, fuel, food, fodder, and fertiliser and for such activities as thatching and weaving. These plant communities are dwindling, however, sometimes giving way to firewood monocultures. Kambikudi tank already has become alarmingly deficient in plant resources.

Animals

There are many domesticated animals such as cattle and sheep in these wetlands systems. Consumers of water and plant resources, they in turn benefit humans and the land. Fish constitute a naturally occurring resource that is exploited locally and sold when the water recedes; this occurs in all water bodies. Some wild animals are hunted for food or trade. The guana excretions of birds are of special importance in that they add great fertility to the soil, partlculartv from October to February.

Human Ecology

There are 5-14 villages around these water bodies whose 200-2,000 inhabitants comprise landowners, daily wage earners, and the unemployed. Some of these inhabitants encroach on common lands. Consequently, the current tanks retain only part of their past stature. Nevertheless, agriculture, aquaculture, and social and wetland forestry, in addition to direct use of tank soil, water, plants, and animals, continue around every tank. The people also have their own perceptions regarding the socioeconomic aspects of the tanks.

Agriculture and Aquaculture

As soon as the rains set in, rice is planted in all of the wetlands using channelled water or groundwater. Addition of fertilisers and pesticides follows. This scenario of delta culture is unsuitable to these basically semiarid areas, where the emphasis should be on water economy, soil conservation, and equal access to the common resource of water. In these water-scarce societies, water should be retained for long periods in tanks and/or community wells, not privatised through tube wells. There should be dry-land farming requiring minimum water per unit area, which alone increases the arability of land by increasing the available area and facilitating double cropping. In such cases it would be easier to develop long-term fertility strategies such as composting, administration of biofertilisers, and pest control through biological means-plants, birds, and other agents. Water bodies should be fully utilised for aquaculture by natural means with inputs of only seed and planktonic cultures. The existing scenario is the opposite of the ideal. Wells impede the tanks' resourcefulness. Through their selfishness, private water users pirate common property and destroy its ecological health.

Social and Wetland Forestry

As for tree cultures, they should be separated into plantations within and outside tank systems. Those within are inundated by water for various periods and serve as animal habitats. Those outside are plantations on wastelands receiving only natural rainfall. The former must be regulated because although they yield greater biomass, enrich soil fertility, and provide habitat for animals, they also cause gradual reduction in tank area; this, however, can be resolved through engineering.

Perceptions

Local people's socioeconomic status and perceptions regarding the tanks are being studied to evolve locally relevant ecological management strategies. Such surveys help us understand the impacts on the local economy of tank irrigation, forestry plantations, dry-land agriculture, land use patterns, and other conditions. These insights can lead to the emergence of a perspective for long-term restoration of the tanks. However, the present study was limited to a sample gathering of local perceptions, which has revealed sufficient information on the degraded state of tank systems to help us discern what they were and should be, and what is the common scenario; It is a sad tale of neglect and land grabbing.

Valuing Wetlands

Accounting all resources harboured in tank ecosystems and valuing them in relative and absolute terms may give us an ecological and economic perspective for development options. In the current attempt, values for 13 items were converted to a fraction of 1,the intrinsic value. Values obtained for the present tanks ranged from 0.9 to 0.6. Tanks in the lower portion of the range need correspondingly more conservation inputs; otherwise, they will gradually lose ecological resilience and economic utility. If the value is reduced to 0.5, either the tank has to be abandoned or restoration efforts are warranted. Tanks obtaining higher values, on the other hand can, accommodate development activities.

Conservation

Conservation has two facets: (1) maintaining the resourcefulness of soil and water; and (2) enriching biodiversity and preserving habitats such as water, bodies, inlet channels, and catchments that are affected by and part of agriculture, aquaculture, wetland forestry, and animal husbandry.

Villages draw sustenance from tank-connected resources, which therefore need greater care to enable human settlements to enjoy a longer and richer balance in the resource bank. Unfortunately, there have been no conservation efforts, let alone restorative exercises, to preserve any of the water bodies. Even the sluices, regulators, supply channels, and bunds remain unattended and in disrepair. Biologically rich thickets are removed in favour of monocultures. But everywhere people want more - plants, more water for longer periods, and more fertile soil. Fortunately, however, wetland forestry has turned out to be conservative. Water that would normally go to private properties through tube wells is consumed by common forests, which in turn become habitats for animals. Together, they gradually enrich the soil. Because this is the present state of several tanks, conservation of what is still left and restoration of whatever has been lost can be achieved only Onder the authority of local people and their *panchayats*. A few examples are given below.

Land: Identification and quantification of land use classes should be carried out so that crops appropriate for summer and winter and quality soil suitable for construction purposes can be selected.

Water: Existing data appear unreliable. Before conservation measures are taken, new data shouldbe obtained on rainfall; on variations in runoff, catchment, storage capacity, seepage, and groundwater recharge; on irrigation efficiency; and on the economics of well and channel irrigation.

Plants: Varieties of cultivated plants and others of ecological and economic significance are the objects of survey, collection, and preservation. Locally used cultivators carry special importance. Although traditional varieties may have been lost, chances of their occurrence in some pockets cannot be ruled out. Germplasm of such cultivators should be maintained. Many dwindling medicinal species also need to be conserved.

Animals: Efforts to increase the populations of both domesticated and wild animals are needed, for, these animals have ecological as well as economic uses. Such increases will be possible only by declaring the water bodies mini-sanctuaries or refugea.

Development

Assessment of all of the resources in the wetlands ecosystems is a prerequisite for development planning. Water dynamics must be estimated first, including quantification of rainfall, evaporation, groundwater, and surface water. Qualitative assessments to determine potability and other characteristics then need to be made on a monthly basis for a few years.

Resource Inventories

Surveys of land and water, and of plant, animal, and human ecologies, around the tanks described here constitute resource inventories. When these surveys are integrated with other data available from national and regional agencies, the result will be a composite, reliable database. There is not yet much data for any single wetland, and there are more than 35,000 wetlands of different sizes, constituents, and characteristics to be studied. These wetlands are associated with thousands of villages and several million rural people. This is no small matter but still remains neglected.

People's Initiatives

People consistently desire development through government efforts, not through their own involvement. Government activities are mostly confined to implementing so-called social forestry, allowing borewells, providing fertilisers and pesticides, and extending the services of agricultural agencies. Thus some development is seen around every tank.

The villages around these water bodies practice agriculture, aquaculture, and social forestry. If large- scale permaculture, sericulture, apiculture, and vermiculture involving grasses, sedges, and perennial forbes are added, keeping in mind the minimal water requirements of plants, sustainable development will have been achieved. Everything will have been protected and conserved while economic development continues. This should be the ideal for wetlands.

Government Inputs

Managerial inputs needed for the revival of tanks as useful wetlands can be made only with the support of government infrastructures and extension services-autonomous bodies such as the *khadi* and the Village Industries Board, in association with local *panchayats,* nongovernmental organisations, and academicians of each region. Formal and informal education of local people regarding every aspect of these water bodies is a prerequisite for initiation 6f these inputs. Meanwhile, declaring these wetlands systems protected areas-resource sanctuaries or bird sanctuaries-and reforming the *panchayat raj* institutions around them is an urgent political imperative in our semiarid tropical region. Otherwise, Tamil Nadu's dependence on neighbouring states for water may become unbearably perennial. This could lead to dangerous geopolitical tensions, with which we became familiar in post- independent India.

Perspectives Tank Ecosystems

A tank ecosystem consists of all areas around a water body, such as catchments, *ayacuts,* villages, supply channels, and wells; all organic life, including soil, water, plants, and animals; and all farming practices, such as agriculture, aquaculture, animal husbandry, and social forestry. These systems have some features of irrigation reservoirs, natural lakes, shallow wetlands, and riverine shorelines. Consequently, subsystems vary among tanks. A few may even have microhabitats, as in the case of Kaliveli tank. But in all tank areas, the water body functions as a cornerstone component of the region, meeting the water, soil, plant, and animal needs of the surrounding villages. In other words, if the tanks were not there, many villages would not exist. History also bears this out. Human settlements are known to have disappeared along the ancient Mangamma Salai in southern Tamil Nadu because the tanks apparently ran out of water every year for some time. Such mishaps can be averted through modern science and technology.

Conservation and Development

A natural corollary of the above concerns is quantification of land and water dynamics and biotic resources. It is imperative to conserve whatever still exists and restore whatever is possible so that the system comes to life for future development. Conversely, the region could be developed only in some spheres in such a way that other resources are conserved. In other words, conservation for development and development for conservation should emerge as the middle-path wisdom forwetlands. But this principle must be based on accounting, valuation, and diagnosis of the system.

Tragedy of the Commons

It has been seen that all of the resources of a wetlands area are interconnected-among themselves and with the rural SOCietyas a whole. The tank lands and their water are the most important of these common-property resources. With the decline in tank rights, duties, and management due to planning and politics, water and land have gradually and systematically been privatised.

Water Markets: Water retention periods, which are.ephemeral anyway, have been further reduced due to such factors as tube well extraction and excessive water use. The tube wells around the tanks symbolise privatisation of the common surface water, which is extracted mechanically and sold to neighbouring farmers for a profit. And the electricity to privately extract this common water is subsidised!

Land Grabbing: In the absence of managerial systems to replace the traditional ones, tank lands are encroached on by neighbouring landowners, local landlords, and political forces. Sometimes the government itself "encroaches" on the land in the name of social forestry, which actually should be called wetland forestry. Consequently, many tanks are apparently no more than temporary ponds and puddles. This anarchy is beneficial to a few and detrimental to most. However, there is an interesting variation to this common trend. In Kaliveli tank in the South Arcot district, the offshore land is encroached on by a large number of villagers, apparently from the lower economic classes, and the government has gradually been legitim ising these encroachments by awarding *pattas*. Results of this practice are expected to be inconsequential due to the vastness of the wetlands area. But for how long? Socialism through such land reforms at the cost of ecology also may dwindle in the face of the East Coast Road, which is rapidly nearing completion.

Wetland Forestry

Silvicultural practices using leguminous plants in tank beds improve both soil quality and diversity in animal populations. But detailed enquiries need to be made about production, marketing, and management because this is a rare case of doing the best in the worst of times. Economics seem to have been totally ignored in the erroneous assumption that silviculture in the tank bed is equal to social forestry outside it.

Ecoagriculture

When water is scarce it is not proper to cultivate water-intensive crops. Yet paddy is grown, seemingly with no attempt to study the economics involved. Still worse is the growing practice by farmers of cultivating sugarcane with common tank water obtained through borewells. Borewells seem to be the single most unjust policy input-ecologically and technologically, as well as economically-for they privatise common properties, spoil ecology,and cause social inequities by applying a good technology in an unsuitable place (i.e., around tanks).

Bird Sanctuaries

To different degrees and over varying periods, tanks already are a form of bird sanctuary. Birds influence all other life through food chains, reproductive needs, and nutritional ethologies, some of which are of economic significance to tank ecosystems. Their excreta contribute to soil fertility and they bring in plankton from other water bodies. Some of these birds prey on insect crop pests. To ensure the continuity of these benefits it is necessary to regreen barren areas with permacultures, preferably from patches of natural vegetation. This will result in increased productivity and animal diversity, for nutrition as a limiting factor no longer exists. Aquatic productivity also will become accelerated, leading to an increase in migratory bird populations and associated benefits such as pest control and guanal deposits in agricultural fields. All of these will be possible only if water bodies are declared bird sanctuaries and given to local educational institutions for adoption.

Bird poaching should be curbed by appointing local people as guards.

Urban Wetlands

Wetlands seem to have become the easiest and most justifiable victims of private property ownership and speculative profiteering. In this connection one may recall instances of "converting water into soil" in many small towns by dumping solid wastes for "reclaiming." This private lane!is now used for raising concrete jungles, with the consequence that rainwater drainage has been reduced and underground aquifer recharge hampered. What is the gain? What is the loss? And for whom?

Imperatives

Having reached the conclusion that conservation and development must go hand in hand, we must develop a framework of actions along with certain catalysts or agents of change, ensuring cooperation among local people and coordination among government bodies. We feel that the success of ecologically oriented development depends on complementary inputs from government bodies, NGOs,' local people, and academicians.

Empowerment of Beneficiaries

Tank irrigation thrived until a few decades ago because water .distribution was carried out by local bodies of farmers in *ayacuts* or *zamindars.* In some tanks farmers no longer have any authority. Tail- end farmers have had to shift to groundwater irrigation. People are not involved in tank maintenance. This trend can be reversed only by returning tanks to the village *panchayats* and rejuvenating traditional water management bodies.

Policy Inputs

Policies should be based on sound philosophy, since government programmes have long-lasting and indirect effects on agriculture and land use and, through them, on the daily lives of people. Therefore all decisions must be based on the ecological wisdom of sustainable growth. Agricultural policies are the most important because they regulate land use through such means as revenue subsidies, extension activities, training, expert guidance, and irrigation policies. The ecological suitability of all crops should be evaluated. Drought-resistant plants should be introduced through agriculture and social forestry policies. Water-intensive cropping patterns should be prevented through implementation of fiscal policies. Long-term silvicultural practices should be given greater priority. Regulations for creation of deep bore wells in the vicinity of tanks, support for alternative agricultural methods such as crop rotation and organic farming, and legal instruments for declaring these water bodies protected areas are urgently needed.

Land-based Actions

Villagers are aware of the economic but not the ecological importance of tanks. Only when full awareness is achieved can effective local participation in sustainable utilisation of tank resources be ensured. Although strategies for restoration and conservation vary between nonsystem and system tanks because of differences in water retention periods, sound policies and result-oriented, land-based actions can and must be developed for both types. These include the following

- Reinforcement of embankments and repair of regulators, sluices, and supply and feeder channels; desiltation of water bodies.
- Protection of tanks from poaching, provision of fishing and grazing rights, and removal of encroachments.
- Regulation of land use in areas surrounding tanks so that all rainwater drains into the tanks, increasing their water-holding capacity
- Provision of financial support to NGOs involved in development and/or conservation activities in areas around tanks
- Establishment of initiatives favouring such activities as organic farming, cultivation of medicinal plants, ecotourism, wetland forestry, and aquaculture
- Education of local people in all aspects of tank systems to motivate them to manage their common property

NGOs

NGOs are recognised as major agents of change. These voluntary bodies have motivated people, built bridges of understanding, and achieved goals, and most are ecologically oriented. Therefore it is appropriate to draw them into tank restoration and conservation.

Cooperatives and Panchayats

Most government efforts are in vain because they fail to involve local people. Therefore people should be assisted in forming cooperatives to centralise all operations, especially social forestry, by means of which villagers could obtain cheap firewood and regular incomes. Later, such mechanisms could be extended to other areas such as dairy operation, vermiculture, sericulture, apiculture, floriculture, management of plant and animal refugia, gardening, and above all water sharing. Initially, people could take up development activities yielding produce and income. To sustain these activities for long periods, conservation of water, soil, plants, and animals could then be undertaken. However, villages around tanks could not be expected to perform all of these activities; they would need assistance from trained extension workers and other experts.

Updating Records

Background data on water bodies provided by the Revenue, Irrigation, and Agriculture departments differ from data obtained on the ground for a variety of reasons, including natural degradation (siltation, aridity), human-induced degradation (encroachment), and emphasis on alternatives (wells) and destructive policies and practices (reclamation, poaching, deforestation). How much rainfall is there? How much goes to the wetlands, how much to the wells? What was the original area of each tank, and what is it now? How much land has been encroached on and how much encroachment is legalised? What is the waterspread area of each tank and the volume of water it can hold? Restoring land and water equity among local people by initiating proper management techniques is a challenging problem with economic and political significance.

Panchayati Raj

Tank irrigation requires strong local authority to generate collective action for tank building, efficiently distribute water through optimal allocation among beneficiaries and over seasons, and properly maintain the irrigation system. The water dynamics encompass the entire catchment area, supply channels, the command area, wells, impediments, and adjuncts. The villages are intimately connected with this web; therefore conservation and development have to go hand in hand. Through a shift from direct social control to indirect economic hegemony by subtle ownership of water and soil, tanks have become severely degraded. Nucleating each tank along with its dependent villages into a unit-an ecopolitical unit-has thus become a necessity. Empowering each unit with the responsibility to regenerate water bodies-catalysed by political power, social consciousness, and academic inputs-is the chief imperative emerging from the present stud\!o If this regeneration occurs a turnaround will have begun with far-reaching positive consequences for the wetland country as well as for its 50,000 villages and 10-20 million people. But can the wetland resources lost during the last 50 years be accounted for, let alone restored? Sadly, the concepts and values responsible for human progress over many millennia seem to be missing from our dictionaries.

National Tank Authority

The subtle interrelationships among agriculture, social forestry, land and water dynamics, biodiversity, and the socioeconomic milieu, and above all the political undertones running through the entire tank system, must be realised if these water bodies are to be resuscitated. Although the foregoing is the story of only six of these tanks, there is no reason to expect that the others are significantly different. Since these water bodies constitute a major natural irrigation and drainage source, we must radically change our approach towards their management-that is, from an engineering perspective to an ecosystem approach, that of a guiding spirit. This can be done in the interests of the wetlands and their people through establishment of a national tank authority, which should be mandated to protect all of India's wetlands. Tank care should encompass conservation and restoration of resources as well as development on an ecologically sustainable scale.

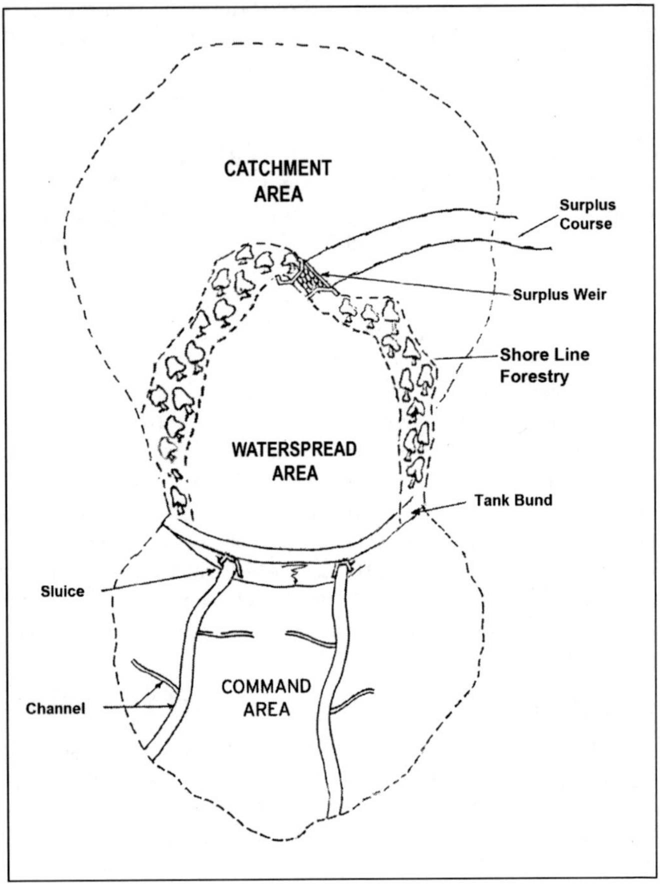

Fig. 1: A Typical Non System Tank

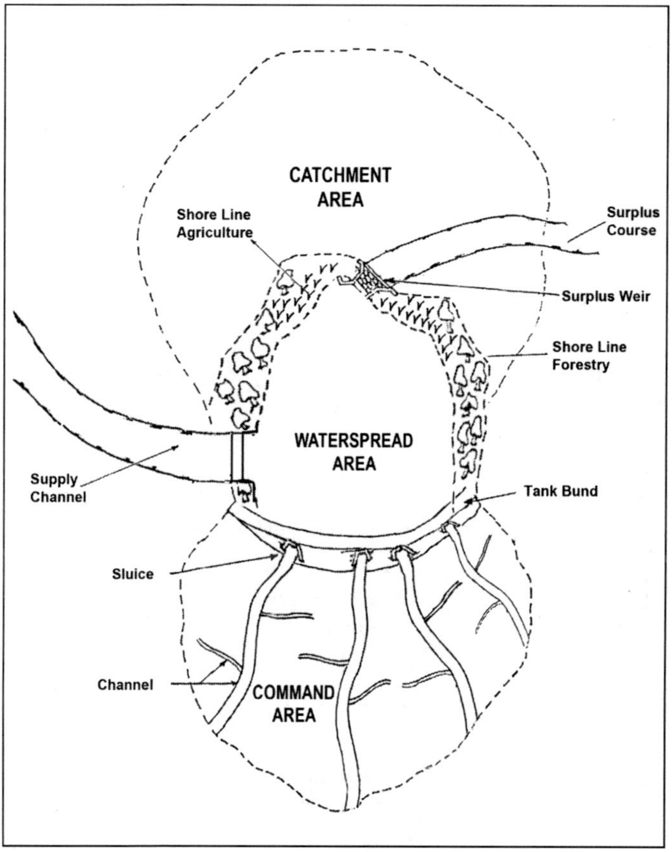

Fig. 2: A Typical System Tank

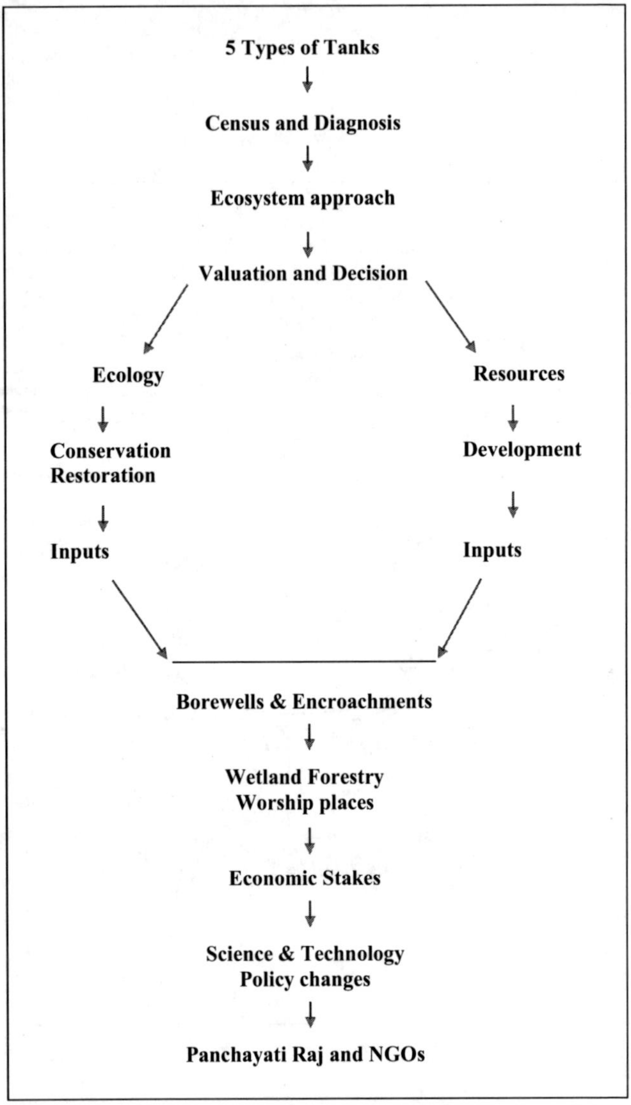

Fig. 3: Ecological Security Through Small Water-Bodies: Issues at a Glance.

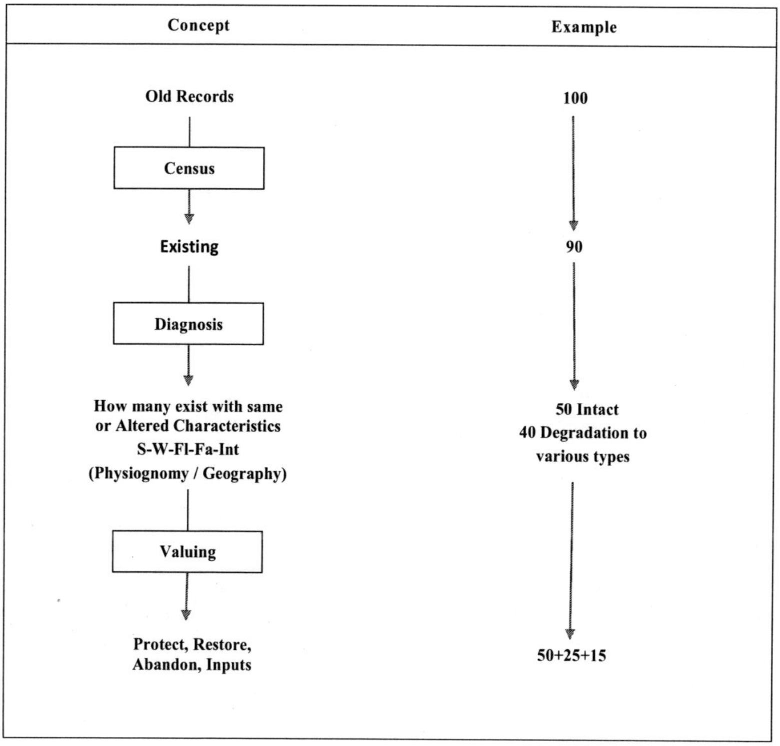

Fig. 4: Sequence of tank evaluations for Conservation and Development.

Wtr-16 Ecosystem Approach to the Management of Traditional Irrigation systems

T.R.K. Yoganand, C.B.S.R. Sharma
Salim Ali School of Ecology and Environmental Sciences
Pondicherry University, Pondicherry - 605 014

Water bodies constitute a traditional system of rainfall conservation for cropland Irrigation and other ephemeral or perennial uses of water. Many others on the other hand receive water through engineered channels from an apex reservoir mostly built after damming rivers. The nature of these reservoirs depend upon the water receipts from local catchments and supply channels, com-mand area, density of human populations, range of uses, rainfall, water and soil nature and plant and animal life. All these bestow on the tank, with all its webs of activity, a holistic character, To understand this ecoism, studies on two tanks were undertaken, so that they may throw some insights into managerial inputs. Our current work pertains to water, soil, plants, animals, agriculture, aquaculture and perceptions on these in the human settlements associated with a system tank - Ousteri and a non-system reservoir, Kaliveli.

Ousteri situated about 10 Kms west of Pondicherry is fed by local catchments of about 10 Sq. Km. and a supply channel from the nearby dam on the river Varahanadhi. It supports more than 100 species of plants - emergent and submergent and animals, terrestrial and aquatic - including thousands of migratory birds. The soil is clayey and slightly alkaline, water is also slightly alkaline. A multi crop agricul-ture of about 1500 hectares is supported by the tank water distributed through canals. Seven villages are spread over this area and they use this water body for a variety of pur-poses.

Kaliveli is a 7000 ha expanse of water, beginning 20Km north of Pondicherry on the coastline for l0 Km further and interior. At the northeast point it drains through a creek into an estuary. On the surface the soil is sandy, and in the sub-surface and bed it is clayey -loamy and has a gradient in pH from neutral to alkaline. Water shows a spatio-temporal variation from pH 7 at one extreme to 9 where there is an estuarine influence. The plant species indicate clay and saline conditions. More than 50 species of migrant birds were recorded. The wetland is extensively used for agriculture at the periphery. Several villages are associated with this. It is a major destination-cum-stopover site for migratory birds using the Asian flyway.

Ousteri studies suggest that the system tank has to be treated on a geographical basis spanning from the channel origins to the outreaches of irrigation water. The only engineering input is a little dredging of the bed and maneuvering the rainwater into the tank. Aqua-cultural inputs can be initiated along with percolation facilities and extensive vegetating. The interdependence of people and the tank

---

[In] Congress on Traditional Sciences and Technologies of India, Section: Water Management. 28 Nov-3 Dec 1993, Indian Institute of Technology, Bombay.

can be increased by expanding agriculture through less water utilizing crops and eco-recreation. This is a self-sufficient system- an ecosystem around a system tank can be developed and maintained, with considerable economic benefits to locals.

Kaliveli has extensive ramifications reaching upto estuary on one side and fertile fields interior. This system supporting a high population of local and migratory birds should be totally preserved with a few policy inputs in this direction. Technology Inputs should be limited to its marine contacts. Percolation spots could be identified to recharge the water table, rather than losing out water through evaporation or flooding into the sea. This also will preserve the agriculture on one side and ecological balances on the other while preventing the water from excessive estuarine salinity. A fringe benefit can be aqua-culture on the estuarine side and food chain studies on plankton, plants, fishes and birds, which is rare in India. This can serve as a development model for a conserved, therefore secure, ecological future

Finally it is our considered opinion that no management inputs shall be made without fully studying the ecological aspects covering the system as a whole. A revision of ecostatuses of traditional systems are a pre-requisite of modernising efforts. This may lead as a result from I standpoint to reclamation of tanks for other purposes at one extreme or restoration to the past level of existence at the other. The emphasis is that, there cannot be any common approach to the management of all tanks. The input has to be system specific - taking all ecological aspects into account.

Our work commenced in June 1993 supported by Madras Institute of Development Studies (MIDS) and Ministry of Environment and Forests. The concerned data will be presented. Thanks are due to Prof. Vaidyanathan, Prof. S. Neelakantan and Dr. Paul Appasamy of MIDS Madras.

6. CONFESSIONS

1. Origin of the Project

Tanks, innovated when the riverine man moved away into interior regions, were realized as a great extant source, when the deterioration of environment was realized, about 50 years ago which made the UNDP to goad the relevant countries to study and resurrect their water bodies. DOEF was financed for this initiative. It has in turn asked a PC Member, Vaidyanathan of MIDS, Chennai, to undertake this project. He has given me the task of improving some tanks with current scientific inputs. We tried to update all data and knowledge of tanks from British times and elevated the Tanks to a status of Ecosystems, by adding ecological features. Consequently ours is a Pioneering Study of water Storage Systems, fast depleting due to usury by money and power.

2. Carriage of Project

As a duty, I told the then VC about this project. He responded by confiscating my lab-room, ignoring my need for that room for the project [The contents taken by them were never returned to me, sharing them among themselves!] consequently, I had to request MIDS to subcontract the work to me than granting as a Project. I took a sabbatical leave. The work began from my house– with 3 post PG students and 1 PG student from our department, my current Co-Authors.

3. Interference

The VC [Agnanam] tried to prevent this project first by confiscating my space and materials and by interfering with MIDS, Which rebuffed him. Then he took away the Camera used by us for field work to give to a Lecturer [Parthasaradhy] whose work does not require Photography. Then He ordered me to submit periodical reports to the HOD, a Reader [Deviprasad] . One of us, Amruth, was much harmed by most faculty especially Poyyamoli, for working with me!

No where in the world a Senior Professor was subordinated to 8 lecturers and Readers.

4. Credits

As the Project Leader, the Report was submitted in my name; students getting due recognition in the text. But the all data were given to them for publishing in journals, on their own. Dr. Manimekalan took the relevant materials on behalf ofthem. Hope they did publish.

5. Money Matters

The grant made was very meager- Rs.150,000 The students worked excellently despite low stipends. At the close of the work I had to put about Rs. 20000. The work was simply a labour of love. Contributions of Yoganand and Amruth, who used to be better than most faculty, were superlative.

Project leaders often swallow funds; here funds were contributed by the workers, who are paid less than the norm. Prof. Vaidyanathan got a million- worth data and info at 10% of its cost! Such ratios are normally the reverse, in Indian Universities!

6. The work

Planning of the work was initially done at MIDS, taking advices from Profs. Vaidyanathan, Neelakantan, Appasamy and others. This is modified at PU by Yoganand, Amrut and Cyril Antony, the chief of INTACH at Pondy. The plans were always reviewed after the field visits, initially. Once settled, everything is routine. Reports were sent periodically to MIDS for suggestions.

7. The Peers

About 25 copies were sent to important academicians such as Swaminathan, Gadgil, Ramakrishnan, Anil Gupta, Nandita Krishnan and all VCs in Tamil Nadu. Most people replied with suggestions and laudatory remarks. MIDS was very happy. Its Director,

The Director of MIDS remarked *"Our pioneering work has to be referred to by all future workers"*.

8. "Hari likes Rain"

I went to VC's [Gnanam] house along with Yoganand, to plead for keeping the camera for field work and Parthasaradhy can borrow whenever he needs. We were standing outside the entry gate. He came out to say an emphatic "NO". It was drizzling, increasing gradually. He suddenly said "Hari likes to stroll in rain." Came running was a Giant Dog; driver opened the door of car; both drove away with the canine jutting its head towards both of us ! The VC went in and we into the rain.

9. Unsatisfactory Biodata

Despite my Objectives and Work [Oxbridge Values], the damages caused by 2 VCs and 2 Gangs of Colleague–G3&G5, for 30 yrs, at Pondicherry stifled my Contributions.

A. Papers

1. 31 Research Papers in UK, USA, Holland, Switzerland, Italy, Germany, Japan =230p
2. 51 Research Papers in India = 445p

B. Reviews : Chemicals, Pollutants and Mutagenesis =154p

1. 1971 - India – Journal of Sci. Ind. Res. =17p
2. 1987 – Malaysia - SAM-APPEN = 15p
3. 1990 – U S A - Critical Reviews in Plant Sciences =34p
4. 1990 – U K – Mutagenesis = 21p
5. 1993 – On *in situ* Mutagenesis, UNPUBLISHED = 67p

C. Reports / Projects*

1. Monozite Belt Floristics -UGC
2. Maize Germplasm Collection for CYMMYT at Mexico - CYMMYT
3. Phulbani : Medicinal Plants used by Tribals - UGC
4. Drugs with Heavy Metals : Genetic Toxicity in Rodents - ICMR

5. Fungicides : Genetic Toxicity of Commonly used Fungicides -CSIR
6. *In situ* mutagenicity ; DOEF; *VCs and Colleagues destroyed this, mid- stream*
7. Small Water Bodies :UNDP– DOEF–MIDS. Most successful Report
8. East Coast of Tamil Nadu :INTACH – CAG - PU
9. Vision 2020 Pondichery, GOP,

   *Assisted by 12 Students, 8 obtaining Doctorates

D. Books Published

1. Sharks on Campus: Compilation of 41 Articles mostly on Higher Education; p. 371, 2015, Notion Press.
2. Ecology, Environment and Politics: Compilation of 38 Public Lectures in Ecology & Environment at 35 Institutions in India; p. 412, 2018, Kalpaz.
3. Teaching Labours of Sisyphus: Synopses of 190 Class Lectures From 10 Branches of Environmental Sciences, p. 802, 2020, Gyan in 2 Volumes.
4. Irrigation Tanks in Semi-arid Ecosystems, A Survey of 6 small water bodies in Pondy –TN; p. 380, 2020, Gyan, [with 2 Others]

E. Books In Different stages of Preparation

1. Keeping The Asphidistra Alive
2. From Genetic Toxicology To Environmental Mutagenesis
3. Piranhas on the Prowl in Higher Education Systems
4. PLANTS in Medicine, Energy, Plant Protection and Environmental Monitoring,
5. Ecography of Coromandel Coast of Tamilnadu from Markanam to Koodangulam
6. Learners Perceptions of Ecology & Environment –A10 -Volume Treatise

F. Others

1. Studied and worked at BITS [Pilani], IISc [Bangalore], ICAR [Coimbatore] and Universities at Berhampur, Madurai, Coimbatore and Pondicherry.
2. Countries Visited: Italy, Hungary, UK, Thailand, Malaysia and USA.
3. Resource Person to : ICSSR, MHRD, DOEF, UGC, UPSC etc

Index

B

D

G

N

O

P

Q

R

S

T

Y

Z